32⁰⁰
70ᶜ
6

D1266118

NOTES AND PROBLEMS
IN MICROECONOMIC THEORY

ADVANCED TEXTBOOKS IN ECONOMICS

VOLUME 15

Editors:

C. J. BLISS

M. D. INTRILIGATOR

Advisory Editors:

S. M. GOLDFELD

L. JOHANSEN

D. W. JORGENSON

M. C. KEMP

J.-C. MILLERON

NORTH-HOLLAND PUBLISHING COMPANY
AMSTERDAM · NEW YORK · OXFORD

NOTES AND PROBLEMS
IN MICROECONOMIC THEORY

PETER B. DIXON
La Trobe University

SAMUEL BOWLES
University of Massachusetts at Amherst

DAVID KENDRICK
University of Texas at Austin

in collaboration with

LANCE TAYLOR
Massachusetts Institute of Technology

MARC ROBERTS
Harvard University

NORTH-HOLLAND PUBLISHING COMPANY
AMSTERDAM · NEW YORK · OXFORD

©NORTH-HOLLAND PUBLISHING COMPANY — 1980

ISBN for this series: 0 7204 3600 1
ISBN for this volume: 0 444 85325 1
First edition 1980
1st reprint 1983

Publishers

NORTH-HOLLAND PUBLISHING COMPANY
AMSTERDAM · NEW YORK · OXFORD

Sole distributors for the U.S.A. and Canada

ELSEVIER/NORTH-HOLLAND, INC.
52 VANDERBILT AVENUE
NEW YORK, N.Y. 10017

Library of Congress Cataloging in Publication Data

Dixon, Peter B
   Notes and problems in microeconomic theory.

   (Advanced textbooks in economics ; 15)
   Based on earlier work by S. Bowles and
D. Kendrick.
   1. Microeconomics. I. Bowles, Samuel,
joint author. II. Kendrick, David A., joint
author. III. Title.
HB171.5.D549   338.5   79-22681
ISBN 0-444-85325-1

PRINTED IN THE NETHERLANDS

INTRODUCTION TO THE SERIES

The aim of the series is to cover topics in economics, mathematical economics and econometrics, at a level suitable for graduate students or final year under-graduates specializing in economics. There is at any time much material that has become well established in journal papers and discussion series which still awaits a clear, self-contained treatment that can easily be mastered by students without considerable preparation or extra reading. Leading specialists will be invited to contribute volumes to fill such gaps. Primary emphasis will be placed on clarity, comprehensive coverage of sensibly defined areas, and insight into fundamentals, but original ideas will not be excluded. Certain volumes will therefore add to existing knowledge, while others will serve as a means of communicating both known and new ideas in a way that will inspire and attract students not already familiar with the subject matter concerned.

The Editors

CONTENTS

x *Contents*

B. Static optimization 235

C. An introduction to linear models 258

D. Theoretical developments underlying modern production function
econometrics 273

INTRODUCTION

In 1968–69 I was a first-year graduate student in Harvard's economics programme. Among the many excellent courses that I attended, Sam Bowles' and David Kendrick's microeconomic theory 201a was outstanding. The course was built around a series of problems. In the summer of 1969 Bowles and Kendrick gathered the problems and other course materials into book form. I was lucky enough to be their editorial assistant. The book, under the same title as the present one, was published in 1970 in Chicago by the Markham Publishing Company.

More recently, I was very pleased when David Kendrick suggested that I prepare a new book using the Bowles–Kendrick work as a starting point. I saw my assignment as one of updating and supplementing the earlier material to reflect some of the major developments and changes in emphasis in microeconomic theory of the last ten years. The overall objectives and structure of the new book are as before, and therefore they are accurately described by Bowles and Kendrick's introduction (reproduced below) to the original book. Thus, all that remains for me to do in introducing the new book is briefly to outline its distinctive features.

I have retained about two-thirds of the old book and that material represents about half of this one. In terms of broadly defined areas, the coverage of the new book (as with the old one) is mathematical programming, the theory of consumer demand, the theory of production, and welfare economics. I have, however, given greater emphasis to the role of microeconomic theory in applied econometrics. Over the last decade there has been a general recognition of the need for rigorous theoretical specifications as a basis for empirical research. A fundamental equation of applied econometrics can be expressed as

results = data + theory.

Theory has been receiving more attention in this equation for at least two reasons. First, the economic disturbances of the early seventies — for example the changes in the international monetary system, the sudden escalation in energy prices, and the dramatic increase in real wages — left many econometric models floundering. They were unable to provide useful simulations of the effects of the shocks or to give guidance on the appropriate policy responses. It became apparent that while many models can fit available time series data, it is only by close attention to theory that one can hope to create models capable of giving insight into the implications of disturbances which carry the economy away from previously established historic trends. A second factor in the expanding role of microeconomic theory has been the demands by economic policy-makers for more and more detail. Besides the traditional macro aggregates, governments have become concerned with individual industries, regions, and occupational groups. The required rate of growth on the left-hand side of the research equation has been outstripping the growth of data availability. As a consequence there has been a proliferation of tightly constrained disaggregated models where data deficiencies are covered by strong assumptions from microeconomic theory. A recurring theme of this book is that assumptions such as utility maximization and cost minimization reduce the number of free parameters for which estimates must be derived from limited data.

In comparison with the old book I have, in parts of this book, demanded a little more perseverance with mathematical arguments. This was unavoidable given the increasingly technical nature of the subject. I should make clear, however, that the formal mathematical prerequisites for using the materials presented here are no more than those for the original book. Most of the material continues to be accessible to readers with a knowledge of elementary calculus and matrix algebra (first-year college level). On the other hand, it cannot be denied that some rather lengthy sequences of mathematical steps are involved in developing some of the new topics, e.g. intertemporal utility maximization, duality, flexible functional forms, CRESH production functions, and integrability. Since a key to successfully negotiating a long argument is to have a clear view of the end point, I have prefaced the chapters and many of the exercises with introductory notes which attempt to set the scene. I have also expanded the purely mathematical section of the original book. In addition to their primary objective, i.e. to help students to acquire some relevant mathematical theory, I hope that the exercises on mathematical programming (Problem Set 1) will provide some experience in the art of reaching conclusions via fairly extended sequences of elementary mathematical steps.

There are two final points concerning the organization of the book. I am sure that students will agree that if they use the answers too early, the exercises will lose much of their value. I was tempted to place the answers in a separate part of the book to encourage students not to refer to them before trying to work the exercises for themselves. The question—answer format of the original book is retained only because it allows a less disjointed presentation. The second point also concerns the order in which the material is arranged. The chapter on mathematical programming comes first. This seems logical. The chapter provides some basic tools for the study of microeconomic theory. Nevertheless, students should not feel that it is necessary to conquer all of Chapter 1 before moving on to the other material. In general, students can choose their own path through the book. With few exceptions, the later exercises are not formally dependent on earlier ones, although there is some quickening in pace as the book progresses.

In preparing the book I have received generous assistance from several people. Michael Intriligator, in particular, provided detailed and valuable comments on earlier drafts. David Emmons spotted many typographical and other errors. Naturally, he is not responsible for those that remain. Alan Powell has been a constant source of encouragement. Much of my faith in the importance of microeconomic theory in applied economics has been derived from my association with him while working on the IMPACT Project. Orani Dixon, Jan White and Elvine Moore did expert secretarial work through three drafts. Finally, all the authors wish to thank the Rand McNally College Publishing Company (which bought out the Markham Publishing Company) for surrendering their copyright to the original book.

Melbourne, December 1978

PETER B. DIXON

INTRODUCTION TO THE MARKHAM EDITION

This book contains a set of materials for supplementary work on or self-teaching of microeconomic theory. The materials consist of annotated reading lists and sets of problems complete with rather detailed answers. The reading lists have been developed under the assumption that students of microeconomic theory approach the material with rather diverse levels of training and experience. For example, there is an increasing number of students of this subject who are innocent of economics but who are well trained in mathematics. There are others who have just the reverse kind of preparation, and there is yet a third group which enjoys strong preparation in both fields. Also, students who begin studying in this field always approach it with rather different preferences about the emphasis which they wish to place on the various parts of the material. By providing liberal reading notes we have attempted to let the student find his own way through the course of study, keeping his personal background and interest always in mind as a guide to his reading and study.

The problem sets and answers embody the notion that a thorough grasp of microeconomic theory can be obtained only by the participation of the student beyond the level of simply giving intellectual assent to the ideas in lectures, textbooks, and journal articles. A large set of problems are provided here to help the student (1) become thoroughly versed in the fundamentals of the subject and (2) discover for himself the strengths and weaknesses of the current state of development of microeconomic theory. Detailed answers to the problems are included in the hope that the student will attempt to solve them first on his own and then that he will benefit as much from the answers as from the problems themselves.

We also hope that the problems and answers included with these materials will be of particular help to graduate students who are preparing for their general examinations in microeconomic theory. The procedure in many graduate schools is for the exams to be given at the end of the second year of graduate studies, and students frequently prepare for the exams by working sets of problems and discussing the solutions with one another. The problems and answers given here should provide an increment to the stock of problems currently circulating in most graduate schools.

These materials were developed for use in the introductory graduate-level microeconomic theory course at Harvard University taught by the two of us with assistance from Lance Taylor in 1967–68 and Marc Roberts in 1968–69. To engage the student as an active participant in the learning process and to help each student progress through the materials according to his own background and interest, a rather different format was employed. The class was divided into groups of five students each, and the teaching was done on a tutorial basis without lectures. The groups met once a week for two hours. Alternate weeks were devoted to a discussion of the readings and accompanying problem sets. Reading and problem sets were completed prior to the classes so that the sessions could be devoted to give-and-take among students and teachers on problems and concepts that were not clear or that were debatable. Students were encouraged to follow different paths through the reading materials depending on background and interest.

We have tried to devote a problem or a major part of one to what we considered to be the fundamental concepts of microeconomic theory. It is clear, however, that the method itself tends to bias the choice of subject matter. By concentrating on solvable problems and by confining ourselves largely to exercises which can be posed and solved mathematically, we have diverted attention away from those areas in which there are no simple answers and where the present state of the theory does not admit precise mathematical formulation. Although we have tried to give attention to the frontier fields in microeconomic theory, our main thrust has unavoidably been in the familiar areas of the conventional wisdom where the level of theoretical development (whatever its other weaknesses) allows the presentation of the main body of knowledge as a set of puzzles to be worked out.

Of course, the reduction of economic theory to puzzle-making and puzzle-solving has its weaknesses. The successes rather than the failures of the theory are emphasized. Large areas of potentially fruitful study are excluded altogether. And it may be that the students are brought to regard theorizing and theorists as nothing more than puzzle-solving and puzzle-solvers. Theorists are certainly this, but good theorists are sometimes more. By viewing economic behavior broadly as part of a complex system of social relationships, theorists such as Schumpeter, Bohm–Bawerk, Marx, and many of the classic writers have vastly enriched our understanding of economic theory. But to capture the full contributions of any of these writers in a simply manipulated mathematical problem is virtually impossible. Therefore we have avoided attempts to formulate these kinds of problems and have relied more heavily on readings to impart a sense of this type of theory.

Much of what is useful and interesting about the current state of microeconomic theory can be successfully taught via the medium of problems. But the above serves as a warning not to identify the study of economic theory with the mastery of the types of theoretical problems known to have simple solutions in the body of received wisdom.

The present state of microeconomic theory is not presented as a finished product, but rather as part of an evolutionary process in which today's answers are often tomorrow's mistakes and today's burning problems will appear to future economists (and some present ones) as arid intellectual exercises. We would like students to be able to use microeconomic theory, be critical of it, and contribute to it, as it unfolds during their professional careers. In part this means that some of our problems require the use of certain mathematical tools that may be little used at present but that we anticipate will be common procedures in economics in the years to come.

Many of the materials presented here could hardly be called original. We have learned much both about economics and about teaching from our teachers, particularly Robert Bishop, Robert Dorfman, Alexander Gerschenkron, Louis Lefeber, Wassily Leontief, and Paul Samuelson. Many of the problems themselves have circulated as part of the oral tradition of teachers and students of microeconomics. Where the original author of a problem could be determined, we have thanked him by name in the text. But in many cases it was impossible to determine the precise authorship, in part because problems and exercises are often of diverse parentage. To the few thoroughbred and the many mongrelized problems, we have added many of our own new creations. In developing them, we have worked jointly with Marc Roberts and Lance Taylor and have been ably assisted by Elisha Pazner and Peter Dixon, both of whom first worked on these materials as students in the course and later as editorial assistants, and authors of new problems. Finally, we are grateful to the Department of Economics and the Project for Quantitative Research in Economic Development of Harvard for assistance in developing these materials.

SAMUEL BOWLES
DAVID KENDRICK

Chapter 1

NOTES AND PROBLEMS IN THE THEORY OF MATHEMATICAL PROGRAMMING

1.1. Introduction

The most important mathematical prerequisite for the study of modern micro-economics and economic planning is mathematical programming. Mathematical programming is concerned with finding the values for variables to maximize functions subject to constraints. Typical economic applications include the determination of production levels which will maximize profits subject to the availability of fixed plant, the determination of a consumption pattern which will maximize household satisfaction but will be consistent with the household budget, and the allocation of development spending across sectors so as to maximize economic growth subject to satisfying income distribution, employment, inflation, and balance of trade targets.

There are two distinct uses of mathematical programming techniques in economics. The first is in the computation of numerical solutions for empirically specified models. The second is as a means for drawing out the implications of basic behavioral assumptions. For example, if we start by assuming that households behave as if they maximize their satisfaction subject to a budget constraint, then the algebraic solution of the household programming problem leads to a testable theory concerning household consumption responses to changes in prices and incomes. However, it should be emphasized that a knowledge of mathematical programming techniques does not make a micro or planning economist, it is a prerequisite only. It does not show us how to formulate interesting and revealing models, but merely how to generate some of the implications of the models which we do formulate.

The aim of this chapter is to give a reasonably rigorous but brief coverage of the Lagrangian and Kuhn—Tucker theories of constrained optimization.[1] We try

---

[1] We will not be concerned with dynamic optimization via calculus of variations or control theoretic techniques. For a complete but elementary treatment of these topics see Intriligator (1971, part IV).

to do this in three ways: (i) with a reading guide, (ii) with a problem set, and (iii) with a set of notes (sections 1.3–1.8) describing the theory. The material in sections 1.3–1.8 is incomplete in the sense that we do not give proofs. On the other hand, we have attempted to be rigorous by explicitly confronting various 'exceptional cases' and difficulties with the theory. Thus, our presentation will not be suitable for all students and we have suggested some alternative approaches in Reading Guide 1. In particular, students who are capable mathematicians and who have some available time will benefit from a more advanced approach. Students who do not have much background in calculus or matrix algebra may prefer a slower approach. We hope, however, that most students will find that the problem set and the detailed answers are useful, whatever route they choose through the literature.

Our attitude to mathematics in this chapter and throughout the rest of the book is pragmatic. This is a book about economics, not mathematics. We are not interested in detailed proofs, provided convincing diagrammatic demonstrations are available. But we are interested in a full understanding of basic theorems. Without that, and without the ability to argue from simple diagrams, the student of economics will find himself severely handicapped. In attempting to provide rigorous statements of propositions, we find that the use of stylized mathematical language is unavoidable. In any case, this language is now common in the literature which students must eventually read. Perseverance will be required with phrases such as 'there exists $\lambda_1 \geqslant 0$ such that', '$\bar{x}$ is a solution if and only if there exists...', etc.

The chapter is short. We have not considered the so-called second order conditions, Hessians and related areas. Our guess is that students can get by for a while in innocence of these topics. In most economic applications it is obvious whether a stationary point is a local maximum or minimum, and when this is not true, then reference to the second order conditions is likely to be impractical.

1.2. Goals, reading guide and references

By the time you finish with this chapter, we hope that you will have attained the following goals:

(1) a facility to use and interpret contour–gradient diagrams;

(2) an understanding of the necessary conditions for the solution of a constrained maximization problem where the constraints are equalities, sign constraints or inequality constraints;

(3) an ability to use the necessary conditions in the computation of solutions for simple numerical problems;

(4) familiarity with the ideas of convexity of the constraint set and quasi-

Reading Guide 1*

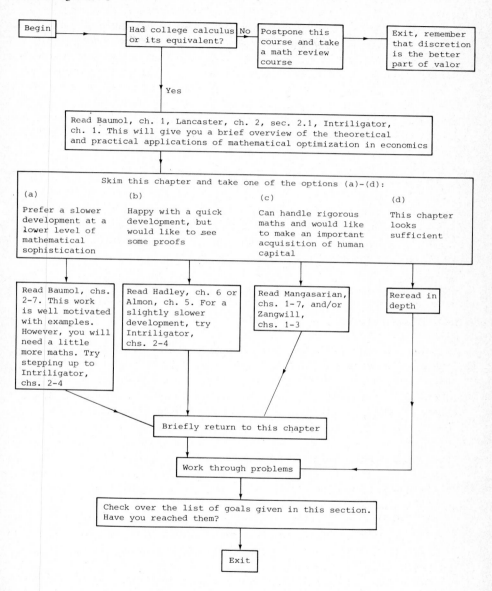

concavity of the objective function, and their relationship to 'sufficiency' propositions;

(5) a working knowledge of the Lagrangian method, including an appreciation of the conditions under which it breaks down;

(6) an ability to interpret the Lagrangian multiplier, including an understanding of the situations in which the usual interpretation is invalid; and

(7) a familiarity with the idea of duality in the linear programming context.

Reading Guide 1 gives some alternative approaches to achieving these goals. The readings are referred to in abbreviated form. Full citations are in the reference list. The list also contains other references appearing in the chapter.

References for Chapter 1

Almon, C. (1967) *Matrix Methods in Economics*, Addison-Wesley.
Baumol, W.J. (1972) *Economic Theory and Operations Analysis*, 3rd edn., Prentice-Hall.
Hadley, G. (1964) *Non-Linear and Dynamic Programming*, Addison-Wesley.
Intriligator, M.D. (1971) *Mathematical Optimization and Economic Theory*, Prentice-Hall.
Lancaster, K. (1968) *Mathematical Economics*, Macmillan.
Mangasarian, O.L. (1969) *Nonlinear Programming*, McGraw-Hill.
Zangwill, W.I. (1969) *Nonlinear Programming, A Unified Approach*, Prentice-Hall.

1.3.   Formal statement of the problem

We wish to maximize a function of n variables subject to m constraints. Formally our maximand or objective function is

$$f(x_1, x_2, ..., x_n).$$

By defining the vector x as[2]

$$x = (x_1, ..., x_n)',$$

we can rewrite our maximand more compactly as $f(x)$, which is a single-valued function of the n vector, x.

We denote the constraints on the values of x by m inequalities

$$g^1(x_1, ..., x_n) \leq 0,$$

$$\vdots$$

$$g^m(x_1, ..., x_n) \leq 0.$$

---

[2]   It is easier to print row vectors. However, x is conventionally a column vector. Therefore we have included the prime to denote transposition.

More compactly, we may write

$$g(x) \leqslant 0,$$

where

$$g(x) = \begin{bmatrix} g^1(x) \\ \vdots \\ g^m(x) \end{bmatrix}.$$

That is, $g(x)$ is a vector of m elements, each of which is a function of the n elements of x: $g(x)$ is an m-vector-valued function of the n vector x. The right-hand side of the last inequality above is to be read as an m vector of zeros.

In summary, our problem* is to choose x to maximize

$$f(x) \tag{1.3.1}$$

subject to

$$g(x) \leqslant 0$$

where, for convenience, we assume throughout this chapter that f and g are defined for all values of $x \in R^n$. In E1.19[3] you are asked to think about the implications of restrictions on the domains of f and g.[4]

Problem (1.3.1) can be said to be in standard form. Minimization problems, and problems with equality constraints, can always be rewritten in the format of (1.3.1). For example, assume that we wish to choose x_1, x_2 to *minimize*

$$x_1 + x_2$$

subject to

$$x_1 x_2 = 1.$$

This problem may be solved by choosing x_1 and x_2 to maximize

$$-(x_1 + x_2)$$

subject to

$$x_1 x_2 - 1 \leqslant 0$$

Note: In maximization problems the reference number between parentheses on the right-hand margin refers to the *entire* problem, not just the quantity to be maximized.

[3] We use the notation E 1.19 to refer to exercise 19 in Problem Set 1.

[4] The domains of f and g are the sets of vectors x for which $f(x)$ and $g(x)$ are defined. Thus, if f and g are defined for all possible values of x, then the domains of f and g are R^n, the set of n-component real valued vectors. In E 1.19 you will be concerned with a situation in which the domains of f and g are a subset of R^n.

and

$$-x_1 x_2 + 1 \leqslant 0.$$

Hence, if we learn how to solve a problem in the standard form (1.3.1), we will also know how to solve a variety of other constrained optimization problems. Do exercise El.1 to be sure you understand how to convert problems to the standard form (1.3.1).

Throughout our analysis of problem (1.3.1) we will assume that the functions f, g^1,...,g^m are differentiable. Mangasarian (1969, ch. 5) discusses optimization problems without differentiability. In economic problems, differentiability is almost always present, and therefore we will take advantage of it in developing the optimization theory.

Under the differentiability assumption, a very useful method for illustrating the solution technique for problem (1.3.1) is the contour—gradient diagram. The next section is a digression to describe that device.

1.4. The gradient vector and contour diagrams

Fig. 1.4.1 illustrates a contour or isovalue curve for a function f of two variables x_1 and x_2. $f(x)$ has the same value, k, for all x's represented by points on the solid line. That is, the equation for the isovalue curve is

$$f(x) = k,$$

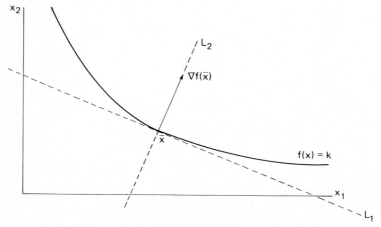

Figure 1.4.1

where k is a constant. The line L_1 is tangent to the isovalue curve at the point $\bar{x}$, and L_2 is perpendicular to L_1. Our eventual concern is to specify the points on the dotted line L_2. However, first we describe the line L_1, and then we consider the line L_2.

The slope of the line L_1 is the same as that of the isovalue curve at $\bar{x}$. We find the slope of the isovalue curve by considering small changes in x_1 and x_2 away from $\bar{x}$ which leave us on the isovalue curve. Hence, the slope of the isovalue curve is given by dx_2/dx_1, where dx_2 and dx_1 satisfy

$$\frac{\partial f(\bar{x})}{\partial x_1} dx_1 + \frac{\partial f(\bar{x})}{\partial x_2} dx_2 = 0,$$

i.e. the slope of L_1 is

$$\frac{dx_2}{dx_1} = - \frac{f_1}{f_2},$$

where

$$f_1 = \frac{\partial f}{\partial x_1} \; ; \quad f_2 = \frac{\partial f}{\partial x_2},$$

and it is understood that the derivatives are evaluated at $\bar{x}$.

At this stage, it will be recalled that if two lines cross at right angles, and the first has a slope of a, then the second has a slope of $-1/a$. Fig. 1.4.2 may be a

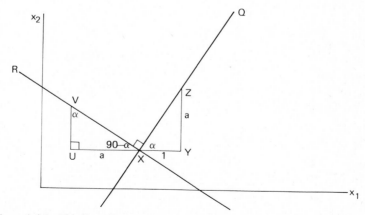

Figure 1.4.2 The lines RVX and XZQ cross at right angles at X. The slope of XZQ is a. We construct the line UXY parallel to the horizontal axis and make XY have length 1 and UX have length a. Then XYZ and VUX are similar triangles and length VU = length XY = 1. Hence the slope of RVX is $-1/a$.

convenient reminder. Hence, the slope of line L_2 is f_2/f_1. Now that we know that the slope of L_2 is f_2/f_1, we can see that z is a point on the line L_2 if and only if there exists a scalar ρ such that

$$z = \bar{x} + \rho(f_1, f_2)'.$$

That is, the points on L_2 form the set[5]

$$\{z \mid z = \bar{x} + \rho \nabla f, \rho \in R\},$$

where $\nabla f = (f_1, f_2)'$ and R is the set of real numbers.

$\nabla f(\bar{x})$ is known as the gradient vector of f at $\bar{x}$. It is often marked on contour diagrams as in fig. 1.4.1. The arrow shows the direction in which we would move if we were to add *positive* multiples of the vector $\nabla f(\bar{x})$ to $\bar{x}$.[6] It should also be noted that unless $\nabla f = 0$, the gradient direction is a direction of *increase* in f. In fact, it is the direction of maximum increase in f (see E1.7). However, for the present, it is sufficient to point out that the change in the value of f for a small movement in the gradient direction is

$$df = f_1 dx_1 + f_2 dx_2,$$

where dx_1, dx_2 are set so that

$$(dx_1, dx_2)' = \rho \nabla f,$$

with ρ being a small positive number. Hence, as we move in the gradient direction, the change in the value of f is given by

$$df = \rho\{(f_1)^2 + (f_2)^2\} \geqslant 0,$$

i.e. the change in the value of f is non-negative, and will be positive unless we are at a point where $f_1 = f_2 = 0$.

We can summarize this section as follows. The gradient direction at $\bar{x}$ for a function f is normal to the isovalue curve through $\bar{x}$. Also, the gradient direction is a direction of increase in f. If this material has been unfamiliar, you should pause here to attempt E1.2.

1.5.   The necessary conditions for a constrained maximum

We consider a special case of problem (1.3.1) where n, the number of variables, is 2 and m, the number of constraints, is 1, i.e. we wish to find x_1 and x_2 to maximize

---

[5]   The notation ' | ' in the set description below means 'such that'.

[6]   There is of course nothing in fig. 1.4.1 to indicate whether the arrow should point northeast or southwest along the line L_2. Our drawing implies that f_1 and f_2 are positive.

$$f(x_1, x_2)$$

subject to

$$g^1(x_1, x_2) \leqslant 0.$$

The problem is illustrated in fig. 1.5.1. The shaded area represents the feasible set of x's, i.e. the x's which satisfy the constraint. The boundary of the feasible set is the contour of g^1 defined by

$$g^1(x_1, x_2) = 0.$$

We have also marked on some contour lines $f(x) = a$, $f(x) = b$, and $f(x) = c$, for the function f and we assume that f is increasing as we move north-east, i.e. $a < b < c$.

By inspection of the diagram, we see that the problem solution is at $\bar{x}$. We also notice that at $\bar{x}$ the gradient directions for both f and g^1 coincide. In fig. 1.5.1 we have marked $\nabla f(\bar{x})$ and $\nabla g^1(\bar{x})$ on the same arrow. This is not meant to imply that $\nabla f(\bar{x})$ equals $\nabla g^1(\bar{x})$. What it implies is that if we add positive multiples of either the vector $\nabla f(\bar{x})$ or the vector $\nabla g^1(\bar{x})$ to $\bar{x}$, then we move in the direction indicated by the arrow, i.e. the direction normal to both the contours of f and g^1. Thus, $\nabla f(\bar{x})$ is a non-negative multiple of $\nabla g^1(\bar{x})$, i.e. there exists $\lambda_1 \geqslant 0$ such that

$$\nabla f(\bar{x}) = \lambda_1 \nabla g^1(\bar{x}).$$

(Be sure to understand why the gradient directions for f and g^1 coincide. For example, how do we know that the gradient direction for g^1 is to the northeast, rather than the southwest?)[7]

Let us consider a second two-variable problem. This time, however, we will assume that there are two constraints,

$$g^1(x_1, x_2) \leqslant 0,$$
$$g^2(x_1, x_2) \leqslant 0.$$

The feasible set, or constraint set, i.e. the set of x's which satisfy both constraints, is represented by the shaded area in fig. 1.5.2. The boundary of the feasible set is formed by particular contours of the constraint functions, g^1 and g^2. Some contours of f are marked, and it is assumed that f is increasing as we move northeast. Inspection of the diagram indicates that the problem solution is

---

[7] Remember that if we move in the gradient direction, g^1 increases. As we move southwest from $\bar{x}$, g^1 is decreasing — we are crossing points where $g^1(x) \leqslant 0$, whereas $g^1(\bar{x}) = 0$.

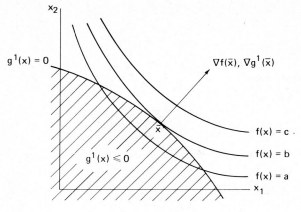

Figure 1.5.1

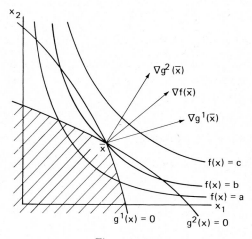

Figure 1.5.2

at $\bar{x}$. Notice that at $\bar{x}$ the gradient direction for f is between those for g^1 and g^2, i.e. there exist $\lambda_1, \lambda_2 \geqslant 0$ such that

$$\nabla f(\bar{x}) = \lambda_1 \nabla g^1(\bar{x}) + \lambda_2 \nabla g^2(\bar{x}).$$

Fig. 1.5.3 is another illustration of a two-variable, two-constraint problem. It shows only one of the constraints as binding at the solution $\bar{x}$. The existence of the second constraint has no influence on the problem solution. Once more, we see that there exists $\lambda_1, \lambda_2 \geqslant 0$ such that

$$\nabla f(\bar{x}) = \lambda_1 \nabla g^1(\bar{x}) + \lambda_2 \nabla g^2(\bar{x}).$$

We simply set $\lambda_2 = 0$.

At this point we might be tempted to suggest that a set of necessary conditions for $\bar{x}$ to be a solution to problem (1.3.1) are that there exist $\lambda_1, \lambda_2, ..., \lambda_m \geqslant 0$ such that

$$\nabla f(\bar{x}) = \sum_i \lambda_i \nabla g^i(\bar{x}),$$

$$g^i(\bar{x}) \leqslant 0, \quad i = 1, ..., m$$

and

$$\lambda_i = 0, \quad \text{if } g^i(\bar{x}) < 0.$$

This is almost right, but not quite. Inspection of fig. 1.5.4 reveals an exceptional case. Here the feasible region consists of just one point, and this point, $\bar{x}$, is obviously the problem solution. There is no non-negative linear combination of $\nabla g^1(\bar{x})$ and $\nabla g^2(\bar{x})$ which equals $\nabla f(\bar{x})$, i.e. there exists no non-negative values for λ_1 and λ_2 such that

$$\nabla f(\bar{x}) = \lambda_1 \nabla g^1(\bar{x}) + \lambda_2 \nabla g^2(\bar{x}).$$

Another exceptional case is illustrated in fig. 1.5.5. The feasible region is a cusp, and the solution is at $\bar{x}$. Again it is clear that there are no non-negative values for λ_1 and λ_2 such that

$$\nabla f(\bar{x}) = \lambda_1 \nabla g^1(\bar{x}) + \lambda_2 \nabla g^2(\bar{x}).$$

A theorem which is true is as follows.

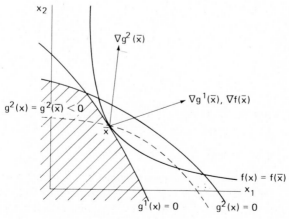

Figure 1.5.3

Theorem 1. Let $\bar{x}$ be a solution for problem (1.3.1). Then there exist $\lambda_0, \lambda_1, ..., \lambda_m \geqslant 0$, with at least one λ_i being nonzero, such that

$$\lambda_0 \nabla f(\bar{x}) = \sum_i \lambda_i \nabla g^i(\bar{x}),$$

$$g^i(\bar{x}) \leqslant 0, \quad \text{for } i = 1, ..., m$$

and

$$\lambda_i = 0, \qquad \text{if } g^i(\bar{x}) < 0.$$

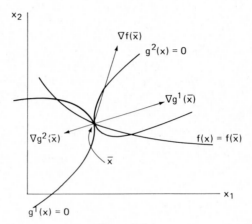

Figure 1.5.4

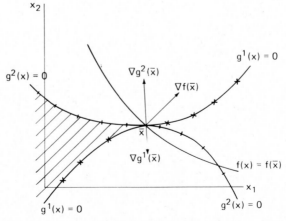

Figure 1.5.5

The exceptional cases illustrated in figs. 1.5.4 and 1.5.5 are now handled by setting $\lambda_0 = 0$. In both situations it is possible to find non-negative values for λ_1 and λ_2, not both zero, such that

$$0 = \lambda_1 g^1(\overline{x}) + \lambda_2 g^2(\overline{x}).$$

In figs. 1.5.1–1.5.3, λ_0 can be assigned the value 1.

We will not attempt to prove theorem 1. Mathematically motivated readers are referred to Mangasarian, ch. 7, see Reading Guide 1. We hope that other readers have gained a strong intuitive grasp of what it means from our diagrams.

Unfortunately, while true, theorem 1 is not completely discriminating. Many points can satisfy the conditions of theorem 1, and yet not solve problem (1.3.1). In fig. 1.5.6 both the points $\overline{x}$ and y satisfy the conditions of theorem 1, yet only $\overline{x}$ is a solution to problem (1.3.1). Similarly, both the points $\overline{x}$ and z in fig. 1.5.7[8] satisfy the conditions of theorem 1, but z is not a problem solution. Finally, all the points on the line XYZ in fig. 1.5.8 satisfy the conditions of theorem 1, but only Z is a problem solution.

The idea being emphasized is that theorem 1 provides some *necessary* conditions for $\overline{x}$ to solve problem (1.3.1), but they are not sufficient. Hence, in solving problem (1.3.1) it may not be enough simply to find any $\overline{x}$ which

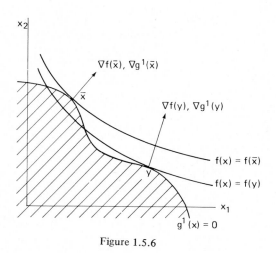

Figure 1.5.6

[8] Fig. 1.5.7 may be thought of as being similar to a topographical map on which there are two adjacent hills.

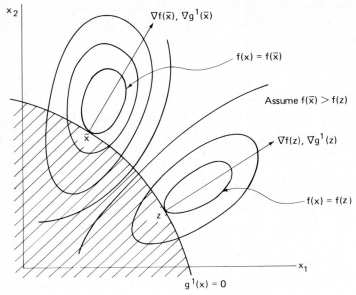

Figure 1.5.7

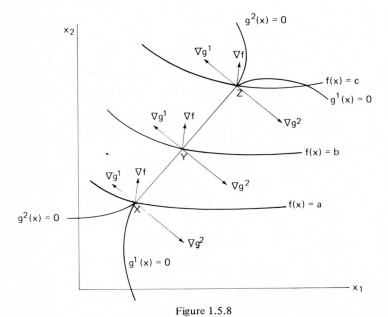

Figure 1.5.8

satisfies the conditions of theorem 1. All that we know is that the solution(s), if any, of problem (1.3.1) does satisfy the conditions of theorem 1.

Before proceeding to the next section, we suggest that you check your understanding of theorem 1 by working El.3—El.9.

1.6.   The role of convexity

What conditions on the functions f and g would rule out the possibility of having a point $\bar{x}$ which satisfies the conditions of theorem 1, but is not a solution of problem (1.3.1)? That is to say, in what circumstances can we know that the conditions of theorem 1 are sufficient as well as necessary.

Let us assume that the feasible region is *convex*. This means that if two points x and y satisfy the constraints, i.e.

$$g(x) \leqslant 0$$

and

$$g(y) \leqslant 0,$$

then the point

$$\alpha x + (1 - \alpha)y$$

also satisfies the constraints, i.e.

$$g(\alpha x + (1 - \alpha)y) \leqslant 0,$$

where α is any number in the interval 0 to 1, i.e. $\alpha \in [0, 1]$. ($\alpha \in [0, 1]$ means that $\alpha \geqslant 0$ and $\alpha \leqslant 1$.)

A convex set is illustrated in fig. 1.6.1, while fig. 1.6.2 shows a nonconvex set. From a geometric point of view, a set is convex if a straight line joining any two points within the set lies completely within the set.

Next we assume that f is a *quasiconcave* function. f is quasiconcave if for any number, γ, the set defined by $\{x \mid f(x) \geqslant \gamma\}$ is a convex set. In other words, if

$$f(y) \geqslant \gamma$$

and

$$f(z) \geqslant \gamma,$$

then

$$f(\alpha y + (1 - \alpha)z) \geqslant \gamma, \text{ for all } \alpha \in [0, 1].$$

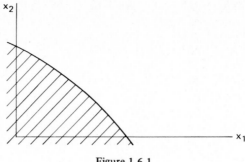

Figure 1.6.1

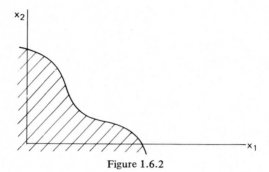

Figure 1.6.2

Fig. 1.6.3 shows the isovalue lines for a quasiconcave function and fig. 1.6.4 illustrates a nonquasiconcave function.

Our final assumption is that the constraint set contains an interior, i.e. we assume that there is at least one point x such that $g(x) < 0$. This assumption is known as Slater's *constraint qualification*. The role of constraint qualifications, of which Slater's is one example, is to rule out situations such as that illustrated in fig. 1.5.8. Notice that in fig. 1.5.8 the feasible region is convex (it is a straight line) but there is no point x in the feasible region which satisfies the constraints as strict inequalities.

Under the three assumptions — convex constraint set, quasiconcave objective function, and Slater's constraint qualification — the conditions in theorem 1 become sufficient, as well as necessary. We state the following theorem.

Theorem 2.   If f is a quasiconcave function, and the constraint set is both convex and satisfies Slater's constraint qualification, then $\bar{x}$ is a solution of

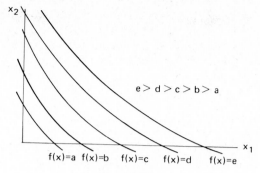

Figure 1.6.3

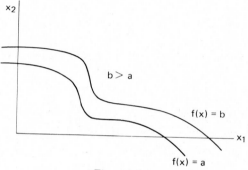

Figure 1.6.4

problem (1.3.1) if and only if there exist non-negative values for $\lambda_1,...,\lambda_m$ such that

$$\nabla f(\bar{x}) = \sum_i \lambda_i \nabla g^i(\bar{x}),$$

$$g^i(\bar{x}) \leqslant 0, \quad i = 1,...,m,$$

$$\lambda_i = 0, \quad \text{if } g^i(\bar{x}) < 0.$$

We will not prove theorem 2. However, we ask the reader to make certain he has a good intuitive grasp of it by checking over figs. 1.5.6–1.5.8. Notice that each of the three assumptions (convex constraint set, quasiconcave objective function, and Slater's constraint qualification) plays a role in making the conditions of theorem 2 sufficient (the 'if' part). Convexity of the constraint set rules out the problem illustrated in fig. 1.5.6. In fig. 1.5.7 the objective function is not quasiconcave, and again theorem 2 is inapplicable. Finally, as already mentioned, Slater's constraint qualification eliminates the problem illustrated in fig. 1.5.8.

Slater's constraint qualification also eliminates the problem illustrated in fig. 1.5.4, and in fig. 1.5.5 the constraint set is not convex. This dispenses with the 'exceptional' cases mentioned in the last section, and explains why in theorem 2 we have not had to include the possibility of λ_0 being zero.

1.7. The Lagrangian function

Many readers will be familiar with the method of Lagrange multipliers. A standard problem in college calculus courses is as follows: choose $x_1,...,x_n$ to maximize

$$f(x) \tag{1.7.1}$$

subject to

$$g^1(x) = 0,$$
$$\vdots$$
$$g^h(x) = 0.$$

The suggested solution method is to form the Lagrangian, and put the partial derivatives equal to zero, i.e. we define a function

$$L(x,\lambda) \equiv f(x) - \sum_{i=1}^{h} \lambda_i g^i(x).$$

Then we look for a solution for the x's and λ's in the system of $n + h$ equations

$$\frac{\partial L}{\partial x_j} \equiv \frac{\partial f}{\partial x_j} - \sum_{i=1}^{h} \lambda_i \frac{\partial g^i}{\partial x_j} = 0, \quad j = 1,...,n, \tag{1.7.2}$$

$$\frac{\partial L}{\partial \lambda_i} \equiv -g^i = 0, \qquad\qquad i = 1,...,h. \tag{1.7.3}$$

Why does the method work? According to theorem 1.1 (see E1.9 and its answer) if $\bar{x}$ is a solution to problem (1.7.1), then there exist numbers $\lambda_0,\lambda_1,...,\lambda_h$, not all zero, with $\lambda_0 \geqslant 0$, but $\lambda_1,...,\lambda_h$ of no predetermined sign, such that $\bar{x}$ and the λ's simultaneously satisfy

$$\lambda_0 \nabla f(\bar{x}) = \sum_{i=1}^{h} \lambda_i \nabla g^i(\bar{x}) \tag{1.7.4}$$

and

$$g^i(\bar{x}) = 0, \quad i = 1,...,h. \tag{1.7.5}$$

Apart from the troublesome λ_0, systems (1.7.4)–(1.7.5) is precisely the same as (1.7.2)–(1.7.3). The Lagrangian function acted as a mnemonic device. It can be used simply to remind us how to generate the list of necessary conditions for a constrained maximum.

There are two obvious questions. First, what can be done about λ_0? Secondly, can the Lagrangian function provide a useful memory aid for problems in which there are inequality and sign constraints?

Strictly, the λ_0 should be included. Without further information on the form of the f and the g^i we cannot be sure that (1.7.2)–(1.7.3) are a set of necessary conditions for a solution of problem (1.7.1), i.e. $\bar{x}$ could be a solution for problem (1.7.1), but there may exist no values for $\lambda_1, \lambda_2, ..., \lambda_h$ such that $\bar{x}$ and the λ's jointly satisfy (1.7.2)–(1.7.3). We can refer back to figs. 1.5.4, 1.5.5 and 1.5.8 for examples of situations in which the set of conditions generated by the Lagrangian would be inadequate. We could also try using the Lagrangian method to solve the trivial problem: choose x to maximize

$$x$$

subject to

$$x^2 = 0.$$

Despite the examples given in the last paragraph, λ_0 is usually ignored. It is implicitly set at 1. This is because in economic applications the 'exceptional' cases rarely arise. Notice that if we set $\lambda_0 = 0$ in the system (1.7.4)–(1.7.5), then the objective function f has no role. It would be a very strange economic problem which could be solved via a set of equations which involved no information about the objective function![9]

It is probably worth pointing out that after we have assumed that $\lambda_0 \neq 0$, then there is no further loss of generality in setting $\lambda_0 = 1$. If (1.7.4)–(1.7.5) are satisfied with $\lambda_0 = 2$, say, then they can be satisfied with $\lambda_0 = 1$ by simply halving the original choices for $\lambda_1, ..., \lambda_h$. When the convention of setting $\lambda_0 = 1$ is followed, then the resulting $\lambda_1, ..., \lambda_h$ are known as Lagrangian multipliers. In section 1.8 we will see that the Lagrangian multipliers have an interesting and important interpretation.

Our second question was concerned with the applicability of the Lagrangian function in problems in which there are sign and inequality constraints as well as equality constraints. We consider the problem: choose $x_1, x_2, ..., x_n$ to maximize

---

[9]   More formally, the exceptional cases can be ruled out by appealing to constraint qualifications. For example, in the last section we mentioned the Slater constraint qualification. While Slater's condition is not applicable in problems with equality constraints or in which the constraint set is nonconvex, there are various other conditions which are. See Mangasarian (1969, ch. 7).

$$f(x) \tag{1.7.6}$$

subject to

$$g^i(x) \leqslant 0, \quad i = 1,...,m,$$

$$g^i(x) = 0, \quad i = m + 1,...m + r,$$

$$x_j \geqslant 0, \quad j = 1,...,s.$$

Again we form the Lagrangian

$$L(x, \lambda) \equiv f(x) - \sum_{i=1}^{m+r} \lambda_i g^i(x).$$

Now we perform two operations. First we treat the λ's as given and write the necessary conditions for L to be maximized with respect to the choice of the x's, keeping in mind the sign constraints. This yields

$$\frac{\partial L(x, \lambda)}{\partial x_j} \equiv \frac{\partial f}{\partial x_j} - \sum_{i=1}^{m+r} \lambda_i \frac{\partial g^i}{\partial x_j} \leqslant 0, \quad j = 1,...,s, \tag{1.7.7a}$$

with

$$x_j = 0, \quad \text{if } \frac{\partial L(x, \lambda)}{\partial x_j} < 0, \qquad j = 1,...,s, \tag{1.7.7b}$$

and

$$\frac{\partial f}{\partial x_j} - \sum_{i=1}^{m+r} \lambda_i \frac{\partial g^i}{\partial x_j} = 0, \qquad j = s+1,...,n. \tag{1.7.8}$$

Next we treat the x's as given and write the necessary conditions for L to be minimized with respect to the choice of the λ's. This time we insist that $\lambda_i, i = 1,...,m$ are non-negative. This yields

$$\frac{\partial L(x, \lambda)}{\partial \lambda_i} \equiv -g^i \geqslant 0, \quad i = 1,...,m, \tag{1.7.9a}$$

with

$$\lambda_i = 0, \quad \text{if } -g^i > 0, \qquad i = 1,...,m, \tag{1.7.9b}$$

and

$$-g^i = 0, \qquad i = m + 1,...,m + r. \tag{1.7.10}$$

On combining the results of E1.8 and E1.9 we see that (apart from the λ_0), (1.7.7)–(1.7.10) are a set of necessary conditions for the solution of problem

(1.7.6.). Thus, if we assume away the exceptional case, the necessary conditions for a solution of problem (1.7.6) can be generated by writing the necessary conditions for a saddle point[10] of

$$L(x, \lambda),$$

where the λ_i corresponding to the less-than-or-equal-to constraints and the relevant x_i are restricted to being non-negative. Again it appears that the Lagrangian can be a useful mnemonic device.

1.8. Displacement analysis and the interpretation of the Lagrangian multipliers

Consider the problem of choosing x to maximize

$$f(x) \tag{1.8.1}$$

subject to

$$g^i(x) = b_i, \quad i = 1,...,h,$$

where the b_i are parameters. In previous sections we have written the constraints with zeros on the right-hand side. In this section it will be convenient, for notational reasons, to denote the right-hand sides by b_i's. We will be concerned with the question: how does the value of the objective function vary with the values of the b's or, more technically, what are the values of

$$\partial f/\partial b_j, \quad j = 1,...,h \ ?$$

This sort of question arises quite frequently in mathematical and quantitative economics. For example, we might be choosing output levels to maximize profits subject to the availability of a fixed amount of different types of equipment. In deciding whether to buy another machine, i.e. increase one of the b_i's, we will want to know the effect on our objective function, f. One approach would be to solve the problem several times with the b_i's set at different levels and then to compare the resulting values for the objective function. However, if we are concerned only with small variations in the b_i's, it turns out that the relevant information is usually contained in one solution of the problem.

We assume[11] that if $\bar{x}$ solves (1.8.1), then there exists a *unique*[12] set of

---

[10] $\bar{a}, \bar{b}$ is a saddle point of $\psi(a,b)$ if $\bar{a}$ maximizes $\psi(a,\bar{b})$ and $\bar{b}$ minimizes $\psi(\bar{a},b)$.
[11] We assume away the exceptional case.
[12] The assumption that the λ_i are unique is crucial in the argument and conclusions of this section. In E1.16 you will encounter an example in which more than one set of λ_i can satisfy (1.8.2) for a given solution, $\bar{x}$. However, before becoming involved in this non-standard case, you should complete your reading of this section.

numbers $\lambda_1, \lambda_2, ..., \lambda_h$, the Langrangian multipliers, such that $\bar{x}$ and the λ's jointly satisfy

$$\nabla f(\bar{x}) = \sum_{i=1}^{h} \lambda_i \nabla g^i(\bar{x}), \tag{1.8.2}$$

and

$$g^i(\bar{x}) = b_i, \quad i = 1, ..., h. \tag{1.8.3}$$

If we make a small change in the b_i's, and we are to continue to satisfy the constraints, then provided that the resulting change, dx, in the problem solution is small,[13] we can write

$$(\nabla g^i(\bar{x}))' dx = db_i, \quad i = 1, ..., h, \tag{1.8.4}$$

where the db_i are the changes in the b_i's. [14] Also, the change in the value of the objective function will be

$$df = (\nabla f(\bar{x}))' dx. \tag{1.8.5}$$

When we combine (1.8.2), (1.8.4) and (1.8.5) we find that

$$df = \sum_{i=1}^{h} \lambda_i \, db_i. \tag{1.8.6}$$

In the special case where only one, say the jth, b is moved,

$$df = \lambda_j \, db_j$$

and so

$$\partial f / \partial b_j = \lambda_j, \tag{1.8.7}$$

where we use the partial derivative notation to emphasize that (1.8.7) is concerned with the rate of change of f with respect to changes in b_j, holding all the other b's constant.

The λ's not only play an important role in the solution of constrained optimization problems, in 'standard' cases, they can also answer questions concerning the sensitivity of the value of the objective function to changes in resource availabilities. In some nonstandard situations, where small changes in the b_i's

---

[13]   In some problems, a small change in the b_i's can produce a discontinuous jump in the solution. E 1.17 is an example. This is, however, a fairly unusual case and you should complete this section before worrying about it.
[14]   We assume that the small changes in the b_i's do not render the problem (1.8.1) infeasible, i.e. we assume that there exist values for dx which satisfy (1.8.4). This is in fact implied by the assumption that the Lagrangian multipliers are unique, see E1.16 and its answer.

produce discontinuous 'jumps' in the problem solution, or where the λ's are not uniquely determined or where the assumption that $\lambda_0 > 0$ is invalid, (1.8.7) does not apply.

El.15–El.17 are designed to increase your familiarity with the ideas of this section. Then in El.18, you are asked to check whether result (1.8.7) generalizes to problems in which there are inequality constraints. Since inequality constraints are important in economics, we urge you to work through to El.18.

PROBLEM SET 1

Exercise 1.1. *Standard form*

Rewrite the following problem in standard form.

Choose non-negative values for x to minimize $f(x)$ subject to $g^1(x) \leqslant 0$, $g^2(x) = 0$, $g^3(x) \geqslant 0$.

Our answer is given below. We hope that with this problem, as with all others in the book, you will make an effort to provide your own answer, before looking at ours.

Answer. Textbooks vary as to which problem they call standard. We have chosen maximization subject to less-than-or-equal-to constraints. Exercise 1.1 asks you to rewrite a minimize problem with equality, greater-than-or-equal-to, less-than-or-equal-to and sign constraints in standard form. This can be done as follows: choose x to maximize

$$-f(x)$$

subject to

$$g^1(x) \leqslant 0,$$
$$g^2(x) \leqslant 0,$$
$$-g^2(x) \leqslant 0,$$
$$-g^3(x) \leqslant 0$$

and

$$-x \leqslant 0.$$

Exercise 1.2. *Contour–gradient diagram*

Consider the function

$$f(x_1, x_2) = x_1^2 + x_2^2.$$

What is the value of the gradient vector at $(x_1, x_2) = (2, 1)$? What is the slope of a line in the gradient direction? (Let x_2 be on the vertical axis and x_1 be on the horizontal.) What is the slope of the contour at $(2, 1)$? Make the relevant sketch and mark on the gradient direction at $(2, 1)$.

Answer.

$$\nabla f(x)' = (2x_1, 2x_2),$$

When

$$x' = (2, 1); \quad \nabla f(x)' = (4, 2).$$

Hence, at $(2, 1)$ the slope of the line in the gradient direction is 2/4, i.e. 1/2. The slope of the contour is $-f_1/f_2 = -2x_1/2x_2$. Thus, at $x' = (2, 1)$ the slope of the contour is $-4/2$, i.e. -2. Fig. E1.2.1 is the relevant contour–gradient diagram.

Exercise 1.3. Necessary conditions for a constrained maximum

In each of the figs. E1.3.1–E1.3.4, does $\bar{x}$ satisfy the necessary conditions (theorem 1) for a constrained maximum? Is $\bar{x}$ in fact a constrained maximum? The shading indicates the feasible set.

Obviously a 'no' answer to the first question implies a 'no' answer to the second. It is possible, however, for you to answer 'yes' for the first question, but 'no' for the second.

Answer. Fig. E1.3.1, no, no.

At $\bar{x}$ neither constraint is binding. Therefore, λ_1 and λ_2 must be set at zero. Then zero would be the only value for λ_0 such that

$$\lambda_0 \nabla f(\bar{x}) = \lambda_1 \nabla g^1(\bar{x}) + \lambda_2 \nabla g^2(\bar{x}).$$

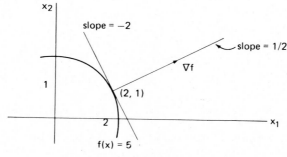

Figure E1.2.1

However, not all the λ_i, $i = 0,...,m$ are allowed to be zero. Hence $\bar{x}$ does not satisfy the conditions of theorem 1.

Fig. E1.3.2, yes, no.
At $\bar{x}$, $\nabla f(x) = 0$. Hence, we can choose $\lambda_0 = 1$, say, and $\lambda_1 = 0$ and satisfy the condition

$$\lambda_0 \nabla f(\bar{x}) = \lambda_1 \nabla g^1(\bar{x}).$$

$\bar{x}$, and our values for the λ_i's clearly satisfy the remaining conditions of theorem 1, and thus $\bar{x}$ satisfies the necessary conditions for a constrained maximum.

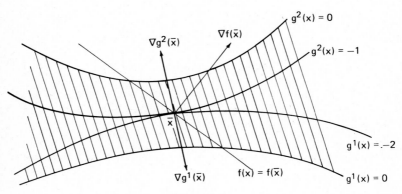

Figure E1.3.1

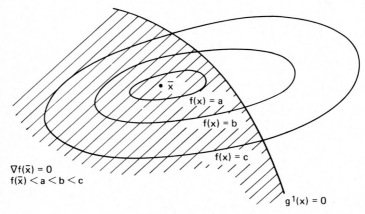

Figure E1.3.2

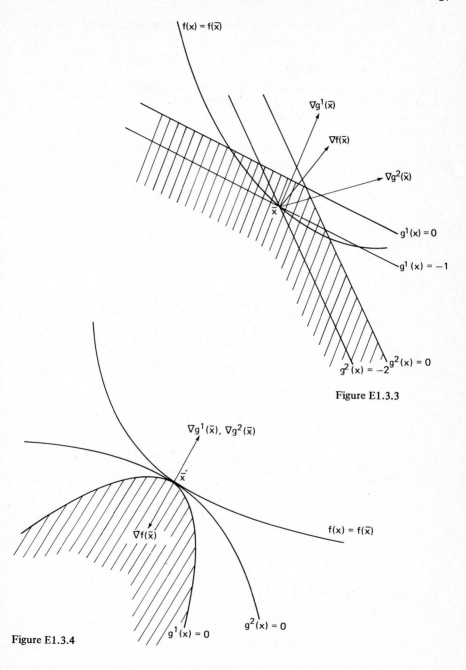

Figure E1.3.3

Figure E1.3.4

However, $\bar{x}$ is not a constrained maximum. It is a minimum rather than a maximum. When you have studied theorem 2 (see section 1.6), you could consider the following question: how does theorem 2 rule out the problem illustrated in fig E1.3.2?

(Answer. $f(x)$ is not quasiconcave. For any number, γ, the set defined by $\{x \mid f(x) \geqslant \gamma\}$ is not convex. In fact, f is quasiconvex, i.e. for any number, γ, the set defined by $\{x \mid f(x) \leqslant \gamma\}$ is convex.)

Fig. E1.3.3, no, no.
The argument here is the same as for fig. E1.3.1.

Fig. E1.3.4, no, no.
It is not possible to find non-negative values, not all zero, for $\lambda_0, \lambda_1, \lambda_2$, such that

$$\lambda_0 \nabla f(\bar{x}) = \lambda_1 \nabla g^1(\bar{x}) + \lambda_2 \nabla g^2(\bar{x}).$$

Exercise 1.4. An easy optimization problem

Find values for x_1 and x_2 which maximize

$$x_1 + x_2$$

subject to

$$x_1^2 + x_2^2 - 1 \leqslant 0.$$

Solve the problem by looking for values of (x_1, x_2) which satisfy the conditions of theorem 1.

Answer. If (x_1, x_2) is a constrained maximum, then there exist $\lambda_0, \lambda_1 \geqslant 0$, with not both λ_0 and λ_1 equal to zero, such that

$$\lambda_0 = \lambda_1 2x_1, \tag{i}$$

$$\lambda_0 = \lambda_1 2x_2, \tag{ii}$$

$$x_1^2 + x_2^2 - 1 \leqslant 0, \tag{iii}$$

$$\lambda_1(x_1^2 + x_2^2 - 1) = 0. \tag{iv}$$

(Notice that the last condition is an alternative way of writing $\lambda_1 = 0$ if $x_1^2 + x_2^2 - 1 < 0$.)

Is it possible that $\lambda_0 = 0$? If λ_0 were zero, then λ_1 could not be zero since not both λ_0 and λ_1 are allowed to be zero. Hence we would have $(x_1, x_2) = 0$.

However, then the constraint would not be binding, and we would have to set $\lambda_1 = 0$. We may conclude that there is no x satisfying the necessary conditions for a constrained maximum with $\lambda_0 = 0$.

We assume, without loss of generality, that $\lambda_0 = 1$. If $\lambda_1 = 0$, then neither (i) nor (ii) could be fulfilled. Therefore λ_1 must be greater than zero and the constraint must be binding. Hence the constrained maximum can be found by solving for x_1, x_2 and $\lambda_1 > 0$, in the system

$$1 = \lambda_1 2x_1,$$

$$1 = \lambda_1 2x_2,$$

$$x_1^2 + x_2^2 - 1 = 0.$$

This gives the solution

$$x_1 = x_2 = \lambda_1 = 1/\sqrt{2}.$$

(Notice that $x_1 = x_2 = -1/\sqrt{2}$ is not a solution. It fails to give a positive λ_1.)

While it is clear that $x = (1/\sqrt{2}, 1/\sqrt{2})$ satisfies the necessary conditions for a constrained maximum, can we be sure that it is a constrained maximum? We could appeal to theorem 2, section 1.6. Our problem has a quasiconcave objective function, a convex constraint set, and satisfies the constraint qualification. Perhaps a simpler, and more general argument is as follows. Provided that we are sure that the problem has a solution at all, then $(1/\sqrt{2}, 1/\sqrt{2})$ must be it. It is the only point which satisfies the necessary conditions. The *Weierstrass theorem* assures us that the problem does have a solution.[15]

Exercise 1.5. *A more difficult optimization problem*

Find values for x_1 and x_2 which maximize

$$8x_1 + 9x_2$$

subject to

$$x_1^2 + x_2^2 - 1 \leqslant 0$$

and

$$(x_1 + 1)(x_2 + 1) - 2 \leqslant 0.$$

---

[15] This theorem says that if the constraint set is nonempty and compact (i.e. the constraint set contains its boundary points and is bounded) and the objective function is continuous, then problem (1.3.1) has a solution. See Intriligator (1971, p. 13).

Be sure to check that you do have a problem solution. It is not sufficient merely to find a point which satisfies the conditions of theorem 1.

Answer.   The easiest way to solve the problem is by drawing a diagram. From fig. E1.5.1 it is clear that the solution is at $x' = (0, 1)$. However, to illustrate the use of theorem 1, we will solve the problem mechanically. We look for values of $x_1, x_2, \lambda_0, \lambda_1, \lambda_2$, with the λ_i being non-negative and not all zero, such that

$$\lambda_0 8 = \lambda_1 2x_1 + \lambda_2 (x_2 + 1), \tag{i}$$

$$\lambda_0 9 = \lambda_1 2x_2 + \lambda_2 (x_1 + 1), \tag{ii}$$

$$x_1^2 + x_2^2 - 1 \leqslant 0, \tag{iii}$$

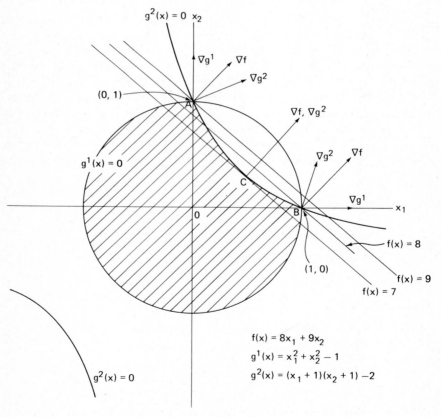

$$f(x) = 8x_1 + 9x_2$$
$$g^1(x) = x_1^2 + x_2^2 - 1$$
$$g^2(x) = (x_1 + 1)(x_2 + 1) - 2$$

Figure E1.5.1

$$(x_1 + 1)(x_2 + 1) - 2 \leqslant 0, \tag{iv}$$

$$\lambda_1(x_1^2 + x_2^2 - 1) = 0, \tag{v}$$

$$\lambda_2((x_1 + 1)(x_2 + 1) - 2) = 0. \tag{vi}$$

Our strategy will be as follows. First we will set $\lambda_0 = 0$, and ask whether there are any solutions to (i)–(vi) with this condition satisfied. Then we will set $\lambda_0 = 1$ and consider in turn the cases in which both constraints are binding, no constraints are binding, and one constraint is binding. More specifically, we will be examining each of the cases shown in table E1.5.1. The result column anticipates the working which is to follow.

Is it possible to find a solution for (i)–(vi) with $\lambda_0 = \lambda_1 = 0$? Assume that such a solution exists. Then $\lambda_2 \neq 0$. (Not all the λ_i are allowed to be zero.) Hence (i) and (ii) imply that $(x_2 + 1) = (x_1 + 1) = 0$. Then (vi) implies that $\lambda_2 = 0$. This contradicts our previous assertion that $\lambda_2 \neq 0$. Therefore we can conclude that there are no solutions for (i)–(vi) with $\lambda_0 = \lambda_1 = 0$. By a similar argument, the reader can establish that there are no solutions with $\lambda_0 = \lambda_2 = 0$.

Is it possible to find a solution for (i)–(vi) with $\lambda_0 = 0$, but λ_1 and λ_2 both strictly greater than zero? If such a solution exists, we know from (v) and (vi) that it must satisfy

$$x_1^2 + x_2^2 - 1 = 0, \tag{vii}$$

$$(x_1 + 1)(x_2 + 1) - 2 = 0. \tag{viii}$$

From fig. E1.5.1, or otherwise, the reader will find that (vii) and (viii) imply that either[16]

$$(x_1, x_2) = (1, 0)$$

Table E1.5.1

Case	λ_0	λ_1	λ_2	Result
1	0	0	+	no solution
2	0	+	0	no solution
3	0	+	+	no solution
4	1	+	+	two solutions
5	1	0	0	no solution
6	1	+	0	no solution
7	1	0	+	one solution

[16] These are the only real roots of (vii) and (viii). There are some complex roots which we will ignore. We are interested in real solutions only.

or

$$(x_1, x_2) = (0, 1).$$

However, if $(x_1, x_2) = (1, 0)$ and $\lambda_0 = 0$, then (i) and (ii) imply that

$$0 = \lambda_1 2 + \lambda_2$$

and

$$0 = 0 + \lambda_2 2,$$

which would mean that $\lambda_1 = \lambda_2 = 0$. Also, if $(x_1, x_2) = (0, 1)$ and $\lambda_0 = 0$, then (i) and (ii) imply that

$$0 = 0 + \lambda_2 2$$

and

$$0 = \lambda_1 2 + \lambda_2.$$

Again, we would have $\lambda_1 = \lambda_2 = 0$. Hence we may conclude that there are no solutions to (i)–(vi) with $\lambda_0 = 0$ and $\lambda_1, \lambda_2 > 0$. In fact, the argument so far has established that there are no solutions with $\lambda_0 = 0$.

From here on, without loss of generality, we assume that $\lambda_0 = 1$. With $\lambda_0 = 1$, is it possible to find a solution to (i)–(vi) in which both λ_1 and λ_2 are positive? In the last paragraph, we found that if both constraints are binding, then either

$$(x_1, x_2) = (1, 0) \quad \text{or} \quad (x_1, x_2) = (0, 1).$$

With $(x_1, x_2) = (1, 0)$ and $\lambda_0 = 1$, (i) and (ii) imply that

$$\left.\begin{array}{l} 8 = \lambda_1 2 + \lambda_2 \\ 9 = 0 + \lambda_2 2 \end{array}\right\} \implies \lambda_2 = 4\tfrac{1}{2}, \quad \lambda_1 = 1\tfrac{3}{4}.$$

Hence $x_1 = 1, x_2 = 0, \lambda_0 = 1, \lambda_1 = 1\tfrac{3}{4}, \lambda_2 = 4\tfrac{1}{2}$ satisfy (i)–(vi), i.e. $x_1 = 1, x_2 = 0$ satisfy the necessary conditions for a constrained maximum. In fig. E1.5.1 we have located point B. Similarly we can show that $x_1 = 0, x_2 = 1, \lambda_0 = 1, \lambda_1 = 2\tfrac{1}{2}$, $\lambda_2 = 4$ also satisfy the necessary conditions for a constrained maximum (point A in the diagram).

We still have not finished. There are three more cases to consider. Is it possible to find a solution to (i)–(vi) with neither constraint being binding? This would imply that $\lambda_1 = \lambda_2 = 0$. From (i) and (ii) we obtain $\lambda_0 = 0$, contradicting our assumption that $\lambda_0 = 1$. Next, is it possible that just the first constraint is binding, i.e. $\lambda_1 > 0, \lambda_2 = 0$ and

$$x_1^2 + x_2^2 - 1 = 0? \tag{ix}$$

With $\lambda_2 = 0$ and $\lambda_0 = 1$, (i) and (ii) imply that

$$8 = \lambda_1 2x_1,$$
$$9 = \lambda_1 2x_2.$$

Hence

$$8/9 = x_1/x_2. \tag{x}$$

By using (ix) and (x) we find that

$$((8/9)^2 + 1)x_2^2 = 1,$$

i.e.

$$x_2 = \pm 1/\sqrt{(1 + (8/9)^2)}$$

and

$$x_1 = \pm 8/9\sqrt{(1 + (8/9)^2)}.$$

The negative values for (x_1, x_2) can be ignored because they are inconsistent with a non-negative value for λ_1. The positive solutions for (x_1, x_2) are also inconsistent with (i)–(vi). Notice that they violate the second constraint because

$$(1 + 1/\sqrt{(1 + (8/9)^2)})(1 + 8/9\sqrt{(1 + (8/9)^2)}) - 2 > 0.$$

Hence there are no solutions for (i)–(vi) with $\lambda_0 = 1$, $\lambda_2 = 0$, and $\lambda_1 > 0$.
The last case to consider is $\lambda_0 = 1$, $\lambda_1 = 0$ and $\lambda_2 > 0$. This would imply

$$8 = \lambda_2(x_2 + 1), \tag{xi}$$
$$9 = \lambda_2(x_1 + 1) \tag{xii}$$

and

$$(x_1 + 1)(x_2 + 1) - 2 = 0. \tag{xiii}$$

We find that $x_1 = \frac{1}{2}, x_2 = \frac{1}{3}$ and $\lambda_2 = 6$ satisfy (xi)–(xiii). There are also some negative solutions for x_1 and x_2, but some arithmetic shows that these violate (iii). We check that $x_1 = \frac{1}{2}, x_2 = \frac{1}{3}$ is consistent with the first constraint by noting that

$$(\tfrac{1}{2})^2 + (\tfrac{1}{3})^2 - 1 < 0.$$

Hence, we have found a third solution to (i)–(vi), point C in fig. E1.5.1. To summarize, our three solutions are:

$$x_1 = 1; \quad x_1 = 0; \quad x_1 = \tfrac{1}{2},$$

$$x_2 = 0; \quad x_2 = 1; \quad x_2 = \tfrac{1}{3},$$

$$\lambda_0 = 1; \quad \lambda_0 = 1; \quad \lambda_0 = 1,$$

$$\lambda_1 = 1\tfrac{3}{4}; \quad \lambda_1 = 2\tfrac{1}{2}; \quad \lambda_1 = 0,$$

$$\lambda_2 = 4\tfrac{1}{2}; \quad \lambda_2 = 4; \quad \lambda_2 = 6.$$

The first of these solutions gives a value of 8 for the objective function. The second gives a value of 9 and the third gives a value of 7. Hence, the problem solution is $x_1 = 0, x_2 = 1$.[17]

Exercise 1.6. *An exceptional case*

Find values for x_1 and x_2 which maximize

$$2x_1 + x_2$$

subject to

$$x_1^2 + x_2^2 - 1 \leqslant 0 \quad \text{and} \quad x_1 x_2 \geqslant \tfrac{1}{2}.$$

Again, the easiest way to solve the problem is by drawing a diagram. From fig. E1.6.1, it appears that the feasible set consists of just two points: $(1/\sqrt{2}, 1/\sqrt{2})$ and $(-1/\sqrt{2}, -1/\sqrt{2})$. Both these points satisfy the necessary conditions for a constrained maximum, but it is clear that the problem solution is the former.

As in the previous exercise, we illustrate the application of theorem 1 by solving the problem mechanically. We look for values of $x_1, x_2, \lambda_0, \lambda_1, \lambda_2$, with the λ_i being non-negative and not all zero, such that

$$\lambda_0 2 = \lambda_1 2x_1 - \lambda_2 x_2, \tag{i}$$

$$\lambda_0 = \lambda_1 2x_2 - \lambda_2 x_1, \tag{ii}$$

$$x_1^2 + x_2^2 - 1 \leqslant 0, \tag{iii}$$

$$-x_1 x_2 + \tfrac{1}{2} \leqslant 0, \tag{iv}$$

$$\lambda_1(x_1^2 + x_2^2 - 1) = 0, \tag{v}$$

$$\lambda_2(-x_1 x_2 + \tfrac{1}{2}) = 0. \tag{vi}$$

---

[17] The ultra-careful reader will notice that we have *assumed* that the problem does have a solution. Given that it has a solution, then we have shown that the solution must be $(x_1, x_2) = (0, 1)$. The assumption that a solution exists is justified by the Weierstrass theorem.

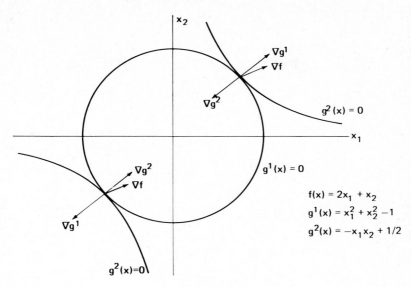

Figure E1.6.1

(*Note:* the second constraint has been rewritten as a less-than-or-equal-to constraint.)

We follow the strategy of the previous exercise and work through the cases listed in table E1.5.1. In case 1, i.e. $\lambda_0 = \lambda_1 = 0$, $\lambda_2 > 0$, we obtain $x_1 = x_2 = 0$. This violates (iv). Hence there is no solution to (i)–(vi) with $\lambda_0 = \lambda_1 = 0$. Similarly, there is no solution for case 2. However, for case 3, i.e. $\lambda_0 = 0$, λ_1, $\lambda_2 > 0$, we have

$$x_1^2 + x_2^2 - 1 = 0,$$

$$-x_1 x_2 + \tfrac{1}{2} = 0.$$

This implies that either

$$(x_1, x_2) = (1/\sqrt{2}, 1/\sqrt{2})$$

or

$$(x_1, x_2) = (-1/\sqrt{2}, -1/\sqrt{2}).$$

If $(x_1, x_2) = (1/\sqrt{2}, 1/\sqrt{2})$, then (i) and (ii) imply

$$0 = \lambda_1 2/\sqrt{2} - \lambda_2/\sqrt{2}$$

No

and

$$0 = \lambda_1 2/\sqrt{2} - \lambda_2/\sqrt{2}.$$

$\lambda_1 = 1$, $\lambda_2 = 2$ are among the possible solutions of these last two equations. Similarly, if $(x_1, x_2) = (-1/\sqrt{2}, -1/\sqrt{2})$, we find $\lambda_1 = 1$, $\lambda_2 = 2$ will satisfy (i) and (ii). Hence, we have found two distinct [18] solutions to (i)–(vi). They are

$$x_1 = 1/\sqrt{2}; \quad x_1 = -1/\sqrt{2},$$
$$x_2 = 1/\sqrt{2}; \quad x_2 = -1/\sqrt{2},$$
$$\lambda_0 = 0; \quad \lambda_0 = 0,$$
$$\lambda_1 = 1; \quad \lambda_1 = 1,$$
$$\lambda_2 = 2; \quad \lambda_2 = 2.$$

In case 4 we again find that $(x_1, x_2) = \pm (1/\sqrt{2}, 1/\sqrt{2})$. By substituting the positive solutions into (i) and (ii), we obtain

$$2 = \lambda_1 2/\sqrt{2} - \lambda_2/\sqrt{2},$$
$$1 = \lambda_1 2/\sqrt{2} - \lambda_2/\sqrt{2}.$$

These two equations are inconsistent. Similarly if we substitute the negative solutions for x_1 and x_2 into (i) and (ii) we generate inconsistent equations. Hence case 4 yields no solutions.

Case 5 is quickly dispensed with by looking at either (i) or (ii). In case 6 we have

$$2 = \lambda_1 2x_1,$$
$$1 = \lambda_1 2x_2,$$
$$x_1^2 + x_2^2 - 1 = 0.$$

This implies that $(x_1, x_2) = \pm (2/\sqrt{5}, 1/\sqrt{5})$. The negative solutions are inconsistent with λ_1 being positive and the positive solutions violate (iv). Hence case 6 yields no solutions.

In case 7, i.e. $\lambda_0 = 1, \lambda_1 = 0, \lambda_2 > 0$,

$$2 = -\lambda_2 x_2,$$
$$1 = -\lambda_2 x_1$$

[18]   The scale of the λ_i's is arbitrary. We will consider solutions to be distinct only if they differ in the x's.

and

$$-x_1 x_2 + \tfrac{1}{2} = 0.$$

This implies that $(x_1, x_2) = \pm (1/2, 1)$. Both of these solutions violate (iii).

We conclude that the only solutions to (i)–(vi) were those generated in case 3. From these it is clear that the problem solution is $x_1 = 1/\sqrt{2}$, $x_2 = 1/\sqrt{2}$. Footnote 17 is again applicable.

Why is this problem 'exceptional'? Could we have solved it via the Lagrangian function? (See section 1.7.)

Exercise 1.7.   Direction of steepest ascent

Choose values for $r_1,...,r_n$ to maximize

$$\sum_i r_i f_i$$

subject to

$$\sum_i r_i^2 \leqslant 1.$$

Assume that not all the f_i are zero.

Answer.   If $r_1,...,r_n$ is a constrained maximum, then there exists λ_0, λ_1 such that $r_1,...,r_n$ and λ_0, λ_1 jointly satisfy

$$\lambda_0 f_i = 2\lambda_1 r_i, \quad i = 1,...,n,$$

$$\sum_i r_i^2 - 1 \leqslant 0,$$

$$\lambda_1 = 0, \qquad \text{if } \sum_i r_i^2 - 1 < 0,$$

$$\lambda_0, \lambda_1 \geqslant 0, \quad \text{with not both being equal to zero.}$$

Is it possible that $\lambda_0 = 0$? If λ_0 were zero, then λ_1 could not be zero. Hence, each of the r_i would be zero. But this would mean that

$$\sum_i r_i^2 - 1 < 0$$

and λ_1 would therefore be zero. Hence λ_0 is not zero.

Since λ_0 is not zero, and not all the f_i are zero, (by assumption) we may conclude that λ_1 is not zero. Thus

$$r_i = \frac{\lambda_0}{2\lambda_1} f_i, \quad \text{for all } i$$

and

$$\sum_i r_i^2 = 1.$$

Hence

$$1 = \sum_i r_i^2 = \frac{\lambda_0^2}{4\lambda_1^2} \sum_i f_i^2$$

and

$$\frac{\lambda_0}{2\lambda_1} = \sqrt{(1/\sum f_i^2)}.$$

(The λ's must both be positive. Therefore we can ignore the negative root.) Thus

$$r_i = f_i/\sqrt{\sum f_i^2}, \quad i = 1,...,n.$$

We know that this must be the problem solution. It is the only set of values for the r_i which satisfy the necessary conditions. (Again footnote 17 applies.)

Are you sure that this problem justifies the assertion that the gradient direction is the direction of steepest ascent?

Exercise 1.8.   Sign constraints

Consider the problem of choosing x to maximize

$$f(x)$$

subject to

$$g(x) \leqslant 0$$

and

$$x \geqslant 0.$$

Using theorem 1, show that if $\bar{x}$ is a problem solution, then there exists a nonzero, non-negative vector

$$\lambda' = (\lambda_0, \lambda_1,...,\lambda_m)$$

such that

$$\lambda_0 \nabla f(\bar{x}) \leqslant \sum_i \lambda_i \nabla g^i(\bar{x}),$$
$$\bar{x}'\left\{\lambda_0 \nabla f(\bar{x}) - \sum_i \lambda_i \nabla g^i(\bar{x})\right\} = 0,$$
$$g(\bar{x}) \leqslant 0, \quad -\bar{x} \leqslant 0,$$

and

$$\widetilde{\lambda}' g(\bar{x}) = 0,$$

where

$$\widetilde{\lambda}' = (\lambda_1,...,\lambda_m).$$

Answer. In standard form, the problem is to choose x to maximize

$$f(x)$$

subject to

$$g(x) \leqslant 0$$

and

$$-x \leqslant 0.$$

From theorem 1, it follows that if $\bar{x}$ is a problem solution, then there exist $(\lambda_0, \lambda_1, ..., \lambda_m, \lambda_{m+1}, ..., \lambda_{m+n})$, non-negative and not all zero, such that the λ's and $\bar{x}$ jointly satisfy

$$\lambda_0 \nabla f(\bar{x}) = \sum_{i=1}^{m} \lambda_i \nabla g^i(\bar{x}) + \lambda_{m+1} \begin{pmatrix} -1 \\ 0 \\ \vdots \\ 0 \end{pmatrix} + \lambda_{m+2} \begin{pmatrix} 0 \\ -1 \\ \vdots \\ 0 \end{pmatrix} + ... + \lambda_{m+n} \begin{pmatrix} 0 \\ 0 \\ \vdots \\ -1 \end{pmatrix}, \quad \text{(i)}$$

$$g(\bar{x}) \leqslant 0, \tag{ii}$$

$$\tilde{\lambda}' g(\bar{x}) = 0, \tag{iii}$$

$$-\bar{x} \leqslant 0 \tag{iv}$$

and

$$\lambda_{m+j} = 0, \quad \text{if } -\bar{x}_j < 0.$$

Since each of the $\lambda_{m+1}, ..., \lambda_{m+n}$ is non-negative, we may replace the first condition by

$$\lambda_0 \nabla f(\bar{x}) \leqslant \sum_{i=1}^{m} \lambda_i \nabla g^i(\bar{x}). \tag{v}$$

Furthermore, if the jth component of this relationship holds as a strict inequality, then λ_{m+j} must be greater than zero and $\bar{x}_j = 0$, i.e. if

$$\lambda_0 \frac{\partial f(\bar{x})}{\partial x_j} < \sum_{i=1}^{m} \lambda_i \frac{\partial g^i(\bar{x})}{\partial x_j}$$

then

$$\bar{x}_j = 0.$$

Hence

$$\bar{x}_j \left\{ \lambda_0 \frac{\partial f(\bar{x})}{\partial x_j} - \sum_{i=1}^{m} \lambda_i \frac{\partial g^i(\bar{x})}{\partial x_j} \right\} = 0, \quad \text{for all } j = 1,...,n$$

and therefore,

$$\bar{x}' \left\{ \lambda_0 \nabla f(\bar{x}) - \sum_{i=1}^{m} \lambda_i \nabla g^i(\bar{x}) \right\} = 0. \tag{vi}$$

Conditions (ii)–(vi) establish the required proposition.

Exercise 1.9.   Equality constraints

Consider the problem of choosing x to maximize

$$f(x) \tag{E1.9.1}$$

subject to

$$g^1(x) = 0.$$

Rewrite the problem into standard form, and then use theorem 1 to generate the necessary conditions for $\bar{x}$ to be a problem solution. This set of necessary conditions is not very useful. Why?

Answer.   In standard form, the problem is to choose x to maximize

$$f(x)$$

subject to

$$g^1(x) \leqslant 0$$

and

$$-g^1(x) \leqslant 0.$$

According to theorem 1, if $\bar{x}$ is a solution, then there will exist $\lambda_0, \lambda_1, \lambda_2$, non-negative and not all zero, such that $\lambda_0, \lambda_1, \lambda_2$ and $\bar{x}$ jointly satisfy

$$\lambda_0 \nabla f(\bar{x}) = \lambda_1 \nabla g^1(\bar{x}) + \lambda_2(-\nabla g^1(\bar{x})), \tag{i}$$

$$g^1(\bar{x}) \leqslant 0, \quad \text{with } \lambda_1 = 0, \text{ if } g^1(\bar{x}) < 0,$$

$$-g^1(\bar{x}) \leqslant 0, \quad \text{with } \lambda_2 = 0, \text{ if } -g^1(\bar{x}) < 0. \tag{ii}$$

This does not, however, form a useful set of necessary conditions. *Any* x^* which merely satisfies the constraint will satisfy the necessary conditions! We simply put $\lambda_0 = 0$, $\lambda_1 = \lambda_2 = 1$. Then (i) is satisfied; both sides are zero. Clearly (ii) is satisfied since

$$g^1(x^*) = 0$$

and

$$-g^1(x^*) = 0.$$

How can we sharpen theorem 1 so that it provides information about the problem solution when there are equality constraints? One approach is to consider a problem which is very close to the original problem. We choose x to maximize

$$f(x) \tag{E1.9.2}$$

subject to

$$g^1(x) - \epsilon \leqslant 0$$

and

$$-g^1(x) - \epsilon \leqslant 0,$$

where ϵ is an arbitrarily small positive number.

The constraints in problem (E1.9.2) do not force $g^1(x)$ to be precisely zero, but they do force $g^1(x)$ to be between $-\epsilon$ and $+\epsilon$. We can choose ϵ as small as we like, so that if $\bar{x}$ is a solution to the original problem (E1.9.1), it will approximately satisfy the necessary conditions for a solution to the new problem (E1.9.2). The necessary conditions for x^*, say, to be a solution for the new problem, (E1.9.2), are that there exist λ_0^*, λ_1^* and λ_2^*, non-negative and not all zero, such that x^* and the λ_i^*'s jointly satisfy

$$\lambda_0^* \nabla f(x^*) = \lambda_1^* \nabla g^1(x^*) - \lambda_2^* \nabla g^1(x^*),$$

i.e.

$$\lambda_0^* \nabla f(x^*) = (\lambda_1^* - \lambda_2^*) \nabla g^1(x^*),$$

$$g^1(x^*) - \epsilon \leqslant 0,$$

$$-g^1(x^*) - \epsilon \leqslant 0,$$

$$\lambda_1^* = 0, \quad \text{if } g^1(x^*) - \epsilon < 0$$

and

$$\lambda_2^* = 0, \quad \text{if } -g^1(x^*) - \epsilon < 0.$$

It is clear that at least one of the λ_1^*, λ_2^* must be zero since not both the conditions

$$g^1(x^*) - \epsilon = 0$$

and

$$-g^1(x^*) - \epsilon = 0$$

can hold simultaneously. Hence, if we form a new variable, λ^*, defined as

$$\lambda^* = \lambda_1^* - \lambda_2^*,$$

we can be sure that not both λ_0^* and λ^* are zero. [19] On the other hand, we cannot be sure of the sign of λ^*. We can conclude that if x^* is a solution to problem (E1.9.2), then there will exist $\lambda_0^* \geqslant 0$ and λ^*, whose sign is not predetermined, such that not both λ_0^* and λ^* are zero, and such that λ_0^*, λ^* and x^* simultaneously satisfy the conditions

$$\lambda_0^* \nabla f(x^*) = \lambda^* g^1(x^*),$$

$$g^1(x^*) - \epsilon \leqslant 0,$$

$$-g^1(x^*) - \epsilon \leqslant 0,$$

with

$$\lambda^* \leqslant 0, \quad \text{if } g^1(x^*) - \epsilon < 0$$

and

$$\lambda^* \geqslant 0, \quad \text{if } -g^1(x^*) - \epsilon < 0.$$

As we let ϵ approach zero, this last set of conditions reduces to a set of necessary conditions for a solution of the original problem (E1.9.1). In fact, $\overline{x}$ is a solution for (E1.9.1) only if there exist $\lambda_0 \geqslant 0$ and λ, whose signs is not predetermined, such that not both λ_0 and λ are zero, and such that λ_0, λ and $\overline{x}$ simultaneously satisfy the conditions

$$\lambda_0 \nabla f(\overline{x}) = \lambda \nabla g^1(\overline{x})$$

and

$$g^1(\overline{x}) = 0.$$

In general, we can extend theorem 1 as follows.

Theorem 1.1.   Consider the problem of choosing x to maximize

$$f(x)$$

---

[19]   If λ^* is zero, then both λ_1^* and λ_2^* must be zero. Hence if λ^* is zero, then λ_0^* cannot be zero.

subject to

$$g^i(x) \leqslant 0, \quad i = 1,...,m$$

and

$$g^i(x) = 0, \quad i = m+1,...,m+r.$$

If $\bar{x}$ is a problem solution, then there exist numbers $\lambda_0, \lambda_1,...,\lambda_{m+r}$, not all zero and with $\lambda_0, \lambda_1,...,\lambda_m$ non-negative, such that

$$\lambda_0 \nabla f(\bar{x}) = \sum_{i=1}^{m+r} \lambda_i \nabla g^i(\bar{x}),$$

$$g^i(\bar{x}) \leqslant 0, \quad i = 1,...,m,$$

$$g^i(\bar{x}) = 0, \quad i = m+1,...,m+r$$

and

$$\lambda_i = 0, \quad \text{if } g^i(\bar{x}) < 0, \quad i = 1,...,m.$$

In summary, if the *j*th constraint is an equality rather than a less-than-or-equal-to constraint, then we modify theorem 1 by not requiring the *j*th λ to be non-negative. Naturally, we also insist that in the list of necessary conditions the *j*th constraint holds as an equality.

Exercise 1.10. Linear constraints

Demonstrate that the constraint set defined as follows is convex:

$$g(x) \equiv Ax - b \leqslant 0,$$

where A is an $m \times n$ matrix and b is an $m \times 1$ vector.

Answer. Let x and y be any two vectors which satisfy the constraints. Then

$$A(\alpha x) - \alpha b \leqslant 0$$

and

$$A((1-\alpha)y) - (1-\alpha)b \leqslant 0,$$

where α is any scalar in the interval [0, 1]. Hence

$$A(\alpha x + (1-\alpha)y) - b \leqslant 0.$$

Thus, the vector $\alpha x + (1-\alpha)y$ satisfies the constraints. This is sufficient to establish that the constraint set is convex.

Exercise 1.11.   Linear objective function

Demonstrate that the function

$$f(x) = c'x$$

is quasiconcave where c' is a $1 \times n$ vector.

Answer.   Let y and z be any two vectors satisfying

$$c'y \geqslant \gamma$$

and

$$c'z \geqslant \gamma.$$

Then, where α is any scalar in the interval $[0, 1]$, we have

$$c'(\alpha y) \geqslant \alpha \gamma$$

and

$$c'((1-\alpha)z) \geqslant (1-\alpha)\gamma.$$

Hence

$$c'(\alpha y + (1-\alpha)z) \geqslant \gamma.$$

We have shown that the set

$$\{x \mid c'x \geqslant \gamma\}$$

is convex for any choice of γ. This is sufficient to demonstrate that the function

$$f(x) = c'x$$

is quasiconcave.

Exercise 1.12.   A nonquasiconcave objective function

Explain why the objective function illustrated in fig. 1.5.7 is not quasiconcave.

Answer.   We consider the set

$$S = \{x \mid f(x) \geqslant f(z)\}.$$

$\bar{x}$ and z both belong to this set. If we draw a straight line connecting $\bar{x}$ and z, it passes through some points, at least near z, which do not lie in S. Thus, S is nonconvex and f is nonquasiconcave.

Exercise 1.13. Nonuniqueness of the problem solutions

We start with some definitions.

The function, f, is *strictly quasiconcave* if and only if for any number, γ,

$$f(y) \geqslant \gamma \quad \text{and} \quad f(z) \geqslant \gamma \quad (y \neq z)$$

imply that $f(\alpha y + (1-\alpha)z) > \gamma$ for all $\alpha \in (0,1)$. ($\alpha \in (0,1)$ means that $\alpha > 0$ and $\alpha < 1$.)

The assumption of strict quasiconcavity excludes the possibility of linear segments in the isovalue curves. In particular, the function in E1.11 is quasiconcave, but not strictly quasiconcave.

The constraint set is *strictly convex* if and only if any point, r, of the form

$$r = \alpha x + (1-\alpha)y \quad (x \neq y).$$

where $\alpha \in (0,1)$, and x and y are in the constraint set, both belongs to the constraint set and is not a boundary point, i.e. r is in the interior of the constraint set. Geometrically, if we draw a straight line joining any two points x and y in the constraint set, then with the possible exceptions of x and y, none of the points on the straight line is a boundary point. The assumption of strict convexity rules out the constraint set in E1.10.

Now imagine that we have a problem which satisfies the conditions of theorem 2, the quasiconcave objective function, the convex constraint set, and Slater's constraint qualification. Show diagrammatically that the problem solution may not be unique. Prove that the problem solution (if it exists) is unique provided that the constraint set is convex and the objective function is *strictly quasiconcave*. Will the solution necessarily be unique if the constraint set is *strictly convex* and the objective function is quasiconcave?

Answer.   Fig. E1.13.1 illustrates a problem with multiple solutions, a convex constraint set which satisfies Slater's constraint qualification, and a quasiconcave objective function. Solutions occur anywhere along the line x, y.

Now we suppose that the objective function is strictly quasiconcave and the constraint set is convex. Fig. E1.13.1 is excluded. The objective function is not *strictly* quasiconcave. More generally we can demonstrate that the problem solution is unique, as follows: assume that y and z are problem solutions with

$$y \neq z.$$

Since y and z are problem solutions, we know that

$$g(y) \leqslant 0$$

$$g(z) \leqslant 0$$

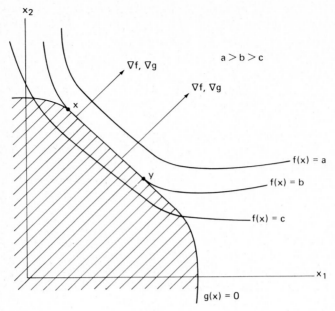

Figure E1.13.1

and

$$f(y) = f(z).$$

We consider the point

$$r = \alpha y + (1-\alpha)z, \quad \text{where } \alpha\epsilon(0, 1).$$

The convexity of the constraint set implies that

$$g(r) \leqslant 0, \tag{E1.13.1}$$

and the strict quasiconcavity of the objective function implies that

$$f(r) > f(y) = f(z). \tag{E1.13.2}$$

Eq. (E1.13.1) means that r is within the constraint set and therefore (E1.13.2) contradicts the assumption that y and z are problem solutions. We may conclude that it is not possible to have more than one problem solution.

We now turn to the case where the constraint set is strictly convex, but the objective function is merely quasiconcave.

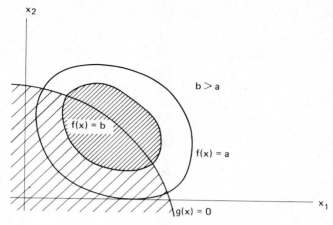

Figure E1.13.2

Fig. E1.13.2 illustrates a rather strange case in which the objective function has a plateau. It reaches an *unconstrained* maximum at any point in the heavily shaded region. This situation is consistent with quasiconcavity and thus it appears that fig. E1.13.2 illustrates a situation where there are multiple solutions despite the strict convexity of the constraint set and the quasiconcavity in the objective function. If, however, we assume that there is at most one point x which is both in the constraint set, and also satisfies

$$\nabla f(x) = 0,$$

then it is not hard to show that strict convexity of the constraint set and quasiconcavity of the objective function are sufficient to ensure that there is no more than a single problem solution.

Exercise 1.14. Linear programming, primal and dual

Consider the following problem, known as the primal problem: choose x_1, x_2 to maximize

$$c_1 x_1 + c_2 x_2 \tag{E1.14.1}$$

subject to

$$a_{11}x_1 + a_{12}x_2 \leqslant b_1,$$

$$a_{21}x_1 + a_{22}x_2 \leqslant b_2$$

and

$$x_1, x_2 \geqslant 0,$$

where the c_i, a_{ij} and b_i are parameters.

It is clear that the objective function is quasiconcave and that the constraint set is convex, see E1.10 and E1.11. We will assume that the constraint qualification is met.[20] Hence the conditions of theorem 2 are fulfilled.

Use theorem 2 and the result from E1.8 (i.e. cover the sign constraints by appropriate inequality conditions) to give a set of necessary and sufficient conditions for a solution.

Next, consider the *dual* problem. The dual problem is to choose y_1, y_2 to minimize

$$b_1 y_1 + b_2 y_2 \qquad\qquad\qquad \text{(E1.14.2)}$$

subject to

$$a_{11} y_1 + a_{21} y_2 \geqslant c_1,$$

$$a_{12} y_1 + a_{22} y_2 \geqslant c_2$$

and

$$y_1, y_2 \geqslant 0.$$

Again, write down necessary and sufficient conditions for a solution.

Discuss the relationship between the two problems.

Answer.   In the notation of theorem 2 we have

$$\nabla f = \begin{pmatrix} c_1 \\ c_2 \end{pmatrix}; \ \nabla g^1 = \begin{pmatrix} a_{11} \\ a_{12} \end{pmatrix}; \ \nabla g^2 = \begin{pmatrix} a_{21} \\ a_{22} \end{pmatrix}.$$

Hence, the non-negative vector $\bar{x}' = (\bar{x}_1, \bar{x}_2)$ is a solution if and only if there exists a non-negative vector [21] $\bar{y}' = (\bar{y}_1, \bar{y}_2)$ such that $\bar{x}$ and $\bar{y}$ simultaneously satisfy

---

[20]   Actually, there is no need to worry about the constraint qualification in linear programming problems. The exceptional cases, see figs. 1.5.4, 1.5.5 and 1.5.8, cannot arise. The ambitious reader might check in Mangasarian (1969, pp. 102–103) to see which of the constraint qualifications mentioned there is automatically satisfied in the linear programming situation.

[21]   The use of y's rather than λ's will facilitate the comparison between the primal problem, (E1.14.1), and the dual problem, (E1.14.2).

$$\begin{pmatrix} c_1 \\ c_2 \end{pmatrix} \leqslant \bar{y}_1 \begin{pmatrix} a_{11} \\ a_{12} \end{pmatrix} + \bar{y}_2 \begin{pmatrix} a_{21} \\ a_{22} \end{pmatrix},$$

$$(\bar{x}_1, \bar{x}_2) \left[\begin{pmatrix} c_1 \\ c_2 \end{pmatrix} - \bar{y}_1 \begin{pmatrix} a_{11} \\ a_{12} \end{pmatrix} - \bar{y}_2 \begin{pmatrix} a_{21} \\ a_{22} \end{pmatrix} \right] = 0,$$

$$a_{11}\bar{x}_1 + a_{12}\bar{x}_2 - b_1 \leqslant 0,$$

$$a_{21}\bar{x}_1 + a_{22}\bar{x}_2 - b_2 \leqslant 0$$

and

$$(\bar{y}_1, \bar{y}_2) \begin{pmatrix} a_{11}\bar{x}_1 + a_{12}\bar{x}_2 - b_1 \\ a_{21}\bar{x}_1 + a_{22}\bar{x}_2 - b_2 \end{pmatrix} = 0.$$

In matrix and vector notation we can rewrite the necessary and sufficient conditions as follows: $\bar{x}$, where $\bar{x} \geqslant 0$, is a solution if and only if there exists $\bar{y} \geqslant 0$ such that $\bar{x}$ and $\bar{y}$ simultaneously satisfy

$$\left.\begin{aligned} & c \leqslant A'\bar{y}, \\ & \bar{x}'(c - A'y) = 0, \\ & A\bar{x} - b \leqslant 0, \\ & \bar{y}'(A\bar{x} - b) = 0, \end{aligned}\right\} \tag{i}$$

where

$$A = \begin{pmatrix} a_{11} & a_{12} \\ a_{21} & a_{22} \end{pmatrix}; \quad b = \begin{pmatrix} b_1 \\ b_2 \end{pmatrix} \quad \text{and} \quad c = \begin{pmatrix} c_1 \\ c_2 \end{pmatrix}.$$

The second problem, (E1.14.2), can be written as: choose y_1, y_2 to maximize

$$-b_1 y_1 - b_2 y_2$$

subject to

$$-a_{11}y_1 - a_{21}y_2 \leqslant -c_1,$$

$$-a_{12}y_1 - a_{22}y_2 \leqslant -c_2$$

and

$$y_1, y_2 \geqslant 0.$$

The non-negative vector $\bar{\bar{y}}' = (\bar{\bar{y}}_1, \bar{\bar{y}}_2)$ is a solution for this problem if and only if there exists a non-negative vector $\bar{\bar{x}}' = (\bar{\bar{x}}_1, \bar{\bar{x}}_2)$ such that $\bar{\bar{y}}$ and $\bar{\bar{x}}$ simultaneously satisfy

$$-\begin{pmatrix} b_1 \\ b_2 \end{pmatrix} \leqslant -\bar{\bar{x}}_1 \begin{pmatrix} a_{11} \\ a_{21} \end{pmatrix} - \bar{\bar{x}}_2 \begin{pmatrix} a_{12} \\ a_{22} \end{pmatrix},$$

$$(\bar{\bar{y}}_1, \bar{\bar{y}}_2) \left[-\begin{pmatrix} b_1 \\ b_2 \end{pmatrix} + \bar{\bar{x}}_1 \begin{pmatrix} a_{11} \\ a_{21} \end{pmatrix} + \bar{\bar{x}}_2 \begin{pmatrix} a_{12} \\ a_{22} \end{pmatrix} \right] = 0,$$

$$-a_{11}\bar{\bar{y}}_1 - a_{21}\bar{\bar{y}}_2 \leqslant -c_1,$$

$$-a_{12}\bar{\bar{y}}_1 - a_{22}\bar{\bar{y}}_2 \leqslant -c_2$$

and

$$(\bar{\bar{x}}_1, \bar{\bar{x}}_2) \begin{pmatrix} -a_{11}\bar{\bar{y}}_1 - a_{21}\bar{\bar{y}}_2 + c_1 \\ -a_{12}\bar{\bar{y}}_1 - a_{22}\bar{\bar{y}}_2 + c_2 \end{pmatrix} = 0.$$

In matrix notation these conditions are as follows: $\bar{\bar{y}}$, where $\bar{\bar{y}} \geqslant 0$, is a solution if and only if there exists $\bar{\bar{x}} \geqslant 0$ such that $\bar{\bar{y}}$ and $\bar{\bar{x}}$ simultaneously satisfy

$$\left. \begin{array}{l} A\bar{\bar{x}} - b \leqslant 0, \\[4pt] \bar{\bar{y}}'(A\bar{\bar{x}} - b) = 0, \\[4pt] c \leqslant A'\bar{\bar{y}}, \\[4pt] \bar{\bar{x}}'(c - A'\bar{\bar{y}}) = 0. \end{array} \right\} \tag{ii}$$

The relationship between problems (E1.14.1) and (E1.14.2) can be seen from the two sets of necessary and sufficient conditions (i) and (ii). These are identical. If $\bar{x}$ and $\bar{y}$ satisfy (i), then $\bar{\bar{y}}$ and $\bar{\bar{x}}$ satisfy (ii). Hence, if a solution exists for problem (E1.14.1), then a solution exists for problem (E1.14.2) and vice versa.[22] Also, the optimal value for the objective function in problem (E1.14.1) is the same as that in problem (E1.14.2). For example, if $\bar{x}$ and $\bar{y}$ satisfy conditions (i), then the optimal value for the objective function in problem (E1.14.1) is $c'\bar{x}$, and the optimal value for the objective function in problem (E1.14.2) is $b'\bar{y}$. However, either from conditions (i) or (ii) we see that

$$\bar{x}'c = \bar{x}'A'\bar{y}$$

and

$$\bar{y}'A\bar{x} = \bar{y}'b.$$

---

[22]   What does it mean to say that a solution does not exist? It might be useful to draw two diagrams showing linear-programming problems with no solution. In the first case the constraint set would be empty. In the second, the problem would be unbounded.

Therefore[23]

$$c'\bar{x} = b'\bar{y}.$$

If you would like more information on the theory of primal and dual problems, you could look at Intriligator (1971, ch. 5) or Lancaster (1968, ch. 3). However, for readers who are pressed for time, it is worth pointing out that the primal–dual relationship is important for two reasons. First, it is the basis of some efficient computational techniques; any linear-programming problem can be solved either via its primal or dual. Secondly, in practical applications, both problems often have interesting economic interpretations. See, for example, Baumol (1972, ch. 6).

Exercise 1.15. On the interpretation of the Lagrangian multipliers

Assume that x_1 and x_2 are chosen so as to maximize

$$f(x_1, x_2) \equiv -(x_1-2)^2 - (x_2-2)^2$$

subject to

$$x_1 + x_2 = b,$$

where b is a parameter.

Express x_1, x_2 and the optimal value of f as functions of b. Derive an expression for $\partial f/\partial b$. Check that this is the same as the Lagrangian multiplier associated with the problem.

Answer.   If $\bar{x}$ is a solution, then there exist $\lambda_0 \geq 0$ and λ_1 such that not both are zero, and such that

$$-2(\bar{x}_1-2)\lambda_0 = \lambda_1, \tag{i}$$

$$-2(\bar{x}_2-2)\lambda_0 = \lambda_1 \tag{ii}$$

and

$$\bar{x}_1 + \bar{x}_2 = b. \tag{iii}$$

Certainly $\lambda_0 \neq 0$. (If $\lambda_0 = 0$, then $\lambda_1 = 0$, but not both can be zero.) Therefore, we may set $\lambda_0 = 1$. Then on the basis of (i) and (ii) we may conclude that

$$\bar{x}_1 = \bar{x}_2.$$

---

[23] $\bar{y}'A\bar{x}$ is a scalar. Therefore

$$\bar{y}'A\bar{x} = (\bar{y}'A\bar{x})' = \bar{x}'A'\bar{y}.$$

Finally, via (iii) we see that

$$\bar{x}_1 = b/2,$$
$$\bar{x}_2 = b/2,$$
$$\lambda_1 = -2(b/2 - 2)$$

and

$$f = -2(b/2 - 2)^2.$$

We note that

$$\partial f/\partial b = -2(b/2 - 2)$$

which is the same as λ_1.

Exercise 1.16.   *An example of nonunique Lagrangian multipliers*

Consider the problem of choosing x_1 and x_2 to maximize

$$f(x_1, x_2) \equiv x_1 x_2$$

subject to

$$g^1(x_1, x_2) \equiv x_1 + x_2 - 1 = 0$$

and

$$g^2(x_1, x_2) \equiv x_1^2 + x_2^2 - \tfrac{1}{2} = 0.$$

Sketch the relevant gradient—contour diagram and convince yourself that the problem solution occurs at

$$\bar{x}_1 = \tfrac{1}{2}; \quad \bar{x}_2 = \tfrac{1}{2}.$$

Show that at $\bar{x}$ any pair of values for λ_1 and λ_2, with $\lambda_1 + \lambda_2 = \tfrac{1}{2}$, will, together with $\bar{x}$, satisfy the conditions

$$\nabla f(\bar{x}) = \lambda_1 \nabla g^1(\bar{x}) + \lambda_2 \nabla g^2(\bar{x})$$

and

$$g^i(\bar{x}) = 0, \quad i = 1, 2.$$

Answer.   Fig. E1.16.1 illustrates the problem solution. We note that at $\bar{x} = (\tfrac{1}{2}, \tfrac{1}{2})$,

$$\nabla f = \begin{pmatrix} \overline{x}_2 \\ \overline{x}_1 \end{pmatrix} = \begin{pmatrix} \frac{1}{2} \\ \frac{1}{2} \end{pmatrix},$$

$$\nabla g^1(\overline{x}) = \begin{pmatrix} 1 \\ 1 \end{pmatrix}$$

and

$$\nabla g^2(\overline{x}) = \begin{pmatrix} 2\overline{x}_1 \\ 2\overline{x}_2 \end{pmatrix} = \begin{pmatrix} 1 \\ 1 \end{pmatrix}.$$

It follows immediately that if $\lambda_1 + \lambda_2 = \frac{1}{2}$, then

$$\nabla f(\overline{x}) = \lambda_1 \nabla g^1(\overline{x}) + \lambda_2 \nabla g^2(\overline{x}).$$

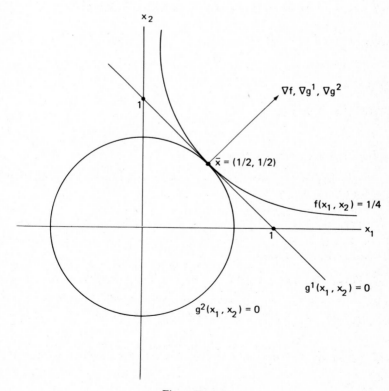

Figure E1.16.1

The nonuniqueness of the Lagrangian multipliers reflects the fact that in the region of $\bar{x}$ one of the constraints is redundant. In this particular problem either of the constraints could be removed without affecting the problem solution. More generally, in the h-equality-constraints problem, (1.8.1), the Lagrangian multipliers associated with any particular solution, $\bar{x}$, will be nonunique if and only if the vectors $\nabla g^i(\bar{x})$, $i = 1,...,h$, are *linearly dependent*.[24] This is shown as follows: if $\nabla g^i(\bar{x})$, $i = 1,...,h$ are linearly dependent, then there exist numbers $\alpha_1,..., \alpha_h$, not all zero, such that

$$\sum_{i=1}^{h} \alpha_i \nabla g^i(\bar{x}) = 0. \tag{i}$$

Hence if we have a set of Lagrangian multipliers, $\bar{\lambda}_1,...,\bar{\lambda}_h$, such that

$$\nabla f(\bar{x}) = \sum_{i=1}^{h} \bar{\lambda}_i \nabla g^i(\bar{x}), \tag{ii}$$

then we can make another, and different set, which also satisfies (ii), by forming $\bar{\bar{\lambda}}_i$, $i = 1,...,h$, where

$$\bar{\bar{\lambda}}_i = \bar{\lambda}_i + \alpha_i, \quad i = 1,...,h.$$

Going the other way around, if we have two different sets of Lagrangian multipliers such that

$$\nabla f(\bar{x}) = \sum_{i=1}^{h} \bar{\lambda}_i \nabla g^i(\bar{x})$$

and

$$\nabla f(\bar{x}) = \sum_{i=1}^{h} \bar{\bar{\lambda}}_i \nabla g^i(\bar{x}),$$

then

$$0 = \sum_{i=1}^{h} (\bar{\lambda}_i - \bar{\bar{\lambda}}_i) \nabla g^i(\bar{x}),$$

and thus the $\nabla g^i(\bar{x})$ are linearly dependent.

In situations where the Lagrangian multipliers are nonunique, it is clear that they cannot be used to indicate the effects of marginal relaxations in the constraints. On the other hand, the importance of the nonuniqueness should not be overemphasized. In fact, it is only likely to arise in rather poorly specified

---

[24]   Vectors $v_1,..., v_s$, are said to be linearly dependent if there exist numbers $\alpha_1,...,\alpha_s$, not all zero, such that

$$\sum_{i=1}^{s} \alpha_i v_i = 0.$$

economic problems, problems in which at least one of the constraints can be thought of as 'locally redundant'. If the $\nabla g^i(\overline{x}), i = 1,...,h$, are linearly dependent, we can rearrange (i) so that

$$\nabla g^1(\overline{x}) = \sum_{i=2}^{h} \beta_i \nabla g^i(\overline{x}), \tag{iii}$$

where $\beta_i = -\alpha_i/\alpha_1$ and we assume without loss of generality that $\alpha_1 \neq 0$.[25] This means that in the region of $\overline{x}$ we can think of the first constraint as being redundant. Any small movement, dx, away from $\overline{x}$, which is compatible with all the constraints $2,...,h$, i.e. it satisfies

$$(\nabla g^i(\overline{x}))'dx = 0, \quad i = 2,...,h,$$

is automatically compatible with constraint 1.

Another implication of (iii) is that, at least in the region of $\overline{x}$, problem (1.8.1) is on the verge of becoming infeasible. Notice that if b_1 is changed, then it is impossible to change the x's so that

$$(\nabla g^1(\overline{x}))'dx = db_1 \neq 0$$

and

$$(\nabla g^i(\overline{x}))'dx = 0, \quad i = 2,...,h.$$

Only if the $\nabla g^i(\overline{x})$ are *linearly independent*, i.e. only if the λ_i are unique, can we be sure that a small change in the b_i's can be made without rendering our problem infeasible.[26]

Exercise 1.17.   A problem with multiple unconnected solutions

Examine fig. E1.17.1. It is a contour–gradient diagram for the problem of choosing x_1, x_2 to maximize

$$f(x_1, x_2) \equiv -x_1^2 - x_2^2 \tag{E1.17.1}$$

[25]   At least one of the α_i is nonzero. If initially $\alpha_1 = 0$, we simply renumber the constraints.
[26]   It can be shown that if the $\nabla g^i(\overline{x}), i = 1,...,h$, are linearly independent, then there exists at least one solution, dx, for the system (1.8.4), for any choice of the db_i. If you wish to follow up on this point, then you will find that the steps in the mathematics are: (1) any $h \times n$ matrix A with h linearly independent rows has h linearly independent columns, see Lancaster (1968, p. 244); and (2) if A has h linearly independent columns, then we can always find a solution, x, for the system

$$Ax = b.$$

(See Lancaster (1968, p. 248).)

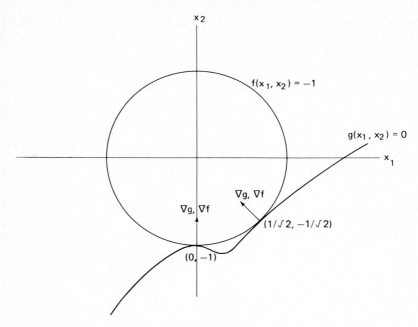

Figure E1.17.1

subject to

$$g(x_1, x_2) \equiv x_2 - h(x_1) = 0, \qquad \text{(E1.17.2)}$$

where h is a function. (For the purposes of this exercise, it will not be necessary to give h an explicit form.)

The diagram shows that the problem has alternative global optima at

$$\bar{x}' = (0, -1) \quad \text{and} \quad \bar{\bar{x}}' = (1/\sqrt{2}, -1/\sqrt{2}).$$

Both points give a value of -1 for the objective function. What is the value of the Lagrangian multiplier associated with each of the solutions? Show[27] that if the constraint is relaxed slightly, i.e. it is replaced by

$$x_2 - h(x_1) = \epsilon, \qquad \text{(E1.17.3)}$$

where ϵ is a positive number, then the problem solution is unique at

$$x^* = (0, -1 + \epsilon)'.$$

---

[27]   Do not attempt to do this formally. Simply argue in terms of the diagram.

What is the value of $\partial f/\partial b$ at $b = 0$, where b is the right-hand constant in constraint (E1.17.2)?

Answer. From (E1.17.1) and (E1.17.2) we see that

$$\nabla f(x) = (-2x_1, -2x_2)'$$

$$\nabla g(x) = \left(-\frac{dh(x_1)}{dx_1}, 1\right)'.$$

At $\bar{x}$, $\nabla f = (0, 2)'$ and at $\bar{\bar{x}}$, $\nabla f = (-\sqrt{2}, \sqrt{2})'$. Hence, at $\bar{x}$, the Lagrangian multiplier, $\bar{\lambda}$, must satisfy

$$\bar{\lambda} = 2,$$

whereas at $\bar{\bar{x}}$ we have

$$\bar{\bar{\lambda}} = \sqrt{2}.$$

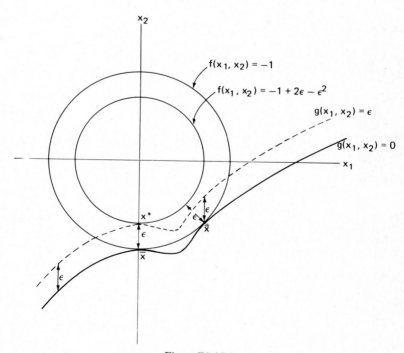

Figure E1.17.2

Under the new constraint, (E1.17.3), the constraint contour is shifted verti-
cally upwards by the distance ϵ (see fig. E1.17.2). We observe that there is a
point of tangency between a contour of the objective function, i.e. a circle, and
the contour of the constraint function at the point

$$x^* = (0, -1 + \epsilon)'.$$

There is another point of tangency, but on a larger circle, in the region of $\bar{\bar{x}}$.
Hence the new solution is at x^*.

The change in the value of the objective function is

$$df = f(x^*) - f(\bar{x})$$

$$= -1 + 2\epsilon - \epsilon^2 + 1$$

$$= 2\epsilon - \epsilon^2.$$

However, if you jump to the conclusion that

$$\left(\frac{\partial f}{\partial b}\right)_{b=0} = 2 = \bar{\lambda},$$

you are being a little hasty. What is true is that

$$\lim_{\substack{\epsilon \to 0 \\ \epsilon > 0}} \frac{df}{\epsilon} = 2,$$

i.e.

$$\left(\frac{\partial f}{\partial b}\right)^R_{b=0} = 2,$$

where

$$\left(\frac{\partial f}{\partial b}\right)^R_{b=0}$$

is the *right* derivative of f with respect to b. The *left* derivative is in fact $\bar{\bar{\lambda}}_2 = \sqrt{2}$. If we decrease b, i.e. we make the constraint

$$x_2 - h(x_1) = -\epsilon,$$

then the problem solution stays in the region of $\bar{\bar{x}}$, and it can be shown that

$$\lim_{\substack{\epsilon \to 0 \\ \epsilon < 0}} \frac{df}{\epsilon} = \sqrt{2}.$$

We can conclude as follows. If a small change in the b_i's can cause large
changes in the problem solution — a situation which can arise if we initially have

alternative optima — then result (1.8.6) cannot be applied uncritically. It will be valid provided we choose the appropriate set of Langrangian multipliers. However, we will not know which set is appropriate unless we first determine the relevant region for the problem solution, and this will depend on the particular variation in the b_i's.

Exercise 1.18. The interpretation of the Lagrangian multipliers when there are inequality constraints

Consider the problem of choosing $x_1,...,x_n$ to maximize

$$f(x) \tag{E1.18.1}$$

subject to

$$g^i(x) \leqslant b_i, \quad i = 1,...,m.$$

Assume that if $\bar{x}$ is a solution, then there exists a unique list of numbers $\lambda_1,...,\lambda_m$, all non-negative, such that[28]

$$\nabla f(\bar{x}) = \sum_{i=1}^{m} \lambda_i \nabla g(\bar{x}),$$

$$g^i(\bar{x}) \leqslant b_i, \quad i = 1,...,m$$

and

$$\lambda_i = 0, \quad \text{if } g^i(\bar{x}) < b_i.$$

Show that if the b_i are changed by small amounts, db_i, $i = 1,...m$, and the resulting change in the problem solution is small, then the change, df, in the optimal value of the objective function satisfies

$$df = \sum_{i=1}^{m} \lambda_i db_i.$$

Answer. The argument is similar to that in section 1.8. However, we note that if

$$g^i(\bar{x}) = b_i$$

then

$$(\nabla g^i(\bar{x}))'dx \leqslant db_i, \tag{i}$$

---

[28] We assume away the exceptional cases. This amounts to assuming that the vectors $\nabla g^i(\bar{x})$, $i \epsilon E$, are linearly independent, where E is the set of indexes for the constraints which hold as equalities at $\bar{x}$.

and if

$$g^i(\overline{x}) < b_i$$

then

$$(\nabla g^i(\overline{x}))' dx \lessgtr db_i, \tag{ii}$$

where dx is the vector of changes in the problem solution resulting from the change in the b_i's.

Expression (i) recognizes that although the ith constraint was met as an equality in the original situation, after the change in the b_i's it may become a strict inequality. Expression (ii) reflects the idea that if the ith constraint was initially slack, i.e. $\overline{x}$ satisfied it as a strict inequality, then we will be free to increase g^i beyond db_i.

Now we proceed as in section 1.8:

$$df = (\nabla f(\overline{x}))' dx.$$

Hence

$$df = \sum_{i=1}^{m} \lambda_i (\nabla g^i(\overline{x}))' dx.$$

If in the original situation

$$g^i(\overline{x}) < 0,$$

then

$$\lambda_i = 0.$$

Hence, despite (ii), when we substitute from (i) and (ii), and remember that the λ_i are non-negative, we find that

$$df \leqslant \sum_{i=1}^{m} \lambda_i db_i. \tag{iii}$$

Is a strict inequality in (iii) really a possibility? It would appear from (i) that it might occur if the change in the b_i's induces a previously 'tight' constraint, with a nonzero λ, to become slack. However, if a small perturbation in the b_i's induces a tight constraint to become slack, then we will see that the relevant λ_i is arbitrarily close to zero, and in fact (iii) can be written as an equality. To establish this we consider the problem of choosing x, in the region of $\overline{x}$ (see fig. E1.18.1) to maximize

$$f(x) \tag{E1.18.2}$$

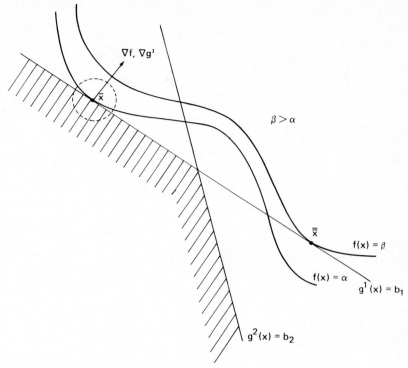

Figure E1.18.1   The solution for problem (E1.18.1) is at $\bar{x}$. Constraint 2 is slack and $E = \{1\}$. If we failed to specify that the solution of problem (E1.18.2) had to be in the region of $\bar{x}$, i.e. we restrict our search to an area such as the dotted circle, then the solution for (E1.18.2) would be at $\bar{\bar{x}}$. Constraint 2 is slack in the region of $\bar{x}$, but not elsewhere.

subject to

$$g^i(x) = b_i, \quad i \in E,$$

where $i \in E$ if and only if

$$g^i(\bar{x}) = b_i,$$

i.e. E is the set of indexes for the tight constraints at the solution for the original problem (E1.18.1).

It is clear[29] that $\bar{x}$ is a solution for the new problem (E1.18.2), and that the associated Lagrangian multipliers are

[29]   Notice that in problem (E1.18.2) we restrict the solution to being in the region of $\bar{x}$. The relevance of this restriction is explained in fig. E1.18.1.

$\lambda_i, \ i \in E,$

i.e. the multipliers on the tight constraints in the original problem.

From section 1.8 we know that the value of the change in the objective function in problem (E1.18.2) produced by a small change in the b_i's, $i \in E$, is given by

$$(\mathrm{d}f)_N = \sum_{i \in E} \lambda_i \mathrm{d}b_i, \tag{iv}$$

where the subscript N is used to denote the 'new' problem (E1.18.2). Since the λ_i on the slack constraints are zero, we may rewrite (iv) as

$$(\mathrm{d}f)_N = \sum_{i=1}^{m} \lambda_i \mathrm{d}b_i. \tag{v}$$

The final step is to recognize that

$$(\mathrm{d}f) \geqslant (\mathrm{d}f)_N. \tag{vi}$$

Notice that in the original problem we have more freedom to move. The increase in the value of the objective function resulting from a given perturbation of the b_i's must be at least as great as that which would arise in the more restricted problem (E1.18.2). From (iii), (v) and (vi) it follows that

$$\mathrm{d}f = \sum_{i=1}^{m} \lambda_i \mathrm{d}b_i.$$

Exercise 1.19.   *Restrictions on the domain of f and g*

Return to the standard problem (1.3.1). However, assume that the search for a solution is not only restricted by the constraints

$g(x) \leqslant 0,$

but also by the necessity for x to be in an *open* subset, S, of R^n, i.e. we rewrite (1.3.1) as: choose x to maximize

$$f(x) \tag{E1.19.1}$$

subject to

$g(x) \leqslant 0$

and

$x \in S \subset R^n.$

This situation arises when f or g are not defined for all values of x. For example, assume that $n = 2$, and that $f(x_1, x_2) = \log x_1 + \log x_2$. Then f is defined only for positive values of x_1 and x_2, i.e. f is defined for

$$x \in S = \{(x_1, x_2) \mid x_1 > 0, x_2 > 0\}.$$

Discuss the modifications which should be made to theorems 1 and 2 to accommodate the additional restriction that x must be in the open set S. While a complete discussion would require some mathematical sophistication, you should not have too much difficulty in giving an adequate intuitive answer. Those readers who work through Mangasarian (1969) will be able to provide some rigor.

Answer.   Very little modification is necessary for theorem 1. We simply add the condition that

$$\overline{x} \in S. \tag{i}$$

It is important, however, that S be open. Since S is open, restriction (i) can never be binding at a problem solution.

More care is needed with theorem 2. First we modify the definition of quasiconcavity. We will say that f is quasiconcave over the *open, convex* set S if and only if the sets, $\Lambda(\gamma)$, where

$$\Lambda(\gamma) = \{x \mid x \in S, \; f(x) \geqslant \gamma\},$$

are convex for all choices of γ. Notice that we are now assuming that S is convex. If S were not convex, then our definition would become rather meaningless. For example, if we choose a very small (large negative) value for γ, we might find that

$$\Lambda(\gamma) = S.$$

If S were not convex, it would not be possible for f to be quasiconcave over the set S.

Now we restate theorem 2 as follows.

Theorem 2.1.   If f is a quasiconcave function, defined on the open, convex set S, and the constraint set, defined by

$$g(x) \leqslant 0$$

and

$$x \in S$$

is both convex and satisfies Slater's constraint qualification, then $\overline{x}$ is a solution of problem (E1.19.1) if and only if there exists non-negative values for $\lambda_1, ..., \lambda_m$ such that

$$\nabla f(\bar{x}) = \sum_i \lambda_i \nabla g^i(\bar{x}),$$

$$g^i(\bar{x}) \leqslant 0, \quad i = 1, ..., m,$$

$$\lambda_i = 0, \quad \text{if } g^i(\bar{x}) < 0$$

and

$$\bar{x} \in S.$$

Chapter 2

THEORY OF THE CONSUMER: INTRODUCTION

2.1. Goals, reading guide and references

The theory of consumer demand is a basic building block for many economic studies. It plays a particularly important role in welfare economics, international trade theory, general equilibrium theory and the theory of public finance. In addition, the techniques required in consumer demand analysis are readily applicable to other parts of economic theory. You will find, for example, that the theory of production is very similar from a mathematical point of view to the theory of consumption.

The objective of this chapter is to introduce you to some of the main ideas of consumer theory and to give you a chance to practise the relevant techniques of analysis. We hope that by the time you have completed the readings and problems that you will have reached the following goals:

(1) a thorough understanding of the procedure for deriving demand functions from the model of consumer maximization of utility subject to a budget constraint;

(2) an ability to discuss clearly the meaning of the uniqueness of a utility function up to a monotonic transformation;

(3) an ability to establish the triad, i.e. the Engel aggregation, the homogeneity restriction, and the symmetry restriction;

(4) an understanding of the Hicks—Slutsky partition and an ability to prove that the own-price substitution effect is negative;

(5) an understanding of how preference orderings could be constructed using observed market behavior (revealed preference);

(6) a familiarity with the basic ideas of the pure theory of exchange, including some of the geometric tools used in general equilibrium analysis, e.g. offer curves, contract curves, and the Edgeworth box;

(7) an understanding of how consumer theory is used to provide restrictions on parameter values in the estimation of a complete system of commodity

demand functions. In particular, you should be familiar with the restrictions which flow from the adoption of an additive utility function.

Reading Guide 2 provides a suggested path through the readings to cover these concepts. Sections 2.2–2.4 are some short notes stating some of the principal definitions and theoretical results encountered in the problem set. Readings and references are given in abbreviated terms in the reading guide and in the rest of the chapter; full citations are in the reference list.

Reading Guide*

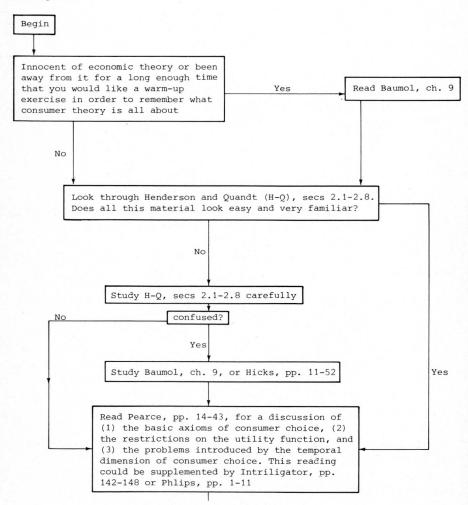

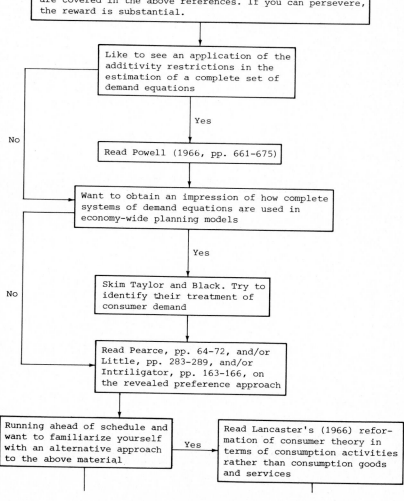

An important use of consumer theory is in the
estimation of systems of demand equations. Here,
the theory often allows the econometrician to place
sufficient restrictions on parameter values to render estimation possible in the presence of data
limitations. Read Powell (1974, chs. 1 and 2) and/or
Theil (1967, pp. 182-200), or Theil (1975, pp. 1-30),
or Phlips, pp. 32-66. Phlips contains some interesting
problems which you might like to attempt.

This reading will be rather difficult for many of you.
However, most of the main results of classical consumer
theory and the recent work on the underlying theory
for the estimation of consistent sets of demand equations
are covered in the above references. If you can persevere,
the reward is substantial.

Like to see an application of the
additivity restrictions in the
estimation of a complete set of
demand equations

Yes

No

Read Powell (1966, pp. 661-675)

Want to obtain an impression of how complete
systems of demand equations are used in
economy-wide planning models

Yes

No

Skim Taylor and Black. Try to
identify their treatment of
consumer demand

Read Pearce, pp. 64-72, and/or
Little, pp. 283-289, and/or
Intriligator, pp. 163-166, on
the revealed preference approach

Running ahead of schedule and
want to familiarize yourself
with an alternative approach
to the above material

Yes

Read Lancaster's (1966) refor-
mation of consumer theory in
terms of consumption activities
rather than consumption goods
and services

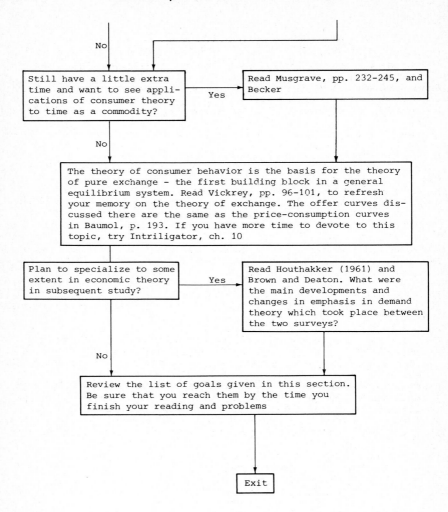

No

| Still have a little extra time and want to see applications of consumer theory to time as a commodity? | → Yes → | Read Musgrave, pp. 232-245, and Becker |

No

The theory of consumer behavior is the basis for the theory of pure exchange – the first building block in a general equilibrium system. Read Vickrey, pp. 96-101, to refresh your memory on the theory of exchange. The offer curves discussed there are the same as the price-consumption curves in Baumol, p. 193. If you have more time to devote to this topic, try Intriligator, ch. 10

| Plan to specialize to some extent in economic theory in subsequent study? | → Yes → | Read Houthakker (1961) and Brown and Deaton. What were the main developments and changes in emphasis in demand theory which took place between the two surveys? |

No

Review the list of goals given in this section. Be sure that you reach them by the time you finish your reading and problems

Exit

*   For full citations, see reference list in this section.

References for Chapter 2

Baumol, W.J. (1972) *Economic Theory and Operations Analysis*, 3rd edn., Prentice-Hall.

Becker, Gary S. (1965) 'A Theory of the Allocation of Time', *Economic Journal*, 74, September, 493–517.

Brown, J.A.C. and A. Deaton (1972) 'Surveys in Applied Economics: Models of Consumer Behavior', *Economic Journal*, 82, 1145–1236.

Ferguson, C.E. and S.M. Maurice (1974) *Economic Analysis*, revised edn., Richard D. Irwin, Inc.

Henderson, J.M. and R.E. Quandt (1971) *Microeconomic Theory*, second edn., McGraw-Hill.

Hicks, J.R. (1962) *Value and Capital*, 2nd edn., Oxford.

Hilton, P.J. (1960) *Partial Derivatives*, Routledge & Kegan Paul Ltd. and Dover Publications Inc.

Hirshleifer, J. (1976) *Price Theory and Applications*, Prentice-Hall.

Houthakker, H.S. (1957) 'An International Comparison of Household Expenditure Patterns, commemorating the Centenary of Engel's Law', *Econometrica*, 25, 532–551.

Houthakker, H.S. (1961) 'The Present State of Consumption Theory', *Econometrica*, 29(4), 704–740.

Intriligator, M.D. (1971) *Mathematical Optimization and Economic Theory*, Prentice-Hall.

Lancaster, K. (1966) 'A New Approach to Consumer Theory', *Journal of Political Economy*, 74, April, 132–157.

Lancaster, K. (1968) *Mathematical Economics*, Macmillan.

Little, I.M.D. (1958) *A Critique of Welfare Economics*, 2nd edn., Oxford.

Musgrave, R.A. (1959) *The Theory of Public Finance: A Study in Public Economy*, McGraw-Hill.

Pearce, I.F. (1964) *A Contribution to Demand Analysis*, Oxford.

Phlips, L. (1974) *Applied Consumption Analysis*, North-Holland/American Elsevier.

Powell, A.A. (1966) 'A Complete System of Consumer Demand Equations for the Australian Economy Fitted by a Model of Additive Preferences', *Econometrica*, 34, 661–675.

Powell, A.A. (1974) *Empirical Analytics of Demand Systems*, Lexington Books, D.C. Heath.

Taylor, L. and S.L. Black (1974) 'Practical General Equilibrium Estimation of Resource Pulls under Trade Liberalization', *Journal of International Economics*, 4(1), 35–58.

Theil, H. (1967) *Economics and Information Theory*, Rand McNally.

Theil, H. (1975) *Theory and Measurement of Consumer Demand*, vol. 1, North-Holland/American Elsevier.

Vickrey, W.S. (1964) *Microstatics*, Harcourt.

2.2. Notes on utility maximizing

Much theoretical and applied economics starts with the hypothesis that household preferences over alternative consumption bundles can be represented by a *utility function*. That is, we assume that a continuous function U can be defined so that

$$U(x) > U(y)$$

if and only if the household prefers commodity bundle x to commodity bundle y.[1]

There is no requirement, of course, that U be unique. In fact, if a household's preferences are representable by any function, then they are representable by many functions. If U is a valid utility function, then so is kU, where k is any positive number. In general, if f is a monotonically increasing[2] function, then $f(U)$ will provide a valid representation of the household's preferences. Notice that

$$f(U(x)) > f(U(y))$$

if and only if

$$U(x) > U(y),$$

i.e.

$$f(U(x)) > f(U(y))$$

if and only if the household prefers x to y.

On the other hand, not all sets of household preferences can be accommodated by a utility function. For example, if a household prefers x to y and y to z, but it also prefers z to x, then a utility function representation is ruled out. Because x is preferred to y, we require that U has the property that

$$U(x) > U(y). \tag{2.2.1}$$

Similarly, we require that

$$U(y) > U(z) \tag{2.2.2}$$

and

$$U(z) > U(x). \tag{2.2.3}$$

Clearly, it is impossible to define a function U which satisfies (2.2.1)–(2.2.3). Hence, by adopting a utility function representation, we are assuming that

---

[1] x and y are non-negative n-vectors whose components represent the household consumption levels for each commodity. We assume that U is defined for all $x \geqslant 0$, $x \in R^n$. Hence, we assume that commodities are divisible, i.e. any non-negative vector can be consumed.

[2] f is a monotonically increasing function if and only if

$$f(a) > f(b)$$

wherever

$$a > b.$$

household preferences are *transitive*, i.e. if the household prefers commodity bundle x to y and y to z, then the household will prefer x to z.

While transitivity is the most obvious restriction imposed by the utility function representation, there are others. If you want to know what these are, we suggest that you check either Phlips (1974, pp. 1–8) or Intriligator (1971, pp. 142–145). Both these readings give straightforward and complete statements of the conditions under which a set of preferences can be represented by a utility function. Our own view is that if we are happy to assume that preferences are transitive, then we should also be happy to accept the assumption that preferences are representable by a utility function. You will find when you read Phlips and Intriligator, that the assumptions (beyond transitivity) required to ensure the existence of a utility function have little practical significance.[3]

If we accept that it is reasonable to represent household preferences by a utility function, then the natural next step is to assume that households behave as if they choose their purchases of goods and services to maximize the utility derivable from their total budgets. We assume that the representative household chooses $x \geqslant 0$ to maximize

$$U(x) \tag{2.2.4}$$

subject to

$$p'x \leqslant y,$$

where x is an n-vector whose components are the amounts of each commodity purchased, p is the vector of commodity prices, y is the total household budget, and U is the household's utility function.

Many of you will have some familiarity with model (2.2.4), at least in its two-commodity form.[4] Where $n = 2$, we can illustrate the household utility-maximizing problem as in fig. 2.2.1. $\alpha\alpha$, $\beta\beta$ and $\gamma\gamma$ are contours (usually called indifference curves) of the utility function. $A'B$ is the budget line defining the household's feasible set of purchases and $\bar{x}$ is the problem solution, i.e. the commodity bundle which maximizes utility subject to the budget constraint. You will recall that the purpose of diagrams such as fig. 2.2.1 is to facilitate the discussion of how households are likely to react to changes in prices, p, and income, y.[5] Such changes generate shifts in the position of the budget line and many exercises in elementary courses are concerned with tracing out the implica-

---

[3]   We return to this idea in Chapter 3, especially E3.4.

[4]   Standard textbook treatments include Ferguson and Maurice (1974, chs. 3 and 4), Baumol (1972, ch. 9) and Hirshleifer (1976, chs. 3 and 4).

[5] y might be more appropriately referred to as the household's level of expenditure. In this book we follow conventional practice and call y 'income'.

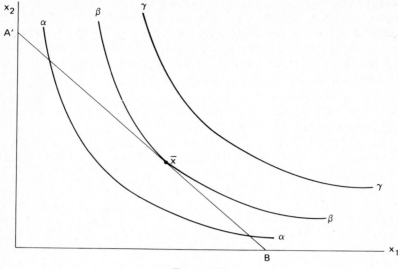

Figure 2.2.1

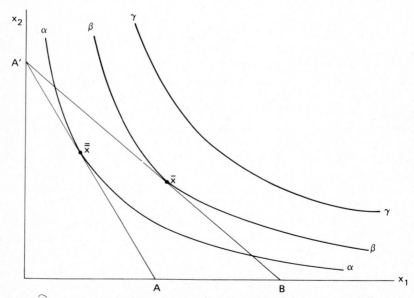

Figure 2.2.2. The increase in the price of good 1 shifts the budget line from $A'B$ to $A'A$. Household consumption moves from $\bar{x}$ to $\bar{\bar{x}}$.

tions for household consumption. For example, fig. 2.2.2 illustrates the impact on household purchases of goods 1 and 2 of an increase in p_1, with p_2 and y held constant. (Can you remember how to separate out the income and substitution effects? If not, look at Intriligator (1971, p. 161).) More generally, model (2.2.4) provides a theoretical structure for investigations of systems of household demand equations.

2.3. Systems of demand equations

On the basis of (2.2.4) we can write the system of household demand equations as

$$x_i = g_i(p_1, p_2, ..., p_n; y), \quad i = 1, ..., n, \tag{2.3.1}$$

where $g_i(p_1, ..., p_n; y)$ denotes the solution for x_i in problem (2.2.4) when prices and income are at the levels $p_1, ..., p_n$ and y. It is usual to assume that the g_i are functions, i.e. for each value of p and y the solution for (2.2.4) is unique. It is also usual to assume that the g_i are continuous. (Figs. 2.3.1 and 2.3.2 show counter-cases.) Both uniqueness and continuity are assured if the utility function is *strictly quasiconcave* (see E1.13). In this chapter we will not attempt a rigorous justification of the strict quasiconcavity assumption. We simply ask you to rely

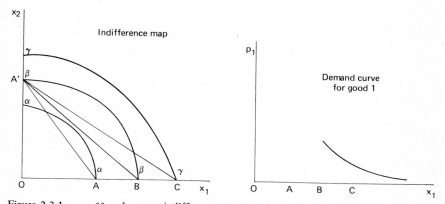

Figure 2.3.1. $\alpha\alpha$, $\beta\beta$ and $\gamma\gamma$ are indifference curves exhibiting the 'wrong' curvature. When the budget line is $A'A$, household consumption is completely specialized in good 2. (The solution to the consumer problem is at A'.) As we lower the price of good 1 (holding p_2 and y constant) consumption stays at A' until the budget line reaches $A'B$. At this stage the consumer is indifferent between points A' and B. As p_1 falls further, the consumer specializes in good 1. The resulting demand curve (illustrated on the right) exhibits a discontinuity at the price–income combination implied by budget line $A'B$.

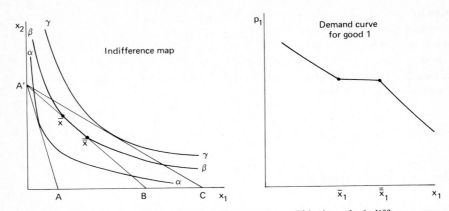

Figure 2.3.2. Again $\alpha\alpha$, $\beta\beta$ and $\gamma\gamma$ are indifference curves. This time, the indifference curve $\beta\beta$ has a linear segment. With the particular price–income combination implied by the budget line $A'B$, the household is indifferent over the range of consumption bundles from $\underline{x}$ to $\overline{x}$, i.e. the consumption bundle is not uniquely determined. The demand curve for good 1 is illustrated on the right.

on the traditional story of diminishing marginal rates of substitution (see, for example, Ferguson and Maurice (1974, pp. 74–79), Hirshleifer (1976, pp. 68–69) and Baumol (1972, ch. 9)). In chapter 3 (see E3.4) we will be more ambitious. We will argue that if observable household behavior is consistent with any utility-maximizing model, then it is consistent with one in which the utility function is strictly quasiconcave. In other words, there is no set of data which would support the utility-maximizing model but at the same time allow us to reject the assumption that the utility function is strictly quasiconcave. Thus, if we are prepared to assume utility maximizing, then there is no reason to be shy about the additional assumption that the utility function is strictly quasiconcave.

A final assumption to be noted here is that the g_i are differentiable. This assumption does not really need to be justified independently of the continuity assumption. If the g_i are continuous, then there can be no harm in assuming them to be differentiable. If the 'truth' is that the g_i are continuous but not differentiable, then the truth can be approximated to any degree of precision by a model in which the g_i are assumed to be differentiable. The differentiability assumption is convenient because it allows us to define elasticities. We describe the responsiveness of the demand for good i to changes in the price of good j by

$$e_{ij} = \frac{\partial g_i}{\partial p_j} \frac{p_j}{g_i}, \quad \text{for all } i \text{ and } j, \tag{2.3.2}$$

where e_{ij} is called the elasticity of demand for good i with respect to price j. If $i = j$, then e_{ij} is an 'own' price elasticity. Otherwise it is a 'cross' price elasticity. e_{ij} gives the percentage rate of change in the demand for good i per percentage increase in p_j with all other prices and the expenditure level held constant. Similarly, we describe the responsiveness of demand to changes in income by income elasticities (E_i):

$$E_i = \frac{\partial g_i}{\partial y} \frac{y}{g_i}, \quad i = 1,...n. \tag{2.3.3}$$

The focus of most applied work in demand systems is on the measurement of the elasticities e_{ij} and E_i.[6]

2.4. The implications of utility maximizing for demand systems

Most of the material in this chapter concentrates on the relationship between the model (2.2.4) and the system of demand equations (2.3.1). Some readers may, however, be wondering why we bother with (2.2.4). If our ultimate interest is in studying household demand, why do we not simply start with (2.3.1)? An objective of this chapter is to answer that question. Briefly, one role of model (2.2.4) is to suggest restrictions on the form of the functions g_i. For example, it can be shown that the model (2.2.4) implies the following three relationships between the elasticities e_{ij} and E_i:

$$\sum_k \alpha_k E_k = 1, \tag{2.4.1}$$

$$\sum_k e_{ik} = -E_i, \quad i = 1,...,n, \tag{2.4.2}$$

$$\alpha_i(e_{ij} + E_i\alpha_j) = \alpha_j(e_{ji} + E_j\alpha_i), \quad \text{for all } i \neq j, \tag{2.4.3}$$

where the E_k's and e_{ij}'s were defined by (2.3.2) and (2.3.3) and the α's are budget shares defined by

$$\alpha_i = p_i g_i/y,$$

i.e. α_i is the share of household expenditure devoted to good i. In E2.1, E2.2 and E2.6 you are asked to derive (2.4.1)–(2.4.3) from the model (2.2.4). For the present, however, we need only note the power of these restrictions. They provide $1 + n + (n^2-n)/2$ relationships between the elasticities. If n were 10, say,

[6] The elasticities are not normally assumed to be constants. Usual practice is to report elasticity estimates at sample mean values for p and y.

this would reduce the number of 'free' elasticities from 110 (n^2 price elasticities and n income elasticities) to 54. That is to say, given 54 of the e's and E's, we could compute the remaining 56 using (2.4.1)–(2.4.3) and observations of the budget shares.[7] Even greater economizing of free parameters in the demand system is possible if we are prepared to restrict the form of the utility function. In E2.17 you will find that if the utility function is additive, i.e.

$$U(x) = \sum_{i=1}^{n} U^i(x_i),$$

then (2.4.3) may be replaced by

$$e_{ij} = -E_i \alpha_j \left(1 + \frac{E_j}{\omega}\right), \qquad \text{for all } i \neq j, \tag{2.4.4}$$

where ω is a scalar, independent of i and j. With (2.4.1), (2.4.2) and (2.4.4) we have $1 + n + (n^2 - n - 1) = n^2$ restrictions.[8] If $n = 10$, the number of free elasticities is reduced from 110 to 10. Since data on prices, income and consumption levels is always scarce, prior information such as (2.4.1)–(2.4.4) plays a critical role in econometric studies of demand systems. The smaller the number of free parameters to be estimated, the greater the chance that our limited data will yield statistically satisfactory results.[9]

A second role of model (2.2.4) is to give demand theory some normative as well as descriptive content. In many applications we will want to make descriptive statements, e.g. statements of the form 'household demand for clothing will increase by 2 percent in response to a 1 percent increase in income'. We may also want to make normative statements, e.g. 'a 10 percent increase in the price of food will reduce household welfare by the same amount as a 1 percent reduction in income'. Once we begin to make statements about consumer welfare, some form of welfare or utility function becomes essential. In this chapter we will touch on the role of model (2.2.4) in welfare economics. E2.16, for example, involves the concept of Pareto optimality. Our emphasis, however, will be on the first use of model (2.2.4), i.e. its role in econometrics. Applications to welfare economics will be taken up more fully in Chapter 3.

---

[7]   Obviously not any 54 e's and E's would be adequate. For example, the 54 should not include all 10 of the E's.

[8]   (2.4.4) consists of $n^2 - n$ equations, but it introduces one new parameter, ω. Thus, the number of restrictions is effectively $(n^2 - n - 1)$.

[9]   For a short statement on this point see Phlips (1974, p. 56).

PROBLEM SET 2

Exercise 2.1. The Engel aggregation

Consider a consumer who chooses his consumption bundle, $x_1,...,x_n$, to maximize his utility

$$U(x_1,...,x_n) \tag{E2.1.1}$$

subject to his budget constraint

$$\sum_k p_k x_k \leqslant y. \tag{E2.1.2}$$

Prove the so-called Engel aggregation property, that the sum of the products of each income elasticity with its budget proportion must equal 1, i.e.

$$\sum_k \alpha_k E_k = 1, \tag{E2.1.3}$$

where

$$E_k = \frac{\partial x_k}{\partial y} \frac{y}{x_k}$$

and

$$\alpha_k = p_k x_k / y, \quad k = 1,...,n.$$

Answer.   We assume that the consumer spends his entire budget. (This follows from the usual assumption that marginal utilities are strictly positive.) Then by totally differentiating (E2.1.2) we find that

$$\sum_k (\mathrm{d}p_k)x_k + \sum_k (\mathrm{d}x_k)p_k = \mathrm{d}y.$$

If all prices are held constant and only income is varied, then

$$\sum_k (\mathrm{d}x_k)p_k = \mathrm{d}y.$$

Hence

$$\sum_k \frac{\partial x_k}{\partial y} p_k = 1. \tag{i}$$

Eq. (i) may be rewritten as

$$\sum_k \frac{\partial x_k}{\partial y} \frac{y}{x_k} \frac{x_k p_k}{y} = 1,$$

i.e.

$$\sum_k E_k \alpha_k = 1.$$

Exercise 2.2. Homogeneity restriction

Show that the demand equations of the form

$$x_i = \phi_i (p_1,...,p_n, y),$$

which can be derived from the model (E2.1.1)–(E2.1.2), are homogeneous of degree zero in prices and income. Now prove the 'homogeneity restriction', i.e.

$$\sum_k e_{ik} = -E_i, \quad i = 1,...,n, \tag{E2.2.1}$$

where

$$e_{ik} = \frac{\partial x_i}{\partial p_k} \frac{p_k}{x_i}$$

and

$$E_i = \frac{\partial x_i}{\partial y} \frac{y}{x_i} .$$

Answer.   The demand functions are homogeneous of degree zero if

$$\phi_i(\beta p_1,...,\beta p_n, \beta y) = \phi_i(p_1,...,p_n, y) \tag{i}$$

for all $\beta > 0$. This means that if all prices and income are doubled, say, i.e. $\beta = 2$, then there is no change in commodity demands.

To show that the demand functions derived from the constrained utility maximizing model (E2.1.1)–(E2.1.2) are homogeneous of degree zero, we multiply the prices and income by a common factor $\beta > 0$. Then the constraint (E.2.1.2) becomes

$$\sum_k \beta p_k x_k \leqslant \beta y.$$

However, the constraint region is unaffected. The consumer's choice of consumption bundles is still restricted to the original set. Therefore, the utility-maximizing consumption bundle will remain unchanged. This is sufficient to justify (i).

(E2.2.1) may be derived as follows: by totally differentiating the demand functions we have

$$dx_i = \sum_k \frac{\partial x_i}{\partial p_k} \, dp_k + \frac{\partial x_i}{\partial y} \, dy, \quad i = 1,\ldots,n.$$

These equations may be rewritten as

$$\frac{dx_i}{x_i} = \sum_k \frac{\partial x_i}{\partial p_k} \frac{p_k}{x_i} \frac{dp_k}{p_k} + \frac{\partial x_i}{\partial y} \frac{y}{x_i} \frac{dy}{y},$$

i.e.

$$\frac{dx_i}{x_i} = \sum_k e_{ik} \frac{dp_k}{p_k} + E_i \frac{dy}{y}, \quad \text{for all } i.$$

If we set

$$\frac{dy}{y} = \frac{dp_k}{p_k} = \beta, \quad \text{for all } k,$$

then we know from (i) that $dx_i = 0$. Hence

$$0 = \sum_k e_{ik} \beta + E_i \beta,$$

i.e.

$$\sum_k e_{ik} = -E_i, \quad i = 1,\ldots,n.$$

Exercise 2.3.   *The linear expenditure system*

(a) Here is a problem to test your facility at deriving the demand functions implied by a specific utility maximizing model. Assume that a consumer has an income of $\$y$ to divide between goods 1 and 2. What will be his demand for each good as a function of y, p_1 and p_2, where p_1 and p_2 are the commodity prices, if his utility function is

$$U(x_1, x_2) = \ln x_1 + 2 \ln x_2 \tag{E2.3.1}$$

and x_1 and x_2 are quantities of goods 1 and 2? (Check that the utility function is strictly quasiconcave over the positive orthant.)

(b) Answer the same question for another consumer whose utility function is

$$V(x_1, x_2) = x_1 x_2^2. \tag{E2.3.2}$$

Do you obtain the same results? Why? Can you be sure that (E2.3.2) is strictly quasiconcave?

(c) Now consider the more general case where

$$U(x_1, x_2) = \beta_1 \ln (x_1 - \gamma_1) + \beta_2 \ln (x_2 - \gamma_2) \tag{E2.3.3}$$

and $\beta_1, \beta_2, \gamma_1$ and γ_2 are parameters with $\beta_1, \beta_2 > 0$ and $\Sigma_i \beta_i = 1$.[10] Derive the demand functions for goods 1 and 2. Can you suggest why applied workers like to include the γ_i? *Hint*: what is the income elasticity of demand for each of the goods when the utility function has the form

$$U(x_1, x_2) = \beta_1 \ln x_1 + \beta_2 \ln x_2? \tag{E2.3.4}$$

Answer.   (a) The first problem is to check that the utility function (E2.3.1) is strictly quasiconcave over the positive orthant. We consider any two positive consumption bundles $x = (x_1, x_2)$ and $y = (y_1, y_2)$. Assume that both $U(x)$ and $U(y)$ are greater than or equal to γ. Then we will have shown that U is strictly quasiconcave over the positive orthant if we find that

$$U(\alpha x + (1-\alpha)y) > \gamma$$

for any α in the open interval (0, 1).

Under (E2.3.1),

$$U(\alpha x + (1-\alpha)y) = \ln (\alpha x_1 + (1-\alpha)y_1) + 2 \ln (\alpha x_2 + (1-\alpha)y_2).$$

If $\alpha \epsilon$ (0, 1), then

$$U(\alpha x + (1-\alpha)y) > \alpha \ln x_1 + (1-\alpha) \ln y_1 + \alpha\, 2 \ln x_2 + (1-\alpha)\, 2 \ln y_2.$$

(Draw a sketch to convince yourself that if $\alpha \epsilon$ (0, 1) then

$$\ln (\alpha a + (1-\alpha)b) > \alpha \ln a + (1-\alpha) \ln b.)$$

Thus,

$$U(\alpha x + (1-\alpha)y) > \alpha\, U(x) + (1-\alpha)\, U(y) \geqslant \gamma.$$

This not only establishes that the utility function is *strictly* quasiconcave over the positive orthant, but also that it is *strictly* concave. U is said to be strictly concave if

$$U(\alpha x + (1-\alpha)y) > \alpha\, U(x) + (1-\alpha)\, U(y)$$

for all x and y, where $\alpha \epsilon$ (0, 1).

---

[10]   This is a convenient normalization. No loss of generality is implied. Why?

Turning now to the main problem, we note that the consumer will choose positive values for x_1 and x_2 to maximize

$$\ln x_1 + 2 \ln x_2$$

subject to

$$p_1 x_1 + p_2 x_2 \leqslant y.$$

The objective function is strictly quasiconcave over the positive orthant, the constraint set is convex and satisfies a constraint qualification. We can proceed with the Lagrangian method in confidence that it will yield the unique solution for the optimal values of x_1, x_2. On forming the Lagrangian

$$L(x, \lambda) = \ln x_1 + 2 \ln x_2 - \lambda(p_1 x_1 + p_2 x_2 - y),$$

and equating the derivatives to zero, we find that at the consumption optimum

$$1/x_1 - \lambda p_1 = 0, \tag{E2.3.5}$$

$$2/x_2 - \lambda p_2 = 0 \tag{E2.3.6}$$

and

$$p_1 x_1 + p_2 x_2 = y. \tag{E2.3.7}$$

(We can ignore the sign restrictions on x_1 and x_2 and the possibility of the budget constraint being a strict inequality. Utility is $-\infty$ if either x_1 or x_2 is zero, and all the budget will be spent since $\partial U/\partial x_i > 0$ for $i = 1, 2$ and any values of the x_i.)

From (E2.3.5) and (E2.3.6) we find that

$$\frac{x_2}{2x_1} = \frac{p_1}{p_2} .$$

On substituting into (E2.3.7) we obtain

$$x_1 = y/3p_1 \tag{E2.3.8a}$$

and

$$x_2 = 2y/3p_2 . \tag{E2.3.8b}$$

(E2.3.8) is the system of demand equations arising from the utility function (E2.3.1). Check that these demand equations are homogeneous of degree zero in prices and expenditure level.

(b) For the second consumer, the one having the utility function (E2.3.2), we notice that[11]

$$\ln (V(x_1, x_2)) = \ln x_1 + 2 \ln x_2 = U(x_1, x_2).$$

[11] It becomes tedious continually to mention that x_1 and x_2 are restricted to the positive orthant. For the remainder of this answer we will take that as understood.

Hence, ln V is exactly the same as the utility function, U, we had initially. Now ln V is a positive (or increasing) *monotonic transformation* of V. In general, $F(V)$ is said to be such a transformation if

$$\frac{\mathrm{d}F(V)}{\mathrm{d}V} > 0, \quad \text{for all values of } V.$$

This in turn implies

$$F(V_1) \gtreqless F(V_2)$$

if and only if $V_1 \gtreqless V_2$. In the particular case which we are studying in this problem, we have

$$\frac{\mathrm{d}F(V)}{\mathrm{d}V} = \frac{\mathrm{d}\ln V}{\mathrm{d}V} = \frac{1}{V} > 0.$$

Because U is a positive monotonic transformation of V, the demand systems derived from the two utility functions will be the same or, to put the same point another way, for given prices and incomes, the consumption pattern that maximizes a given utility function also maximizes all positive monotonic transformations of that function. See Henderson and Quandt (1971, sec. 2.3) if you need a fuller discussion.

Given that $F(V(x)) = U(x)$, that $U(x)$ is strictly quasiconcave, and that F is a positive monotonic transformation, can we be sure that $V(x)$ is strictly quasiconcave? Let x and y be any two consumption bundles such that

$$V(x) > \gamma \quad \text{and} \quad V(y) > \gamma.$$

Then because F is a monotonically increasing function, we can write

$$U(x) = F(V(x)) > F(\gamma)$$

and

$$U(y) = F(V(y)) > F(\gamma).$$

Now since U is strictly quasiconcave,

$$U(\alpha x + (1-\alpha)y) > F(\gamma)$$

for all $\alpha \epsilon\ (0, 1)$. Therefore

$$F(V(\alpha x + (1-\alpha)y)) > F(\gamma)$$

and again, because F is monotonically increasing, we can conclude that

$$V(\alpha x + (1-\alpha)y) > \gamma.$$

This is sufficient to establish that V is strictly quasiconcave. Hence, we have shown that the property of strict quasiconcavity is preserved under positive monotonic transformations. On the other hand, the property of strict concavity is not necessarily preserved. Notice that while (E2.3.1) is strictly concave, (E2.3.2) is not.

(c) We form the Lagrangian

$$L(x, \lambda) = \beta_1 \ln (x_1 - \gamma_1) + \beta_2 \ln (x_2 - \gamma_2) - \lambda(p_1 x_1 + p_2 x_2 - y).$$

The first-order conditions are

$$\frac{\beta_1}{x_1 - \gamma_1} = \lambda p_1, \tag{i}$$

$$\frac{\beta_2}{x_2 - \gamma_2} = \lambda p_2 \tag{ii}$$

and

$$p_1 x_1 + p_2 x_2 = y. \tag{iii}$$

From (i) and (ii) we see that

$$\beta_i = \lambda(p_i x_i - p_i \gamma_i), \quad i = 1, 2.$$

Hence,

$$\sum_i \beta_i = 1 = \lambda \left(y - \sum_i p_i \gamma_i \right)$$

and

$$\lambda = 1 \Big/ \left(y - \sum_i p_i \gamma_i \right). \tag{iv}$$

Finally, we use (iv) in (i) and (ii) to obtain

$$x_k = \gamma_k + \frac{\beta_k \left(y - \Sigma_i p_i \gamma_i \right)}{p_k}, \quad k = 1, 2,$$

or alternatively

$$p_k x_k = p_k \gamma_k + \beta_k \left(y - \sum_i p_i \gamma_i \right), \quad k = 1, 2. \tag{v}$$

The equations (v) are the so-called *linear expenditure system* (LES). Expenditure $p_k x_k$ on each good k is a *linear* function of prices and income. This explains much of the popularity in applied work of the n-commodity version of the utility function (E2.3.3); see for example Powell (1974, ch. 2) and the references given there. Notice that the γ_k play the key role of allowing expenditure elasticities of demand to differ from 1. If each of the γ_k is zero, i.e. the utility function is (E2.3.4), then

$$x_k = \frac{\beta_k y}{p_k}$$

and

$$E_k \equiv \frac{\partial x_k}{\partial y} \frac{y}{x_k} = 1.$$

A utility specification which forces expenditure elasticities to 1 is unsatisfactory in empirical applications. Expenditure elasticities are comparatively easily estimated. Typically, expenditure elasticities for 'food' are less than 1, whereas for 'recreation' they are more than 1. For a pioneering study of expenditure elasticities, see Houthakker (1957).

A common interpretation of the linear expenditure system (v) is as follows. γ_k is said to be the 'subsistence' requirement for good k. Then $\Sigma_i p_i \gamma_i$ is the subsistence level of expenditure and $(y - \Sigma_i p_i \gamma_i)$ is supernumerary expenditure, i.e. expenditure above subsistence requirements. β_k is the marginal budget share, i.e. β_k is the additional expenditure on good k associated with an additional dollar of total expenditure. Thus, system (v) is interpreted as meaning that expenditure on good k consists of two parts: a subsistence part, $p_k \gamma_k$, and a supernumerary part, $\beta_k(y - \Sigma_i p_i \gamma_i)$, with supernumerary expenditure on good k being proportional to total supernumerary expenditure. It should be pointed out, however, that this interpretation of the linear expenditure system frequently breaks down in empirical work. Often we find negative estimates for the γ_k's. Such results are incompatible with the idea that the γ_k's are subsistence quantities. As explained above, the key role of the γ's is to give system (v) flexibility with respect to the implied expenditure elasticities. Empirically and theoretically unjustified restrictions on the values of the expenditure elasticities can be introduced by attempts to restrict the γ's to positive values.

Exercise 2.4. The marginal utility of income

Return to the consumer described in the first part of E2.3. Assuming that the utility function is (E2.3.1), express the marginal utility of income as a function of p_1, p_2 and y. Repeat this exercise for the utility function (E2.3.2). Does the marginal utility of income change as we switch between the two utility functions? On the basis of your answer to that question, would you say that marginal utility is an ordinal or cardinal concept?

Answer.   First we recall the analysis of Chapter 1, section 8. On the basis of that argument we know that the Lagrangian multiplier may be interpreted as the marginal utility of income, i.e.

$$\partial U/\partial y = \lambda,$$

where $\partial U/\partial y$ is the marginal utility of income, i.e. the rate of increase in utility per unit increase in y, and λ is the Lagrangian multiplier associated with the solution to the utility maximizing problem. Then from (E2.3.5) and (E2.3.6) we find that

$$\lambda p_1 x_1 = 1$$

and

$$\lambda p_2 x_2 = 2.$$

Hence

$$\lambda y = 3$$

and

$$\lambda = 3/y. \tag{i}$$

With the utility function (E2.3.2), the first-order conditions are

$$x_2^2 - \lambda^* p_1 = 0,$$
$$2x_1 x_2 - \lambda^* p_2 = 0$$

and

$$p_1 x_1 + p_2 x_2 = y.$$

These give

$$\lambda^* p_1 x_1 = x_1 x_2^2$$

and

$$\lambda^* p_2 x_2 = 2x_1 x_2^2. \tag{ii}$$

Hence

$$p_2 x_2 = 2p_1 x_1,$$
$$x_1 = y/3p_1$$

and

$$x_2 = 2y/3p_2.$$

Substituting back into (ii), we obtain

$$\lambda^* = \frac{4y^2}{9p_2^2 p_1}. \tag{iii}$$

By comparing (iii) and (i) we see that although a positive monotonic transformation of the utility function leaves the demand system unchanged, it *does* change the marginal utility of income. Thus, we may conclude that marginal utility is a *cardinal* concept. It depends on which particular utility function is selected from the family of equivalent utility functions describing the consumer's given set of preferences.

Exercise 2.5. Displacement analysis, an example

Consider the consumer described in the first part of E2.3. Adopting the utility function (E2.3.1), but without deriving the demand functions, find equations suitable for evaluating the changes in x_1, x_2 and λ, the marginal utility of income, which will result from small changes in the prices p_1 and p_2 and in income y.[12] From these equations, determine the income effects $\partial x_1 / \partial y$, $\partial x_2 / \partial y$, and the effects of changes in p_1 on x_1 and x_2, i.e. $\partial x_1 / \partial p_1$ and $\partial x_2 / \partial p_1$. What are the signs of the income effects? What property of the utility function is responsible for this result? Show that the cross substitution effect, $\partial x_2 / \partial p_1$, is zero. You may check your calculations of the various partial derivatives by making appropriate differentiations of the demand functions which you derived in E2.3.

Answer. We assume that when prices and income change, the consumer reorganizes his purchases so that he maximizes his utility subject to his new budget constraint. At his new consumption levels, $x_1(N)$, $x_2(N)$, there will exist $\lambda(N)$ such that

$$\frac{1}{x_1(N)} - \lambda(N) \, p_1(N) = 0, \tag{i}$$

$$\frac{2}{x_2(N)} - \lambda(N) \, p_2(N) = 0 \tag{ii}$$

and

$$p_1(N) \, x_1(N) + p_2(N) \, x_2(N) = y(N), \tag{iii}$$

where $p_1(N)$, $p_2(N)$ and $y(N)$ are the new levels for p_1, p_2 and y.

Next, we compare the original first-order conditions (E2.3.5)–(E2.3.7) with the new first-order conditions (i)–(iii). By subtracting (E2.3.5) from (i) we obtain

---

[12] If you have difficulty with this problem, you should review the relevant theory in Intriligator (1971, ch. 7, esp. sec. 7.4).

$$\left(\frac{1}{x_1(N)} - \frac{1}{x_1}\right) - (\lambda(N)\,p_1(N) - \lambda p_1) = 0$$

i.e.

$$d(1/x_1) - d(\lambda p_1) = 0,$$

where $d(1/x_1)$ and $d(\lambda_1 p_1)$ are the changes in $1/x_1$ and λp_1. If the changes are small, this last equation becomes

$$\frac{\partial(1/x_1)}{\partial x_1}\,dx_1 - \frac{\partial(\lambda p_1)}{\partial \lambda}\,d\lambda - \frac{\partial(\lambda p_1)}{\partial p_1}\,dp_1 = 0,$$

i.e.

$$-\frac{1}{x_1^2}\,dx_1 - p_1\,d\lambda - \lambda dp_1 = 0. \tag{iv}$$

Similarly, by totally differentiating (E2.3.6) and (E2.3.7) we find that

$$-\frac{2}{x_2^2}\,dx_2 - p_2\,d\lambda - \lambda dp_2 = 0 \tag{v}$$

and

$$p_1\,dx_1 + p_2\,dx_2 + (dp_1)x_1 + (dp_2)x_2 = dy. \tag{vi}$$

The three equations (iv)–(vi) may be set out in a convenient matrix format as

$$\begin{bmatrix} -\dfrac{1}{x_1^2} & 0 & p_1 \\[2mm] 0 & -\dfrac{2}{x_2^2} & p_2 \\[2mm] p_1 & p_2 & 0 \end{bmatrix} \begin{bmatrix} dx_1 \\[2mm] dx_2 \\[2mm] -d\lambda \end{bmatrix} = \begin{bmatrix} \lambda dp_1 \\[2mm] \lambda dp_2 \\[2mm] dy - \sum_i (dp_i)x_i \end{bmatrix}. \tag{vii}$$

We 'solve' (vii) by writing

$$\begin{bmatrix} dx_1 \\[2mm] dx_2 \\[2mm] -d\lambda \end{bmatrix} = \begin{bmatrix} -\dfrac{1}{x_1^2} & 0 & p_1 \\[2mm] 0 & -\dfrac{2}{x_2^2} & p_2 \\[2mm] p_1 & p_2 & 0 \end{bmatrix}^{-1} \begin{bmatrix} \lambda dp_1 \\[2mm] \lambda dp_2 \\[2mm] dy - \sum_i (dp_i)x_i \end{bmatrix}.$$

The matrix to be inverted is the so-called bordered Hessian of the utility function (E2.3.1). On carrying out the inversion we find that

$$
\begin{bmatrix} dx_1 \\ dx_2 \\ -d\lambda \end{bmatrix} = \cfrac{1}{\left(\cfrac{p_2}{x_1}\right)^2 + 2\left(\cfrac{p_1}{x_2}\right)^2} \begin{bmatrix} -p_2^2 & p_1 p_2 & \cfrac{2p_1}{x_2^2} \\[2mm] p_1 p_2 & -p_1^2 & \cfrac{p_2}{x_1^2} \\[2mm] \cfrac{2p_1}{x_2^2} & \cfrac{p_2}{x_1^2} & \cfrac{2}{x_1^2 x_2^2} \end{bmatrix}
$$

$$
\times \begin{bmatrix} \lambda dp_1 \\[2mm] \lambda dp_2 \\[2mm] dy - \sum_i (dp_i) x_i \end{bmatrix}. \tag{viii}
$$

(If you have trouble with inverting matrices, check that we have the right answer by multiplying our inverse by the original bordered Hessian. You should generate the identity matrix.)

Eq. (viii) is suitable for evaluating the effects of changes in prices and income on consumption levels and on the marginal utility of income. We have derived it without explicitly obtaining the demand system (E2.3.8). In the present example this is not very useful. However, the technique becomes important when the demand functions cannot be derived explicitly. The point is illustrated in E2.6 and E.2.17.

On the basis of eq. (viii), we can compute the income derivatives, $\partial x_1/\partial y$ and $\partial x_2/\partial y$, as follows: if we consider a situation in which prices are fixed, but income changes, then

$$
\begin{bmatrix} dx_1 \\ dx_2 \\ -d\lambda \end{bmatrix} = \cfrac{1}{\left(\cfrac{p_2}{x_1}\right)^2 + 2\left(\cfrac{p_1}{x_2}\right)^2} \begin{bmatrix} \cfrac{2p_1}{x_2^2} \\[2mm] \cfrac{p_2}{x_1^2} \\[2mm] \cfrac{2}{x_1^2 x_2^2} \end{bmatrix} dy.
$$

Hence,

$$
\frac{\partial x_1}{\partial y} = \frac{2p_1/x_2^2}{(p_2/x_1)^2 + 2(p_1/x_2)^2} \tag{ix}
$$

and

$$\frac{\partial x_2}{\partial y} = \frac{p_2/x_1^2}{(p_2/x_1)^2 + 2(p_1/x_2)^2}$$

Both income derivatives are positive. This result is attributable to the additivity of the utility function. With this type of utility function, quantities consumed of any good do not affect the marginal utility of other goods. Hence, increases in income must result in increases in the purchases of all goods, for otherwise the marginal utility of a dollar's worth of expenditure on some goods would be left higher than that on others. Accordingly, the additive utility function excludes the possibility of inferior goods.

To determine the price derivatives $\partial x_1/\partial p_1$ and $\partial x_2/\partial p_1$, we set dy and dp_2 equal to zero. Then (viii) implies that

$$\begin{bmatrix} dx_1 \\ dx_2 \end{bmatrix} = \frac{1}{(p_2/x_1)^2 + 2(p_1/x_2)^2} \begin{bmatrix} -p_2^2 & 2p_1/x_2^2 \\ p_1 p_2 & p_2/x_1^2 \end{bmatrix} \begin{bmatrix} \lambda dp_1 \\ -x_1 dp_1 \end{bmatrix}.$$

From here we find that

$$\frac{\partial x_1}{\partial p_1} = \frac{1}{(p_2/x_1)^2 + 2(p_1/x_2)^2} \left(-\lambda p_2^2 - \frac{2x_1 p_1}{x_2^2} \right)$$

and

$$\frac{\partial x_2}{\partial p_1} = \frac{1}{(p_2/x_1)^2 + 2(p_1/x_2)^2} \left(\lambda p_1 p_2 - \frac{p_2}{x_1} \right).$$

Finally, if we use the first-order condition (E2.3.5), we see that

$$\lambda = 1/p_1 x_1$$

so that the cross substitution effect, $\partial x_2/\partial p_1$, is zero.

The derivations of $\partial x_1/\partial y$, $\partial x_2/\partial y$, etc. can be checked by differentiating in the demand system (E2.3.8). For example, we find that

$$\frac{\partial x_2}{\partial p_1} = 0$$

and

$$\frac{\partial x_1}{\partial y} = \frac{1}{3p_1}.$$

(This last result may be obtained from (ix) by substituting from (E2.3.5) and (E2.3.6) to eliminate the x's and then simplifying.)

Exercise 2.6. Displacement analysis and the symmetry restriction

In E2.5, working with a special case, you obtained an expression for evaluating changes in the consumption of various commodities as a function of changes in prices and income. Now consider the general case where there are n goods $x_1,...,x_n$; their prices are $p_1,...,p_n$; and the consumer has income y and a strictly quasiconcave utility function $U(x_1,...,x_n)$. Show that

$$\begin{bmatrix} H & p \\ p' & 0 \end{bmatrix} \begin{bmatrix} dx \\ -d\lambda \end{bmatrix} = \begin{bmatrix} \lambda dp \\ dy - (dp)'x \end{bmatrix}, \qquad (E2.6.1)$$

where H is the Hessian matrix of the utility function, i.e.

$$H \equiv [U_{ij}]_{n \times n}, \quad \text{with } U_{ij} \equiv \frac{\partial^2 U}{\partial x_i \, \partial x_j},$$

p and x are vectors of prices and consumptions, and λ is the marginal utility of income.

Adopt the notation

$$R \equiv \begin{bmatrix} H & p \\ p' & 0 \end{bmatrix}^{-1} \equiv \begin{bmatrix} r_{11}, & \cdots & r_{1n}, & r_{1\,n+1} \\ \vdots & & & \\ r_{n1}, & \cdots & r_{nn}, & r_{nn+1} \\ r_{n+1\,1}, \cdots & & & r_{n+1\,n+1} \end{bmatrix}.$$

Note that R is a symmetric matrix. (Why?) Now prove the symmetry restriction, i.e.

$$\alpha_i(e_{ij} + E_i\alpha_j) = \alpha_j(e_{ji} + E_j\alpha_i), \quad \text{for all } i \neq j, \qquad (E2.6.2)$$

where the α's, E's and e's are defined as in E2.1 and E2.2.

Answer.   We assume that the consumer chooses $x_1, x_2,...,x_n$ to maximize

$$U(x_1,...,x_n)$$

subject to

$$\sum_k p_k x_k = y.$$

At a constrained maximum there will exist λ, which may be interpreted as the marginal utility of income, such that $\lambda, x_1, ..., x_n$, jointly satisfy

$$\frac{\partial U}{\partial x_i} = \lambda p_i, \quad i = 1, ..., n \tag{i}$$

and

$$\sum_k p_k x_k = y. \tag{ii}$$

By totally differentiating (i) and (ii) we find that

$$\sum_k \frac{\partial}{\partial x_k} \left(\frac{\partial U}{\partial x_i} \right) dx_k = (d\lambda) p_i + \lambda (dp_i), \quad i = 1, ..., n,$$

and

$$\sum_k (dp_k) x_k + \sum_k p_k (dx_k) = dy.$$

In matrix notation, these equations may be presented as

$$
\begin{bmatrix}
U_{11}, & \cdots & U_{1n}, & p_1 \\
& & & \\
U_{n1}, & \cdots & U_{nn}, & p_n \\
& & & \\
p_1, & \cdots & p_n, & 0
\end{bmatrix}
\begin{bmatrix}
dx_1 \\
\vdots \\
dx_n \\
-d\lambda
\end{bmatrix}
=
\begin{bmatrix}
\lambda dp_1 \\
\vdots \\
\lambda dp_n \\
dy - \sum_k (dp_k) x_k
\end{bmatrix}, \tag{iii}
$$

i.e.

$$
\begin{bmatrix}
H & p \\
p' & 0
\end{bmatrix}
\begin{bmatrix}
dx \\
-d\lambda
\end{bmatrix}
=
\begin{bmatrix}
\lambda dp \\
dy - (dp)' x
\end{bmatrix}.
$$

The bordered Hessian,

$$
\begin{bmatrix}
H & p \\
p' & 0
\end{bmatrix},
$$

is symmetric (from Young's theorem[13] $U_{ij} = U_{ji}$ for all i and j). Thus, R, the inverse of the bordered Hessian, is also symmetric.[14] (If A is any symmetric matrix, then A^{-1}, if it exists, is symmetric.)[15]

On solving (iii) we obtain

$$
\begin{bmatrix} dx \\ \\ -d\lambda \end{bmatrix} = R \begin{bmatrix} \lambda dp \\ \\ dy - (dp)'x \end{bmatrix}
$$

or, more fully,

$$
\begin{bmatrix} dx_1 \\ dx_2 \\ \vdots \\ dx_n \\ -d\lambda \end{bmatrix} = \begin{bmatrix} r_{11}, & \cdots & r_{1n}, & r_{1n+1} \\ & & & \\ r_{n1}, & \cdots & r_{nn}, & r_{nn+1} \\ r_{n+11} & \cdots & & r_{n+1\,n+1} \end{bmatrix} \begin{bmatrix} \lambda dp_1 \\ \vdots \\ \lambda dp_n \\ dy - \sum_k (dp_k)x_k \end{bmatrix} . \qquad \text{(iv)}
$$

From (iv) we can deduce the derivatives of the demand functions. In particular

$$
\frac{\partial x_k}{\partial y} = r_{kn+1}, \quad k = 1,\dots,n \qquad \text{(v)}
$$

(set $dy = 1$, and $dp_i = 0$, $i = 1,\dots,n$) and

$$
\frac{\partial x_k}{\partial p_s} = \lambda r_{ks} - (r_{kn+1})x_s, \quad \text{for all } k \text{ and } s \qquad \text{(vi)}
$$

(set $dp_s = 1$, and all the other price changes and dy to zero). Because $r_{ij} = r_{ji}$, eq. (vi) implies that

$$
\frac{\partial x_i}{\partial p_j} - \frac{\partial x_j}{\partial p_i} = -(r_{in+1})x_j + (r_{jn+1})x_i. \qquad \text{(vii)}
$$

---

[13]   See, for example, Hilton (1960, pp. 49–51).

[14]   The strict quasiconcavity of U ensures that the consumer's utility-maximizing problem has one, and only one, solution for each choice of $p > 0$ and $y > 0$. This in turn ensures the existence of R. However, we usually make the additional assumption that H^{-1} exists. This is convenient, but it does not follow from the assumption of strict quasiconcavity (or even strict concavity). For example, consider the problem of choosing the scalar, x, to maximize the strictly quasiconcave objective function $(x-1)^3$ subject to $x \leqslant 1$. You will find that at the optimum value for x, $(x = 1)$, the Hessian is zero, but that the R matrix exists.

[15] $(A^{-1})'A' = (AA^{-1})' = I$. Hence, $(A')^{-1} = (A^{-1})'$. If A is symmetric then it follows that $A^{-1} = (A^{-1})'$. Hence, A^{-1} is symmetric.

Then from (v) and (vii) we obtain

$$\frac{\partial x_i}{\partial p_j} - \frac{\partial x_j}{\partial p_i} = -\frac{\partial x_i}{\partial y} x_j + \frac{\partial x_j}{\partial y} x_i. \tag{viii}$$

The final step in the derivation of the symmetry restriction is to translate the derivatives into elasticities. In (ix) the terms of the original equation (viii) are displayed in square brackets. The translation to elasticities is made in the usual way by multiplying and dividing through by prices, income and quantities:

$$\frac{x_i p_i}{y} \frac{p_j}{x_i} \left[\frac{\partial x_i}{\partial p_j}\right] \frac{y}{p_j p_i} - \frac{x_j p_j}{y} \frac{p_i}{x_j} \left[\frac{\partial x_j}{\partial p_i}\right] \frac{y}{p_i p_j}$$

$$= -\frac{x_i p_i}{y} \frac{y}{x_i} \left[\frac{\partial x_i}{\partial y}\right] \frac{[x_j] p_j}{y} \frac{y}{p_i p_j} + \frac{x_j p_j}{y} \frac{y}{x_j} \left[\frac{\partial x_j}{\partial y}\right] \frac{[x_i] p_i}{y} \frac{y}{p_i p_j}, \tag{ix}$$

i.e.

$$\alpha_i e_{ij} - \alpha_j e_{ji} = -\alpha_i E_i \alpha_j + \alpha_j E_j \alpha_i,$$

and this last equation can be rearranged to give (E2.6.2).

Exercise 2.7. The triad

Alan Powell (1974) has referred to the three results, the Engel aggregation (E2.1.3), the homogeneity restriction (E2.2.1), and the symmetry restriction (E2.6.2), as the 'triad'. Some appreciation of the power of the triad can be gained by completing the following scheme:[16]

$\alpha_1 = \frac{1}{2}$,	$\alpha_2 = \frac{1}{4}$,	$\alpha_3 = \frac{1}{4}$	
$e_{11} = -1$,	$e_{12} = ?$,	$e_{13} = 0$	$E_1 = \frac{1}{2}$
$e_{21} = ?$,	$e_{22} = ?$,	$e_{23} = ?$	$E_2 = ?$
$e_{31} = ?$,	$e_{32} = -\frac{1}{4}$,	$e_{33} = ?$	$E_3 = 1$

[16]   The E's, α's and e's are defined as in E2.1 and E2.2.

Answer.   The completed table is shown below:

$\alpha_1 = \frac{1}{2}$,	$\alpha_2 = \frac{1}{4}$,	$\alpha_3 = \frac{1}{4}$	
$e_{11} = -1$,	$e_{12} = \frac{1}{2}$,	$e_{13} = 0$	$E_1 = \frac{1}{2}$
$e_{21} = \frac{1}{4}$,	$e_{22} = -1\frac{3}{4}$,	$e_{23} = -\frac{1}{2}$	$E_2 = 2$
$e_{31} = -\frac{1}{4}$,	$e_{32} = -\frac{1}{4}$,	$e_{33} = -\frac{1}{2}$	$E_3 = 1$

Starting from the incomplete table, we used the homegeneity restriction to find e_{12}, i.e.

$$e_{12} = -E_1 - e_{11} - e_{13}.$$

E_2 was computed from the Engel aggregation, i.e.

$$E_2 = (1 - E_1\alpha_1 - E_3\alpha_3)/\alpha_2,$$

The symmetry restriction allowed us to compute e_{21} from knowing e_{12}, the E's and the α's:

$$e_{21} = \frac{\alpha_1(e_{12} + E_1\alpha_2)}{\alpha_2} - E_2\alpha_1.$$

Similarly, we used the symmetry restriction to generate e_{31} and e_{23}. Finally, e_{22} and e_{33} were deduced from the homogeneity restriction.

On the basis of knowing the budget shares, the α_i's, and five of the elasticities, we were able to deduce the other seven elasticities. The triad provides $1 + n + n(n-1)/2$ restrictions. When $n = 3$ the triad suggests seven independent relationships between the elasticities.

The estimation of demand elasticities, E_i and e_{ij}, has been the objective of intensive econometric activity. Excellent survey texts are available, for example, Powell (1974) and Phlips (1974). Both these references emphasize the importance of prior restrictions in econometric work. It is too much to ask 'the data' to reveal $n^2 + n$ elasticities without some help from economic theory. The imposition of the triad restrictions, and perhaps some additional restrictions (see E2.17), has made possible the estimation of complete systems of demand elasticities.

Exercise 2.8. The Cournot aggregation

Prove that

$$\sum_i \alpha_i e_{ik} = -\alpha_k \quad \text{for all } k.$$

Is this a further restriction on the demand elasticities, or is it implied by the triad?

Answer. We assume that

$$\sum_i p_i x_i = y.$$

By total differentiation we obtain

$$\sum_i (\mathrm{d}p_i) x_i + \sum_i (\mathrm{d}x_i) p_i = \mathrm{d}y.$$

Now we set all the price and income changes to zero with the exception of $\mathrm{d}p_k$. Thus,

$$(\mathrm{d}p_k) x_k + \sum_i (\mathrm{d}x_i) p_i = 0$$

and

$$-x_k = \sum_i \frac{\partial x_i}{\partial p_k} p_i. \tag{i}$$

Finally, we translate into elasticities and budget shares by rewriting (i) as

$$\frac{[-x_k] p_k}{y} = \sum_i \left[\frac{\partial x_i}{\partial p_k} \right] \frac{p_k}{x_i} \frac{x_i [p_i]}{y},$$

i.e.

$$-\alpha_k = \sum_i e_{ik} \alpha_i. \tag{ii}$$

Restriction (ii) cannot be counted as additional to the triad. It can be deduced as follows: the symmetry restrictions imply

$$\sum_i e_{ik} \alpha_i = \sum_i [\alpha_k (e_{ki} + E_k \alpha_i) - E_i \alpha_i \alpha_k]$$

$$= \alpha_k \sum_i e_{ki} + \alpha_k E_k \sum_i \alpha_i - \alpha_k \sum_i \alpha_i E_i$$

$$= -\alpha_k E_k + \alpha_k E_k - \alpha_k.$$

(We have used the homogeneity restriction, the Engel aggregation and the fact that $\sum_i \alpha_i = 1$.) Hence,

$$\sum_i e_{ik} \alpha_i = -\alpha_k.$$

The Cournot aggregation suggests an interesting question. Can we be sure that the triad contains all the useful restrictions which flow from the utility-maximizing model in which the utility function is strictly quasiconcave and differentiable, but otherwise unrestricted? Even though we have found that the Cournot aggregation is implied by the triad, perhaps there are other restrictions which are independent of the triad? The answer is that apart from some restrictions on the signs of various price elasticities (see E2.10), the triad *does* summarize the complete set of restrictions on the demand elasticities. This is a principal conclusion from the literature on the so-called *integrability* problem. But since integrability is rather a difficult topic, we will delay consideration of it until Chapter 3.

Exercise 2.9.   The Hicks–Slutsky partition

Show that for all i and j,

$$\frac{\partial x_i}{\partial p_j} = \left(\frac{\partial x_i}{\partial p_j} \right)_{dU=0} - x_j \frac{\partial x_i}{\partial y} \tag{E2.9.1}$$

or, equivalently,

$$e_{ij} = e_{ij}^c - E_i \alpha_j, \tag{E2.9.2}$$

where $(\partial x_i / \partial p_j)_{dU=0}$ is the *compensated* derivative of the demand for good i with respect to changes in price j, i.e. $\partial x_i / \partial p_{j\,dU=0}$ is the effect on the demand for good i when there is a change in both p_j and a change in y which is sufficient to allow the consumer to maintain his initial level of utility. e_{ij}^c is the compensated elasticity, i.e.

$$e_{ij}^c = \frac{p_j}{x_i} \left(\frac{\partial x_i}{\partial p_j} \right)_{dU=0}.$$

Hint: the first step is to find the change in income, dy, which is necessary to compensate for a change, dp_j, in price j. This can be done by noting that

$$dU = \sum_k \frac{\partial U}{\partial x_k} \, dx_k = \sum_k \lambda p_k \, dx_k = 0 \tag{E2.9.3}$$

and

$$dy = \sum_k p_k \, dx_k + (dp_j) x_j, \tag{E2.9.4}$$

where dU is the change in utility and the dx_k, dy are the changes in consumption levels and income arising from the compensated change in p_j. λ is the marginal utility of income

Answer. From (E2.9.3) and (E.2.9.4) we see that the compensation, dy, necessary to allow the consumer to retain his initial level of utility is given by

$$dy = (dp_j)x_j.$$

Therefore the change in x_i arising from both a change in p_j and a utility compensating change in income is

$$\left(dx_i\right)_{dU=0} = \frac{\partial x_i}{\partial p_j}\,dp_j + \frac{\partial x_i}{\partial y}\,(dp_j)x_j,$$

i.e.

$$\left(\frac{\partial x_i}{\partial p_j}\right)_{dU=0} = \frac{\partial x_i}{\partial p_j} + \frac{\partial x_i}{\partial y}\,x_j. \tag{E2.9.5}$$

This equation can quickly be rearranged to give (E2.9.1) and (E2.9.2).

The Hicks—Slutsky partition divides the total effect on x_i of a change in p_j into two parts. Referring to (E2.9.1), the first term on the right is the substitution effect. In terms of the usual diagram,[17] the substitution effect arises from the movement around the initial indifference curve. The second term is the *income effect*. It captures the idea that an uncompensated change in p_j will affect the consumer's purchases of good i by affecting the real value of his total budget.

Exercise 2.10. The negativity of the own-price substitution effect

Demonstrate that

$$\left(\frac{\partial x_i}{\partial p_i}\right)_{dU=0} \leqslant 0, \quad \text{for all } i.$$

This can be done by appealing to the second-order conditions, see for example Lancaster (1968, pp. 56—58). However, a simpler and more direct argument is available using ideas from the theory of revealed preference, see for example Lancaster (1968, pp. 125—127) or Baumol (1972, pp. 231—232).

Answer. We assume that the consumer chooses his consumption vector x to maximize a strictly quasiconcave, differentiable utility function, $U(x)$, subject to

---

[17] See, for example, Intriligator (1971, p. 161).

his budget constraint $p'x = y$.[18] We consider two situations in both of which the consumer achieves the same utility level. The two situations can be thought of as the initial and final situations after a compensated change in prices. In the first situation the price vector is $\bar{p}$ and income is $\bar{y}$. In the second, the price vector is $\bar{\bar{p}}$, not equal to $\bar{p}$, and income is $\bar{\bar{y}}$.[19] Where $\bar{x}$ and $\bar{\bar{x}}$ are the optimum consumption vectors for each situation, we have

$$U(\bar{x}) = U(\bar{\bar{x}}),$$

with $\bar{x} \neq \bar{\bar{x}}$.

Fig. E2.10.1 illustrates the two situations for the two-good case. It will be noticed that the indifference curve is 'smooth' with no linear segments or 'corners' and with the right convexity. The *strict* quasiconcavity assumption rules out the possibility of linear segments and the differentiability assumption excludes indifference curves of the type shown in fig. E2.10.2. (After you have understood the argument given here, you might work out what modifications are necessary if the utility function is not strictly quasiconcave or has nondifferentiable points.)

We note that

$$\bar{p}'\,\bar{\bar{x}} > \bar{y} = \bar{p}'\,\bar{x} \tag{i}$$

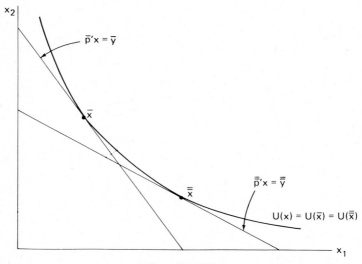

Figure E2.10.1

18   We assume that the consumer spends his entire budget.
19   We assume that relative prices have changed, i.e. $\bar{p} \neq \beta\bar{\bar{p}}$, where β is a scalar.

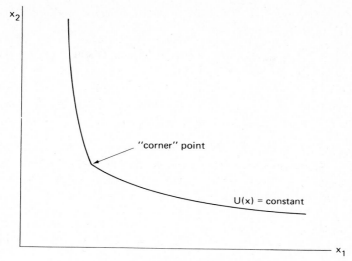

Figure E2.10.2

and

$$\bar{p}'\,x > \bar{\bar{y}} = \bar{p}'\,\bar{\bar{x}}.$$

(ii)

The first of these inequalities means that when the consumer was faced with the initial prices, $\bar{p}$, and income, $\bar{y}$, he could not afford the consumption vector $\bar{\bar{x}}$. If $\bar{p}'\,\bar{\bar{x}}$ were equal to or less than $\bar{y}$, then $\bar{x}$ and $\bar{\bar{x}}$ would be alternative optima for the initial consumer problem. However, the assumption of *strict* quasiconcavity implies that the consumer problem has a unique solution. The justification for inequality (ii) is similar to that for (i).

From (i) and (ii) we find that

$$\bar{p}'\,(\bar{\bar{x}} - \bar{x}) > 0$$

and

$$\bar{\bar{p}}'\,(\bar{x} - \bar{\bar{x}}) > 0.$$

Hence

$$\bar{p}'\,(\bar{\bar{x}} - \bar{x}) + \bar{\bar{p}}'\,(\bar{x} - \bar{\bar{x}}) > 0,$$

i.e.

$$(\bar{\bar{p}}' - \bar{p}')\,(\bar{x} - \bar{\bar{x}}) > 0$$

and

$$(\bar{\bar{p}}' - \bar{p}')\,(\bar{\bar{x}} - \bar{x}) < 0.$$

This final inequality can be written as

$$(\mathrm{d}p)'\,(\mathrm{d}x) < 0, \tag{iii}$$

where $\mathrm{d}p$ and $\mathrm{d}x$ are the vectors of price and consumption changes between the final and initial situations. In the special case where only price i changes, then

$$(\mathrm{d}p_i)\,(\mathrm{d}x_i) < 0.$$

Hence a compensated increase in p_i produces a reduction in x_i; $(\mathrm{d}p_i)$ and $(\mathrm{d}x_i)$ are of opposite signs. We can conclude that

$$\left(\frac{\partial x_i}{\partial p_i}\right)_{\mathrm{d}U=0} \leqslant 0. \tag{E2.10.1}$$

It is usual to conclude that

$$\left(\frac{\partial x_i}{\partial p_i}\right)_{\mathrm{d}U=0} < 0.$$

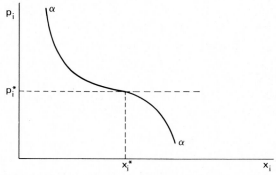

Figure E2.10.3. $\alpha\alpha$ is the compensated demand curve for good i, i.e. it shows the demand for good i as we vary p_i holding all other prices and the utility level constant. The curve is consistent with having

$$(\mathrm{d}p_i)\,(\mathrm{d}x_i) < 0.$$

But it is also true that

$$\left(\frac{\partial x_i}{\partial p_i}\right)_{\mathrm{d}U=0} = 0$$

at the point where $x_i = x_i^*$.

Our argument, however, has not explicitly ruled out the case illustrated in fig. E2.10.3. Hence, we will be content with (E2.10.1).

For future reference (see E3.14) it will be useful to note that in addition to (E2.10.1), (iii) implies that the matrix of compensated own and cross price derivatives is negative semidefinite. (A symmetric matrix A is said to be negative semidefinite if $x'Ax \leqslant 0$ for all choices of the vector x.) To obtain this result we write

$$dx = G dp, \tag{iv}$$

where dx is the vector of changes in consumption arising from a compensated change in prices dp, and G is the matrix of compensated own and cross price derivatives,[20] i.e.

$$G_{ij} = \left(\frac{\partial x_i}{\partial p_j} \right)_{dU=0}, \quad \text{for all} \ \ i,j.$$

If $dp = \beta p$, where β is a scalar, then

$$dx = 0. \tag{v}$$

(A compensated proportionate change in all prices leaves consumption unchanged.) If $dp \neq \beta p$, then according to (iii) we have

$$(dp)' dx < 0. \tag{vi}$$

On combining (iv)–(vi) we see that

$$(dp)' G dp \leqslant 0 \tag{E2.10.2}$$

for all choices of dp.

Exercise 2.11. *The inferiority of Giffen goods*

Are all Giffen goods inferior?

Answer.   For Giffen goods we have

$$0 < \frac{\partial x_i}{\partial p_i} = \left(\frac{\partial x_i}{\partial p_i} \right)_{dU=0} - x_i \frac{\partial x_i}{\partial y}.$$

---

[20] G is the matrix of derivatives whose typical element is defined by (E2.9.5). Notice that G is symmetric, i.e.

$$\left(\frac{\partial x_i}{\partial p_j} \right)_{dU=0} = \left(\frac{\partial x_j}{\partial p_i} \right)_{dU=0}.$$

This follows from (E2.9.5) and the symmetry restriction – see in particular eq. (viii) in (E2.6).

Given the nonpositivity of the own-price substitution effect, the above inequality implies that

$$\frac{\partial x_i}{\partial y} < 0.$$

Hence, Giffen goods are inferior.

Exercise 2.12. The sign of cross-elasticities of demand

Although two goods i and j may be substitutes, the cross-elasticity of demand for i with respect to changes in the price of j can be negative. Explain with the aid of a suitable diagram.

Answer.   Two goods i and j are said to be substitutes if and only if

$$\left(\frac{\partial x_i}{\partial p_j}\right)_{dU=0} \geqslant 0. \tag{i}$$

Inequality (i) may also be written as

$$e_{ij}^c \geqslant 0. \tag{ii}$$

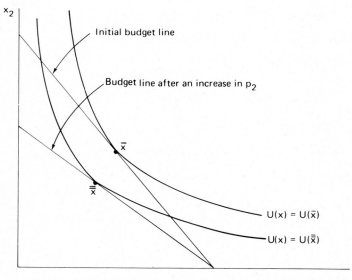

Figure E2.12.1.   An increase in p_2 moves the consumer equilibrium from $\bar{x}$ to $\bar{\bar{x}}$. In particular an increase in p_2 *reduces* x_1, i.e. $e_{12} < 0$.

The Hicks–Slutsky partition implies that

$$e_{ij} = e_{ij}^c - \alpha_j E_i$$

(see (E2.9.2)).

If $\alpha_j E_i > e_{ij}^c$, then despite (ii), e_{ij} will be negative. Fig. E2.12.1 illustrates a situation, for the two-good model, in which goods 1 and 2 are substitutes (in view of E2.13, they could not be anything else), yet the cross-elasticity of demand e_{12} is negative.

Exercise 2.13.   Substitutes, the two-good case

Show that in the two-good case, all goods must be substitutes.

Answer.   For the two-good case we consider a compensated increase in p_1 with p_2 constant. Then the changes in x_1 and x_2 are

$$dx_1 = \left(\frac{\partial x_1}{\partial p_1}\right)_{dU=0} dp_1$$

and

$$dx_2 = \left(\frac{\partial x_2}{\partial p_1}\right)_{dU=0} dp_1.$$

The change in utility is given by

$$\dot{d}U = \frac{\partial U}{\partial x_1}\ dx_1 + \frac{\partial U}{\partial x_2}\ dx_2 = 0.$$

Hence

$$\left(\frac{\partial U}{\partial x_1}\right)\left(\frac{\partial x_1}{\partial p_1}\right)_{dU=0} dp_1 + \left(\frac{\partial U}{\partial x_2}\right)\left(\frac{\partial x_2}{\partial p_1}\right)_{dU=0} dp_1 = 0. \qquad \text{(i)}$$

We assume that $\partial U/\partial x_1$ and $\partial U/\partial x_2$ are positive. In fact, they are equal to the marginal utility of income multiplied by the respective prices. We also know that the own-price substitution effect is nonpositive. We may conclude from (i), that

$$\left(\frac{\partial x_2}{\partial p_1}\right)_{dU=0} \geqslant 0.$$

Hence goods 1 and 2 are substitutes.

Exercise 2.14.   Consumer behavior under rationing

Assume that a consumer has the utility function

$$U(x_1, x_2) = x_1 x_2,$$

where x_1 and x_2 represent the amounts of two goods, 1 and 2, consumed in a given time period. Find his utility-maximizing consumption levels subject to the budget constraint

$$5x_1 + 4x_2 \leqslant 50 \quad (p_1 = 5, p_2 = 4 \text{ and } y = 50).$$

Now suppose that a rationing system is imposed on the consumer. The ration point 'prices' of x_1 and x_2 are 3 and 6, respectively, and the consumer is issued a total of 40 ration points. Find his optimum consumption levels. Are both the ration and budget constraints binding? What is the effect on the consumer's utility of having respectively one more ration point and one more dollar.

Demonstrate that the existence of a market for ration points will improve the consumer's welfare. In particular, calculate the consumer's utility, optimum consumption levels, and the number of ration points which he buys or sells when the price of a ration point is $p_3 = 0.5$.

Answer.   In the initial situation, i.e. before the imposition of rationing, the consumer will choose non-negative values for x_1 and x_2 to maximize

$$x_1 x_2$$

subject to

$$5x_1 + 4x_2 \leqslant 50.$$

We may assume that the constraint is binding and that the optimal values for x_1 and x_2 are strictly positive. Thus, the first-order conditions for a solution are

$$\left. \begin{array}{l} x_2 - 5\lambda = 0, \\ x_1 - 4\lambda = 0 \\ 5x_1 + 4x_2 = 50. \end{array} \right\} \qquad \text{(i)}$$

From (i), we find that

$$x_1 = 5, \quad x_2 = 6\tfrac{1}{4} \quad \text{and} \quad \lambda = 1\tfrac{1}{4}.$$

With the imposition of rationing, the consumer's problem becomes that of choosing non-negative values for x_1 and x_2 to maximize

$$x_1 x_2 \qquad \text{(ii)}$$

subject to

$$5x_1 + 4x_2 \leqslant 50$$

and

$$3x_1 + 6x_2 \leqslant 40.$$

It is obvious that the optimal values of x_1 and x_2 will be strictly positive. On the other hand, it is not obvious which of the constraints will be binding. Hence we cannot take any short cuts.

On applying the Lagrangian method to generate the first-order conditions, we find that at a solution for problem (ii) there will exist non-negative values for λ_1 and λ_2 such that

$$\left.\begin{aligned}
x_2 - 5\lambda_1 - 3\lambda_2 &= 0, \\
x_1 - 4\lambda_1 - 6\lambda_2 &= 0, \\
5x_1 + 4x_2 - 50 &\leqslant 0, \\
3x_1 + 6x_2 - 40 &\leqslant 0, \\
\lambda_1 (5x_1 + 4x_2 - 50) &= 0, \\
\lambda_2 (3x_1 + 6x_2 - 40) &= 0.
\end{aligned}\right\} \qquad \text{(iii)}$$

Certainly, not both λ_1 and λ_2 can be zero. This would imply that x_1 and x_2 are both zero, giving a value of zero for the objective function. There is no doubt that the consumer can do better than that.

Can we have $\lambda_2 = 0$ with $\lambda_1 > 0$? If $\lambda_1 > 0$, then the first constraint holds as an equality, i.e.

$$5x_1 + 4x_2 - 50 = 0.$$

Also, with $\lambda_2 = 0$ the first two equations in (iii) imply that

$$5x_1 - 4x_2 = 0.$$

From here we obtain

$$x_1 = 5 \quad \text{and} \quad x_2 = 6\tfrac{1}{4}.$$

However, these values for x_1 and x_2 violate the second constraint.

Can we have $\lambda_1 = 0$ with $\lambda_2 > 0$? Under these conditions, we find that

$$3x_1 + 6x_2 = 40$$

and

$$x_1 - 2x_2 = 0.$$

This gives

$$x_1 = 6\tfrac{2}{3}; \quad x_2 = 3\tfrac{1}{3},$$

and these values of x_1 and x_2, together with

$$\lambda_1 = 0 \quad \text{and} \quad \lambda_2 = 1\tfrac{1}{9}$$

satisfy (iii).

The final case to be checked is $\lambda_1 > 0$, $\lambda_2 > 0$. This would imply that both constraints were binding, giving

$$x_1 = \tfrac{70}{9} \quad \text{and} \quad x_2 = \tfrac{25}{9}.$$

Then from the first two equations in (iii) we would have

$$\tfrac{25}{9} = 5\lambda_1 + 3\lambda_2$$

and

$$\tfrac{70}{9} = 4\lambda_1 + 6\lambda_2,$$

i.e.

$$\lambda_1 = -\tfrac{10}{27} \quad \text{and} \quad \lambda_2 = \tfrac{125}{81}.$$

Negative values for the λ's are not allowed. We may conclude that the problem solution occurs in the second case examined, i.e. with $\lambda_1 = 0$ and $\lambda_2 > 0$, giving $x_1 = 6\tfrac{2}{3}$ and $x_2 = 3\tfrac{1}{3}$.

The marginal utilities of dollars and ration points are given by the Lagrangian multipliers. An additional dollar generates no utility. (Notice that the consumer is not using all his dollar budget.) On the other hand, an additional ration point will yield $1\tfrac{1}{9}$ units of utility.

It is now clear that the consumer must benefit from the existence of a market for ration points. At the margin, dollars are of no value to him. If he can trade dollars for ration points, he will be able to achieve a higher level of utility. In particular, if ration points can be bought and sold for $\$\tfrac{1}{2}$, then he is free to choose non-negative values for x_1 and x_2 to maximize

$$x_1 x_2 \tag{iv}$$

subject to

$$(5 + 1\tfrac{1}{2})x_1 + (4 + 3)x_2 \leqslant 50 + 20.$$

The price of good 1 is $\$ 5$ plus 3 ration points, or effectively $\$ 6\tfrac{1}{2}$. The price of good 2 is $\$ 4$ plus 6 ration points, or effectively $\$ 7$. The consumer's budget is $\$ 50$ plus 40 ration points, or effectively $\$ 70$. Alternatively we could work in ration points. Then the budget constraint would be

$$(10 + 3)x_1 + (8 + 6)x_2 \leqslant 100 + 40.$$

The price of good 1 would be 13 ration points, etc.

Proceeding with problem (iv) we find that the first-order conditions are

$$x_2 - 6\tfrac{1}{2}\lambda = 0,$$
$$x_1 - 7\lambda = 0$$

and

$$6\tfrac{1}{2}x_1 + 7x_2 = 70,$$

and thus

$$x_1 = \tfrac{70}{13} \quad \text{and} \quad x_2 = 5.$$

With the existence of the market for ration points, the consumer has increased his utility from

$$U_1 = (6\tfrac{2}{3})(3\tfrac{1}{3}) = 22\tfrac{2}{9},$$

where U_1 is his initial utility under rationing, to

$$U_2 = (\tfrac{70}{13})(5) = 26\tfrac{12}{13}.$$

He has done this by trading dollars for ration points. He now uses

$$(\tfrac{70}{13})(3) + (5)(6) = 46\tfrac{2}{13}$$

ration points. Of his $ 50 budget, he has used

$$(6\tfrac{2}{13})(\tfrac{1}{2}) = \$ 3\tfrac{1}{13}$$

to buy additional ration points and

$$(5)(\tfrac{70}{13}) + (4)(5) = \$ 46\tfrac{12}{13}$$

to meet the dollar prices of his purchases of goods 1 and 2.

Exercise 2.15. The allocation of time

A self-sufficient farmer lives on produce he grows himself under conditions of diminishing marginal productivity of labor. The length of his working time can be explained in terms of a utility-maximizing choice between agricultural produce and leisure. There is a minimum real hourly wage rate which could just induce him to quit farming and become a hired worker. If this minimum wage were offered to him, and he became a hired worker, would the length of his working time (1) remain the same, (2) become shorter, or (3) become longer than when he was a self-sufficient farmer?

What institutional assumptions are implicit in your response? Note that for the farmer, who owns all the necessary means of production, the labor–leisure choice is a real possibility. Under what conditions will the wage laborer have control over his hours of work?

Answer.   The solution to this problem can be seen immediately in fig. E2.15.1. uu is an indifference curve for the farmer's produce–leisure choice; LP is his consumption possibilities curve while he remains self-employed. (What is the relationship of LP to the total product of labor curve?) The curvature of LP exhibits diminishing marginal product. The farmer's utility-maximizing combination of leisure and product is at A. If the farmer becomes a wage-earner, his consumption possibilities curve changes to a straight line; i.e. we are assuming that the farmer is paid a fixed amount of 'product' per hour. The slope of LB represents the minimum hourly wage rate which could induce him to quit farming; the corresponding consumption possibilities line LB just allows him to reach uu. It is clear that as a wage-earner the farmer will work longer than when he was self-employed. His utility-maximizing bundle is at B, giving him more product but less leisure than at A.

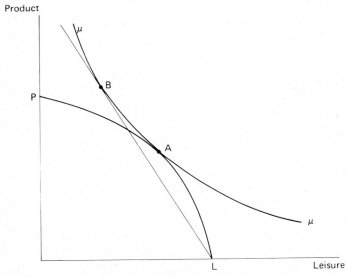

Figure E2.15.1

Be sure you understand why the answer depends crucially on the fact that for the self-employed farmer the marginal rate of transformation of leisure into product is diminishing, but when he hires his labor out on the market, he faces a constant marginal rate of transformation of leisure into product.

Exercise 2.16. *Pure exchange and Pareto optimality*

Consider an economy of two men who consume just two goods, x and y. Man 1 has an intitial endowment of 40 units of x and 160 of y while man 2 has 240 and 120 units of x and y, respectively. Assume that the men have the following utility functions:

$$U_1 = x_1 y_1 = \text{utility of man 1}$$

$$U_2 = x_2 y_2^2 = \text{utility of man 2},$$

where x_i and y_i are the amounts of goods x and y consumed by man i.

(a) Using the standard geometrical apparatus (the 'Edgeworth–Bowley box'), show that in general there exists some exchange (trade) between the two which will result in their both obtaining a higher level of utility.

(b) We define a situation to be *efficient* or *Pareto optimal* if there is no reallocation of commodities between the two men which gives one of them higher utility without lowering the utility of the other. Show that a necessary condition for efficiency is

$$\frac{\partial U_1}{\partial x_1} \Big/ \frac{\partial U_1}{\partial y_1} = \frac{\partial U_2}{\partial x_2} \Big/ \frac{\partial U_2}{\partial y_2} \, .$$

Is the assumption of efficiency sufficient to determine what trading will be done between man 1 and man 2?

(c) Under the assumption of competition, each man faces a common set of prices p_x and p_y. Each maximizes his utility subject to his budget constraint and prices adjust so that supply equals demand for all goods. Determine the competitive values for x_1, y_1, x_2, y_2 and p_y. We may assume that $p_x = 1$. (Why?) If the algebra becomes a little tedious, you may prefer to limit yourself to writing down the relevant equations and checking that $x_1 = 140$, $x_2 = 140$, $y_1 = 93\frac{1}{3}$, $y_2 = 186\frac{2}{3}$ and $p_y = 1\frac{1}{2}$ is the solution. Is the competitive allocation of goods Pareto optimal?

Answer.

(a) Consider fig. E2.16.1. A represents the initial endowments. Both men gain welfare by any trade which moves them into the shaded area.

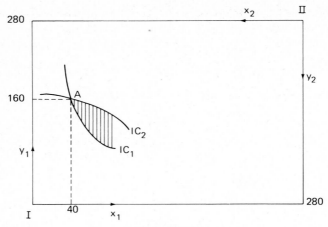

Figure E2.16.1

(b) Goods x and y can be allocated efficiently only if x_1, y_1, x_2 and y_2 maximize

$$U_1(x_1, y_1) \tag{i}$$

subject to

$$\bar{U}_2 = U_2(x_2, y_2),$$

$$x_1 + x_2 = \bar{x}_1 + \bar{x}_2$$

and

$$y_1 + y_2 = \bar{y}_1 + \bar{y}_2,$$

where $\bar{U}_2$ is a predetermined level of utility for consumer 2 and the $\bar{x}_i, \bar{y}_i$ are the initial endowments. In other words, given the utility level of man 2, efficiency implies that the available goods must be allocated so that the utility level for man 1 is a maximum. Alternatively, we could work with a problem in which man 2's utility is maximized subject to achieving a given level of utility for man 1 and subject to the availability of goods.

Necessary conditions for the solution of problem (i) can be generated by differentiating the Lagrangian,

$$L = U_1(x_1, y_1) - \lambda(\bar{U}_2 - U_2(x_2, y_2))$$
$$- \Pi_x(x_1 + x_2 - \bar{x}_1 - \bar{x}_2) - \Pi_y(y_1 + y_2 - \bar{y}_1 - \bar{y}_2),$$

where λ, Π_x and Π_y are the Lagrangian multipliers. Hence, for an efficient allocation, we will have

$$\frac{\partial U_1}{\partial x_1} - \Pi_x = 0,$$

$$\frac{\partial U_1}{\partial y_1} - \Pi_y = 0,$$

$$\lambda \frac{\partial U_2}{\partial x_2} - \Pi_x = 0$$

and

$$\lambda \frac{\partial U_2}{\partial y_2} - \Pi_y = 0,$$

as well as the initial constraints. By carrying out the obvious divisions we find that

$$\frac{\Pi_x}{\Pi_y} = \frac{\partial U_1}{\partial x_1} \bigg/ \frac{\partial U_1}{\partial y_1} = \frac{\partial U_2}{\partial x_2} \bigg/ \frac{\partial U_2}{\partial y_2} . \qquad (E2.16.1)$$

Efficiency alone is not sufficient to determine the trading pattern between man 1 and man 2. Efficiency merely locates us on the *contract curve*, see fig. E2.16.2. Different points on the contract curve may be generated by changing

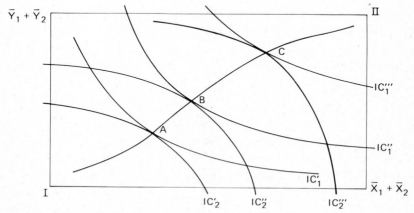

Figure E2.16.2. IC_1', IC_1'' and IC_1''' are three indifference curves for man 1 and IC_2', IC_2'' and IC_2''' are three indifference curves for man 2. The contract curve or locus of efficient points, i.e. those satisfying (E2.16.1), is shown as A, B, C.

the value of $\bar{U}_2$ in problem (i). As we increase $\bar{U}_2$ the solution of problem (i) moves along the contract curve towards I. To attain a unique solution for the trading problem, we need some additional information or restrictions. These might be provided by having some rule which allows us to evaluate alternative distributions of utility (a social welfare function) and to choose the one we like best. But in the absence of a social welfare function (or some other device), the indeterminacy remains.

(c) Man 1 chooses x_1 and y_1 to maximize

$$x_1 y_1$$

subject to

$$p_x x_1 + p_y y_1 = p_x 40 + p_y 160.$$

The first-order conditions are

$$y_1 = \lambda p_x,$$
$$x_1 = \lambda p_y$$

and

$$p_x x_1 + p_y y_1 = p_x 40 + p_y 160.$$

On eliminating λ we obtain

$$x_1 = \left(\frac{p_y}{p_x}\right) y_1 \tag{ii}$$

and

$$x_1 + \left(\frac{p_y}{p_x}\right) y_1 = 40 + 160 \left(\frac{p_y}{p_x}\right).^{21} \tag{iii}$$

Similarly we find that for man 2,

$$2x_2 = \left(\frac{p_y}{p_x}\right) y_2 \tag{iv}$$

and

$$x_2 + \left(\frac{p_y}{p_x}\right) y_2 = 240 + 120 \left(\frac{p_y}{p_x}\right). \tag{v}$$

---

[21] Eq. (iii) is simply a rearrangement of the budget constraint. This form will be convenient for our explanation of why the competitive equilibrium determines relative prices, but not absolute prices.

Finally, we note that total consumption must equal the total supplies, i.e.

$$x_1 + x_2 = 280 \ (= \bar{x}_1 + \bar{x}_2) \tag{vi}$$

and

$$y_1 + y_2 = 280 \ (= \bar{y}_1 + \bar{y}_2). \tag{vii}$$

To summarize, we have found that x_1, x_2, y_1, y_2 and p_y/p_x are consistent with the competitive equilibrium only if they satisfy eqs. (ii)–(vii). Notice that relative prices, (p_y/p_x), not absolute prices, appear in the equations. Hence we can assume that $p_x = 1$ (or any other positive number) and determine p_y. Also, it is worth pointing out that any one of the equations (iii), (v), (vi) and (vii) can be derived from the remaining three. For example, we can derive (vii) from (iii), (v) and (vi). Rewriting (iii), (v) and (vi) with the notation $k = p_y/p_x$, we have

$$x_1 + ky_1 = \ \ 40 + 160k,$$

$$x_2 + ky_2 = 240 + 120k$$

and

$$x_1 + \ \ x_2 = 280.$$

Adding the first two of these equations and using the third, we find that

$$280 + ky_1 + ky_2 = 280 + 160k + 120k,$$

i.e.

$$y_1 + y_2 = 280,$$

which is precisely eq. (vii). Hence in determining the competitive values for the five variables x_1, x_2, y_1, y_2 and k, we need use only the five equations (ii)–(vi). The last of the supply and demand equations will be satisfied automatically if we find a solution for the first five equations.[22]

To solve the five-equation system (ii)–(vi) we proceed as follows: first we substitute from (ii) and (iv) into (iii), (v) and (vi), to eliminate x_1 and x_2. This gives.

$$2ky_1 = 40 + 160k,$$

$$1\tfrac{1}{2} ky_2 = 240 + 120k$$

and

$$ky_1 + \tfrac{1}{2} ky_2 = 280.$$

---

[22] Our elimination of one of the demand-equals-supply equations is an example of the application of Walras's law.

Next we eliminate y_1, reducing our system to

$$1\tfrac{1}{2} ky_2 - 120k = 240$$

and

$$80k + \tfrac{1}{2} ky_2 = 260.$$

Finally, we eliminate k and we find that

$$\frac{1\tfrac{1}{2} y_2 - 120}{80 + \tfrac{1}{2} y_2} = \frac{240}{260}.$$

Hence

$$y_2 = 186\tfrac{2}{3}$$
$$y_1 = \ \ 93\tfrac{1}{3}$$
$$x_1 = 140$$
$$x_2 = 140$$

and

$$k \ = 1\tfrac{1}{2} = (p_y/p_x).$$

The competitive mechanism resolves the indeterminacy discussed in part (b). Under competitive conditions, each man, i, organizes his purchases so that

$$\frac{\partial U_i}{\partial x_i} \Big/ \frac{\partial U_i}{\partial y_i} = \frac{p_x}{p_y}.$$

Thus (E2.16.1) is satisfied and the competitive equilibrium is Pareto optimal. Compared with part (b), we have the additional information that consumers must satisfy their budgets. This is sufficient to determine at which point on the contract curve the equilibrium will occur.[23]

Exercise 2.17. *Additive utility functions*

A popular assumption in empirical work is that the utility function is additive, i.e. it can be written in the form

$$U(x_1,...,x_n) = U^1(x_1) + U^2(x_2) + ... + U^n(x_n),$$

---

[23]   In a more general example, it is possible that there are several competitive equilibria. Hence, even the adoption of competitive assumptions may not completely eliminate the indeterminacy of the pure exchange model.

where each of U^1, U^2,...,U^n is a strictly concave function of a single argument. The log-linear utility function, (E2.3.3), is an example. Under the additivity assumption, the symmetry condition (E2.6.2) can be replaced by the stronger restriction

$$e_{ij} = -E_i \alpha_j \left(1 + \frac{E_j}{\omega} \right), \quad \text{for all } i \neq j, \tag{E2.17.1}$$

where ω is a scalar, independent of i and j. ω is often referred to as the 'Frisch parameter'.

(a) Is an additive utility function likely to be an adequate description of consumer preferences in a very detailed model where the commodity classifications include, for example, fruit, vegetables, meat, fish, cotton shirts, synthetic shirts, etc.? Would the additivity assumption be more easily sustainable in an aggregative model based on commodity classifications such as food, clothing, etc.?

(b) Check that (E2.17.1) is in fact a more severe restriction than (E2.6.2), i.e. check that (E2.17.1) implies (E2.6.2), but not vice versa.

(c) The derivation of (E2.17.1) is fairly time consuming. However, it illustrates a general method of translating restrictions on the utility function (in this case the zeros in the Hessian) into empirically useful restrictions on the demand elasticities. As a first step, prove that

$$\begin{bmatrix} H & p \\ p' & 0 \end{bmatrix}^{-1} = \frac{1}{p' H^{-1} p} \left[\begin{array}{c|c} (p' H^{-1} p) H^{-1} - H^{-1} pp' H^{-1} & H^{-1} p \\ \hline p' H^{-1} & -1 \end{array} \right]. \tag{E2.17.2}$$

The relevance of this step will be apparent from (E2.6.1). Once you have established (E2.17.2), you will be able to show that

$$\frac{\partial \lambda}{\partial y} = \frac{1}{p' H^{-1} p}, \tag{E2.17.3}$$

$$\frac{\partial x_i}{\partial y} = (H^{-1} p)_i \frac{\partial \lambda}{\partial y} \tag{E2.17.4}$$

and

$$\frac{\partial x_i}{\partial p_j} = (H^{-1})_{ij} \lambda - \frac{\partial \lambda}{\partial y} (H^{-1} p)_i (H^{-1} p)_j \lambda$$

$$- \frac{\partial \lambda}{\partial y} (H^{-1} p)_i x_j \quad \text{for all } i \text{ and } j, \tag{E2.17.5}$$

where the notations $(\cdot)_j$ and $(\cdot)_{ij}$ denote the jth and ijth components of the bracketed vector and matrix.

Next, recognize that under the additivity assumption, H and H^{-1} are diagonal matrices. Now use (E2.17.4) and (E2.17.5) to obtain (E2.17.1).

(d) What is the interpretation of the Frisch parameter, ω?

(e) Consider the utility function

$$V(x_1, x_2,...,x_n) = \prod_{i=1}^{n} V^i(x_i). \tag{E2.17.3}$$

Would you expect restriction (E2.17.1) to be applicable? How about the interpretation of ω, would it still be the same as in the additive case?

(f) Can you complete the following scheme under the assumption that the consumer's preferences are additive?

$\alpha_1 = \frac{1}{3},$	$\alpha_2 = \frac{1}{3},$	$\alpha_3 = \frac{1}{3}$	
$e_{11} = -\frac{13}{48}$	$e_{12} = ?$	$e_{13} = ?$	$E_1 = \frac{1}{2}$
$e_{21} = ?$	$e_{22} = ?$	$e_{23} = ?$	$E_2 = \frac{1}{2}$
$e_{31} = ?$	$e_{32} = ?$	$e_{33} = ?$	$E_3 = ?$

Answer. (a) Under additivity we are assuming that the consumer behaves as if his marginal utility of good i is independent of his consumption of good j, $j \neq i$. This assumption is hard to justify for a very detailed study. The consumer's marginal utility for cotton shirts is likely to depend on both the number of cotton and synthetic shirts which he has. On the other hand, it may be acceptable to assume that the marginal utility for 'food' is independent of quantities of 'clothing'. Very intuitively, the additivity assumption rules out the possibility of 'special' substitution effects. It is not applicable when we have a situation in which i and j are extremely close substitutes, but i and k are only weakly substitutable.

(b) From (E2.17.1) we have

$$\alpha_i (e_{ij} + E_i \alpha_j) = -\frac{E_i \alpha_j E_j \alpha_i}{\omega}, \quad i \neq j,$$

and

$$\alpha_j (e_{ji} + E_j \alpha_i) = -\frac{E_j \alpha_i E_i \alpha_j}{\omega}, \quad i \neq j.$$

Hence

$$\alpha_i (e_{ij} + E_i \alpha_j) = \alpha_j (e_{ji} + E_j \alpha_i), \quad \text{for } i \neq j,$$

and we have shown that (E2.17.1) implies the symmetry condition (E2.6.2). On the other hand, the symmetry condition certainly does not imply (E2.17.1). In E2.7 you generated a scheme of elasticities which satisfied (E2.6.2). A little arithmetic will show that they do not satisfy (E2.17.1). For example, you will find that

$$\frac{\alpha_1 (e_{12} + E_1 \alpha_2)}{\alpha_1 (e_{13} + E_1 \alpha_3)} \neq \frac{E_1 E_2 \alpha_1 \alpha_2}{E_1 E_3 \alpha_1 \alpha_3} \,.$$

(c) One way to prove (E2.17.2) is by multiplying the bordered Hessian by our proposed inverse and checking that the result is the identity matrix. A more instructive method is as follows: let

$$\begin{bmatrix} H & p \\ p' & 0 \end{bmatrix}^{-1} = \begin{bmatrix} A & b \\ b' & \tau \end{bmatrix} \tag{i}$$

where A is an $n \times n$ matrix, b is an $n \times 1$ vector, and τ is a scalar.

We have written (i) so that the partitioning in the inverse is the same as that in the initial bordered Hessian. We have also used the symmetry of the bordered Hessian. Notice that we have taken account of the fact that the $(n + 1)$th row and $(n + 1)$th column of the inverse are the same.

From (i) we have

$$\begin{bmatrix} H & p \\ p' & 0 \end{bmatrix} \begin{bmatrix} A & b \\ b' & \tau \end{bmatrix} = \begin{bmatrix} I & 0 \\ 0 & 1 \end{bmatrix}. \tag{ii}$$

Our objective now is to manipulate (ii) so as to express A, b and τ in terms of H and p. By multiplying out the left-hand side of (ii) we find that

$$HA + pb' = I, \tag{iii}$$

$$Hb + p\tau = 0, \tag{iv}$$

$$p'A = 0, \tag{v}$$

$$p'b = 1. \tag{vi}$$

We assume that H has an inverse so that (iii) can be solved for A, i.e.

$$A = H^{-1} (I - pb'), \tag{vii}$$

and (iv) can be solved for b, i.e.

$$b = -H^{-1} p\tau. \tag{viii}$$

Multiplying (viii) by p' and using (vi), we obtain

$$\tau = -1/(p'H^{-1}p).$$

Substitution back into (viii) yields

$$b = \frac{1}{p'H^{-1}p} H^{-1}p,$$

and finally, substitution into (vii) gives

$$A = H^{-1} - \frac{1}{p'H^{-1}p} H^{-1}pp'H^{-1}.$$

(Since H and H^{-1} are symmetric, $(H^{-1}p)' = p'H^{-1}$.) Returning to (i) we see that

$$
\begin{bmatrix} H & p \\ p' & 0 \end{bmatrix}^{-1} = \left(\frac{1}{p'H^{-1}p} \right) \left[\begin{array}{c|c} (p'H^{-1}p)H^{-1} - H^{-1}pp'H^{-1} & H^{-1}p \\ \hline p'H^{-1} & -1 \end{array} \right].
$$

At this stage we can rewrite the matrix equation (E2.6.1) as

$$
\begin{bmatrix} dx \\ -d\lambda \end{bmatrix} = \frac{1}{p'H^{-1}p} \left[\begin{array}{c|c} (p'H^{-1}p)H^{-1} - H^{-1}pp'H^{-1} & H^{-1}p \\ \hline p'H^{-1} & -1 \end{array} \right] \begin{bmatrix} \lambda dp \\ dy - (dp)'x \end{bmatrix}.
$$

If we set $dy = 1$ and $dp = 0$, we find that

$$-d\lambda = - \frac{1}{p'H^{-1}p}$$

and

$$dx_i = \frac{1}{p'H^{-1}p} (H^{-1}p)_i.$$

Hence

$$\frac{\partial \lambda}{\partial y} = \frac{1}{p'H^{-1}p}$$

and

$$\frac{\partial x_i}{\partial y} = (H^{-1}p)_i \frac{\partial \lambda}{\partial y}.$$

Similarly, if we set $dp_j = 1$ with dy and $dp_k = 0$, for all $k \neq j$, we can derive (E2.17.5). Notice that the i, jth element of the matrix $H^{-1}pp'H^{-1}$ is the ith element of the vector $H^{-1}p$ multiplied by the jth element of the vector $p'H^{-1}$, i.e.

$$(H^{-1}pp'H^{-1})_{ij} = (H^{-1}p)_i (H^{-1}p)_j.$$

The time has now arrived for us to use the additivity assumption. Additivity implies that

$$\frac{\partial^2 U}{\partial x_i \, \partial x_j} = 0, \quad \text{for all } i \neq j.$$

Hence the Hessian, H, and its inverse, are diagonal, and for $i \neq j$, the first term on the right-hand side of (E2.17.5) is zero. Thus (E2.17.5) reduces to

$$\frac{\partial x_i}{\partial p_j} = -\frac{\partial \lambda}{\partial y} (H^{-1}p)_i (H^{-1}p)_j \lambda - \frac{\partial \lambda}{\partial y} (H^{-1}p)_i x_j, \quad i \neq j. \tag{ix}$$

From (E2.17.4), we have

$$(H^{-1}p)_k = \left(\frac{\partial x_k}{\partial y}\right) \Big/ \left(\frac{\partial \lambda}{\partial y}\right), \quad \text{for all } k,$$

and by substitution into (ix) we obtain

$$\frac{\partial x_i}{\partial p_j} = -\frac{\partial x_i}{\partial y} \frac{\partial x_j}{\partial y} \left(\frac{\lambda}{\partial \lambda / \partial y}\right) - \frac{\partial x_i}{\partial y} x_j, \quad \text{for all } i \neq j. \tag{x}$$

Eq. (x) is translated into a relationship between elasticities by multiplying and dividing by prices and quantities in the usual way:

$$\left[\frac{\partial x_i}{\partial p_j}\right] \frac{p_j}{x_i} = -\left[\frac{\partial x_i}{\partial y}\right] \frac{y}{x_i} \left[\frac{\partial x_j}{\partial y}\right] \frac{y}{x_j} \frac{p_j x_j}{y} \left[\frac{\lambda}{\partial \lambda / \partial y}\right] \frac{1}{y}$$

$$- \left[\frac{\partial x_i}{\partial y}\right] \frac{y}{x_i} \frac{[x_j] p_j}{y},$$

i.e.

$$e_{ij} = -\frac{E_i E_j \alpha_j}{\omega} - E_i \alpha_j \quad \text{for all } i \neq j,$$

where

$$\omega = \frac{\partial \lambda}{\partial y} \frac{y}{\lambda}. \tag{xi}$$

On rearranging, we obtain (E2.17.1).

(d) From (xi) we see that ω can be interpreted as the elasticity of the marginal utility of income with respect to income, i.e. it shows the percentage effect on the marginal utility of income of a one percent increase in income.

(e) Utility function (E2.17.3) becomes additive under a positive monotonic transformation. Note that

$$\ln V = \sum_i \ln V^i.$$

Since the preferences described by the utility function, U, where

$$U = \ln V = \sum_i \ln V^i$$

are precisely the same as those described by the initial utility function, V, the demand responses to price and income movements will be unchanged by the replacement of V by U. (E2.17.1) is valid when the utility function is U. It will also be valid when the utility function is V.

With the multiplicative utility function V, ω cannot be interpreted as the elasticity of the marginal utility of income. However, that interpretation is valid when the utility function is additive. Hence

$$\omega = \frac{\partial(\partial \ln V/\partial y)}{\partial y} \frac{y}{\partial \ln V/\partial y},$$

i.e.

$$\omega = \frac{\partial\left(\dfrac{1}{V}\dfrac{\partial V}{\partial y}\right)}{\partial y} \frac{y}{\dfrac{1}{V}\dfrac{\partial V}{\partial y}}$$

$$= -\frac{\partial V}{\partial y}\frac{y}{V} + \frac{\partial(\partial V/\partial y)}{\partial y} \frac{y}{\partial V/\partial y}.$$

We can conclude that with the multiplicative utility function (E2.17.3), ω can be interpreted as the difference between the elasticity of *marginal* utility with respect to income and the elasticity of *total* utility with respect to income.

To summarize, if there exists F, a monotonically increasing function, such that $F(V)$ is additive, where V is the utility function, then restriction (E2.17.1) is applicable. However, the standard interpretation (but not the numerical value) of ω depends on the utility function being additive.

(f) From the Engel aggregation, (E2.1.3), we find that

$$E_3 = \frac{1 - \alpha_1 E_1 - \alpha_2 E_2}{\alpha_3} = 2.$$

Next, we use the homogeneity restriction (E2.2.1) to write

$$e_{11} + e_{12} + e_{13} = -E_1.$$

Under additivity, this last equation may be rewritten as

$$e_{11} - E_1 \alpha_2 \left(1 + \frac{E_2}{\omega}\right) - E_1 \alpha_3 \left(1 + \frac{E_3}{\omega}\right) = -E_1.$$

Now, by using the values for the α's, E's and e_{11} as shown in the table, we find that

$$\omega = -4.$$

From here we can use (E2.17.1) to generate the e_{ij} for all $i \neq j$ and the homogeneity restriction to fill in the diagonal terms e_{22} and e_{33}. The completed table is as follows:

$\alpha_1 = \frac{1}{3}$,	$\alpha_2 = \frac{1}{3}$,	$\alpha_3 = \frac{1}{3}$	
$e_{11} = -\frac{13}{48}$	$e_{12} = -\frac{7}{48}$	$e_{13} = -\frac{4}{48}$	$E_1 = \frac{1}{2}$
$e_{21} = -\frac{7}{48}$	$e_{22} = -\frac{13}{48}$	$e_{23} = -\frac{4}{48}$	$E_2 = \frac{1}{2}$
$e_{31} = -\frac{28}{48}$	$e_{32} = -\frac{28}{48}$	$e_{33} = -\frac{40}{48}$	$E_3 = 2$

On the basis of knowing the budget shares and two of the expenditure elasticities, plus one price elasticity, we were able to deduce the other nine elasticities. In general, we have $n^2 + n$ price and income elasticities. Under the assumption that the utility function is additive, we have

$$1 + n + (n(n-1) - 1) = n^2$$

restrictions: one restriction for the Engel aggregation, n restrictions for homogeneity and $n(n-1) - 1$ restrictions for additivity. Notice that (E2.17.1) determines the $n(n-1)$ cross-elasticities, but introduces one new elasticity ω. With $n = 3$, the additivity model provides $1 + 3 + 5 = 9$ restrictions applying to 12 elasticities. With $n = 20$, we have 400 restrictions applying to 420 elasticities.

Chapter 3

THEORY OF THE CONSUMER: EXTENSIONS

3.1. Goals, reading guide and references

The material in this chapter falls under seven general headings; revealed preference, economic surplus, aggregation, integrability, obstacles to Pareto optimality, intertemporal models of household behavior, and decisions under uncertainty. With a few exceptions, the problems and readings on later topics are independent of the earlier ones. If at first you find a particular topic to be difficult or of little interest, it might be sensible to skip over it and to return to it at another time.

The chapter has several objectives. The first is to extend the theory developed in Chapter 2. Extensions include the introduction of time into the utility-maximizing framework, i.e. we will consider models in which households are viewed as planning the time-path of their purchases so as to maximize the value of an intertemporal utility function. The time element is important if our theory is to explain household savings and investment in durables. Secondly, we will be asking you to deepen your understanding of consumer theory. For example, we have included material on the integrability problem and on the relationship between the theory of revealed preference and the theory of utility maximization. Finally, we hope to give you an introduction to the applications of consumer theory to welfare economics. Whereas the applications-oriented material of Chapter 2 was mainly on the role of consumer theory in suggesting econometrically useful restrictions on the form of demand functions, in this chapter the welfare applications (especially the idea of consumer surplus) are given more prominence.

By the time you complete the readings and problem set we hope that, at a minimum, you will be able to do all of the following:

(1) use arguments from the theory of revealed preference in discussing the relative merits of alternative economic situations;

(2) explain convincingly, although not necessarily rigorously, that the two

assumptions — (a) that the household behaves in accordance with the strong axiom of revealed preference and (b) that the household is a constrained maximizer of a strictly quasiconcave utility function — are observationally equivalent;

(3) discuss the integrability problem — its nature, the main results in the field, and their significance;

(4) use consumer surplus arguments in discussing the relative merits of alternative economic situations;

(5) explain the theoretical foundations of consumer surplus, including the role of compensated demand curves;

(6) use consumer and producer surplus measures to quantify the costs of inefficiencies in resource use arising from various types of taxes, e.g. tariffs, sales taxes and public utility charges in excess of marginal costs;

(7) discuss the difficulties which arise for traditional welfare economics from the possibility that consumer preferences may be modified by the policy decision whose merits are being assessed;

(8) define what is meant by public goods and to be able to explain the reasons why social (rather than individual) decision-making is necessary in setting their production levels and in deciding how they should be financed;

(9) explain the problems posed by aggregation across households for both the positive and normative applications of the basic utility maximizing model of household behavior;

(10) work with dynamic models of consumer choice — in particular, explain how the demands for durables and savings can be handled in a dynamic framework;

(11) understand the subjective and other reasons for the concept of time preference;

(12) see through the paradox of 'intertemporal inconsistency'; and

(13) compare the Von Neumann and Morgenstern concept of utility with that of the ordinalists.

Reading Guide 3 provides a suggested path through the readings to cover these concepts. The readings are referred to in abbreviated terms in the flow chart and in the problem set; full citations are given in the reference list.

Reading Guide 3*

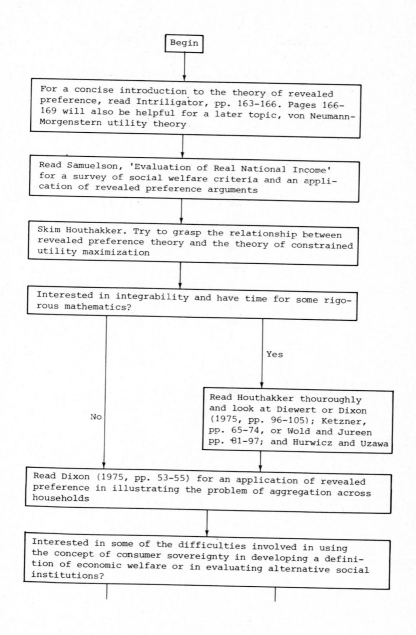

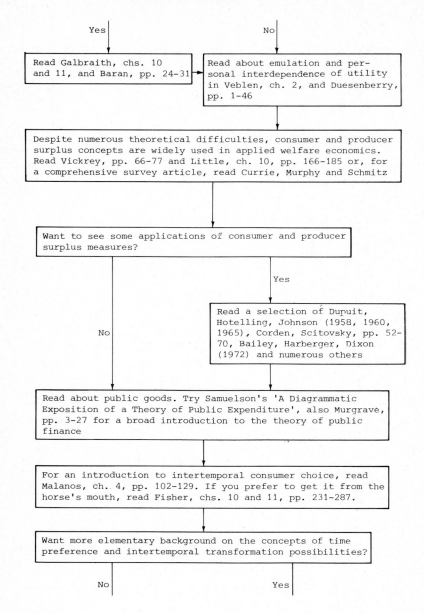

Yes | No

Read Galbraith, chs. 10 and 11, and Baran, pp. 24-31

Read about emulation and personal interdependence of utility in Veblen, ch. 2, and Duesenberry, pp. 1-46

Despite numerous theoretical difficulties, consumer and producer surplus concepts are widely used in applied welfare economics. Read Vickrey, pp. 66-77 and Little, ch. 10, pp. 166-185 or, for a comprehensive survey article, read Currie, Murphy and Schmitz

Want to see some applications of consumer and producer surplus measures?

Yes

Read a selection of Dupuit, Hotelling, Johnson (1958, 1960, 1965), Corden, Scitovsky, pp. 52-70, Bailey, Harberger, Dixon (1972) and numerous others

No

Read about public goods. Try Samuelson's 'A Diagrammatic Exposition of a Theory of Public Expenditure', also Murgrave, pp. 3-27 for a broad introduction to the theory of public finance

For an introduction to intertemporal consumer choice, read Malanos, ch. 4, pp. 102-129. If you prefer to get it from the horse's mouth, read Fisher, chs. 10 and 11, pp. 231-287.

Want more elementary background on the concepts of time preference and intertemporal transformation possibilities?

No | Yes

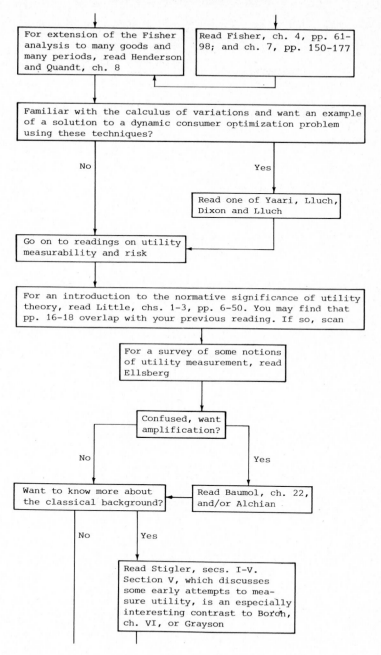

For extension of the Fisher analysis to many goods and many periods, read Henderson and Quandt, ch. 8

Read Fisher, ch. 4, pp. 61-98; and ch. 7, pp. 150-177

Familiar with the calculus of variations and want an example of a solution to a dynamic consumer optimization problem using these techniques?

No

Yes

Read one of Yaari, Lluch, Dixon and Lluch

Go on to readings on utility measurability and risk

For an introduction to the normative significance of utility theory, read Little, chs. 1-3, pp. 6-50. You may find that pp. 16-18 overlap with your previous reading. If so, scan

For a survey of some notions of utility measurement, read Ellsberg

Confused, want amplification?

No

Yes

Want to know more about the classical background?

Read Baumol, ch. 22, and/or Alchian

No

Yes

Read Stigler, secs. I-V. Section V, which discusses some early attempts to measure utility, is an especially interesting contrast to Boren, ch. VI, or Grayson

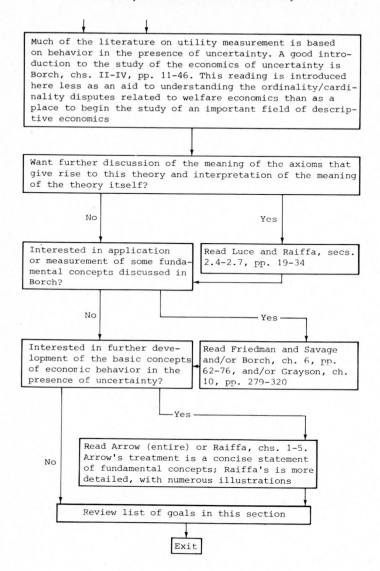

Much of the literature on utility measurement is based on behavior in the presence of uncertainty. A good introduction to the study of the economics of uncertainty is Borch, chs. II-IV, pp. 11-46. This reading is introduced here less as an aid to understanding the ordinality/cardinality disputes related to welfare economics than as a place to begin the study of an important field of descriptive economics

Want further discussion of the meaning of the axioms that give rise to this theory and interpretation of the meaning of the theory itself?

No

Yes

Interested in application or measurement of some fundamental concepts discussed in Borch?

Read Luce and Raiffa, secs. 2.4-2.7, pp. 19-34

No

Yes

Interested in further development of the basic concepts of economic behavior in the presence of uncertainty?

Read Friedman and Savage and/or Borch, ch. 6, pp. 62-76, and/or Grayson, ch. 10, pp. 279-320

Yes

Read Arrow (entire) or Raiffa, chs. 1-5. Arrow's treatment is a concise statement of fundamental concepts; Raiffa's is more detailed, with numerous illustrations

No

Review list of goals in this section

Exit

*For full citations, see reference list in this section

References for Chapter 3

Alchian, A.A. (1953) 'The Meaning of Utility Measurement', *American Economic Review*, Vol. 43, March, 26–50.

Arrow, K.J. (1965) *Aspects of the Theory of Risk-Bearing*, Yrjo Jahnssonin Saatio, Helsinki.

Bailey, M. (1956) 'The Welfare Costs of Inflationary Finance', *Journal of Political Economy*, April, 93–110.

Baran, P. (1957) *The Political Economy of Growth*, Monthly Review Press, New York.

Baumol, W.J. (1972) *Economic Theory and Operations Analysis*, 3rd edn., Prentice-Hall.

Blackorby, C., D. Nissen, D. Primont and R.R. Russell, (1973) 'Consistent Intertemporal Decision Making', *Review of Economic Studies*, 239–248.

Borch, K.H. (1968) *The Economics of Uncertainty*, Princeton University Press.

Corden, W.M. (1957) 'The Calculation of the Cost of Protection', *Economic Record*, 33, April, 29–51.

Currie, J.M., J.A. Murphy and A. Schmitz (1971) 'The Concept of Economic Surplus and its Use in Economic Analysis', *Economic Journal*, 81, 741–799.

Denison, E.F. (1967) *Why Growth Rates Differ*, Brookings Institute.

Diewert, W.E. (1973) 'Afriat and Revealed Preference Theory', *Review of Economic Studies*, July, 419–425.

Dixon, P.B. (1972) 'The Costs of Average Cost Pricing', *Journal of Public Economics*, 1, 245–256.

Dixon, P.B. (1975) *The Theory of Joint Maximization*, North-Holland Publishing Company.

Dixon, P.B. and C. Lluch (1977) 'Durable Goods in the Extended Linear Expenditure System', *Review of Economic Studies*, 44 (2), 381–384.

Dixon, P.B. (1978) 'Economies of Scale, Commodity Disaggregation and the Costs of Protection', *Australian Economic Papers*, 11, June, 63–80.

Duesenberry, J.S. (1962) *Income Savings and the Theory of Consumer Behaviour*, Harvard University Press.

Dupuit, J. (1952) 'On the Measurement of the Utility of Public Works', *International Economic Papers*, 2, 83–110.

Ellsberg, D. (1954) 'Classical and Current Notions of Measurable Utility', *The Economic Journal*, 64, September, 528–556.

Feldstein, M.S. (1972) 'Equity and Efficiency in Public Sector Pricing: the Optimal Two Part Tariff', *Quarterly Journal of Economics*, 86 (2), 175–187.

Fisher, I. (1954) *The Theory of Interest*, Kelly and Millman, New York.

Friedman, M, and L.J. Savage (1948) 'The Utility Analysis of Choices Involving Risk', *Journal of Political Economy*, 56(4), 279–304.

Galbraith, J.K. (1969) *The Affluent Society*, 2nd edn., Houghton Mifflin.

Goldberger, A.S. (1964) *Econometric Theory*, John Wiley and Sons.

Grayson, C.J. (1958) 'Decisions Under Uncertainty', D.B.A. thesis, The Graduate School of Business Administration, George F. Baker Foundation, Harvard University.

Green, J.A. (1960) *Sequences and Series*, Routledge and Kegan Paul.

Harberger, A.C. (1959) 'Using the Resources at Hand More Efficiently', *American Economic Review: Papers and Proceedings*, 49, May, 134–46.

Henderson, J.M. and R.E. Quandt (1971) *Microeconomic Theory*, 2nd edn., McGraw-Hill.

Hicks, J.R. (1939) *Value and Capital*, Oxford.

Hotelling, H. (1938) 'The General Welfare in Relation to Problems of Taxation and of Railway and Utility Rates', *Econometrica*, 6, 242–269.

Houthakker, H.S. (1950) 'Revealed Preference and the Utility Function', *Economica*, 17, 159–174.

Houthakker, H.S. and L.D. Taylor (1970) *Consumer Demand in the United States: Analyses and Projections*, 2nd and enlarged edn., Harvard University Press.

Hurwicz, L. and H. Uzawa (1971) 'On the Integrability of Demand Functions', in: J.S. Chipman, L. Hurwicz, M. Richter and H. Sonnenschein, eds., *Preferences, Utility and Demand*, Harcourt, Brace, Javonovich, Inc., ch. 6.

Intriligator, M.D. (1971) *Mathematical Optimization and Economic Theory*, Prentice-Hall. 1971.

Johnson, H.G. (1958) 'The Gains from Free Trade with Europe: An Estimate', *The Manchester School of Economic and Social Studies*, 26(3), September, 247–255.

Johnson, H.G. (1960) 'The Costs of Protection and the Scientific Tariff', *Journal of Political Economy*, August, 327–345.

Johnson, H.G. (1965) 'The Costs of Protection and Self Sufficiency', *Quarterly Journal of Economics*, August.

Katzner, D. (1970) *Static Demand Theory*, Macmillan.

Lancaster, K. (1958) 'Welfare Propositions in Terms of Consistency and Expanded Choice', *Economic Journal*, 68, September.

Lancaster, K. (1968) *Mathematical Economics*, Macmillan.

Little, I.M.D. (1958) *A Critique of Welfare Economics*, 2nd edn., Oxford, New York.

Lluch, C. (1973) 'The Extended Linear Expenditure System', *European Economic Review*, 4, 21–32.

Luce, R.D. and H. Raiffa (1957) *Games and Decisions*, Wiley, New York.

Malanos, G. (1962) *Intermediate Economic Theory*, Lippincott, Philadelphia.

Musgrave, R.A. (1959) *The Theory of Public Finance*, McGraw-Hill Book Co., Inc.

Peleg, B. and M.E. Yaari (1973) 'On the Existence of a Consistent Course of Action when Tastes are Changing', *Review of Economic Studies*, 341–401.

Phelps, E.S. and R.A. Pollak (1968) 'On Second-best National Savings and Game-Equilibrium Growth', *Review of Economic Studies*, April, 185–199.

Phlips, L. (1974) *Applied Consumption Analysis*, North-Holland/American Elsevier.

Pollak, R.A. (1968) 'Consistent Planning', *Review of Economic Studies*, April, 201–208.

Pratt, J.W. (1964) 'Risk Aversion in the Small and in the Large', *Econometrica*, 32 (1–2), January–April, 122–136.

Pratt, J.W., H. Raiffa and R. Schlaifer (1965) *Introduction to Statistical Decision Theory*, McGraw-Hill.

Raiffa,, H. (1968) *Decision Analysis: Introductory Lectures on Choices under Uncertainty*, Addison-Wesley.

Samuelson, P.A. (1950) 'Evaluation of Real National Income', *Oxford Economic Papers*, NS2, January, 1–29.

Samuelson, P.A. (1955) 'A Diagrammatic Exposition of a Theory of Public Expenditure', *The Review of Economics and Statistics*, 37, November, 350–356.

Scitovsky, T. (1958) *Economic Theory and Western European Integration*, Stanford University Press.

Stigler, G. (1950) 'The Development of Utility Theory', *Journal of Political Economy*, 58, August, October, 307–327, 373–396.

Strotz, R.H. (1955–56) 'Myopia and Inconsistency in Dynamic Utility Maximization', *Review of Economic Studies*, 165–180.

Taylor, L. (1975) 'Theoretical Foundations and Technical Implications', in: C.R. Blitzer, P.B. Clark and L. Taylor, eds., *Economy-Wide Models and Development Planning*, Oxford University Press.

Veblen, T. (1953) *The Theory of the Leisure Class*, New American Library, New York.

Vickrey, W.S. (1964) *Microstatics*, Harcourt, Brace and World.

Wold, H. and L. Jureen (1953) *Demand Analysis*, John Wiley and Sons, Inc.

Yaari, M.E. (1964) 'On the Consumer's Lifetime Allocation Process', *International Economic Review*, 5 (3), 304–317.

Zeckhauser, R. and M. Olson (1966) 'An Economic Theory of Alliances', *Review of Economics and Statistics*, 48, August, 266–279.

1. $\Sigma p_2 q_2 > \Sigma p_2 q_1$ and $\Sigma p_1 q_2 > \Sigma p_1 q_1$.

2. $\Sigma p_2 q_2 = \Sigma p_2 q_1$ and $\Sigma p_1 q_2 > \Sigma p_1 q_1$.

3. $\Sigma p_2 q_2 > \Sigma p_2 q_1$ and $\Sigma p_1 q_2 < \Sigma p_1 q_1$.

4. $\Sigma p_2 q_2 < \Sigma p_2 q_1$ and $\Sigma p_1 q_2 > \Sigma p_1 q_1$.

Can you tell in each case whether the decision-maker views the situation in period 1 as better or worse than in period 2?

(c) (For discussion.) In the context of the theory of the consumer, is there any distinction between 'A is chosen over B' and 'A is preferred to B?' (You may assume that A and B are both attainable.) Would it make any difference if we renamed revealed preference, revealed choice? Introspection might suggest to you that movement to a 'chosen' position does not necessarily yield a greater sense of well-being. E3.20 touches on an aspect of this problem, namely the fact that economic choices may induce changes in the individual preference structure.

Answer.   (a)   See fig. E3.1.1.

(1)   Let O be the initial situation, I the first week's consumption, and II the second week's consumption, and let ARB mean that A is revealed preferred over B. Then $IIRI, IRO$.

(2) II' is the second week's consumption:

  IRO,

  $II'RO$,

  $IRII'$.

But $II'RI$.

Hence I and II' are inconsistent. Assuming Mal traded to reach his most preferred position in each week, we must conclude that his tastes have changed.

(3)   Let II'' be the still newer second week's consumption. Then

  $II''RO$,

  IRO.

But II'' and I are not comparable.

(b) $\Sigma p_2 q_2 > \Sigma p_2 q_1$ implies that in the second period the consumer could have bought the commodity bundle of the first period. Thus, q_2 is revealed to be preferred to q_1. And since $\Sigma p_1 q_2 > \Sigma p_1 q_1$, the bundle bought in the second period could not have been afforded in the first.

(2)   Substituting the equality for the inequality in the first relationship

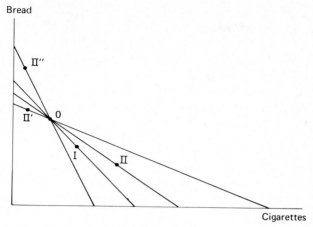

Figure E3.1.1

makes no difference: q_1 could still have been purchased in period 2 and so on.

(3) Now we find q_2 revealed to be preferred to q_1 in the second period, while at the same time q_1 was revealed preferred to q_2 in the first period (i.e. q_1 could have been bought when q_2 was bought and vice versa). This means that our subject is inconsistent or that his tastes have changed; in any case, his behavior violates the revealed preference axiom.

(4) Here q_2 could not have been bought when q_1 was purchased and vice versa. Hence we are unable to say which situation the decision-maker prefers.

Exercise 3.2. *Community welfare decisions (a revealed preference problem)*

The committee on culture in a small town has been given the responsibility of operating the community theater. The costs of running the theater can be met either through taxes or admission fees, or both. Only members of the community can attend the theater. The committee has found that if it levies no tax and charges an admission fee of $ 4.50, each person in the town will attend the theater once per season. If the committee imposes a tax of $ 2.00 per person and charges an admission fee of $ 1.50, each person attends four times, and with a tax of $ 5.00 and an admission of $ 0.50, each person attends seven times. Each of the above proposals covers the cost of operating the theater. Use a revealed preference argument to suggest which of the plans the committee should adopt.

Answer.   Implicit in the statement of the problem is the notion that all individuals behave alike — which is unrealistic and makes the case here unlikely as a model of social decison-making. Making that assumption, however, we can treat this as a revealed preference problem involving the total consumption of all other commodities and theater attendance. Each tax—price combination yields an opportunity set in those variables. See fig. E.3.2.1 (where y denotes the consumer's total budget) and the data set out in table E3.2.1.

Table E3.2.1

Situation	Tax	Admission	Attendance
O	–	–	–
I	0.0	4.50	1
II	2.00	1.50	4
III	5.00	0.50	7

From fig. E3.2.1 we conclude

$IIIRII \quad IIRI \quad IRO.$

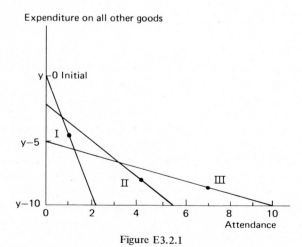

Figure E3.2.1

Exercise 3.3. *International welfare comparisons*

(a) The data in table E3.3.1 are taken from Denison (1967). What can you infer about the levels of welfare and the production possibilities in the various countries, and why? *Note*: you should not attempt to answer this question until you have read Samuelson, 'Evaluation of Real National Income'.

Table E3.3.1 Indexes of real national income (per capita), international comparison, 1960

Area	Indexes based on US commodity prices	Indexes based on European commodity prices
United States	100	100
Northwest Europe	69	48
Belgium	61	54
Denmark	71	47
France	66	48
Germany	73	47
Netherlands	61	50
Norway	64	47
United Kingdom	72	48
Italy	43	26

(b) (For discussion.) A number of writers (e.g. Marx, Marshall, and Veblen and, more recently, Galbraith, Baran, and Duesenberry) have stressed the importance of man's relationship to the productive process and his participation in social life as an influence on the formation of his personality and, more specifically, his preferences. If it is true that the production process itself has significant effects on wants, what can justify the use of individual preferences as the basis for the normative evaluation of the efficiency or, more generally, the desirability of alternative social arrangements relevant to the organization of production?

Answer. (a) We have provided the following possible answer to E3.3 to help readers who have difficulty with this question. Certainly there will be a wide range of alternative approaches.

To simplify matters, let northwest Europe be considered as a single country

(E). Let x_{US} and x_E be the vectors of quantities consumed per head of various goods in the United States and northwest Europe, respectively.

The figures tell us that

$$p_{US}x_{US} > p_{US}x_E \tag{i}$$

and that

$$p_E x_{US} > p_E x_E. \tag{ii}$$

From (i) it appears that from the US point of view, the US consumption bundle is preferred to the European, i.e. for the typical US consumer

$$x_{US}Rx_E.$$

Whether or not the typical European consumer would also prefer x_{US} to x_E is not revealed by the data. Expression (ii) merely implies that the typical European consumer could not afford the US per capita consumption bundle. On the other hand, if we are prepared to assume that resource allocation in the United States and Europe is approximately purely competitive, then from (ii) we can conclude that the European production possiblities frontier (PPF) lies inside that of the United States near x_{US} (see fig. E3.3.1). But this does not mean that the US production possibilities frontier is outside that for Europe at every point, nor in fact that the United States would be capable of producing x_E (as fig. E.3.3.1 shows).

Does (i) contribute any additional information about the European and US production possibilities frontiers? Apparently not. Fig. E3.3.2 is consistent with (i) and (ii) and yet gives us no unambiguous criterion for comparing the productive systems. That is to say, (i) and (ii) cannot alone tell us that one country's

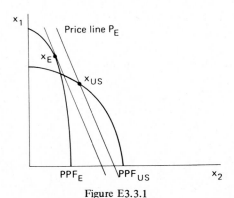

Figure E3.3.1

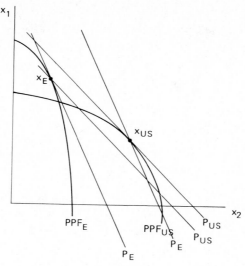

Figure E3.3.2

transformation curve is everywhere inside the others. Therefore, in particular, (i) and (ii) cannot tell us that US consumption possibilities include all European possibilities.

The comparison between the European countries might be easier to make. Here it might be valid to assume that close trade links make p_E the domestic price vector in all countries and that trade makes the budget lines into consumption possibility lines. Now we can conclude that $p_E x_{UK} < p_E x_{Belgium}$ implies that all the consumption possibilities open to the United Kingdom are also open to Belgium, and we might tentatively offer this as an indication of the superior economic welfare of Belgium (see fig. E.3.3.3).

Exercise 3.4.   Revealed preference versus utility maximization

(a)   Consider a household which chooses its consumption vector, c, to maximize a strictly quasiconcave[1] utility function, $U(c)$, subject to $p'c = y$, where p and y are the price vector and the level of expenditure, respectively. For brevity, we

---

[1]   The important word is 'strictly'. Its role is to ensure that for a given p and y, the solution to the consumers utility-maximizing problem is unique. Recall E1.13 and fig. 2.3.2. If multiple solutions are possible, then the observed household consumption behavior could violate the strong axiom of revealed preference. Why?

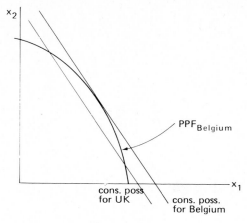

Figure E3.3.3

will say that the household's behavior is consistent with a strictly quasiconcave utility maximizing model (UMM). Show that the household's behavior will satisfy the *strong axiom of revealed preference*.

(b) Sketch some consumption-bundle-budget-line diagrams of the type shown in fig. E.3.4.1. Convince yourself that whenever your diagram is consistent with the strong axiom of revealed preference, then you can always sketch in a set of indifference curves of the usual shape which are consistent with the behavior illustrated in your diagram. (For example, in fig. E.3.4.2 we have superimposed a set of indifference curves on fig. E3.4.1.) This analysis should suggest to you that the reverse of the proposition of part (a) might be true. In fact, it can be shown (apart from a few minor qualifications) that if a household's consumption behavior is consistent with the strong axiom of revealed preference, then it is also consistent with a strictly quasiconcave UMM.[2] Putting this proposition together with the proposition in part (a) we find that the two assumptions, (i) that households behave as if they maximize a strictly quasiconcave utility function and (ii) that household behavior is compatible with the strong axiom of revealed preference, are effectively the same assumption. More formally, but not quite rigorously:

---

[2]   The result alluded to has been proved, with variations, by many authors. The classic article is Houthakker (1950). Modern treatments include Diewert (1973) and Dixon (1975, pp. 96–105). On the general problem of 'integrability', i.e. the problem of identifying conditions on demand behavior which are sufficient to ensure its compatibility with a UMM, mathematically sophisticated students could consult Hurwicz and Uzawa (1971). We hope, however, that it is possible to obtain an intuitive grasp of the main ideas coming from the integrability literature by working on the present exercise and E3.14.

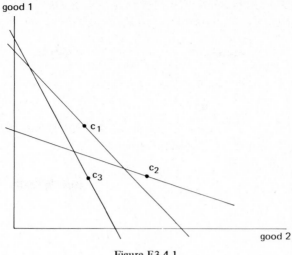

Figure E3.4.1

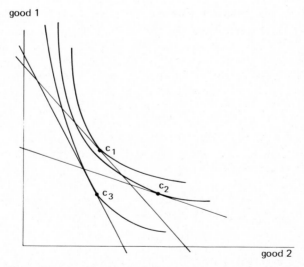

Figure E3.4.2. There are an infinite variety of ways of sketching in a family of indifference curves which are consistent with the illustrated consumption behavior. Can you sketch a set which would imply that $U(c_2) > U(c_1)$?

Household behavior is consistent with the strong axiom of revealed preference if and only if it is consistent with a strictly quasiconcave utility-maximizing model.

(c) What is your reaction to the following viewpoint?

'...Following to its end the path originally slashed by Samuelson through the
jungle of utility and all that, we can entirely dispense with any notion of utility,
cardinal or ordinal, also with indifference curves and preference orderings, and
derive all that can effectively be said concerning consumers' demand from a
single, simple, axiom of consistency' Lancaster (1958, p. 464).

Answer.   (a) Let us assume that the household's behavior is *not* consistent
with the strong axiom. Then it would be possible to have a sequence of distinct
consumption vectors $c_1, c_2,...,c_n$ such that

$$\left.\begin{aligned}
p_1' c_1 &\geqslant p_1' c_2, \\
p_2' c_2 &\geqslant p_2' c_3, \\
&\ \vdots \\
p_{n-1}' c_{n-1} &\geqslant p_{n-1}' c_n
\end{aligned}\right\} \tag{E3.4.1}$$

and

$$p_n' c_n \geqslant p_n' c_1, \tag{E3.4.2}$$

i.e.

$$c_1 R c_2, c_2 R c_3,...,c_{n-1} R c_n$$

and

$$c_n R c_1.$$

If the household's behavior were consistent with a strictly quasiconcave UMM,
then from (E3.4.1) it would follow that

$$U(c_1) > U(c_2) > ... > U(c_n). \tag{E3.4.3}$$

[Since c_i maximizes $U(c)$ subject to the ith budget constraint and c_{i+1} is compatible with the ith budget constraint, it is clear that

$$U(c_i) \geqslant U(c_{i+1}).$$

The possibility of $U(c_i)$ being equal to $U(c_{i+1})$ is ruled out by the assumption of
strict quasiconcavity — the indifference curves contain no 'straight-line' segments, see E1.13 and fig. 2.3.2.] It would also follow from (E3.4.2) that

$$U(c_n) > U(c_1).$$
$$(E3.4.4)$$

(E3.4.3) and (E3.4.4) are contradictory. We may conclude that it is not possible for household behavior to violate the strong axiom of revealed preference, yet be consistent with the strictly quasiconcave UMM. That is, the assumption that household behavior is consistent with the strictly quasiconcave UMM implies that it is consistent with the strong axiom of revealed preference.

(c) Our own reaction is that there is nothing important to choose between utility-maximizing theory and revealed preference theory and that there is no reason to dispense with one or other. In view of the result cited in part (b), the choice between them appears to be merely a matter of convenience. For example, in E2.10 we used a revealed preference type of argument to prove that own price substitution effects are negative. As was pointed out, we could equally well (but with less convenience) have obtained this result by exploiting the properties of utility functions. By contrast, in E2.1, E2.2 and E2.6, where we were concerned with obtaining empirically useful restrictions to be applied to systems of demand equations, we found it convenient to adopt a utility-maximizing model. Alternatively, it would have been possible to work from the strong axiom of revealed preference.

B. Problems using the concept of economic surplus

Exercise 3.5. A consumer surplus approach to the theater problem

Rework E3.2 by calculating the net consumer surplus associated with each of the proposed schemes for operating the theater.

Answer.   In fig. E3.5.1 we have plotted the typical member's demand function for attendances at the community theater. (The crosses are linear interpolations between the known points, the dots.) This demand function shows the number of times the member will attend the theater, at various admission prices, on the assumption that his income is reduced by the necessary theater tax. We will assume that theater charges (taxes and admission costs) are only a small share of the typical member's total budget. This justifies the assumption that the marginal utility of income is approximately unaffected by changes in theater admission prices and theater taxes, i.e. the marginal utility of income is constant along the demand function shown in fig. E.3.5.1. Next, we assume that the willingness of the typical member to pay $ 4.5 for one attendance indicates that he values this attendance at $ 4.5. His valuation of the fourth attendance is $ 1.50 and so on. The significance of the assumption of constancy in the marginal utility of income is that it makes these valuations comparable – under each pricing scheme $ x has the same 'utility' value. Hence we can sum the valuations to obtain the total dollar value of any given number of theater attendances. Table E3.5.1 summarizes the costs and benefits to the typical member under the three theater pricing schemes and supports scheme III over the other two.

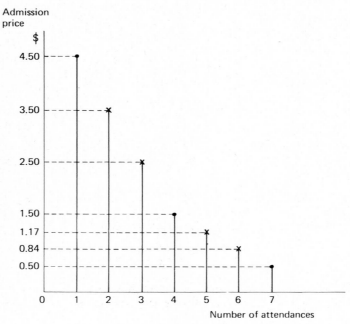

Figure E3.5.1

Table E3.5.1

Scheme	Costs			Benefits		Net benefit or net consumer surplus
	Tax	Admission	Total	No. of attendances	Valuation[a]	
I	0	4.50	4.50	1	4.50	0
II	2.0	6.00	8.00	4	12.00	4.0
III	5.0	3.50	8.50	7	14.50	6.0

[a] Obtained by adding the valuations implied by fig. E3.5.1.

Exercise 3.6. The application of the consumer surplus concept to social decisions through cost—benefit analysis (For discussion).

Consider the following two applications of consumer surplus to problems of social choice:

(1) The US Department of the Interior has invested in new roads, camp grounds, swimming and boating facilities, etc. in a particular national park. Perhaps in part as a result of these new facilities, use of the park has risen more than the national trend (25 percent per year) and in fact triples from 40, 000 user-days per year to 120,000 user-days. A user-day is the use of the park by one person for one day. Since the park, in a policy change, simultaneously lowered admission from \$ 1.25 to \$ 0.25 per person per day, a government economist argues that the increase in the annual consumer surplus from the project can be approximated by

$$\tfrac{1}{2}(\Delta p \Delta q) + q_1 \Delta p.$$

(2) A new aqueduct has brought increased irrigation water to a group of Indian villages that exist almost entirely on nonmarket subsistence farming. With no apparent change in the work force, the total yield per year in the region has gone up by about 25 percent or 10,000 bushels over the previous 40,000. The market value of grain in the nearest significant town is about \$ 4 per bushel. However, the increases in yield are very unevenly distributed over the region, since, to use the water efficiently, over half the water was channeled into a particular plain where only 15 percent of the region's population lived and where the farms were somewhat larger, agricultural techniques more advanced, and general modernization further developed. One economist brought in from the United States to evaluate the project estimated the annual net benefits at

    10,000 bushels × \$ 4/bushel = \$ 40,000.

(a) What difficulties can you see in each case that make the figures a dubious measure of changes in social welfare?

(b) What other data might you want to help you to reach more useful results? How would you incorporate these data into the analysis?

In the literature you will have found several general objections to the consumer surplus concept and its use in measuring social welfare. Rather than supply an answer, we refer you to this literature. In your answers to (a) and (b), try to decide how the objections in the literature relate to the situations described in (1) and (2) and whether they are important or not. Also, pick out particular features of (1) and (2) which might make the use of consumer surplus inappropriate. Finally, be sure to think about the purpose of measuring the change in social welfare. It is impossible to know whether we have a 'good' measure, if we do not know what it is 'good' for.

Exercise 3.7.   Compensated demand functions, consumer surplus and excess burden

Consider a household whose preferences are described by the utility function

$$U(x_1, x_2) = x_1 x_2,$$

where x_1 and x_2 are the household's consumption of goods 1 and 2, respectively.

(a) Derive the household's demand functions for goods 1 and 2.

(b) Derive the household's *compensated* demand functions for goods 1 and 2, i.e. obtain functions of the form

$$x_i = f_i(p_1, p_2, U), \quad i = 1, 2,$$

where U is the household's level of utility. Notice that compared with the usual demand functions, in the compensated demand functions U replaces Y as an argument. Hence, when we differentiate the compensated demand function for good i with respect to p_j (say), we obtain the effect on the household's demand for good i of an increase in p_j where other prices and *utility* (not the expenditure level) are held constant. The expenditure level varies to allow maintenance of the utility level or in other words, the expenditure level varies so as to 'compensate' the household for the price increase.

(c) Assume that in the initial situation the commodity prices, p_1 and p_2, and the household expenditure level, Y, are given by

$$p_1 = 1; \quad p_2 = 1 \quad \text{and} \quad Y = 2.$$

Sketch the compensated and uncompensated demand curves for good 2 with p_1 held constant at the initial level. In the compensated case, U is held constant at the initial level while in the uncompensated case, Y is held constant.

(d) By how much must Y be increased if p_2 increases to 2 (p_1 remains at 1) and our household is to maintain its initial level of utility? (Be sure to check your answer by examining the area under the compensated demand curve.)

(e) Imagine that the increase in p_2, mentioned in part (d), was caused by a tax of 1 on the consumption of good 2. How much revenue would be generated by the tax if we assume, as in (d), that the household makes a compensating increase in its expenditure level? What is the *excess burden* of the tax, i.e. the excess of the compensation required to keep the household at its pretax level of utility over the revenue raised?

Answer.   (a) The first-order conditions are

$$\frac{\partial U}{\partial x_1} = x_2 = \lambda p_1,$$

$$\frac{\partial U}{\partial x_2} = x_1 = \lambda p_2,$$

$$p_1 x_1 + p_2 x_2 = Y.$$

On eliminating λ, we obtain the demand functions

$$x_i = \tfrac{1}{2} Y/p_i, \quad i = 1, 2. \tag{E3.7.1}$$

    (b) To derive the compensated demand functions we add to the system (E3.7.1) the equation

$$U = x_1 x_2. \tag{E3.7.2}$$

Now we substitute from (E3.7.1) into (E3.7.2), obtaining

$$U = \tfrac{1}{4} Y^2 / p_1 p_2, \tag{E3.7.3}$$

i.e.

$$Y = 2\sqrt{(U p_1 p_2)}, \tag{E3.7.4}$$

where (E3.7.4) can be used to show the levels of expenditure required to achieve given levels of utility at given commodity prices. Finally, we substitute from (E3.7.4) into (E3.7.1) to generate the compensated demand functions:

$$x_i = \sqrt{(U p_1 p_2)}/p_i, \quad i = 1, 2.$$

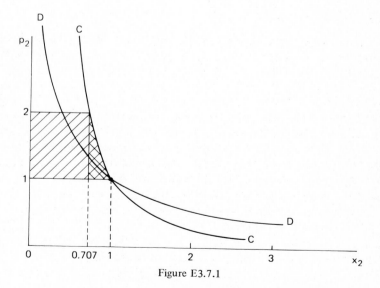

Figure E3.7.1

(c) See fig. E3.7.1. DD is the uncompensated demand curve. It has the equation

$$x_2 = 1/p_2.$$

CC is the compensated demand curve. Its equation is

$$x_2 = 1/\sqrt{p_2}.$$

(*Note*: the initial level of utility is 1, as can be calculated by substitution into (E3.7.3).)

(d) From (E3.7.4) we find that the expenditure level required to maintain the initial utility ($U = 1$) when p_2 increases to 2 is

$$\overline{Y} = 2\sqrt{(1 \times 1 \times 2)} = 2\sqrt{2}.$$

The initial expenditure level was $Y = 2$. Hence, the increase in expenditure necessary to compensate our household for the price increase is $(2\sqrt{2} - 2)$. Notice that the shaded area in fig. E3.7.1 (i.e. the area under the compensated demand curve) is also $(2\sqrt{2} - 2)$. This result is obtainable as follows:

$$\text{shaded area} = \int_1^2 p_2^{-\frac{1}{2}} \, dp_2 = [2p_2^{\frac{1}{2}}]_1^2 = (2\sqrt{2} - 2) \simeq 0.828.$$

(e) The post-tax level of demand for good 2 (assuming compensating increases in expenditure take place) is

$$x_2 = 1/\sqrt{2} = 0.707$$

(see fig. E3.7.1). Thus, the revenue raised is 0.707 (tax × quantity). The compensating increase in expenditure is 0.828 (see part (d)). Hence the excess burden (*eb*) is

$$eb = 0.828 - 0.707 = 0.121.$$

Excess burden is a measure of the inefficiency of the tax as a revenue raiser. The cost of the tax to the household is 0.828 in the sense that Y must be increased by 0.828 for maintenance of the initial level of utility. However, even if Y is increased by 0.828, the revenue from the tax would only be 0.707. A compensated head tax of 0.707 would have raised the same revenue as the tax on commodity 2, but required only a 0.707 compensating increase in Y. Notice that the excess burden (also called the dead weight loss) of the commodity tax is given by the double-shaded triangle in fig. E3.7.1.

In this answer we have considered just one of the possible excess burden measures. Alternative, and just as plausible, measures are possible. We suggest that you look at the discussion in Currie, Murphy and Schmitz (1971) of the four measures of consumer surplus.

Exercise 3.8. *The costs of protection*[3]

Consider an economy in which there are two goods and in which the utility function describing aggregate household preferences has the form

$$U = C_a C_b, \tag{E3.8.1}$$

where C_a and C_b are consumption levels for goods a and b.

   (a) Assume that the economy is capable of producing two units of a and one unit of b; we are not allowing any flexibility in production — the production possibilities frontier is of the form shown in fig. E3.8.1.

If both a and b can be traded internationally with 'world' prices being

$$p_a^w = 1; \quad p_b^w = 1, \tag{E3.8.2}$$

what trading and consumption patterns will emerge? That is, what will our economy import, what will be exported and what quantities of a and b will be consumed?

   (b) Assume that a 20 percent ad valorem tariff is imposed on the import of good b. Thus, provided that good b is imported, its domestic price will be

$$p_b^d = p_b^w (1.2) = 1.2,$$

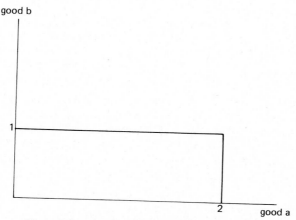

Figure E3.8.1.   Production possibilities frontier.

---

[3]   A pocket calculator will be useful in working this problem and the next two.

while the domestic price of a will remain at 1. Assume that the revenue from the tariff is returned to the economy's consumers in the form of general income subsidy so that the expenditure constraint for the household sector becomes

$$Y = \underbrace{X_a p_a^d + X_b p_b^d}_{\substack{\text{income from} \\ \text{production}}} + \underbrace{T}_{\text{income subsidy}}$$

i.e.

$$Y = 3.2 + T.$$

What will be the new trading and consumption patterns? *Hint*: tariff revenue, T, will satisfy[4]

$$T = 0.2 p_b^w (C_b - X_b).$$

Also,

$$C_a = f_a(p_a^d, p_b^d, Y),$$
$$C_b = f_b(p_a^d, p_b^d, Y),$$

where these last two equations are the commodity demand functions. Once the explicit form for these has been derived, you will have four equations in four unknowns (C_a, C_b, T and Y). The rest should be straightforward.

(c) What is the excess burden of the tariff or the costs of protection, i.e. how much compensation (in addition to the return of the tariff revenue) would the household sector require in order to allow it to achieve the same level of utility with the tariff imposed as it had in the free trade situation.

(d)[5] Continue to assume that community preferences are described by (E3.8.1) and that world commodity prices are given by (E3.8.2). However, assume that the economy's production possibilities frontier is defined by

$$X_a^2 + 2X_b^2 = 6, \qquad\qquad\qquad\qquad (E3.8.3)$$

and that producers choose the combination of a and b which maximizes the value of output in domestic prices. What output levels will be produced under free trade? What will be the free trade consumption and trade patterns? What will be the trade, production and consumption patterns if there is a 20 percent

---

[4] The validity of this equation depends on b not being exported (i.e. $C_b \geqslant X_b$). In part (a) you will have found that b is imported, not exported. Tariff protection for b will at most eliminate imports of b, but it cannot reverse the commodity composition of trade.

[5] If you are totally innocent of production theory, you may prefer to skip this part of the problem until after you have worked through Problem Set 4, parts A and B.

tariff imposed on the import of good b and the tariff revenue is returned to the household sector in the form of an income subsidy? What is the excess burden of the tariff?

Answer.   (a) We assume that the household sector takes domestic commodity prices as given and chooses C_a and C_b to maximize utility subject to the aggregate household budget constraint, i.e. we assume that C_a and C_b maximize

$$C_a C_b \qquad\qquad\qquad\qquad (E3.8.4)$$

subject to

$$p_a^d C_a + p_b^d C_b = Y,$$

where p_a^d and p_b^d are domestic prices of a and b and Y is aggregate household income. From (E3.8.4) we obtain demand functions of the form

$$C_a = \tfrac{1}{2} Y/p_a^d, \qquad\qquad\qquad (E3.8.5a)$$
$$C_b = \tfrac{1}{2} Y/p_b^d. \qquad\qquad\qquad (E3.8.5b)$$

In the absence of transport costs, or other interferences in trade, domestic prices will equal world prices, i.e.

$$p_a^d = p_a^w = 1, \qquad\qquad\qquad (E3.8.6a)$$
$$p_b^d = p_b^w = 1. \qquad\qquad\qquad (E3.8.6b)$$

Finally, we will assume that the household budget is determined by the income arising from production. Thus,

$$Y = p_a^d X_a + p_b^d X_b = 2 + 1 = 3, \qquad\qquad (E3.8.7)$$

where X_a and X_b are the levels of output of a and b.

On substituting from (E3.8.6) and (E3.8.7) into (E3.8.5), we find that free trade consumption is $1\tfrac{1}{2}$ units of a and $1\tfrac{1}{2}$ units of b. Net imports of a and b are

$$M_a = C_a - X_a = 1\tfrac{1}{2} - 2 = -\tfrac{1}{2},$$
$$M_b = C_b - X_b = 1\tfrac{1}{2} - 1 = \tfrac{1}{2}.$$

(Negative imports are to be interpreted as exports.)

(b) Following the 'hint' we can write four equations in four unknowns:

$$Y = 3.2 + T \qquad\qquad \text{(household budget)},$$
$$T = 0.2 p_b^w (C_b - X_b) \qquad \text{(tariff revenue)},$$
$$\left. \begin{array}{l} C_a = \tfrac{1}{2} Y/p_a^d \\[4pt] C_b = \tfrac{1}{2} Y/p_b^d \end{array} \right\} \qquad \begin{array}{l}\text{(commodity demands,} \\ \text{see (E3.8.5)).}\end{array}$$

On solving these equations with $p_a^d = 1$, $p_b^d = 1.2$, $p_b^w = 1$ and $X_b = 1$, we obtain

$C_a = 1.636$; $C_b = 1.363$,

$Y = 3.273$; $T = 0.073$.

The trade pattern is

$M_a = 1.636 - 2 = -0.364$,

$M_b = 1.363 - 1 = 0.363$.

Are you surprised that trade is balanced? Can you explain why

$p_a^w M_a + p_b^w M_b = 0$?

(c) The free trade utility level is

$U = 1\frac{1}{2} \times 1\frac{1}{2} = 2\frac{1}{4}$.

(Free trade consumption of a and b is $1\frac{1}{2}$ and $1\frac{1}{2}$, see part (a).)

Our task is to find D, the compensation required in addition to the return of the tariff revenue, which will allow the household sector to maintain the free trade level of utility ($U = 2\frac{1}{4}$). When compensation is made, we have

$Y = 3.2 + T + D$,

$T = 0.2p_b^w (C_b - X_b)$,

$C_a = \frac{1}{2} Y/p_a^d$,

$C_b = \frac{1}{2} Y/p_b^d$,

with

$2\frac{1}{4} = C_a C_b$ (maintenance of initial utility level).

This gives us five equations in five unknowns (Y, T, D, C_a and C_b). The solution of these equations (assuming $p_a^d = 1, p_b^w = 1, p_b^d = 1.2$ and $X_b = 1$) is

$C_a = 1.643$; $C_b = 1.369$; $Y = 3.286$;

$T = 0.074$; $D = 0.012$.

Hence the costs of protection are 0.012 or about 0.36 percent (0.012/3.286) of the expenditure level. In summary, the tariff on commodity b imposes a welfare loss equivalent to the loss of about 0.36 percent of national income.[6] With the tariff imposed, a source of income worth 0.36 percent of national income would

---

[6] In the model under consideration, national income is income from production plus tariff revenue.

need to be found if the economy were to be able to achieve the free trade level of utility.

In fig. E3.8.2 we have illustrated our answer with the usual[7] consumer surplus costs of protection diagram. cc is the compensated demand curve for good b with p_a held constant at 1 and utility at $2\frac{1}{4}$. The equation for cc is

$$C_b = \sqrt{(2\tfrac{1}{4} \times 1 \times p_b^d)}/p_b^d$$

i.e.

$$C_b = 1\tfrac{1}{2}/\sqrt{p_b^d}.$$

(This can be derived as in E3.7.) ss is the domestic supply curve for good b and in the current problem, ss is vertical or totally inelastic.

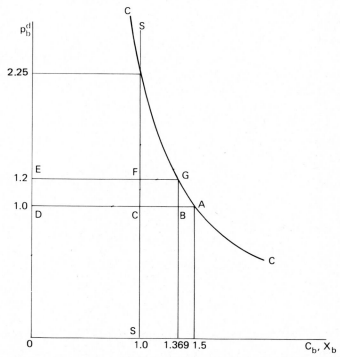

Figure E3.8.2. Loss of consumer surplus arising from the increase in the price of b is the area *ADEG*. However, offsets are the tariff revenue *FGBC* and the increase in producer surplus *EFCD*. The 'triangle' *GAB* is the excess burden or costs of protection.

[7] For a classic presentation, see Corden (1957).

(d) X_a and X_b maximize

$$p_a^d X_a + p_b^d X_b$$

subject to

$$X_a^2 + 2X_b^2 = 6.$$

The Lagrangian is

$$L \equiv p_a^d X_a + p_b^d X_b - \lambda(X_a^2 + 2X_b^2 - 6)$$

and the first order conditions are

$$p_a^d - 2\lambda X_a = 0,$$
$$p_b^d - 4\lambda X_b = 0,$$
$$X_a^2 + 2X_b^2 - 6 = 0.$$

From these three equations we obtain the supply functions:

$$X_a = \sqrt{\left(\frac{12(p_a^d)^2}{2(p_a^d)^2 + (p_b^d)^2} \right)}, \qquad \text{(E3.8.8a)}$$

$$X_b = \sqrt{\left(\frac{3(p_b^d)^2}{2(p_a^d)^2 + (p_b^d)^2} \right)}. \qquad \text{(E3.8.8b)}$$

Under free trade $p_a^d = p_b^d = 1$. Hence, the free trade production levels are

$$X_a = 2 \quad \text{and} \quad X_b = 1.$$

At this stage we can follow the answer in part (a) to obtain the free trade consumption and trade patterns as

$$C_a = 1\tfrac{1}{2}; \quad C_b = 1\tfrac{1}{2}; \quad M_a = -\tfrac{1}{2}; \quad M_b = \tfrac{1}{2}.$$

With the 20 percent tariff on the import of b, p_b^d will be 1.2; p_a^d remains at 1. By substituting into (E3.8.8) we find that the product supplies are

$$X_a = 1.868 \quad \text{and} \quad X_b = 1.121. \qquad \text{(E3.8.9)}$$

Next we use (E3.8.9) to write the household budget as

$$Y = 1.868 + 1.121 \times 1.2 + T,$$

where $T = 0.2(C_b - 1.121).$

C_a and C_b are given by

$C_a = \frac{1}{2} Y$ and $C_b = \frac{1}{2} Y / 1.2$.

On solving these last four equations we obtain

$C_a = 1.630;$ $C_b = 1.358;$

$Y = 3.260;$ $T = 0.047.$

Finally,

$M_a = 1.630 - 1.868 = -0.238,$

$M_b = 1.358 - 1.121 = 0.237.$

To compute the excess burden of the tariff, we find D such that

$Y = 1.868 + 1.121 \times 1.2 + T + D,$

with

$T = 0.2(C_b - 1.121),$

$C_a = \frac{1}{2} Y,$

$C_b = \frac{1}{2} Y / 1.2$

and

$C_a C_b = 2\frac{1}{4}.$

The solution for these five equations is

$C_a = 1.643;$ $C_b = 1.369;$ $Y = 3.286;$

$T = 0.050$ and $D = 0.023.$

Hence the costs of protection are 0.023 or about 0.7 percent (0.023/3.286) of national income. Our solution is illustrated in fig. E3.8.3.

Exercise 3.9. The costs of average cost pricing[8]

The aim of this problem is to sharpen your awareness of some of the issues involved in setting product prices for public utilities when production is subject to increasing returns to scale. While marginal cost pricing may be optimal from some points of view, it leaves the public utility with a loss which must be financed. Average cost pricing (which involves no financial loss) may be preferable if the resource wastage is small.

[8] This problem is based on Dixon (1972).

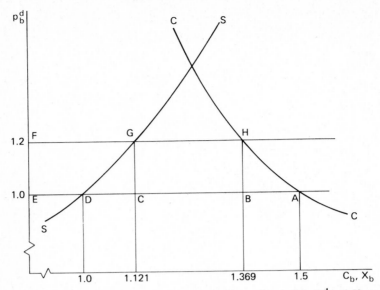

Figure E3.8.3. *cc* is the compensated demand curve for good b. (p_a^d and U are held constant at 1 and $2\frac{1}{4}$, respectively.) *ss* is product b's supply curve. The equations for *cc* and *ss* are

$$C_b = 1\tfrac{1}{2} / \sqrt{p_b^d}$$

and

$$X_b = \sqrt{\left(\frac{3(p_b^d)^2}{2 + (p_b^d)^2}\right)}.$$

The loss in consumer surplus arising from the increase in the price of b is the area *AEFH*. Offsets are the tariff revenue, *GHBC*, and the increase in producer surplus *DEFG*. The two 'triangles' *HAB* and *GCD* are the excess burden or costs of protection. *HAB* is often called the consumption costs of protection, while *GCB* is the production costs of protection.

Imagine that the needs of the community for a particular service can be satisfied by two commodities. For example, city transportation requirements can be met by public or private transport, electricity or oil can be used for home heating. Let the two commodities be a and b and assume that the community requirements can be met by any combination of a and b satisfying the equation

$$g(A,B) \equiv A^{\frac{1}{2}} B^{\frac{1}{2}} = 1, \tag{E3.9.1}$$

where A and B are the consumption levels of a and b.

On the productionside, assume that there are constant returns to scale in the production of commodity a. In particular, assume that the output of a is given by

$$A = L_a,$$

where L_a is the input of 'labor' to the production of a.[9] On the other hand, in the production of b there are strongly increasing returns to scale and

$$B = L_b^2.$$

Assume for convenience that quantity units are defined so that a unit of labor costs $ 1.

(a) What is the minimum labor requirement to produce a combination of a and b which will satisfy the community needs? What are the optimal values of A and B?

(b) Assume that there is average (and marginal) cost pricing in industry a so that the price of a unit of good a is

$$P_a = 1.$$

If the community chooses the values of A and B to minimize $P_a A + P_b B$ subject to (E3.9.1), how should good b be priced?

(c) If P_b is set at the optimum level, what is the profit (or loss) in industry b?

(d) If we are to avoid losses in industry b by insisting on average cost pricing, what will be the price of good b and the quantities sold of a and b? What is the total wastage of labor arising from average as compared with optimal (i.e. marginal) cost pricing in industry b — express your answer as a percentage.

(e) (For discussion.) What are the income distribution assumptions which are implicit in the argument that marginal cost pricing is optimal? Feldstein (1972) is an interesting reference.

Answer.   (a) We choose L_a, L_b, A and B to minimize

$$L_a + L_b$$

subject to

$$A = L_a,$$
$$B = L_b^2$$

and $A^{1/2} B^{1/2} = 1$.

---

[9] In a microeconomic problem, we can assume that factor prices are independent of the production and pricing decisions in industries a and b. Therefore, we can interpret L_a and L_b as the number of dollars of factor use by industries a and b, i.e. L_a and L_b can be thought of as the dollar costs of production.

Although you can probably see quicker ways (via substituting out some variables), we will write out the full Lagrangian. This will be helpful in answering some of the later parts of the problem.

The Lagrangian is

$$Q = L_a + L_b - \lambda_a(L_a - A) - \lambda_b(L_b^2 - B) - \lambda(A^{1/2}B^{1/2} - 1),$$

leading to the first-order conditions

$$\frac{\partial Q}{\partial L_a} = 1 - \lambda_a = 0, \tag{i}$$

$$\frac{\partial Q}{\partial L_b} = 1 - 2\lambda_b L_b = 0, \tag{ii}$$

$$\frac{\partial Q}{\partial A} = \lambda_a - \tfrac{1}{2}\lambda A^{-1/2}B^{1/2} = 0, \tag{iii}$$

$$\frac{\partial Q}{\partial B} = \lambda_b - \tfrac{1}{2}\lambda A^{1/2}B^{-1/2} = 0, \tag{iv}$$

$$\frac{\partial Q}{\partial \lambda} = -A^{1/2}B^{1/2} + 1 = 0, \tag{v}$$

$$\frac{\partial Q}{\partial \lambda_a} = -L_a + A = 0, \tag{vi}$$

$$\frac{\partial Q}{\partial \lambda_b} = -L_b^2 + B = 0. \tag{vii}$$

Using (i), (vi) and (vii) to eliminate L_a, L_b and λ_a, and combining (iii) and (iv) to eliminate λ we obtain

$$\left.\begin{array}{l} 1 = 2\lambda_b B^{1/2} \\[4pt] \lambda_b = (A/B) \end{array}\right\} \Rightarrow 1 = 2A\,B^{-1/2}$$

and

$$A^{1/2}B^{1/2} - 1 = 0.$$

From here we see that

$$A = 2^{-2/3} \simeq 0.630$$

$$B = 2^{2/3} \simeq 1.587$$

$$L_a = A \simeq 0.630$$

$$L_b = \sqrt{B} \simeq 1.260$$

and total labor use is $L_a + L_b \simeq 1.890$.

(b)   The community will choose A and B to minimize

$$A + P_b B$$

subject to

$$A^{1/2} B^{1/2} = 1.$$

This means that the community demands for a and b can be derived from eqs. (iii)–(v), where λ_b is replaced by P_b and $\lambda_a = 1$. Hence, if we wish to set P_b so that the community is induced to demand the combination of a and b which minimizes resource use, we should set P_b at the value revealed for λ_b in answer (a). Eq. (ii) implies that we should set $P_b = 1/2L_b \simeq 0.397$. Notice that the optimal value for P_b is the *marginal cost* of producing good b at the optimal level of production for b.

   (c)   Revenue in industry b $= P_b B = 0.397 \times 1.587 \simeq 0.630$
          Costs in industry b $= L_b$ $\simeq 1.260$
          Loss in industry b $\simeq \overline{0.630}$

Hence revenue covers only 50 percent of costs. Can you rationalize this result?
   (d)   With average cost pricing, P_b is set so that

$$P_b B = L_b,$$

i.e.

$$P_b B = B^{1/2} \quad \text{or} \quad P_b = B^{-1/2}.$$

We set $\lambda_b = B^{-1/2}$, $\lambda_a = 1$ and find A and B from eqs. (iii)–(v). This gives us

$$A = 1; \quad B = 1 \quad \text{and} \quad P_b = 1.$$

Hence, with average cost pricing in industry b, total labor use in the satisfaction of community needs is $L_a + L_b = 2$. The labor wastage implied by average cost pricing (rather than marginal cost pricing) is $2 - 1.890 = 0.110$, or about 5.8 percent of the minimum resource use.

Exercise 3.10.   Economies of scale, intraindustry specialization and the costs of protection [10]

In this exercise we will be assuming that all commodities can be internationally traded at exogenously given world prices. It will also be assumed that it is

---

[10]   This problem is based on the model presented in Dixon (1978). It involves the use of ideas from production theory and some of you may like to skip it until after you have worked through Problem Set 4, parts A and B.

socially optimal to organize the economy's resources so as to maximize the value of *GNP* in world prices; maximizing *GNP* in world prices gives the economy its most favorable budget constraint or consumption possibilities line. However, tariffs or other interferences with trade can induce the economy to produce a suboptimal combination of commodities, i.e. a combination which does not maximize the value of *GNP* at world prices. In the model to be developed here, part of the welfare costs (the part that is often called the production cost) of the tariff distortion will be measured by comparing the world prices value of *GNP* under free trade with that occurring under tariffs. Our particular concern will be to illustrate the potential importance of economies of scale and intraindustry resource shifts in calculations of the costs of protection for small open economies.

We consider a two-industry economy. The first industry, wheat, has a production function of the form

$$X_1 = L_1^{\gamma_1},$$

where X_1 is the output of wheat, L_1 is the input of labor, and γ_1 is a positive parameter, less than 1. Hence, in the wheat industry there are decreasing returns to scale. This might be explained by the presence of a fixed resource, e.g. land.

In the second industry, automotive engineering, there are two processes. The first, the manufacture of complete cars, has a production function

$$X_2 = L_2^{\gamma_2}, \qquad \text{for } L_2 \leqslant \theta_2$$
$$= a_2 L_2, \qquad \text{for } L_2 > \theta_2,$$

where X_2 is the output of cars, L_2 is the input of labor and θ_2, γ_2 and a_2 are positive parameters with $\gamma_2 > 1$ and $a_2 = \theta_2^{\gamma_2 - 1}$. The production function for cars exhibits increasing returns to scale up to the point where the labor input is θ_2. Thereafter, there are constant returns to scale. The value for a_2 is set so that X_2 is a continuous function of L_2.

The second process within industry 2 is the manufacture of engines. The production function is

$$X_3 = L_3^{\gamma_3}, \qquad \text{for } L_3 \leqslant \theta_3$$
$$= a_3 L_3, \qquad \text{for } L_3 > \theta_3,$$

where θ_3, γ_3 and a_3 are positive parameters with $\gamma_3 > 1$ and $a_3 = \theta_3^{\gamma_3 - 1}$. We assume that

$$\theta_3 < \theta_2,$$

i.e. in the manufacture of engines, the minimum efficient scale occurs at a smaller labor input than in the manufacture of complete cars.

Other relevant information concerning the economy is as follows. There is one unit of labor, i.e. L_1, L_2 and L_3 must satisfy

$$L_1 + L_2 + L_3 \leqslant 1.$$

All three goods, wheat, cars and engines are internationally traded and our economy is not large enough to affect 'world' prices. Domestic prices, P_i, are given by

$$P_1 = \overline{P}_1; \quad P_2 = \overline{P}_2(1 + t_2); \quad P_3 = \overline{P}_3,$$

where the $\overline{P}_i$s are world prices and t_2 is the ad valorem tariff (or export subsidy) on good 2. There are no tariffs on goods 1 and 3. Finally, we suppose that producers choose the output levels X_1, X_2 and X_3 which maximize the domestic prices value of *GNP*, i.e. they maximize $\Sigma_{i=1}^{3} P_i X_i$ subject to the production function and labor endowment constraints.[11]

Assume that $\overline{P}_1 = 1$, $\overline{P}_2 = 2\sqrt{(2)}/3$, $\overline{P}_3 = \frac{4}{3}$, $\theta_2 = 1$, $\theta_3 = \frac{1}{2}$, $\gamma_1 = \frac{1}{2}$, $\gamma_2 = \frac{3}{2}$, and $\gamma_3 = \frac{3}{2}$. Notice that we have set

$$\overline{P}_2/\overline{P}_3 = a_3/a_2.$$

Why might this be a reasonable assumption?[12]

Now attempt the following problems. (The figures have been chosen to minimize the arithmetic load. However, some arithmetic is unavoidable. Students who find themselves being overwhelmed by the computations should check with the solution to see if they are on the right track.)

(a) Assume that only goods 1 and 2 can be produced, i.e. ignore good 3. Assume that the tariff, t_2, on good 2 is zero. Compute the labor inputs, L_1, L_2, and the commodity outputs X_1 and X_2 which maximize the value of *GNP*. Make a note of the value of *GNP* in world prices. (In this case, *GNP* in world prices and domestic prices are the same.) You might find it is helpful to sketch the product transformation frontier between goods 1 and 2.

(b) Assume that a 50 percent tariff (or export subsidy) is applied to good 2 so that

$$P_2 = \overline{P}_2 \tfrac{3}{2}.$$

Rework part (a). What is the percentage reduction in the world prices value of *GNP* arising from the interference with trade?

---

[11] Students who enjoy this type of problem could rework it under alternative assumptions. One possibility is that wages equal the value of labor's marginal product in wheat and that the automotive producer is a profit maximizer who acts as a monopsonist in the labor market, recognizing that increases in demands for labor lead to increased wages.
[12] We have set $\overline{P}_2$ and $\overline{P}_3$ so that they reflect relative costs at fully efficient scale. We could expect major exporting countries to have achieved efficient scale.

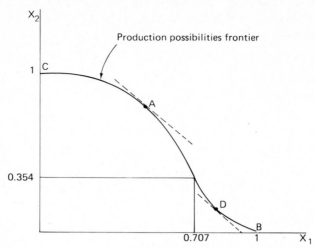

Figure E3.10.1. Where dX_1 and dX_2 are small changes in X_1 and X_2 along the production possibilities frontier,

$$2X_1\,dX_1 + \tfrac{2}{3}X_2^{-1/3}\,dX_2 = 0.$$

Thus, the slope of the production possibilities frontier is

$$\frac{dX_2}{dX_1} = -3X_1\,X_2^{1/3} = -3X_1\,(1 - X_1^2)^{1/2}$$

giving a slope of zero if either X_1 or X_2 is zero. Also, it is not hard to check that

$$\frac{d^2 X_2}{dX_1^2} = 0, \quad \text{when} \quad X_1 = 1/\sqrt{2}.$$

(c) Assume that only goods 1 and 3 can be produced, i.e. ignore good 2. Again compute the labor inputs, L_1, L_3, and commodity outputs, X_1 and X_3 which maximize the domestic prices value of *GNP*. (As in part (a), the domestic and world prices are the same.) What is the value of *GNP* in world prices?

(d) It is obvious that *GNP* maximizing will never require the production of both goods 2 and 3 simultaneously. Why? Assuming that producers maximize the domestic prices value of *GNP*, which good will they produce under free trade? Which will be produced when there is a 50 percent tariff (or export subsidy) on good 2? What is the percentage loss in the world prices value of *GNP* arising from the tariff on good 2.

(e) (For discussion.) Can you explain why the recognition of economies of scale does not by itself have important implications for the measurement of the costs of protection (see the result in part (b))? The dramatic results come when we introduce economies of scale and intraindustry specialization simultaneously.

Answer. (a) The problem is to choose non-negative values for X_1, X_2, L_1 and L_2 to maximize

$$GNP \equiv P_1 X_1 + P_2 X_2 \qquad \text{(E3.10.1)}$$

subject to[13]

$$X_1 = L_1^{1/2}, \qquad \text{(E3.10.2)}$$

$$X_2 = L_2^{3/2} \qquad \text{(E3.10.3)}$$

and $L_1 + L_2 = 1$. $\qquad \text{(E3.10.4)}$

By substituting from (E3.10.2) and (E3.10.3) into (E3.10.4) we obtain

$$X_1^2 + X_2^{2/3} - 1 = 0. \qquad \text{(E3.10.5)}$$

(E3.10.5) is the equation for the production possibilities frontier and is sketched in fig. E3.10.1. It is clear from the figure that we must consider two possibilities: either the solution to problem (E3.10.1)–(E3.10.4) occurs at a tangency point such as A, or it occurs at the corner point B. (Inspection of the diagram rules out the corner point C.) Keeping this information in mind, we proceed as follows. First we rewrite (E3.10.5) as

$$X_1 = (1 - X_2^{2/3})^{1/2}.$$

Now we substitute into (E3.10.1) to obtain

$$GNP = P_1 (1 - X_2^{2/3})^{1/2} + P_2 X_2. \qquad \text{(E3.10.6)}$$

With $P_1 = \bar{P}_1 = 1$ and $P_2 = \bar{P}_2 = 2\sqrt{(2)}/3$, we have

$$GNP = (1 - X_2^{2/3})^{1/2} + 2\sqrt{(2)}X_2/3. \qquad \text{(E3.10.7)}$$

If our problem solution is at a tangency point, then the optimal value of X_2 will satisfy

$$\frac{\partial GNP}{\partial X_2} \equiv - \frac{X_2^{-1/3}(1 - X_2^{2/3})^{-1/2}}{3} + \frac{2\sqrt{2}}{3} = 0,$$

i.e.

$$8(X_2^{2/3})^2 - 8(X_2^{2/3}) + 1 = 0.$$

This implies that either

$$(X_2^{2/3}) = \tfrac{1}{2} + \frac{\sqrt{2}}{4} = 0.854$$

---

[13]   Notice that it is not necessary to consider the constant returns section of production function 2. It cannot be relevant since the economy's total labor endowment is only just equal to θ_2.

or

$$(X_2^{2/3}) = \tfrac{1}{2} - \frac{\sqrt{2}}{4} = 0.146,$$

i.e. either

$$X_2 = 0.789$$

or

$$X_2 = 0.056.$$

The only other possibility that need be considered is the corner solution at B, i.e.

$$X_2 = 0.000.$$

By substitution into (E3.10.7) we find that

$$X_2 = 0.789 \;\; \text{implies} \;\; GNP = 1.126,$$

$$X_2 = 0.056 \;\; \text{implies} \;\; GNP = 0.977$$

and

$$X_2 = 0.000 \;\; \text{implies} \;\; GNP = 1.000.$$

(Notice that in terms of fig. E3.10.1, we have located points A, D and B.) Hence our solution is

$$X_2 = 0.789,$$

with

$$L_2 = 0.854,$$

$$L_1 = 0.146$$

and

$$X_1 = 0.382.$$

(b)   Starting from (E3.10.6), we note that the domestic prices value of *GNP* is now

$$GNP = (1 - X_2^{2/3})^{1/2} + \sqrt{(2)}\,X_2. \tag{E3.10.8}$$

The same sequence of steps as were followed in part (a) generate three possible solutions for X_2:

$$X_2 = 0.913; \;\; X_2 = 0.0143 \quad \text{and} \quad X_2 = 0.$$

Corresponding levels of *GNP* in domestic prices are, respectively, 1.534, 0.990 and 1.000. Hence our solution is

$$X_2 = 0.913,$$

with

$$L_2 = 0.941,$$

$$L_1 = 0.059$$

and

$$X_1 = 0.243.$$

GNP in world prices is

$$GNP_w = 0.243 + (2\sqrt{(2)}/3) \times 0.913 = 1.104.$$

By comparing the solution in this part with that in (a), we find that for the two-commodity model the imposition of a 50 percent tariff on commodity 2 has lowered the world prices value of *GNP* from 1.126 to 1.104, i.e. the world prices value of *GNP* is about 1.95 percent lower.

(c) This time our problem is to choose non-negative values for X_1, X_3, L_1 and L_3 to maximize

$$P_1 X_1 + P_3 X_3$$

subject to

$$L_1 + L_3 = 1$$

$$X_1 = L_1^{\gamma_1}$$

$$X_3 = L_3^{\gamma_3}, \quad L_3 \leqslant \theta_3$$

$$= a_3 L_3, \quad L_3 > \theta_3,$$

i.e. we chose non-negative values for X_1 and X_3 to maximize

$$GNP \equiv X_1 + \tfrac{4}{3} X_3 \qquad\qquad\qquad (E3.10.9)$$

subject to one of the following being valid:

$$X_1^2 + X_3^{2/3} - 1 = 0 \quad \text{and} \quad 0 \leqslant X_3 \leqslant 0.354 \qquad (E3.10.10)$$

or

$$X_1^2 + 1.414 X_3 - 1 = 0 \quad \text{and} \quad 0.354 \leqslant X_3 \leqslant 0.707. \qquad (E3.10.11)$$

Expressions (E3.10.10) and (E3.10.11) describe the production possibilities frontier over the ranges where $X_3 \leqslant \theta_3^{\gamma_3}$ and $X_3 \geqslant \theta_3^{\gamma_3}$.

If the optimal value for X_3 lies in the interval $[0, \theta_3^{\gamma_3}]$, then the value for *GNP* will be given by

$$GNP = (1 - X_3^{2/3})^{1/2} + \tfrac{4}{3} X_3.$$

Either X_3 will be a boundary point, i.e.

$X_3 = 0$ (implies $GNP = 1.0$)

or

$X_3 = 0.354$ (implies $GNP = 1.179$),

or X_3 will satisfy

$$\frac{\mathrm{d}GNP}{\mathrm{d}X_3} = 0. \qquad\qquad\qquad (E3.10.12)$$

By following the method in part (a), the reader will find that the only value for X_3 both in the interval $[0, 0.354]$ and consistent with (E3.10.12) is

$X_3 = 0.0173$ (implies $GNP = 0.989$).

If the optimal value for X_3 lies in the interval $[\theta^{\gamma_3}, a_3]$, then the value for GNP will be given by

$$GNP = (1 - 1.414 X_3)^{1/2} + \tfrac{4}{3} X_3.$$

Again, either X_3 will be a boundary point, i.e.

$X_3 = 0.354$ (implies $GNP = 1.179$)

or

$X_3 = 0.707$ (implies $GNP = 0.942$),

or X_3 will satisfy

$$\frac{\mathrm{d}GNP}{\mathrm{d}X_3} \equiv -0.707(1 - 1.414 X_3)^{-1/2} + \tfrac{4}{3} = 0, \qquad (E3.10.13)$$

i.e.

$X_3 = 0.508$ (implies $GNP = 1.208$).

On comparing the values for GNP associated with the various possibilities for the optimal value of X_3, we find that our problem solution is

$X_3 = 0.508,$

with

$L_3 = 0.718,$

$L_1 = 0.282$

and

$$X_1 = 0.531.$$

GNP in both world and domestic prices is 1.208.

(d) To see why goods 2 and 3 need never be produced simultaneously, we suggest that you sketch the production possibilities frontier for goods 2 and 3 for a fixed labor commitment to the automotive engineering industry. This frontier will be concave from above and a corner solution will always be consistent with *GNP* maximizing.

Under free trade, goods 1 and 3 will be produced. In part (a) we found that when good 2 is produced, without protection, the maximum value for domestic prices *GNP* is only 1.126. However, with the automotive engineering industry specializing in good 3, domestic prices *GNP* is 1.208, see part (c).

With a 50 percent tariff or export subsidy on good 2, the automotive engineering industry will specialize in good 2. In part (b) we found that under protection for good 2, the domestic prices value for *GNP*, with good 2 being produced, is 1.534. With good 3 being produced, the domestic prices value of *GNP* would be 1.208, see part (c).

The tariff on good 2, by inducing specialization in the 'wrong' good, leads to a reduction of about 9 percent in the world prices value of *GNP*, i.e. from 1.208 (see part (c)) to 1.104, see part (b).

C. Some difficulties concerning the use of micro restrictions at the macro level

Exercise 3.11. Aggregation across households

In the standard theory of consumer demand each household is assumed to behave as though it chooses its consumption bundle to maximize a strictly quasiconcave utility function subject to its budget constraint. In applications of the theory, economists have usually assumed that it applies at a macro level, i.e. they have assumed that total household consumption behavior can be described as though the aggregate consumption bundle is chosen to maximize a utility function subject to the aggregate budget constraint. Unfortunately, as you will find in this problem and in E3.12 and E3.13, the aggregate utility-maximizing model cannot be justified simply on the basis of individual utility maximizing.

We consider an economy consisting of two households, 1 and 2. Both have incomes of \$ 10, i.e. $Y_1 = 10$ and $Y_2 = 10$. There are two commodities, a and b, and household i's consumptions of a and b are denoted by C_{ia} and C_{ib}. Assume that we observe the following: when commodity prices, P_a and P_b are given by

$$P_a = 1 \quad \text{and} \quad P_b = 1,$$

then

$$C_{1a} = 1, \quad C_{1b} = 9$$

and

$$C_{2a} = 5, \quad C_{2b} = 5.$$

When commodity prices change to

$$P_a = 2 \quad \text{and} \quad P_b = \tfrac{1}{3}$$

while incomes remain constant at 10, then

$$C_{1a} = 3\tfrac{2}{3}, \quad C_{1b} = 8$$

and

$$C_{2a} = 4\tfrac{1}{2}, \quad C_{2b} = 3.$$

(a) Is the behavior of household 1 consistent with the strong axiom of revealed preference? Is it consistent with a standard utility-maximizing model? How about for household 2?

(b) Can the aggregate behavior of the household sector be described in terms of a utility-maximizing model? That is, does there exist a utility function, U, such that aggregate consumption of a and b, C_a and C_b, has responded to the price changes as though C_a and C_b were chosen to maximize

$$U(C_a, C_b)$$

subject to

$$P_a C_a + P_b C_b \leqslant Y,$$

where

$$Y \equiv Y_1 + Y_2,$$

i.e. Y is the aggregate expenditure of the household sector. *Note*: a careful diagram might be particularly helpful for answering this question.

Answer. Fig. E3.11.1 provides a diagramatic solution. In that figure, AA and BB are the initial and final budget lines for both households. Household 1's initial and final consumption bundles are shown as

$$C^1(1) = (1,9) \quad \text{and} \quad C^1(2) = (3\tfrac{2}{3}, 8),$$

and household 2's consumption bundles are

$$C^2(1) = (5,5) \quad \text{and} \quad C^2(2) = (4\tfrac{1}{2}, 3).$$

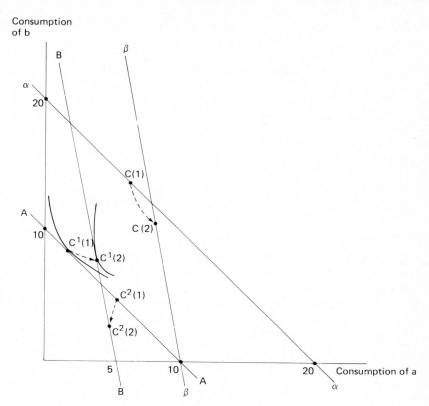

Figure E3.11.1

For household 1, $C^1(2)$ is revealed preferred to $C^1(1)$. However, the reverse does not hold and thus for household 1 the movement from $C^1(1)$ to $C^1(2)$ does not violate the strong axiom of revealed preference. For household 2, $C^2(1)$ is revealed preferred to $C^2(2)$ whereas $C^2(2)$ is not revealed preferred to $C^2(1)$. Hence household 2's behavior also is consistent with the strong axiom of revealed preference. Since the behavior of the households is consistent with the strong axiom of revealed preference, their behavior is consistent with constrained utility maximizing, see E3.4. Indifference curves for a possible utility function for household 1 are sketched on our diagram.

At the aggregate level, the initial budget line is $\alpha\alpha$ and the initial consumption bundle is

$$C(1) = C^1(1) + C^2(1) = (6, 14).$$

The final budget line is $\beta\beta$ with the resulting consumption bundle being

$$C(2) = C^1(2) + C^2(2) = (8\tfrac{1}{6}, 11).$$

From the diagram (or by calculation) we see that $C(1)$ is revealed preferred to $C(2)$ and that $C(2)$ is revealed preferred to $C(1)$. Hence the aggregate behavior is inconsistent with the strong axiom of revealed preference and therefore it is inconsistent with any standard constrained utility-maximizing model.

Exercise 3.12.   *Homogeneity and aggregate demand functions*

Assume that the economy contains n households and that each household is a constrained utility maximizer. That is, each household, i, chooses its consumption vector C_i so as to maximize

$$U_i(C_i)$$

subject to

$$P'C_i = Y_i,$$

where P is the vector of commodity prices and Y_i is i's expenditure level.

(a) What will happen to aggregate commodity demands if all commodity prices and household expenditure levels increase by 10 percent?

(b) How would you modify your last answer if the 10 percent increase in all prices is accompanied by a 10 percent increase in aggregate expenditure (i.e. $\Sigma_i Y_i$ increases by 10 percent) but the expenditure of some households increases by more than 10 percent, while for others the increase is less than 10 percent.

Answer.   (a) A 10 percent increase in Y_i and all prices will leave C_i unchanged. Hence $\Sigma_{i=1}^n C_i$ will also be unchanged.

(b) The assumption that households are constrained utility maximizers implies that aggregate demand functions of the form

$$C_{\cdot j} = f_j(P, Y_1,...,Y_n) \tag{E3.12.1}$$

are homogeneous of degree zero in prices and expenditure levels where $C_{\cdot j}$ denotes aggregate consumption of good j. However, this is certainly not enough to allow us to conclude that demand functions of the form

$$C_{\cdot j} = f_j(P, Y) \tag{E3.12.2}$$

are homogeneous of degree zero in prices and the aggregate expenditure level or in fact that such functions exist at all.[14]

---

[14]   Aggregate demand functions of the form (E3.12.2) are said 'not to exist' if more than one value of $C_{\cdot j}$ can be associated with a single value for (P, Y).

Unless all households have the same marginal propensity to spend on good j, aggregate consumption of good j can change in response to a 10 percent increase in all prices and a nonuniformly distributed 10 percent increase in aggregate expenditure. For example, C_j will increase if households having high marginal propensities to spend on good j experience increases in their expenditure levels relative to households having low marginal propensities to spend on good j.

Exercise 3.13. *The additivity assumption and aggregation across households*

Study the data for a two-household, three-commodity model given in table E3.13.1. Assume that each household behaves as if it were maximizing an additive utility function subject to its budget constraint.

Table E3.13.1

	Household R	Household P
Own-price elasticity for good 1	$e_{11}^{R} = -1$	$e_{11}^{P} = -13/40$
Budget shares	$(\alpha_1^R, \alpha_2^R, \alpha_3^R) = (\frac{1}{2}, \frac{1}{4}, \frac{1}{4})$	$(\alpha_1^P, \alpha_2^P, \alpha_3^P) = (\frac{1}{3}, \frac{1}{3}, \frac{1}{3})$
Expenditure elasticities	$(E_1^R, E_2^R, E_3^R) = (1, 1, 1)$	$(E_1^P, E_2^P, E_3^P) = (\frac{1}{2}, \frac{1}{2}, 2)$
Expenditure level	$Y^R = 1$	$Y^P = 1$

(a) Compute the matrices of own- and cross-price elasticities of demand, i.e. compute the matrices e^P and e^R where

$$e^R = \begin{bmatrix} e_{11}^R & e_{12}^R & e_{13}^R \\ e_{21}^R & e_{22}^R & e_{23}^R \\ e_{31}^R & e_{32}^R & e_{33}^R \end{bmatrix}$$

and e^P is similarly defined for household P.

(b) How should e^P and e^R be combined to form the matrix, e, of own- and cross-price elasticities for the household sector? Compute e. *Hint*: note that

$$e_{ij} = \frac{\partial(x_i^R + x_i^P)}{\partial P_j} \frac{P_j}{x_i^R + x_i^P},$$

where e_{ij} is the aggregate (or market) cross-elasticity of demand for good i with respect to changes in the price, P_j, of good j, and x_i^P and x_i^R are the quantities of i consumed by households P and R.

(c) Assume that the distribution across households in their expenditure levels remains constant, i.e. Y^R/Y^P is fixed. How will commodity demands respond to a 1 percent increase in aggregate expenditure? Compute the aggregate expenditure elasticities of demand, E_i, for $i = 1, 2, 3$, under the assumption of fixed household shares in aggregate expenditure.

(d) Compute the vector of aggregate budget shares, $\alpha = (\alpha_1, \alpha_2, \alpha_3)$.

(e) Are the aggregate elasticities, e_{ij}, E_i, α_i, $i, j = 1, 2, 3$, consistent with a model in which the household sector is viewed as maximizing an additive utility function

$$\sum_{i=1}^{3} U_i(x_i)$$

subject to an aggregate budget constraint

$$P_1 x_1 + P_2 x_2 + P_3 x_3 = Y,$$

where x_1, x_2 and x_3 are aggregate consumption levels, i.e.

$$x_i = x_i^R + x_i^P, \quad i = 1, 2, 3,$$

and Y is the aggregate expenditure level, i.e.

$$Y = Y^R + Y^P?$$

Are the aggregate elasticities consistent with a model in which the household sector is viewed as if it were a single constrained utility maximizer, but in which the utility function is not necessarily additive?

Answer. (a) We recall E2.17(f). In fact, household P's expenditure and price elasticities are the same as those for the consumer in that earlier exercise. By following E2.17, we find that ω^R and ω^P, the Frisch parameters for the two households, are -1 and -4, respectively, and that the e matrices are

$$e^R = \begin{bmatrix} -1 & 0 & 0 \\ 0 & -1 & 0 \\ 0 & 0 & -1 \end{bmatrix} \quad \text{and} \quad e^P = \begin{bmatrix} -\frac{13}{48} & -\frac{7}{48} & -\frac{4}{48} \\ -\frac{7}{48} & -\frac{13}{48} & -\frac{4}{48} \\ -\frac{28}{48} & -\frac{28}{48} & -\frac{40}{48} \end{bmatrix}. \quad \text{(E3.13.1)}$$

(b) Continuing from the 'hint' we note that

$$e_{ij} = \frac{\partial x_i^R}{\partial P_j} \frac{P_j}{x_i^R} \frac{x_i^R}{x_i^R + x_i^P} + \frac{\partial x_i^P}{\partial P_j} \frac{P_j}{x_i^P} \frac{x_i^P}{x_i^R + x_i^P},$$

i.e.

$$e_{ij} = e_{ij}^R S_i^R + e_{ij}^P S_i^P,$$ (E3.13.2)

where S_i^R and S_i^P are the two households' shares in the aggregate consumption of good i, i.e.

$$S_i^R = \frac{x_i^R}{x_i^R + x_i^P} \quad \text{and} \quad S_i^P = \frac{x_i^P}{x_i^R + x_i^P}.$$

The S's can be computed as

$$S_i^Z = \frac{\alpha_i^Z Y^Z}{\alpha_i^R Y^R + \alpha_i^P Y^P}, \quad i = 1,...,3, \quad Z = R, P.$$ (E3.13.3)

From (E3.13.3) we find that

$$(S_1^R, S_2^R, S_3^R) = (\tfrac{3}{5}, \tfrac{3}{7}, \tfrac{3}{7})$$ (E3.13.4a)

and

$$(S_1^P, S_2^P, S_3^P) = (\tfrac{2}{5}, \tfrac{4}{7}, \tfrac{4}{7}).$$ (E3.13.4b)

Finally, using (E3.13.1), (E3.13.2) and (E3.13.4) we obtain

$$e = \begin{bmatrix} -0.708 & -0.058 & -0.033 \\ -0.083 & -0.583 & -0.048 \\ -0.333 & -0.333 & -0.905 \end{bmatrix}.$$ (E3.13.5)

(c) We define E_i as

$$E_i = \frac{\partial(x_i^R + x_i^P)}{\partial Y} \frac{Y}{x_i^R + x_i^P},$$

where

$$Y \equiv Y^P + Y^R.$$

Hence

$$E_i = \frac{\partial x_i^R}{\partial Y} \frac{Y}{x_i^R + x_i^P} + \frac{\partial x_i^P}{\partial Y} \frac{Y}{x_i^R + x_i^P},$$

i.e.

$$E_i = \sum_{Z=P, R} \frac{\partial x_i^Z}{\partial Y^Z} \frac{\partial Y^Z}{\partial Y} \frac{Y}{Y^Z} \frac{Y^Z}{x_i^Z} \frac{x_i^Z}{x_i^R + x_i^P}.$$ (E3.13.6)

Since the distribution across households in their expenditure levels remains constant, the elasticity of household Z's expenditure level with respect to changes in aggregate expenditure is unity, i.e.

$$\frac{\partial Y^Z}{\partial Y} \frac{Y}{Y^Z} = 1, \quad Z = \text{R, P.}$$

Hence (E3.13.6) simplifies to

$$E_i = E_i^R S_i^R + E_i^P S_i^P. \tag{E3.13.7}$$

Expressions (E3.13.4) and (E3.13.7) give

$$(E_1, E_2, E_3) = (0.800, 0.714, 1.571).$$

(d)

$$\alpha_i = \frac{P_i(x_i^R + x_i^P)}{Y}$$

i.e.

$$\alpha_i = \frac{P_i x_i^R}{Y^R} \frac{Y^R}{Y} + \frac{P_i x_i^P}{Y^P} \frac{Y^P}{Y}. \tag{E3.13.8}$$

Hence, the aggregate budget share for good i is a weighted average of the budget shares for each of the households, the weights being the individual household shares in aggregate expenditure. From (E3.13.8) we obtain

$$(\alpha_1, \alpha_2, \alpha_3) = (0.417, 0.292, 0.292).$$

(e) For the aggregate elasticities to be consistent with an *additive* utility maximizing model, it is necessary that there exists ω, the Frisch parameter, such that

$$e_{ij} = -E_i \alpha_j \left(1 + \frac{E_j}{\omega}\right), \quad \text{for all } i \neq j.$$

(Recall E2.17 and (E2.17.1).) That is, it is necessary that the expressions

$$\omega_{ij} = -\frac{\alpha_j E_i E_j}{e_{ij} + \alpha_j E_i}$$

have the same value for all $i \neq j$. After some arithmetic, we find that

$$[\omega_{ij}] = - \begin{bmatrix} * & 0.95 & 1.83 \\ 1.11 & * & 2.04 \\ 1.63 & 2.62 & * \end{bmatrix}.$$

We can conclude that the aggregate elasticities are not consistent with a model in which the household sector is viewed as maximizing an additive utility function.

For the aggregate elasticities to be consistent with any standard utility-maximizing model, it is necessary that they satisfy the symmetry condition, i.e.

$$v_{ij} = v_{ji}, \quad \text{for} \quad i \neq j$$

where

$$v_{ij} \equiv \alpha_i(e_{ij} + E_i\alpha_j).$$

(Recall E2.6 and (E2.6.2).) Again, some arithmetic establishes that

$$v_{ij} = \begin{bmatrix} * & 0.073 & 0.083 \\ 0.063 & * & 0.047 \\ 0.094 & 0.037 & * \end{bmatrix}.$$

Since this matrix is not symmetric, we have shown that the aggregate elasticities are inconsistent with a utility-maximizing model. Are the aggregate elasticities consistent with the homogeneity and Engel aggregation restrictions?

D. An integrability proposition

Exercise 3.14. The triad and integrability

In our answer for E2.8 we raised the question of whether the triad [15] summarizes the complete set of useful restrictions on the demand elasticities which flow from the constrained utility-maximizing model. This exercise is concerned with answering that question. Our method is to prove an integrability proposition. It will be recalled from E3.4 that integrability is concerned with going from demand functions back to utility functions. Given a set of demand elasticities which are consistent with the triad and the sign restriction (E2.10.2), you will be asked to construct a standard utility-maximizing model which is consistent with the demand elasticities. The fact that such a construction is always possible will prove that the triad and the sign restriction contain all the information, relevant for demand functions, flowing from the standard unrestricted utility-maximizing model. Fig. E3.14.1 summarizes the overall strategy.

---

[15] The triad is the Engel aggregation and the homogeneity and symmetry restrictions, see E2.1, E2.2 and E2.6.

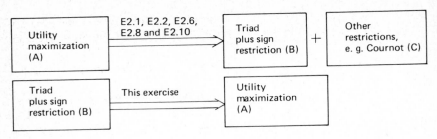

That is $A \Rightarrow B \cup C$

and $\quad B \Rightarrow A$

Thus $\quad B \Rightarrow B \cup C$

Hence $B \Rightarrow C$

We conclude that the Triad plus the Sign restriction imply all other restrictions on demand functions flowing from the utility maximizing model.

Figure E3.14.1

We consider a household whose consumption vector, C, is

$$\bar{C} = \begin{pmatrix} 1 \\ 2 \\ 1 \end{pmatrix} \tag{E3.14.1}$$

when P, the commodity price vector, is

$$\bar{P} = \begin{pmatrix} 1 \\ 1 \\ 1 \end{pmatrix} \tag{E3.14.2}$$

and Y, the level of expenditure, is

$$\bar{Y} = 4. \tag{E3.14.3}$$

Assume the household's consumption response to small changes in P and Y is described by

$$dC = A\,dP + b\,dY, \tag{E3.14.4a}$$

where

$$A = \begin{bmatrix} -3 & 2 & 0 \\ 2\frac{1}{4} & -4 & \frac{3}{4} \\ -\frac{1}{4} & 0 & -1\frac{3}{4} \end{bmatrix} \tag{E3.14.4b}$$

and

$$b = \begin{pmatrix} \frac{1}{4} \\ \frac{1}{4} \\ \frac{1}{2} \end{pmatrix}.$$
(E3.14.4c)

Your overall task is to construct a utility function U, such that the data in (E3.14.1)–(E3.14.4) is consistent with the model: choose C to maximize

$$U(C)$$

subject to

$$P'C = Y.$$

You will find that such a construction is possible, but only because the data satisfies the triad and the sign restriction.

(a) Check that (E3.14.1)–(E3.14.4) are consistent with the triad. (Remember that the elements of A and b are derivatives rather than elasticities.) Compute the matrix G defined by

$$G = A + b\bar{C}',$$

i.e.
(E3.14.5)

$$G_{ij} = A_{ij} + b_i \bar{C}_j, \quad \text{for all } i \text{ and } j,$$

where G_{ij}, A_{ij}, b_j and $\bar{C}_j$ are the ijth and jth components of G, A, b and $\bar{C}$. Note for future reference that (E3.14.4a) can be rewritten as

$$dC = GdP + b(dY - (dP)'\bar{C}).$$
(E3.14.6)

(b) This is not a question, just some parenthetical revision! Recall (E2.6.1), i.e.

$$\begin{bmatrix} H & P \\ P' & 0 \end{bmatrix} \begin{bmatrix} dC \\ -d\lambda \end{bmatrix} = \begin{bmatrix} \lambda dP \\ dY - (dP)'C \end{bmatrix}. {}^{16}$$
(E3.14.7)

This equation was derived from a utility-maximizing model. It describes the relationship between changes in the household's consumption vector and marginal utility of expenditure, and changes in the price vector and expenditure

---

[16] The notation has been brought into line with the present exercise.

level. Recall that H is symmetric and is the Hessian matrix of the utility function. In E2.17, we solved (E3.14.7) and found that

$$\begin{bmatrix} dC \\ -d\lambda \end{bmatrix} = \frac{1}{P'H^{-1}P} \left[\begin{array}{c|c} (P'H^{-1}P)H^{-1} - H^{-1}PP'H^{-1} & H^{-1}P \\ \hline P'H^{-1} & -1 \end{array} \right]$$

$$\times \begin{bmatrix} \lambda dP \\ dY - (dP)'C \end{bmatrix}. \qquad \text{(E3.14.8)}$$

We can rewrite part of (E3.14.8) as

$$dC = \left[\lambda H^{-1} - \frac{\lambda}{P'H^{-1}P} H^{-1}PP'H^{-1} \right] \cdot [dP]$$

$$+ \left[\frac{1}{P'H^{-1}P} H^{-1}P \right] (dY - (dP)'C). \qquad \text{(E3.14.9)}$$

(c) Compute values for the 3×3 matrix $\widetilde{H}$ and the scalar $\widetilde{\lambda} > 0$, such that $\widetilde{H}$ is symmetric and satisfies

$$G = \widetilde{\lambda}\widetilde{H}^{-1} - \frac{\widetilde{\lambda}}{\bar{P}'\widetilde{H}^{-1}\bar{P}} \widetilde{H}^{-1}\bar{P}\bar{P}'\widetilde{H}^{-1} \qquad \text{(E3.14.10)}$$

and

$$b = \frac{1}{\bar{P}'\widetilde{H}^{-1}\bar{P}} \widetilde{H}^{-1}\bar{P}, \qquad \text{(E3.14.11)}$$

where G was computed in part (a) and $\bar{P}$ and b have the values shown in (E3.14.2) and (E3.14.4c).[17] Show that the quadratic utility-maximizing model: choose C to maximize

$$U(C) \equiv v'C + \tfrac{1}{2}C'\widetilde{H}C \qquad \text{(E3.14.12)}$$

subject to

$$P'C = Y,$$

is consistent with (E3.14.4). How should the parameter vector v be chosen so that (E3.14.12) is also consistent with (E3.14.1)–(E3.14.3). That is, compute v

---

[17] *Hint*: substitute from (E3.14.11) into (E3.14.10) and assume that $(\bar{P}'\widetilde{H}^{-1}\bar{P}) = -1$ and $\widetilde{\lambda} = 1$. You will find that other normalizations can be used. They will produce alternative, but equally acceptable values for H.

such that if the utility-maximizing problem (E3.14.12) is confronted with the 'base period' prices, $\bar{P}$, and expenditure level, $\bar{Y}$, then the solution is $\bar{C}$.

Answer.   (a)   First we consider the Engel aggregation, i.e.

$$\sum_k \alpha_k E_k = 1,$$

(E3.14.13)

where α_k and E_k are respectively the budget share and expenditure elasticity for the good k. (E3.14.13) will be satisfied if and only if

$$\sum_k P_k \frac{\partial C_k}{\partial Y} = 1.$$

(E3.14.14)

Since

$$(\bar{P})'b = 1,$$

(E3.14.15)

the data contained in (E3.14.1)–(E3.14.4) is consistent with the Engel aggregation.

Next we check the homogeneity restriction, i.e.

$$\sum_k e_{ik} = -E_i, \quad \text{for all } i,$$

(E3.14.16)

where e_{ik} is the cross-elasticity of demand for good i with respect to changes in price k. (E3.14.16) will be satisfied if and only if

$$\sum_k \frac{\partial C_i}{\partial P_k} P_k = - \frac{\partial C_i}{\partial Y} Y, \quad \text{for all } i.$$

(E3.14.17)

Since

$$A\bar{P} = -b\bar{Y}$$

(E3.14.18)

the data contained in (E3.14.1)–(E3.14.4) is consistent with the homogeneity restriction.

Finally, we check the symmetry restriction. In E2.6 we presented the symmetry restriction in an elasticity form as

$$\alpha_i(e_{ij} + E_i \alpha_j) = \alpha_j(e_{ji} + E_j \alpha_i), \quad \text{for all } i \neq j.$$

(E3.14.19)

In terms of derivatives, we find that (E3.14.19) is valid if and only if

$$\frac{\partial C_i}{\partial P_j} + \frac{\partial C_i}{\partial Y} C_j = \frac{\partial C_j}{\partial P_i} + \frac{\partial C_j}{\partial Y} C_i, \quad \text{for all } i \neq j.$$

(E3.14.20)

Hence, the symmetry restriction is satisfied if and only if the matrix G, defined by (E3.14.5), is symmetric. We compute G, obtaining the symmetric matrix

$$G = \begin{bmatrix} -2\frac{3}{4} & 2\frac{1}{2} & \frac{1}{4} \\ 2\frac{1}{2} & -3\frac{1}{2} & 1 \\ \frac{1}{4} & 1 & -1\frac{1}{4} \end{bmatrix}.$$ (E3.14.21)

It is also worth noting that G is negative semidefinite. [18] Hence we conclude that the data presented in (E3.14.1)–(E3.14.4) not only satisfies the triad, but also is consistent with the sign restriction, (E2.10.2).

(c) By substituting from (E3.14.11) into (E3.14.10) we obtain

$$G = \widetilde{\lambda}\widetilde{H}^{-1} - \widetilde{\lambda}(\bar{P}'\widetilde{H}^{-1}\bar{P})\,bb'.$$ (E3.14.22)

Let us suppose that

$$\bar{P}'\widetilde{H}^{-1}\bar{P} = -1 \quad \text{and} \quad \widetilde{\lambda} = 1,$$ (E3.14.23)

i.e. we will look for an $\widetilde{H}$ and $\widetilde{\lambda}$ which satisfy (E3.14.23) in addition to (E3.14.10) and (E3.14.11).

Under (E3.14.23), (E3.14.22) becomes

$$G = \widetilde{H}^{-1} + bb',$$

i.e.

$$\widetilde{H}^{-1} = G - bb'.$$ (E3.14.24)

This gives

$$\widetilde{H}^{-1} = \begin{bmatrix} -2\frac{13}{16} & 2\frac{7}{16} & \frac{1}{8} \\ 2\frac{7}{16} & -3\frac{9}{16} & \frac{7}{8} \\ \frac{1}{8} & \frac{7}{8} & -1\frac{1}{2} \end{bmatrix} \simeq \begin{bmatrix} -2.81 & 2.44 & 0.13 \\ 2.44 & -3.56 & 0.88 \\ 0.13 & 0.88 & -1.50 \end{bmatrix},$$ (E3.14.25)

and by inversion we obtain

$$\widetilde{H} = \begin{bmatrix} -1.38 & -1.14 & -0.79 \\ -1.14 & -1.27 & -0.85 \\ -0.79 & -0.85 & -1.23 \end{bmatrix}.$$ (E3.14.26)

[18] Most texts in mathematical economics and econometrics contain a section on conditions for negative definiteness and negative semidefiniteness. For example, see Lancaster (1968, pp. 297–300), Goldberger (1964, pp. 34–39), Intriligator (1971, pp. 495–497). Interested readers might check the negative semidefiniteness of G by computing the eigenvalues or the principal minors. Alternatively, they could note the near dominance of the negative diagonal (see Lancaster (1968, pp. 311–312)).

At this stage, you may find that it is reassuring to substitute $\tilde{\lambda} = 1$ and the $\tilde{H}^{-1}$ given by (E3.14.25) into (E3.14.10), (E3.14.11) and (E3.14.23). Apart from rounding errors you will find that we have in fact obtained a $\tilde{\lambda}$ and an $\tilde{H}$ as required. It might also be useful to check through the steps involved in the construction of $\tilde{H}$ to convince yourself that had our data been incompatible with (E3.14.15) or (E3.14.18), or if G had not been symmetric, then it would not have been possible to construct a symmetric $\tilde{H}$ which was compatible with (E3.14.10) and (E3.14.11).

The final part of this exercise is to check that, with a suitable choice for v, the utility-maximizing model (E3.14.12) is compatible with (E3.14.1)–(E3.14.4). From (E3.14.12) we obtain the first-order conditions [19]

$$v + \tilde{H}C = \psi P \tag{E3.14.27a}$$

and

$$P'C = Y, \tag{E3.14.27b}$$

where ψ is the Lagrangian multiplier. If (E3.14.27) is to be compatible with the 'base period' data, then v and ψ will satisfy

$$v + \tilde{H}\overline{C} = \psi \overline{P}$$

and

$$\overline{P}'\overline{C} = \overline{Y}.$$

Thus, v and ψ will satisfy

$$v = \psi \overline{P} - \tilde{H}\overline{C}$$

and

$$\overline{C}'v = \psi \overline{Y} - \overline{C}'\tilde{H}\overline{C},$$

i.e. v and ψ will satisfy

$$\begin{pmatrix} v_1 \\ v_2 \\ v_3 \end{pmatrix} = \begin{pmatrix} \psi \\ \psi \\ \psi \end{pmatrix} + \begin{pmatrix} 4.45 \\ 4.53 \\ 3.72 \end{pmatrix}$$

---

[19] Notice the role of the sign restriction. Since G is negative semidefinite, it follows from (E3.14.24) that H^{-1} and H are negative definite. Consequently, our constructed utility function is strictly quasiconcave and (E3.14.27) are necessary and sufficient conditions for a solution of (E3.14.12).

and $v_1 + 2v_2 + v_3 = 4\psi + 17.23$. These four equations give the solution

$$\bar{\psi} = 1$$

and $(v_1, v_2, v_3) = (5.45, 5.53, 4.72)$.

Returning to (E3.14.27), we obtain

$$\widetilde{H} dC = (d\psi)\bar{P} + \bar{\psi} dP$$

and

$$\bar{P}' dC + \bar{C}' dP = dY,$$

i.e.

$$\begin{bmatrix} \widetilde{H} & \bar{P} \\ \\ \bar{P}' & 0 \end{bmatrix} \begin{bmatrix} dC \\ \\ -d\psi \end{bmatrix} = \begin{bmatrix} dP \\ \\ dY - (dP)'\bar{C} \end{bmatrix}.$$

Hence,

$$dC = \left[\widetilde{H}^{-1} - \frac{1}{\bar{P}' \widetilde{H}^{-1} \bar{P}} \widetilde{H}^{-1} \bar{P} \bar{P}' \widetilde{H}^{-1} \right] dP$$

$$+ \left[\frac{1}{\bar{P}' \widetilde{H}^{-1} \bar{P}} \widetilde{H}^{-1} \bar{P} \right] (dY - (dP)'\bar{C}),$$

i.e.

$$dC = \begin{bmatrix} -2.75 & 2.50 & 0.25 \\ 2.50 & -3.50 & 1.00 \\ 0.25 & 1.00 & -1.25 \end{bmatrix} dP + \begin{bmatrix} 0.25 \\ 0.25 \\ 0.50 \end{bmatrix} dY - \left[\begin{pmatrix} 0.25 \\ 0.25 \\ 0.50 \end{pmatrix} (1 \ \ 2 \ \ 1) \right] dP,$$

i.e.

$$dC = \begin{bmatrix} -3.00 & 2.00 & 0 \\ 2.25 & -4.00 & 0.75 \\ -0.25 & 0 & -1.75 \end{bmatrix} dP + \begin{bmatrix} 0.25 \\ 0.25 \\ 0.50 \end{bmatrix} dY. \qquad \text{(E3.14.28)}$$

Thus, we see that the utility-maximizing model (E3.14.12) is compatible with (E3.14.4).

In summary, we have found that our data, (E3.14.1)–(E3.14.4), is compatible with the model in which C is chosen to maximize

$$U(C) \equiv C' \begin{bmatrix} 5.45 \\ 5.53 \\ 4.72 \end{bmatrix} + \tfrac{1}{2} C' \begin{bmatrix} -1.38 & -1.14 & -0.79 \\ -1.14 & -1.27 & -0.85 \\ -0.79 & -0.85 & -1.23 \end{bmatrix} C \quad \text{(E3.14.29)}$$

subject to

$$P'C = Y.$$

Apart from being compatible with the triad and the sign restriction, there is nothing special about the numbers in (E3.14.1)–(E3.14.4). The method used to construct the utility function (E3.14.29) would have succeeded on any other set of numbers satisfying those conditions. In terms of fig. E3.14.1, we have demonstrated that

$$B \Rightarrow A.$$

E. Obstacles to Pareto optimal market solutions

Even where markets are perfect, there arise obstacles to the achievement of Pareto optimal consumption allocations. (Notice that by confining ourselves to Pareto optimality, we are automatically abstracting from questions of the interpersonal distribution of welfare.) In the next exercise and in E3.16, you are asked to consider two of these obstacles to Pareto optimality: interdependent utilities and public goods.

Exercise 3.15. Interdependent utilities

Assume that our society consists of two individuals 1 and 2, who consume two goods x and y. Let x_i and y_i be the amounts of goods x and y consumed by individual i. Let the individual's utility functions be

$$U_1 = U(x_1, y_1) = x_1 y_1$$

and

$$U_2 = V(x_2, y_2, y_1) = \frac{x_2 y_2^2}{y_1}.$$

How do you interpret the appearance of y_1 in the second person's utility function?

Show that individual utility maximization by both consumers, subject to budget constraints

$$p_x x_i + p_y y_i = B_i, \quad i = 1, 2$$

will, in general, result in a consumption pattern that is not Pareto optimal.

Answer. We derive some necessary conditions for a Pareto optimum. Let $(x_1^0, y_1^0, x_2^0, y_2^0)$ be the consumption levels. Then for $(x_1^0, y_1^0, x_2^0, y_2^0)$ to be Pareto optimal, it must maximize man 1's utility subject to man 2 maintaining his utility level at $K_2 = V(x_2^0, y_2^0, y_1^0)$ and meeting the combined budget constraint. Alternatively, for Pareto optimality $(x_1^0, y_1^0, x_2^0, y_2^0)$ must maximize man 2's utility subject to man 1 maintaining his utility level at $K_1 = U(x_1^0, y_1^0)$ and meeting the combined budget constraint.

Set up the Lagrangian:

$$L = U(x_1, y_1) - \lambda_1 [K_2 - V(x_2, y_2, y_1)]$$
$$- \lambda_2 [p_x(x_1 + x_2) + p_y(y_1 + y_2) - (B_1 + B_2)]. \qquad \text{(E3.15.1)}$$

A necessary condition for $(x_1^0, y_1^0, x_2^0, y_2^0)$ to be Pareto optimal is that there exist λ_1, λ_2 such that

$$\frac{\partial U}{\partial x_1} - \lambda_2 p_x = 0, \qquad \text{(E3.15.2)}$$

$$\frac{\partial U}{\partial y_1} - \lambda_2 p_y + \lambda_1 \frac{\partial V}{\partial y_1} = 0, \qquad \text{(E3.15.3)}$$

$$\lambda_1 \frac{\partial V}{\partial x_2} - \lambda_2 p_x = 0, \qquad \text{(E3.15.4)}$$

$$\lambda_1 \frac{\partial V}{\partial y_2} - \lambda_2 p_y = 0, \qquad \text{(E3.15.5)}$$

where all derivatives are evaluated at $(x_1^0, y_1^0, x_2^0, y_2^0)$. What is the economic interpretation of the third term in (E3.15.3)? (We do not need to make use of the further necessary conditions provided by the constraints.)

At the market equilibrium (i.e. individual maximization point), $(x_1^E, y_1^E, x_2^E, y_2^E)$, there will exist ψ_1, ψ_2 such that

$$\frac{\partial U}{\partial x_1} - \psi_1 p_x = 0, \qquad \text{(E3.15.6)}$$

$$\frac{\partial U}{\partial y_1} - \psi_1 p_y = 0, \qquad \text{(E3.15.7)}$$

$$\frac{\partial V}{\partial x_2} - \psi_2 p_x = 0, \tag{E3.15.8}$$

$$\frac{\partial V}{\partial y_2} - \psi_2 p_y = 0, \tag{E3.15.9}$$

where all derivatives are evaluated at $(x_1^E, y_1^E, x_2^E, y_2^E)$. In general, it is true that if a point satisfies the first-order conditions based on individual utility maximization, i.e. eqs. (E3.15.6)–(E3.15.9), it cannot satisfy eqs. (E3.15.2)–(E3.15.5) and is therefore not Pareto optimal.

Check this assertion by assuming that you have a point which satisfies both sets of conditions. Then you will find that various marginal utilities or prices must be zero. This will not, in general, be true.

Exercise 3.16   Alliance military expenditures as a public good [20]

(a) Consider two countries, each of which feels it necessary to spend money on defence. Suppose the countries' social welfare functions relating to military expenditure (x_i) and defence capability (c_i) are

$$U(x_i, c_i) = -\tfrac{1}{2}x_i^2 + n_i c_i - x_i c_i, \quad i = 1, 2, \tag{E3.16.1}$$

where n_i, gross national product measured in billions of dollars, enters the utility function in such a way as to make the larger country value a given absolute amount of defence more highly. (*Example*: the subjective value of the North American Continental Air Defence System is probably greater to the United States as a country than to Canada as a country, although each gets an 'equal' amount of defence.) Assume that the production function for defence takes the form

$$c_i = ax_i. \tag{E3.16.2}$$

When $a = 1$, find the optimal levels of x_i and c_i for countries with GNPs of 1 and 2 billion, respectively.

(b) Now assume that for political reasons the two countries form an irrevocable alliance. The production function of country 1 now becomes

$$c_1 = ax_1 + ax_2. \tag{E3.16.3}$$

That is to say, country 1 gets ax_2 worth of defence from country 2's expenditure even if it spends no money at all on defence. By maximation of (E3.16.1)

[20] This problem is based in part on the model presented in R. Zeckhauser and M. Olson (1966).

subject to (E3.16.3) we may derive a reaction curve showing country 1's own optimal expenditure on defence as a function of country 2's defence expenditure. Using the data of part (a) find and graph reaction curves for the two countries.

(c) The intersection of the two reaction curves provides a 'stable' equilibrium in the sense that if the countries arrive at the intersection, either one will lose welfare by moving away. [21] What are the countries' levels of military expenditure at the intersection of the reaction curves of part (b)? What relationship do these expenditures bear to the countries' GNPs?

(d) How much of the common defence good do the countries share in the alliance? Do they both gain in welfare by becoming allies? Which country gains the greater welfare?

(e) (For discussion.) Table E3.16.1 gives total GNPs and military expenditures for the NATO countries. Comment on these data in terms of the size versus defence expenditure theory of the previous parts

Table E3.16.1

NATO statistics

Country[a]	GNP, 1964 billions of dollars	Rank	Military budget % of GNP	Rank
United States	569.03	1	9.0	1
Germany	88.87	2	5.5	5
United Kingdom	79.46	3	7.0	2
France	73.40	4	6.7	3
Italy	43.63	5	4.1	9
Canada	38.14	6	4.4	7
Netherlands	15.00	7	4.9	6
Belgium	13.43	8	3.7	11
Denmark	7.73	9	3.3	12
Turkey	6.69	10	5.8	4
Norway	5.64	11	3.9	10
Greece	4.31	12	4.2	8
Luxembourg	0.53	13	1.7	13

Source: R. Zeckhauser and M. Olson (1966).

a Portugal has been omitted, since the bulk of its military effort is concentrated outside the NATO alliance.

[21] If you feel ambitious, try to prove this stability condition.

Answer. (a) Substituting (E3.16.2) into (E3.16.1) and maximizing, we obtain $x_1 = \frac{1}{3}$ and $x_2 = \frac{2}{3}$.

(b) To find country 1's reaction curve, we maximize

$$-\tfrac{1}{2}x_1^2 + (x_1 + x_2) - x_1(x_1 + x_2).$$

This gives $3x_1 = 1 - x_2$. Country 2's reaction curve is $3x_2 = 2 - x_1$. The graphed reaction curves are as shown in fig. E3.16.1.

(c) Solving the two reaction curve equations, we find $x_1 = \frac{1}{8}$ and $x_2 = \frac{5}{8}$. The ratio of defence expenditures to GNP increases with GNP.

(d) It seems clear that the smaller country has made the greater gains. It has reduced its expenditure on defence from one-third to one-eighth, i.e. approximately 60 percent, yet gained an increase in capacity from one-third to three-quarters, i.e. approximately 125 percent.

The larger country has managed to obtain about a 6 percent reduction in expenditure for a 12 percent increase in capacity.

F. Intertemporal Consumer Behavior

In many discussions of consumer behavior, the role of time is given little attention. An explicit dynamic framework is essential, however, if our theory of household behavior is to cope adequately with household savings decisions and decisions to purchase durables.

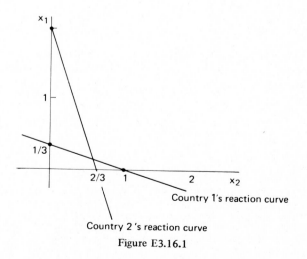

Figure E3.16.1

Exercise 3.17. The elimination of stock variables from demand equations for durables

The presence of durable goods in a set of commodities for which demand equations are to be estimated requires a rather different treatment than might otherwise be used. One problem in the estimation of demand equations for durables is that the stock of the good held at time t is an important determinant of purchases at time t, and yet data on the stock of durables (e.g. clothing) held by consumers are not always easy to come by. Read Phlips (1974, ch. 6) and note the various approaches to the elimination of the 'unobservable' stock variables. Then answer the following questions.

(a) Imagine that we have a model of the form[22]

$$q(t) = \alpha + \beta s(t) + \gamma x(t), \tag{E3.17.1}$$

where $q(t)$ is the volume of purchases of a particular commodity at time t, $s(t)$ is an accumulated stock held at time t, and $x(t)$ is household income at time t. α, β and γ are parameters.[23] Assume that $s(t)$ is unobservable. (Perhaps $s(t)$ is a stock of 'habits'.) However, assume that the stock accumulates according to the relationship

$$s(t) - s(t-1) = q(t) - \delta s(t), \tag{E3.17.2}$$

where δ is a parameter representing the rate of depreciation.[24] Can you use (E3.17.1) and (E3.17.2) to obtain an expression for $q(t)$ which does not involve the unobservable stock variable?

(b) Assume that we have a theory which suggests that 'desired' or 'planned' or 'equilibrium' stock holdings at time t, $s^*(t)$, are described by

$$s^*(t) = f(z(t)), \tag{E3.17.3}$$

where $z(t)$ is a vector of observable variables; for example, $z(t)$ might include prices and income. Next, assume that households make only a partial adjustment towards their desired stock, i.e.

$$s(t) = s(t-1)(1-\delta) + \rho(s^*(t) - s(t-1)(1-\delta)), \tag{E3.17.4}$$

---

[22] The model to be described briefly is that of Houthakker and Taylor (1970, pp. 9–13).

[23] What is the expected sign of β in (i) a habit formation model, and (ii) a durable good model?

[24] In (E3.17.2) we have assumed that depreciation over the period from time t-1 to t is $s(t)\delta$. In (E3.17.4) (E3.17.5) we have made an alternative assumption that depreciation is $s(t-1)\delta$.

where δ is the rate of depreciation and ρ is an adjustment coefficient. We expect that ρ will be between 0 and 1. Finally, we have the stock accumulation relationship

$$s(t) = (1-\delta)s(t-1) + q(t), \qquad (E3.17.5)$$

where $q(t)$ is the level of purchases at time t. Can you obtain an expression for $q(t)$ which does not contain any stock variables?

If you are interested in knowing more about dynamic models of household behavior, we suggest that you read Houthakker and Taylor (1970, pp. 194–200) and Phlips (1974, ch. 7). If you are familiar with the calculus of variations, you could also look at Dixon and Lluch (1977). In each of the various dynamic models, you should be able to identify four steps. First, you will find that there is a theory of 'planned' behavior. This is often derived from an underlying utility-maximizing model. Secondly, there will be a theory of adjustment, i.e. a theory describing the extent to which the households adjust their stocks to bring them into line with their 'planned' stocks. [25] Thirdly, there will be an accumulation relationship such as (E3.17.5). Finally, there will be some algebra aimed at eliminating unobservable variables, e.g. desired stocks and often actual stocks.

Answer.　(a)　From (E3.17.1) we have

$$s(t) = \frac{1}{\beta}(q(t) - \alpha - \gamma x(t)).$$

On substituting into (E3.17.2) we obtain

$$\frac{1+\delta}{\beta}(q(t) - \alpha - \gamma x(t)) = \frac{1}{\beta}(q(t-1) - \alpha - \gamma x(t-1)) + q(t),$$

i.e.

$$q(t) = \frac{\delta\alpha}{1-\beta+\delta} + \frac{1}{1-\beta+\delta}q(t-1) + \frac{(1+\delta)\gamma}{1-\beta+\delta}x(t) - \frac{\gamma}{1-\beta+\delta}x(t-1).$$

$$(E3.17.6)$$

For comparison with Houthakker and Taylor (1970, p. 11, eq.(9)) it might be helpful to rearrange (E3.17.6) as

$$q(t) - q(t-1) = \alpha\delta + (\beta-\delta)q(t) + \gamma(x(t) - x(t-1)) + \gamma\delta x(t).$$

　(b)　We rewrite (E3.17.4) as

$$s(t) = (1-\delta)(1-\rho)s(t-1) + \rho s^*(t). \qquad (E3.17.7)$$

---

[25]　If there is no explicit distinction between desired and actual stocks (as is the case in Houthakker and Taylor) then the adjustment rule can be thought of as (E3.17.4) with $\rho = 1$.

From here we obtain

$$s(t) - (1-\delta)s(t-1) = (1-\delta)(1-\rho)(s(t-1) - (1-\delta)s(t-2))$$
$$+ \rho(s^*(t) - (1-\delta)s^*(t-1)).$$

Now we substitute from (E3.17.5) and find that

$$q(t) = (1-\delta)(1-\rho)q(t-1) + \rho(s^*(t) - (1-\delta)s^*(t-1)).$$

Finally, we use (E3.17.3) and arrive at

$$q(t) = (1-\delta)(1-\rho)q(t-1) + \rho(f(z(t)) - (1-\delta)f(z(t-1))).$$

Exercise 3.18. Savings as a function of the rate of interest

Consider the simplest case of a consumer with a two-period time horizon and an initial income stream which may be altered only through borrowing or lending. He has no bequest motive, i.e. he plans to have no assets at the end of the two periods. Let his utility function be $u = c_0 c_1$ and his initial income stream be $\bar{y}_0$, $\bar{y}_1$, where c_0 and c_1 are his consumption expenditures in periods 0 and 1, and $\bar{y}_0$ and $\bar{y}_1$ are his income levels.

Derive his demand curve for savings as a function of the market rate of interest, r.

Answer. We can set this problem up as a simple constrained maximization. Our constraint is that the present value of any consumption plan (c_0, c_1) must be equal to that of the initial income combination $(\bar{y}_0, \bar{y}_1)$. It is actually computationally simpler to express this by compounding c_0 and $\bar{y}_0$ forward rather than discounting c_1 and $\bar{y}_1$ backward. Hence, we have the Lagrangian

$$L = c_0 c_1 - \lambda[(1+r)c_0 + c_1 - (1+r)\bar{y}_0 - \bar{y}_1].$$

The first-order conditions include

$$\frac{\partial L}{\partial c_0} = c_1 - \lambda(1+r) = 0$$

and

$$\frac{\partial L}{\partial c_1} = c_0 - \lambda = 0,$$

so we have

$$\frac{c_1}{1+r} = c_0.$$

Using the budget constraint, we find

$$c_1 = \tfrac{1}{2}\left[(1+r)\bar{y}_0 + \bar{y}_1\right]$$

and

$$c_0 = \tfrac{1}{2}\left(\bar{y}_0 + \frac{\bar{y}_1}{1+r}\right).$$

Define savings as

$$s = \bar{y}_0 - c_0 = \tfrac{1}{2}\left(\bar{y}_0 - \frac{\bar{y}_1}{1+r}\right).$$

As r increases, savings rise, which can be seen in fig. E3.18.1. Note that because $r''' > r'' > r'$, we have $s''' > s'' > s'$.

The case is somewhat more complicated when the consumer may adjust both his income stream and his consumption stream. This is the 'second approximation' discussed by Fisher and considered in E3.19.

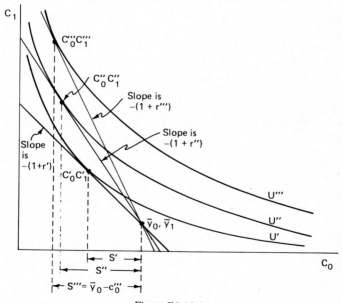

Figure E3.18.1

Exercise 3.19. Intertemporal consumption and investment

A farmer sets aside corn this year to use as seed. He finds that his next harvest Q_1 is related to the year's input of corn Q_0 in the following way:

$$Q_1 = 2Q_0 - 0.001(Q_0^2).$$

Seed is the only resource that is scarce to him. He now has 1000 bushels, and his utility function depends on the quantities of corn he consumes this year and next:

$$U = C_0 C_1,$$

where C_0 is his consumption this year and C_1 his consumption next year.

Answer the following questions, assuming complete divisibility of land and corn.

(a) If there is no capital market, how much should he consume this year and how much next year in order to maximize his utility? What is this rate of time preference at the equilibrium point, i.e. how much corn consumption in period 1 would he be willing to forgo for an extra bushel in period 0? What is the marginal rate of transformation of present into future corn (or the opportunity cost of present corn in terms of future corn) at this point?

(b) If he can borrow or lend any amount at 5 percent per annum, how much corn should be devoted to next year's production? How much should he consume in each year?

To solve this part of the problem, you may use a two-stage method. What is the economic interpretation of the two stages?

Answer. (a) We have $U = C_0 C_1$, and we are also given that the farmer has a stock of 1000 bushels and that the production function is $Q_1 = 2Q_0 - 0.001Q_0^2$. We can write the utility function simply in terms of the farmer's current savings, Q_0, because

$$C_0 = 1000 - Q_0, \tag{i}$$

$$C_1 = 2Q_0 - 0.001Q_0^2, \tag{ii}$$

and hence

$$U = (2Q_0 - 0.001Q_0^2)(1000 - Q_0),$$

i.e.

$$U = 2000Q_0 - 3Q_0^2 + 0.001Q_0^3.$$

The first-order condition for a maximum of U is[26]

$$\frac{\partial U}{\partial Q_0} = 2000 - 6Q_0 + 0.003Q^2 = 0.$$

We solve via the quadratic formula to find

$$Q_0 = \frac{+6 \pm \sqrt{(36 - 4 \times 2000 \times 0.003)}}{2 \times 0.003}$$

$$= \frac{+6 \pm 3.46}{0.006}.$$

The two solutions then are

$$Q_0 = \frac{9.46}{0.006} = 1577, \quad \text{which is impossible, since we must have } Q_0 \leqslant 1000,$$

and

$$Q_0 = \frac{2.54}{0.006} = 423, \quad \text{which is the answer we seek.}$$

This then yields for C_0 and C_1:

$$C_0 = 1000 - Q_0 = 1000 - 423 = 577$$

$$C_1 = 2Q_0 - 0.001Q_0^2 = 846 - 178.9 = 667.$$

The rate of time preference at this point can be defined as the marginal rate of substitution between C_0 and C_1. This rate is

$$-\left[\frac{dC_1}{dC_0}\right]_{U = \text{constant}} = \left[\frac{\partial U/\partial C_0}{\partial U/\partial C_1}\right] = \frac{C_1}{C_0} = 1.156$$

At equilibrium the marginal rate of transformation must be equal to the marginal rate of substitution. We can derive the former from the production function. This also serves as a check on the last calculation. We first re-express the production function in terms of the variables C_0 and C_1. We do this by using eqs. (i) and (ii). We obtain

$$0 = -C_1 + 2(1000 - C_0) - 0.001(1000 - C_0)^2,$$

i.e.

$$0 = -C_1 + 1000 - 0.001C_0^2 = f(C_1, C_0),$$

---

[26] The boundary conditions may be ignored. $Q_0 = 0$ and $Q_0 = 1000$ both imply $U = 0$. Clearly our farmer can do better than that.

which is the transformation locus. Then

$$-\left[\frac{dC_1}{dC_0}\right]_{f=\text{constant}} = 0.002C_0 = 0.002(577) = 1.154,$$

which is close enough to our previous result for the difference to be due to rounding errors.

(b) Now that a capital market is available, the farmer's problem is to choose C_0, C_1, Q_0, Q_1, and B_0 to maximize

$$U = C_0 C_1$$

subject to

$$C_0 = (1000 - Q_0) + B_0,$$
$$C_1 = Q_1 - B_0(1 + 0.05)$$

and

$$Q_1 = 2Q_0 - 0.001Q_0^2,$$

where B_0 is the number of bushels of corn borrowed at time zero. If the farmer lends corn, then B_0 will be negative.

There are several ways to solve this problem, e.g. Lagrangian multipliers, substitution of the constraints into the objective function followed by unconstrained maximization. The approach chosen here is a two-stage procedure.

Stage 1. Arrange productive activity to maximize the present value of surpluses available for lending, debt repayment and consumption:

$$\text{surplus time } 0 = 1000 - Q_0,$$
$$\text{surplus time } 1 = Q_1.$$

Maximize

$$(1000 - Q_0) + \frac{Q_1}{1 + 0.05}$$

subject to

$$Q_1 = 2Q_0 - 0.001Q_0^2.$$

Carrying out the maximization we obtain

$$Q_0 = 475 \quad \text{and} \quad Q_1 = 724.$$

Stage 2. Arrange borrowing and lending to maximize utility subject to the budget constraint, i.e. maximize

$$U = C_0 C_1$$

subject to

$$(1000 - 475) + \frac{724}{1 + 0.05} = C_0 + \frac{C_1}{1 + 0.05}.$$

Carrying out this maximization, we find

$$C_0 = 607 \quad \text{and} \quad C_1 = 638.$$

Solution: farmer should consume 607 and 638 in the two years. 475 should be devoted to the next year's production.

Exercise 3.20. *Vicious circles*

Assume that for a given individual the desired amount of human capital investment k_d depends on the individual's rate of time preference i, i.e. $k_d = k_d(i)$. On the other hand, the individual's rate of time preference is a function of the amount of human capital already invested in himself, k. That is, $i = i(k)$.

Wherever $k_d > k$, the individual invests in additional schooling.

Let the functions be of the form [27]

$$(0.01) (k_d - 10)^3 + (i - 0.6) = 0 \qquad \text{(E3.20.1)}$$

and

$$k + 25(i - 1) = 0, \qquad \text{(E3.20.2)}$$

where k_d and k are measured simply in terms of years of schooling.

(a) Graph the two equations and find the three sets of solutions for k and i, where $k_d = k$.

(b) Assume that the individual begins with no human capital invested in himself. Describe the process by which he would reach an equilibirium amount of human capital investment. At what level would the equilibrium occur?

(c) Assume now that the state imposes a legal restriction on the individual, requiring that he remain in school for at least nine years. What will be the new equilibrium amount of human capital investment?

(d) Answer (c) on the assumption that the legal restriction imposes at least ten years schooling.

(e) Can you determine whether the individual was 'better off' in solution (b) or (d)? Given the above problem, would it be sufficient to assume that all individuals had identical preferences in order to arrive at a normative judgment on the desirability of the ten-year minimum requirement on school attendance?

---

[27] Assume that time preference, i, is defined so that the range of economically meaningful values is $(0,1)$.

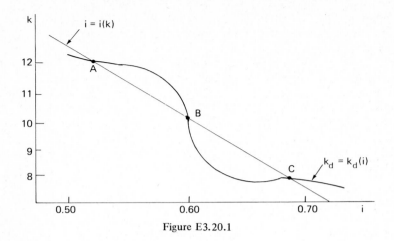

Figure E3.20.1

Answer. (a) The graph of the two equations (E3.20.1) and (E3.20.2) in the relevant range is shown in fig. E3.20.1. There are three solutions as one can find analytically by letting $k' = k - 10$, $i' = i - 0.6$ and substituting into (E3.20.1) and (E3.20.2) to obtain

$$(0.01)(k')^3 + i' = 0$$

and

$$k' + 25i' = 0,$$

which have roots at

$$k' = 0, -2, 2$$

and

$$i' = 0, +0.08, -0.08.$$

Therefore the three sets of solutions to (E3.20.1) and (E3.20.2) for (i,k) are $(0.52, 12)$, $(0.60, 10)$, and $(0.68, 8)$.

(b) When $k < 8$, k_d will exceed k. (In terms of the diagram, the k_d function lies above the i function.) Hence, the individual will desire additional education and go to school until he has $k = 8$ (point C).

(c) With $k = 9$, $k_d < k$. Presumably there is no mechanism for disinvesting in years of schooling. Hence, nine years will be the individual's new equilibrium level for investment in human capital.

(d) If the individual is forced to go to school for ten years, he will reach an equilibrium at point B (see fig. E3.20.1). However, B is an unstable equilibrium.

Any additional education (a PTA 'back-to-school' day, say) will lead him to go back to school for two years more and end up at A, with twelve years of schooling.

(e) Apparently the process of schooling has an effect on individual preferences, in this case upon the individual's rate of time preference. It is not possible, therefore, to infer that the individual is 'better off' when he is in a 'chosen' position. Had the individual chosen to obtain only eight years of schooling as in (b), we would have no reason to believe that he would later have regretted his decision. But the same could be said of the individual who in (d) was forced into a position where the 'choice' of twelve years of schooling became optimal.

Exercise 3.21. *Terminal conditions for multiperiod consumption models*

There are at least two ways to handle the terminal conditions in a finite horizon multiperiod consumption model. One approach is to treat the amount of the terminal bequest as fixed, and the problem becomes one of selecting that consumption path which, given an initial stock of assets and an expected path of noninterest income, will maximize the relevant integral of consumption while providing the required terminal bequest. The model in E3.18 is of this sort, with the terminal bequest set to zero. (How would the results change if the bequest were nonzero?) In a second approach, the amount of the bequest is not set but a value per unit of bequest is chosen. Then the problem is to find that consumption path which, when given the initial stock of assets and the time path of noninterest income, will maximize the relevant integral of consumption plus the value of the terminal bequest. [28] This exercise incorporates the second approach.

Our consumer stands at time zero with the following information:

(1) The net value of his accumulated assets, i.e. $h(0)$.

(2) The expected amount of his noninterest income in years 0, 1, and 2, i.e. $\overline{y(0)}, \overline{y(1)}$, and $\overline{y(2)}$.

(3) The rate of interest δ at which he can either borrow or lend money.

(4) A utility discount rate which reflects his impatience and his uncertainty that he will survive through the three years, i.e. ρ.

(5) A parameter which reflects the diminishing importance which he attaches to marginal units of consumption, i.e. $\eta \in (0,1)$, so that his undiscounted satisfaction in each period can be written as

---

[28] In finite time horizon national planning models, the treatment of terminal conditions often parallels the two approaches described for multiperiod consumption models. The 'bequest' consists of post planning period capital stocks which may be fixed exogenously (approach 1) or given a value in the objective function (approach 2). See Taylor (1975, pp. 105–109).

$$u(t) = \frac{1}{1-\eta} c(t)^{1-\eta}, \quad t = 0, 1, 2,$$

which implies that

$$\frac{\partial u(t)}{\partial c(t)} = c(t)^{-\eta} > 0$$

and

$$\frac{\partial^2 u(t)}{\partial c(t)^2} = -\eta c(t)^{-\eta-1} < 0.$$

(6) A parameter α which reflects the value he attaches to each unit of his asset holdings at time 3, the terminal point of the analysis. It is assumed that he attaches value to these terminal assets either through a bequest motive or through a retirement funds motive.

With this information in mind, the consumer wants to maximize the total value of the discounted sum of his utility from consumption in periods 0, 1, and 2 plus the utility from his bequest at the beginning of period 3.

For the purpose of the exercise, the problem is solved in several steps. At each step you will be asked to formulate or solve a particular part of the problem. Since the steps are cumulative and probably only make sense if you are following our particular method, it would be a good idea to check with our answer as you complete each step.

Step 1. For the first step, set up the constrained maximization problem for the consumer.

Step 2. Derive the necessary conditions for a constrained maximum.

Step 3. For given values of the parameters α, η, ρ, δ, $\overline{h(0)}$, $\overline{y(0)}$, $\overline{y(1)}$ and $\overline{y(2)}$, the system of necessary conditions is very easily solved. How?

Step 4. We refer to the notation in our answer for step 2.

(a) Give an economic interpretation of λ.

(b) Justify (E3.21.8) in words.

(c) Will consumption rise or fall over time? On which parameters will this depend?

(d) There are some very peculiar, unrealistic implications of this model of consumer behavior. Using the following question as a guide, see if you can find and account for them.

Evaluate $\dfrac{\partial c(t)}{\partial \overline{y(\tau)}}$, for any $t, \tau = 0, 1, 2$.

Evaluate $\dfrac{\partial h(3)}{\partial \overline{y(\tau)}}$, $\tau = 0, 1, 2$.

Evaluate $\dfrac{\partial c(0)}{\partial \rho}$, $\dfrac{\partial c(1)}{\partial \rho}$, $\dfrac{\partial c(2)}{\partial \rho}$

and

$$\dfrac{\partial c(0)}{\partial \delta}, \quad \dfrac{\partial c(1)}{\partial \delta}, \quad \dfrac{\partial c(2)}{\partial \delta}.$$

Interpret all your results.

If we assumed that $h(3)$ was no longer a choice variable but that it was set exogenously at zero — we omit (E3.21.8) and drop the $h(3)$ term wherever it appears in (E3.21.4)–(E3.21.7) — then what would be the sign of $\partial c(t)/\partial \overline{y(\tau)}$ for any t, $\tau = 0, 1, 2$?

(e) Continue to assume that $h(3)$ is not a choice variable. Now let the consumer's income stream change to $\overline{y(0)}, \overline{y(1)}$, and $\overline{y(2)}$, where

$$\overline{y(0)} + \frac{\overline{y(1)}}{1+\delta} + \frac{\overline{y(2)}}{(1+\delta)^2} = \overline{y(0)} + \frac{\overline{y(1)}}{1+\delta} + \frac{\overline{y(2)}}{(1+\delta)^2}.$$

What will be the effect on $c(0)$, $c(1)$ and $c(2)$ of this change in the income stream? Which key assumption of the model explains your answer?

(f) Suggest a more realistic description of the borrowing and lending opportunities facing the consumer.

(g) Does your revised description of the consumer's borrowing and lending opportunities lend support to the Keynesian contention that current income is the major determinant of current consumption rather than to the neoclassical emphasis on the rate of interest?

Answer.

Step 1. Choose $c(0)$, $c(1)$, $c(2)$, and $h(3)$ to maximize

$$\alpha h(3) + \sum_{t=0}^{2} \frac{1}{(1+\rho)^t} \frac{1}{1-\eta} c(t)^{1-\eta} \tag{E3.21.1}$$

subject to

$$\overline{h(0)} + \overline{y(0)} + \frac{\overline{y(1)}}{1+\delta} + \frac{\overline{y(2)}}{(1+\delta)^2}$$

$$= c(0) + \frac{c(1)}{1+\delta} + \frac{c(2)}{(1+\delta)^2} + \frac{h(3)}{(1+\delta)^3}, \tag{E3.21.2}$$

where $h(t)$ is the value of assets at time t. This constraint requires that the present value of assets and the income stream equals the present value of the consumption stream and bequest.

Step 2. We form the Lagrangian:

$$L = \alpha h(3) + \sum_{t=0}^{2} \frac{1}{(1+\rho)^t} \frac{1}{(1-\eta)} c(t)^{1-\eta}$$

$$+ \lambda \left[\overline{h(0)} + \overline{y(0)} + \frac{\overline{y(1)}}{1+\delta} + \frac{\overline{y(2)}}{(1+\delta)^2} - c(0) \right.$$

$$\left. - \frac{c(1)}{1+\delta} - \frac{c(2)}{(1+\delta)^2} - \frac{h(3)}{(1+\delta)^3} \right].$$
(E3.21.3)

From here we obtain the necessary conditions for a constrained maximum:

$$\frac{\partial L}{\partial c(0)} = c(0)^{-\eta} - \lambda = 0,$$
(E3.21.4)

$$\frac{\partial L}{\partial c(1)} = \frac{c(1)^{-\eta}}{(1+\rho)} - \frac{\lambda}{(1+\delta)} = 0,$$
(E3.21.5)

$$\frac{\partial L}{\partial c(2)} = \frac{c(2)^{-\eta}}{(1+\rho)^2} - \frac{\lambda}{(1+\delta)^2} = 0,$$
(E3.21.6)

$$\frac{\partial L}{\partial \lambda} = \overline{h(0)} + \overline{y(0)} + \frac{\overline{y(1)}}{1+\delta} + \frac{\overline{y(2)}}{(1+\delta)^2} - c(0)$$

$$- \frac{c(1)}{(1+\delta)} - \frac{c(2)}{(1+\delta)^2} - \frac{h(3)}{(1+\delta)^3} = 0,$$
(E3.21.7)

$$\frac{\partial L}{\partial h(3)} = \alpha - \frac{\lambda}{(1+\delta)^3} = 0.$$
(E3.21.8)

Step 3. (E3.21.8) implies that

$$\lambda = \alpha(1+\delta)^3.$$

Having computed λ, we can compute $c(0)$, $c(1)$ and $c(2)$ immediately from (E3.21.4), (E3.21.5) and (E3.21.6). Finally, with $c(0)$, $c(1)$ and $c(2)$ found, we can use (E3.21.7) to obtain $h(3)$.

Step 4. (a) λ is the marginal utility of a \$ 1 increase in the present value of the income stream plus initial assets. Hence λ is the extra utility gained from a \$ 1 increase in $\overline{h(0)}$ or $\overline{y(0)}$ or a $(1+\delta)$ increase in $\overline{y(1)}$ or a $(1+\delta)^2$ increase in $\overline{y(2)}$.

(b) An increase of \$ 1 in the present value of the income stream can be used to 'buy' $\$(1 + \delta)^3$ of $h(3)$. This gives a gain in utility of $\alpha(1 + \delta)^3$. Hence, the marginal utility of an increase of $\$1$ in the present value of the income stream is $\alpha(1 + \delta)^3$. Therefore $\lambda = \alpha(1 + \delta)^3$.

(c) From (E3.21.4)–(E3.21.6) we find that

$$\frac{c(t+1)}{c(t)} = \left(\frac{1+\delta}{1+\rho}\right)^{1/\eta}, \quad \text{for} \quad t = 0, 1.$$

Hence $c(2) \gtreqless c(1) \gtreqless c(0)$ as $\delta \gtreqless \rho$. Consumption will increase if and only if the rate of interest is greater than the rate of utility discount. The result in no way depends on the time path of income.

(d)

$$\frac{\partial c(t)}{\partial y(\tau)} = 0, \quad \text{for all} \quad t, \tau = 0, 1, 2. \tag{E3.21.9}$$

This result can be seen by following out step 3. From (E3.21.8)

$$\lambda = \alpha(1 + \delta)^3.$$

We substitute into (E3.21.4)–(E3.21.6) to find that

$$c(0) = [\alpha(1 + \delta)^3]^{-1/\eta}, \tag{E3.21.10}$$

$$c(1) = [\alpha(1 + \delta)^2 (1 + \rho)]^{-1/\eta} \tag{E3.21.11}$$

and

$$c(2) = [\alpha(1 + \delta) (1 + \rho)^2]^{-1/\eta}. \tag{E3.21.12}$$

Hence, consumption does not depend on income.

To evaluate $\partial h(3)/\partial y(\tau)$ we can proceed by rearranging (E3.21.7) as

$$\frac{h(3)}{(1+\delta)^3} = \overline{h(0)} + \overline{y(0)} + \frac{\overline{y(1)}}{1+\delta} + \frac{\overline{y(2)}}{(1+\delta)^2}$$

$$- c(0) - \frac{c(1)}{1+\delta} - \frac{c(2)}{(1+\delta)^2}. \tag{E3.21.13}$$

Using the previous result, we have

$$\frac{1}{(1+\delta)^3} \frac{\partial h(3)}{\partial y(\tau)} = \frac{1}{(1+\delta)^\tau}, \quad \tau = 0, 1, 2.$$

That is,

$$\frac{\partial h(3)}{\partial y(\tau)} = (1 + \delta)^{3-\tau}, \quad \tau = 0, 1, 2. \tag{E3.21.14}$$

Finally, we deduce $\partial c(t)/\partial \rho$ and $\partial c(t)/\partial \delta$ from (E3.21.10)–(E3.21.12):

$$\frac{\partial c(t)}{\partial \rho} = \frac{-1}{\eta} \ [\alpha(1+\delta)^{3-t}(1+\rho)^t]^{-1/\eta-1} t\alpha(1+\delta)^{3-t}(1+\rho)^{t-1},$$

$t = 0, 1, 2.$ \hfill (E3.21.15)

$$\frac{\partial c(t)}{\partial \delta} = \frac{-1}{\eta} \ [\alpha(1+\delta)^{3-t}(1+\rho)^t]^{-1/\eta-1}(3-t)\alpha(1+\delta)^{2-t}(1+\rho)^t,$$

$t = 0, 1, 2.$ \hfill (E3.21.16)

How do we interpret and explain the results obtained in (d)? (E3.21.9) and (E3.21.14) indicate that increases in income are entirely devoted to increasing the bequest, never to increasing consumption. We can trace this very unrealistic implication to the asymmetrical treatment of the bequest and consumption in the utility function. Whereas there is diminishing marginal utility for additional units of $c(t)$, $t = 0$, 1, 2, the marginal utility of additional units of $h(3)$ is constant. Hence additional dollars of income will be entirely devoted to increasing $h(3)$, avoiding diminishing marginal utility. (E3.21.15) points up another peculiarity of the model. Increases in the consumers' discount rate will reduce consumption in all periods except the initial period, where it is unchanged. Hence, increases in ρ, which might be expected to increase consumption in early periods and reduce it in later periods, in fact increase the bequest alone. Again the result is attributable to the asymmetrical treatment of the bequest and consumption in the utility function. Increases in ρ reduce the marginal utility of $c(1)$ and $c(2)$ without affecting that of $c(0)$ and $h(3)$. Hence $c(1)$ and $c(2)$ are reduced, and extra resources are devoted to $h(3)$. Although the marginal utility of $c(0)$ was not reduced by the increase in ρ, no extra resources are devoted to it because increases in $c(0)$ yield diminishing marginal utility, whereas $h(3)$ can be increased with constant marginal utility.

From (E3.21.16) we see that an increase in the rate of interest will reduce consumption in all periods. The explanation can again be traced to the bequest term, but we leave it to the reader to work out the details. A more flexible model of consumer behavior would allow for increases in planned consumption in later periods in response to a rise in the rate of interest.

Once $h(3)$ becomes exogenous, then

$$\frac{\partial c(t)}{\partial y(\tau)} > 0, \quad \text{for any } t, \ \ \tau = 0, 1, 2.$$

With $h(3)$ no longer a choice variable, there is no way for the consumer to avoid diminishing marginal utility. Hence, any increases in income will be allocated among $c(0)$, $c(1)$, and $c(2)$.

(e)   There will be no change in $c(0)$, $c(1)$, and $c(2)$. There is no change in the consumer's budget constraint and hence there is no change in the optimal consumption pattern. This implies that the time path of income is not relevant to the consumer, only its present value is important. To obtain this result we have assumed that the consumer works in a perfect capital market. The lending and borrowing rates are the same. On the security of his future income he can borrow as much as he likes at a constant rate of interest. With access to a perfect capital market, the consumer can spread his consumption independently of the time path of income.

(f)   We know that most consumers work in a capital market which is far from perfect. Individuals will find that their borrowing rate is higher than their lending rate. Also, their borrowing rate will rise as they go further into debt. For many individuals the borrowing rate is virtually infinite (i.e. they cannot borrow at all). Imperfections in the capital market are a partial justification for scholarships. In a perfect capital market a student could borrow on the security of future earnings, and the case for subsidizing him with scholarship money would be much weaker.

Perhaps a more realistic specification of the problem facing many consumers is as follows: choose $c(0)$, $c(1)$, and $c(2)$ to maximize

$$\sum_{t=0}^{2} \frac{1}{1-\eta} \, c(t)^{1-\eta} \, \frac{1}{(1+\rho)^t} \tag{E3.21.17}$$

subject to

$$c(0) \leqslant \overline{h(0)} + \overline{y(0)}, \tag{E3.21.18}$$

$$c(1) \leqslant \overline{y(1)} + (1+\delta) \, [\overline{h(0)} + \overline{y(0)} - c(0)] \tag{E3.21.19}$$

and

$$c(2) \leqslant \overline{y(2)} + (1+\delta)^2 \, [\overline{h(0)} + \overline{y(0)} - c(0)]$$
$$+ (1+\delta) \, [\overline{y(1)} - c(1)]. \tag{E3.21.20}$$

For this consumer there is no possibility of borrowing, but he can lend at some low rate of interest δ.

(g)   The description of consumer behavior contained in (E3.21.17)–(E3.21.20) de-emphasizes the role of the rate of interest. The capital market allows the consumer to make only a small earning on funds he is saving to be spent in the future. On the other hand, the inability to borrow makes the current level of income an important determinant of the current level of consumption. A reduction in present income cannot be 'smoothed' over by borrowing. The contention that the current level of income can largely explain present consumption is also strengthened if we assume that future income expectations ($y(1)$, $y(2)$, etc.) are strongly influenced by current income. Now with the rate of interest playing a comparatively minor role and $y(1)$ and $y(2)$ dependent on current income, current income can be used to explain much of current consumption.

Exercise 3.22. Intertemporal inconsistency [29]

At each point of time, t, a particular consumer plans his present and future consumption levels so as to maximize

$$U_t \equiv \sum_{\tau=t}^{\infty} \left(\frac{1}{\tau + 1 - t} \right)^2 \ln\left(C_\tau(t)\right), \qquad \text{(E3.22.1)}$$

where $C_\tau(t)$ is the consumption level planned *at* time t *for* time τ. Notice that our consumer applies a discount factor $(1/(\tau+1-t))^2$ in computing the present utility of consumption to be undertaken τ-t periods into the future. Also, for convenience, we have avoided the 'bequest' problem by assuming that the consumer is young and expects to live for ever.

At time t the consumer's lifetime budget constraint is of the form

$$\sum_{\tau=t}^{\infty} \frac{C_\tau(t)P_\tau(t)}{(1+r)^{\tau-t}} = Z_t, \qquad \text{(E3.22.2)}$$

where Z_t is the expected present value of his future lifetime income stream and current assets, $P_\tau(t)$ is the price (expected at time t) of a unit of consumption at time τ, and r is the expected rate of interest. To simplify the problem, let us assume that

$$P_\tau(t)/(1+r)^{\tau-t} = 1 \text{ (say)}, \quad \text{for all } \tau,$$

i.e. the consumer anticipates a rate of inflation equal to the rate of interest. Thus, the budget constraint can be written as

[29]   The purpose of this problem is to highlight the main points from the famous paper by Strotz (1955). The Strotz problem has had a modern revival. See, for example, Blackorby et al. (1973), Peleg and Yaari (1973), Phelps and Pollak (1968), and Pollak (1968).

$$\sum_{\tau=t}^{\infty} C_{\tau}(t) = Z_t. \tag{E3.22.3}$$

(a) Assuming that $Z_t = 10$, compute $C_t(t)$, $C_{t+1}(t)$, $C_{t+2}(t)$ and $C_{t+3}(t)$. *Hint:* it will be useful to know that

$$\sum_{n=1}^{\infty} (1/n)^2 \simeq 1.645.$$

(b) Assume that the consumer carries out the first step of his plan, i.e. at time t his consumption is 6.079. However, at time $t+1$, he replans his consumption path. He chooses $C_{\tau}(t+1)$, $\tau = t+1,...,\infty$, to maximize

$$U_{t+1} \equiv \sum_{\tau=t+1}^{\infty} \left(\frac{1}{\tau+1-(t+1)} \right)^2 \ln\left(C_{\tau}(t+1)\right) \tag{E3.22.4}$$

subject to

$$\sum_{\tau=t+1}^{\infty} \frac{C_{\tau}(t+1)P_{\tau}(t+1)}{(1+r)^{\tau-(t+1)}} = Z_{t+1}.$$

Assuming that the consumer's expectations concerning prices and his income have been unaltered from those held at time t, we will have

$$Z_{t+1} = (Z_t - P_t(t)C_t(t))(1+r)$$

and

$$P_{\tau}(t+1) = P_{\tau}(t), \quad \tau = t+1, t+2,... .$$

Hence,

$$\frac{P_{\tau}(t+1)}{(1+r)^{\tau-t}} = 1, \quad \text{for all } \tau \geqslant t+1.$$

Under these conditions the consumer's budget constraint for time $t+1$ becomes

$$\sum_{\tau=t+1}^{\infty} C_{\tau}(t+1) = Z_t - C_t(t). \tag{E3.22.5}$$

Compute $C_{t+1}(t+1)$, $C_{t+2}(t+1)$ and $C_{t+3}(t+1)$. Are you surprised that

$$C_{t+s}(t+1) \neq C_{t+s}(t), \quad s = 1, 2, 3?$$

Although nothing has happened to cause our consumer to revise his expectations, when he replans at time $t+1$ he plans a different consumption stream from that planned at time t. Can you account for this apparently paradoxical result?

Answer.　　(a)　We form the Lagrangian:

$$L = \sum_{\tau=t}^{\infty} \left(\frac{1}{\tau+1-t}\right)^2 \ln\left(C_\tau(t)\right) - \lambda\left(\sum_{\tau=t}^{\infty} C_\tau(t) - Z_t\right).$$

From here we generate the first-order conditions

$$\left(\frac{1}{\tau+1-t}\right)^2 \frac{1}{C_\tau(t)} - \lambda = 0, \quad \tau = t, \ t+1,\ldots \qquad \text{(E3.22.6)}$$

and

$$\sum_{\tau=t}^{\infty} C_\tau(t) - Z_t = 0. \qquad \text{(E3.22.7)}$$

On combining (E3.22.6) and (E3.22.7) we obtain

$$\frac{1}{\lambda} \sum_{\tau=t}^{\infty} \left(\frac{1}{\tau+1-t}\right)^2 = Z_t.$$

We note that

$$\sum_{n=1}^{\infty} \left(\frac{1}{n}\right)^2 = 1.645.$$

(See, for example, J.A. Green (1958, p. 60).) Thus, with $Z_t = 10$, we have

$1/\lambda = 6.079,$

$C_t(t) = 6.079,$

$C_{t+1}(t) = \frac{1}{4} \times 6.079 = 1.520,$

$C_{t+2}(t) = \frac{1}{9} \times 6.079 = 0.675$

and

$C_{t+3}(t) = \frac{1}{16} \times 6.079 = 0.380.$

　　(b)　We maximize

$$\sum_{\tau=t+1}^{\infty} \left(\frac{1}{\tau+1-(t+1)}\right)^2 \ln\left(C_\tau(t+1)\right)$$

subject to

$$\sum_{\tau=t+1}^{\infty} C_\tau(t+1) = 10 - 6.079 = 3.921.$$

Applying the same method as in part (a), we obtain

$$C_{t+1}(t+1) = 2.384 \quad (1.520),$$

$$C_{t+2}(t+1) = 0.596 \quad (0.675)$$

and

$$C_{t+3}(t+2) = 0.265 \quad (0.380).$$

The values for $C_{t+1}(t)$, $C_{t+2}(t)$ and $C_{t+3}(t)$, calculated in part (a), are shown in parentheses. The differences between $C_{t+s}(t)$ and $C_{t+s}(t+1)$ show that, on the basis of no new information, our consumer has revised his plans.

The explanation for the paradox is found in a change of tastes or preferences. Obviously, if the consumer's preferences changed between times t and $t+1$, it would not be surprising to find that his consumption plans would be revised, even in the absence of changes in price and income expectations. More precisely, we can say that there have been changes in preferences if there are differences in the preference orderings defined by the utility functions [30]

$$U^t_{t+1} = U_t(\overline{C_t(t)}, C_{t+1}, C_{t+2},...) \tag{E3.22.8}$$

and

$$U^{t+1}_{t+1} = U_{t+1}(C_{t+1}, C_{t+2},...), \tag{E3.22.9}$$

where U^t_{t+1} is U_t (see (E3.22.1)) with the first argument fixed at the consumer's currently optimal consumption level. Hence, U^t_{t+1} reflects the consumer's preferences *at time t* over alternative consumption streams C_{t+1}, C_{t+2},..... U^{t+1}_{t+1}, on the other hand, reflects the consumer's preferences *at time t+1* over alternative consumption streams C_{t+1}, C_{t+2},.... If U^t_{t+1} and U^{t+1}_{t+1} define different preference orderings, then what seemed an optimal plan *at time t* for the consumption stream C_{t+1}, C_{t+2},..., may no longer seem optimal at time $t+1$.

---

[30] There are differences in the preference orderings defined by the two utility functions U^t_{t+1} and U^{t+1}_{t+1} if there are two consumption streams

$$C^*_{t+1}, \quad C^*_{t+2},...$$

and

$$C^{**}_{t+1} \quad C^{**}_{t+2},...$$

such that

$$U^t_{t+1}(C^*_{t+1}, C^*_{t+2},...) \geqslant U^t_{t+1}(C^{**}_{t+1}, C^{**}_{t+2},...)$$

yet

$$U^{t+1}_{t+1}(C^*_{t+1}, C^*_{t+2},...) < U^{t+1}_{t+1}(C^{**}_{t+1}, C^{**}_{t+2},...),$$

i.e. according to the utility function U^t_{t+1} the stream C^{**}_{t+1}, C^{**}_{t+2},.... *is not* preferred to the stream C^*_{t+1}, C^*_{t+2}, ..., while according to the utility function U^{t+1}_{t+1}, the double-star stream *is* preferred to the single-star stream.

What are the specific forms of U_{t+1}^t and U_{t+1}^{t+1} for our particular consumer? From (E3.22.1), (E3.22.4) and the solution in part (a), we find that

$$U_{t+1}^t = \ln 6.079 + \sum_{\tau=t+1}^{\infty} \alpha(\tau - t) \ln (C_\tau) \qquad (E3.22.10)$$

and

$$U_{t+1}^{t+1} = \sum_{\tau=t+1}^{\infty} \alpha(\tau - (t+1)) \ln (C_\tau), \qquad (E3.22.11)$$

where

$$\alpha(r - s) \equiv \left(\frac{1}{r - s + 1} \right)^2, \quad \text{for all } r \geq s. \qquad (E3.22.12)$$

A little arithmetic quickly establishes that U_{t+1}^t and U_{t+1}^{t+1} do not reflect identical preference orderings. For example, consider the streams

$$C^* \equiv (C_{t+1}^*, C_{t+2}^*, ...) = (e, 1, 1, ...)$$

and

$$C^{**} = (e^{1.1}, 0.7, 1, 1, ...).$$

We find that

$$U_{t+1}^t(C^*) = \ln 6.079 + \tfrac{1}{4} \ln (e) + 0 + 0 \ ... = 2.0548$$

and

$$U_{t+1}^t(C^{**}) = \ln 6.079 + \tfrac{1}{4} \ln (e^{1.1}) + \tfrac{1}{9} \ln (0.7) + 0 + 0 + ... = 2.0402.$$

Hence, according to utility function U_{t+1}^t, the stream C^* is preferred to the stream C^{**}. However,

$$U_{t+1}^{t+1} (C^*) = \ln (e) + 0 + 0 \ ... = 1$$

and

$$U_{t+1}^{t+1} (C^{**}) = \ln (e^{1.1}) + \tfrac{1}{4} \ln (0.7) + 0 + ... \simeq 1.0108,$$

and thus according to utility function U_{t+1}^{t+1}, C^{**} is preferred to C^*. Try to explain in words why our consumer at time t prefers C^* to C^{**} as a consumption plan to be executed from time $t+1$ onwards, but when he actually arrives at time $t+1$, he prefers C^{**} to C^*. Would U_{t+1}^t and U_{t+1}^{t+1} reflect identical preferences if the discount factors were defined by the more conventional

$$\alpha(r - s) = \left(\frac{1}{1 + \rho} \right)^{r-s}, \quad \text{for all } r \geq s,$$

rather than by (E3.22.12)?

What is the significance of the Strotz problem? Strotz pointed out that a consumer of the type described in this exercise will know at time t what his preferences at time $t+1$ will be, and that he will know that these preferences will be different from his current preferences. Since the consumer can *fully anticipate* the changes in his preferences, then it would be logical for him to take these changes into account when he is making his current plans, i.e. in forming his consumption plan at time t, he will not maximize (E3.22.1) subject to the budget constraint. He will add other constraints which will allow him to achieve as high a value as possible for (E3.22.1) in view of the fact that when time $t+1$ comes he will not keep to the plan which would be generated simply by maximizing U_t subject to (E3.22.2). Pollak (1968) contains a comparatively simple example of a solution to a planning problem in which anticipated changes in preferences are incorporated. Of course, if preference changes are *unanticipated*, then we can continue to adopt the model in which an intertemporal utility function is maximized subject to the relevant budget constraint. Consumption at each point of time will be the first step on the currently optimal plan.

G. Decisions under uncertainty

The following problems (all on aspects of decision-making under uncertainty) are based on Pratt, Raiffa and Schlaifer (1965).

Exercise 3.23. The determination of utility functions for risky decisions

One way to determine a von Neumann–Morgenstern type of utility function is to pick two arbitrary returns, x_1 and x_2 with $x_2 > x_1$, and assign to each of these returns arbitrary utility values of $u(x_1)$ and $u(x_2)$. Then a complete list of utility values for other returns, x_i, can be determined by answering the following types of questions.

(1) What is the value for x_i that leaves you indifferent between a certainty of x_i and a 50 : 50 chance at x_1 and x_2? Then $u(x_i)$ is such that

$$u(x_i) = 0.5u(x_1) + 0.5u(x_2).$$

(2) What is the value for x_i ($x_i < x_1$) that leaves you indifferent between 60 : 40 chance at x_i and x_2 or a certainty of x_1? Then

$$u(x_1) = 0.6u(x_i) + 0.4u(x_2).$$

(3) What is the value for x_i ($x_i > x_2$) that leaves you indifferent between a 25 : 75 chance at x_1 and x_i or a certainty of x_2? Then

$$u(x_2) = 0.25u(x_1) + 0.75u(x_i).$$

Of course, any one of the x_i's generated by this process (and its associated $u(x_i)$) can be treated as an x_1 or x_2 for further extension or interpolation of the utility function.

(a) Suppose that we have asked a series of questions of the type just described. We find that the following choices are made by our subject where *-I-* indicates indifference and a general lottery of x_1 with probability p_1 and x_2 with probability p_2 is denoted by $[(p_1 : x_1), (p_2 : x_2)]$:

$ 100 *-I-* [(0.5 : -$ 25), (0.5 : $ 300)],

$ 300 *-I-* [(0.5 : $ 600), (0.5 : $ 100)],

$ 100 *-I-* [(0.5 : -$ 100), (0.5 : $ 600)],

-$ 100 *-I-* [(0.5 : -$ 200), (0.5 : $ 300)].

(E3.23.1)

If $u(100) = 0$ and $u(300) = 1$, find the utility values of -25, 600, -100, and -200. Plot these points on a graph [31] and assume that the utility function drawn through them is your own. Answer the following questions on the basis of this function. (You should have found $-1, 2, -2$, and -5.)

(i) What sure return leaves you indifferent between a $50 : 50$ chance at $ 300 and $ 600 and the sure return?

(ii) What sure return leaves you indifferent between a 0.75 chance at $ 400 and a 0.25 chance at $-$ 200 and the sure return?

(iii) What would you pay (i.e. what insurance premium would you pay to avoid having to take a 0.5 chance at $ 0 and a 0.5 chance at $-$ 200?

(iv) What sure sum of money is indifferent to a lottery that offers a 0.375 chance at $ 500, a 0.125 chance at $ 600 and a 0.5 chance at $ 0?

(v) If someone offered to sell you a ticket for the lottery in (iv) for $ 200, would you buy it? What would someone who maximized expected money values do? Why?

(vi) Consider the following lottery: $ 0 with probability 0.2; $ 150 with probability 0.5; and $ 600 with probability 0.3. How much would you be willing to sell this lottery for if you owned it?

(vii) For how much would you be willing to buy the lottery in (vi) if you did not own it? Which is greater, the buying price or the selling price? What does this fact indicate about the shape of the decision-maker's utility function? Why?

(b) Using the method described at the beginning of this exercise, obtain

---

[31]   In our solution to this problem we have joined the plotted points with straight lines. You may prefer to do this, too, simply to facilitate checking your solutions when you have completed the problem.

your preference function for incremental amounts of money between −$ 10 000 and +$ 10 000. Start with $x_1 = \$ 0$, $x_2 = \$ 10\ 000$ and $u(x_1) = 0$, $u(x_2) = 100$. Plot these points on graph paper as you obtain them. After obtaining a 'moderate' number, draw a smooth curve through them.

Answer. (a) We want to determine the utility function for the decision-maker whose choices are indicated in (E3.23.1). Set $u(100) = 0$ and $u(300) = 1$ and utilize the principle that the decision-maker is an expected utility maximizer.

To find $u(-25)$ note

$$u(100) = 0.5u(-25) + 0.5u(300),$$

$$0 = 0.5u(-25) + 0.5.$$

Hence,

$$u(-25) = -1.$$

To find $u(600)$ we have

$$u(300) = 0.5u(600) + 0.5u(100),$$

$$1 = 0.5u(600) + 0.$$

This implies

$$u(600) = 2.$$

To find $u(-100)$ we use the result just obtained, combined with the data that

$$u(100) = 0.5u(-100) + 0.5u(600).$$

Hence,

$$0 = 0.5u(-100) + 1$$

and

$$u(-100) = -2.$$

To find $u(-200)$ we substitute the previous result into

$$u(-100) = 0.5u(-200) + 0.5u(300),$$

obtaining

$$-2 = 0.5u(-200) + 0.5.$$

This implies

$$u(-200) = -5.$$

The graph of this utility function is then as shown in fig. E3.23.1. (We have used linear interpolation.) Now we can use this utility function to answer the rest of the questions.

(i) We must find x_a such that

$$u(x_a) = 0.5u(300) + 0.5u(600),$$

i.e.

$$u(x_a) = 0.5 + 1 = 1.5.$$

Using the graph derived, we find

$$u(x_a) = 1.5 \text{ implies } x_a \simeq 450.$$

Then $ 450 is the sure return whose utility is the same as a 50 : 50 chance at $ 300 and $ 600.

(ii) We must find x_b such that

$$u(x_b) = 0.75u(400) + 0.25u(-200),$$

i.e.

$$u(x_b) = \tfrac{3}{4} \times \tfrac{4}{3} + \tfrac{1}{4} \times -5 = -0.25.$$

We used the graph to find $u(400)$; now we use it to find

$$u(x_b) = -0.25 \text{ implies } x_b \approx \$ 70.$$

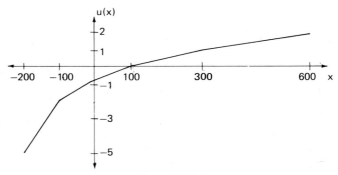

Figure E3.23.1

Then $ 70 is the sure return whose utility is the same as that of the lottery.

(iii) To avoid having to take an unfavorable lottery, you would be willing to incur a loss, x_c, whose utility equals the lottery's expected utility. Use the graph to find $u(0) = -0.8$:

$$u(x_c) = 0.5u(0) + 0.5u(-200),$$

$$u(x_c) = 0.5 \times -0.8 + 0.5 \times -5 = -2.9.$$

Then we use our graph to find

$$u(x_c) = -2.9 \text{ implies } x_c \approx -\$ 130.$$

Therefore, you would be willing to pay up to $ 130 to avoid having to take this lottery. We can look on this an an upper bound on what you would be willing to pay to insure against a 50 percent chance of losing $ 200.

(iv) We want to find x_d such that

$$u(x_d) = 0.375u(500) + 0.125u(600) + 0.5u(0),$$

i.e.

$$u(x_d) = 0.375 \times \tfrac{5}{3} + 0.125 \times 2 + 0.5 \times -0.8 = 0.475,$$

where we used the graph to find $u(500)$ and $u(0)$. Now we use it again to find

$$u(x_d) = 0.475 \text{ implies } x_d \approx \$ 195.$$

Therefore, $ 195 is the sum indifferent to the lottery.

(v) Suppose someone offered to sell you the lottery for $ 200. You would not buy it because the expected utility value of that option is

$$E[u(L)] = 0.375u(500 - 200) + 0.125u(600 - 200) + 0.5u(0 - 200),$$

i.e.

$$E[u(L)] = 0.375u(300) + 0.125u(400) + 0.5u(-200).$$

Using the graph, this implies that buying the lottery for $ 200 is indifferent to losing approximately $ 100. Notice that we subtract the purchase price from each outcome to obtain the net money value for each outcome.

An expected money return maximizer would see the option as simply

$$E(L) = 0.375(500 - 200) + 0.125(600 - 200) + 0.5(-200) = \$ 62.5.$$

And since this option has a positive expected money value, such a decision-maker would buy the lottery for $ 200.

(vi) If you own a lottery, you would sell it for a sum, x_f, just larger than the sure return with the same expected utility value. Thus we find, using our gr to obtain $u(0), u(150)$:

$$u(x_f) = 0.2u(0) + 0.5u(150) + 0.3u(600)$$

$$= 0.2 \times -\tfrac{4}{5} + \tfrac{1}{2} \times \tfrac{1}{4} + \tfrac{3}{10} \times 2$$

$$= 0.565.$$

Using our graph, we obtain $x_f \simeq \$\,212$.

(vii) To find the buying price, b, we have to solve the following equation:

$$0 = -u(0) + 0.2u(0-b) + 0.5u(150-b) + 0.3u(600-b). \qquad \text{(E3.23.2)}$$

The b that solves this equation yields an expected utility for the bought lottery (each outcome minus the cost) equal to the utility of zero.

This is not easy to solve without an analytical expression for $u(x)$. Instead, we must proceed by iteration, using our graph. Convergence is relatively easy to accomplish, however. In solving this, we first tried $b_1 = \$\,150$. Using our graph of $u(x)$, we found that the right-hand side of (E3.23.2) is

$$\text{RHS} = +0.8 + (0.2 \times -3.5) + (0.5 \times -0.8) + (0.3 \times 1.5)$$

$$= 0.15.$$

Therefore, for $b_1 = \$\,150$, the lottery still has positive expected utility value. So we tried $b_2 = \$\,160$. This yields

$$\text{RHS} = +0.8 + (0.2 \times -3.8) + (0.5 \times -0.88) + (0.3 \times 1.47)$$

$$= -0.02,$$

which is close enough to zero. Therefore we can say that the *buying price* of the lottery is $\approx \$\,159$.

The *selling price* was $\approx \$\,212$, which is greater than the buying price and closer to the expected money value of the lottery itself, which is $\$\,255.00$ This demonstrates the phenomena of *decreasing absolute risk aversion*. For more on this point, see Arrow (1965, pp. 33–41), Pratt (1964, pp. 122–136) and Raiffa (1968, pp. 89–93).

Exercise 3.24. *The St. Petersberg paradox*

The famous St. Petersberg paradox that gave rise to Bernoulli's work on utility theory involved the game where a coin was tossed until it came up heads. If heads appeared for the first time on the nth toss, the game paid 2^n (i.e. the payoff doubled on each toss).

(a) Show that a man who maximized expected money value would pay out [en]tire assets for the right to play this game.

(b) How much would you pay for the right to play this game?

(c) Since there is not enough money in the world to make the payoff $\$ 2^{50}$, suppose that we modify the game so that if heads does not come up in the first 25 throws, the player gets nothing. Show that the expected money value of this game is $\$ 25$.

(d) How much would you be willing to pay for the right to play in the modified game? *Hint*: form the geometric series each of whose terms is the value of the game when the first heads occurs on the *n*th toss times the probability that such an outcome will result.

Answer. Consider the value of the St. Petersberg paradox game when heads appears on the *n*th toss. Call this E_n:

$$E_n = 2^n.$$

Let p_n be the probability of a heads occurring first on the *n*th toss. Then

$$p_n = (\tfrac{1}{2})^n.$$

Now the total expected value of the game is the summation over all possible outcomes weighted by probabilities. Therefore,

$$\text{expected value of game} = \sum_{n=1}^{\infty} E_n p_n = \sum_{n=1}^{\infty} 1 = \infty.$$

For a game in which heads counts as a win only if it appears on one of the first 25 tosses, we have

$$\text{expected value of game} = \sum_{n=1}^{25} 1 = 25.$$

Exercise 3.25. The boundedness of the utility function

State the amount of money z such that you are indifferent between the following two options.

Option A. In addition to your regular income, you will receive a tax-free gift of $\$ z$ per year for the rest of your life.

Option B. A single toss of the coin will determine whether you get nothing or the privilege of the unlimited ability to write checks for the purpose of financing consumption by you and your family for the rest of your life. (No foreign-aid programs or solving the world's problems; you must spend the money on yourself and your family.)

The existence of an amount z such that you are indifferent to the above options shows that your utility function (for 'own' consumption) is bounded from above. You should see why this follows. Perhaps this problem also convinces you that the general postulate that utility functions are bounded is empirically plausible.

Having u bounded implies that as $x \to \infty$, $u(x) \to$ some positive limit. The boundedness property also has implications for the 'relative risk aversion' displayed by the decision-maker (see Arrow (1965, pp. 36–37)).

Exercise 3.26.   Measurable utility (a review question)

A number of concepts of utility measurement have been discussed in the literature: the cardinal concepts of the utilitarians; the ordinal version as expressed, for example, by J.R. Hicks (1939, chs. 1–3); the von Neumann–Morgenstern concept of measurability; and the 'cardinality' which arises in the case of additive utility functions. Be able to describe these by indicating the data and/or experimental conditions which would allow the measurement of utility according to each concept. Be prepared to comment on the applicability of each concept to

(1) decision-making under certainty;

(2) decision-making under uncertainty; and

(3) normative economics.

Chapter 4

PRODUCTION THEORY

4.1. Goals, reading guide and references

The material in this chapter is set out under four general headings: properties of production functions, optimization subject to specific production function constraints, linear production models, and the economic theory underlying the modern approach to production function estimation. The primary purpose of the chapter is to introduce you to the theory and application of production functions. The readings and problem set will also give you some insight into the theory of the distribution of rewards between different factors of production.

We hope that you will see applications outside production theory for the technical equipment you will be acquiring. It will be obvious, for example, that mathematical techniques such as logarithmic differentiation and linear programming have applications far beyond those alluded to in this chapter. In addition, you will find that much of production theory is applicable, with simple modifications, to the analysis of consumer demand. Similarly, many of the techniques of consumer theory are reapplied in production theory. Thus, there is a two-way link between this chapter and the two previous ones. On the one hand, your knowledge of consumer theory will allow you to make rapid progress with production theory. On the other hand, as you work through the problems on production theory you will be revising, broadening and deepening your knowledge of consumer theory.

As in the previous chapters, we have made a list of goals. By the time you are finished with the material presented here, we hope that you will be able to do all the following:

(1) handle standard manipulations with linearly homogeneous production functions; for example, you should be confident in applying Euler's theorem;

(2) understand the difference between a homothetic production function and a homogeneous production function;

(3) explain the properties of the Cobb–Douglas, Leontief, CES and CRESH

production functions and know what is meant by a flexible functional form;

(4)   discuss alternative definitions of the elasticity of substitution;

(5)   understand the relevance of the elasticity of substitution to the theory of income distribution;

(6)   derive the factor price frontier from the production function;

(7)   discuss the properties of the factor price frontier — its shape, the interpretation of its slope, how it shifts under various types of technological change, its relationship to the cost function;

(8)   derive the production possibilities frontier given the production functions and the resource endowments;

(9)   discuss the shape of the production possibilities frontier and the conditions on the production functions which will ensure the convexity of the production possibilities set;

(10)   understand the classifications of technical change (namely, embodied or disembodied, and capital saving, labor saving or neutral);

(11)   discuss the attributes of technical change (its biasedness, sectoral distribution, etc.) that are particularly relevant to the theory of the distribution of income, and whether in models of income distribution the pattern of technical change should be taken as exogenous or made endogenous;

(12)   derive the restrictions on the form of the input demand functions which follow from the cost minimizing model;

(13)   outline the formal similarities and differences between the cost minimizing theory of producer behavior and the utility-maximizing theory of consumer behavior;

(14)   set up simple production problems in a linear programming framework, solve them graphically and explain the meaning of the dual variables and their relationship to the 'marginal productivities' of neoclassical production theory;

(15)   derive the properties (e.g. concavity and homogeneity of degree one in prices) of cost functions in the cost minimizing model and explain what is meant by the 'duality' between cost functions and production functions; and

(16)   apply Shepard's lemma and understand its significance for econometric work.

Reading Guide 4 provides a suggested path through the readings to cover these concepts. In section 4.2 we have provided some short additional notes on the theoretical developments underlying recent production function econometrics. These notes may be useful when you tackle section D in Problem Set 4.

Readings and references are given in abbreviated terms in the reading guide and in the rest of the chapter; full citations are in the reference list.

Reading Guide 4*

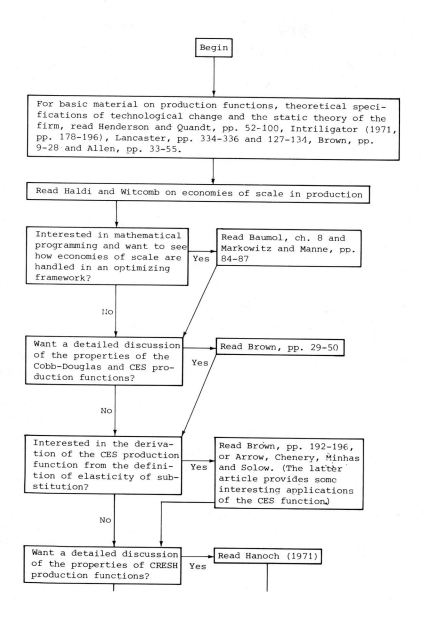

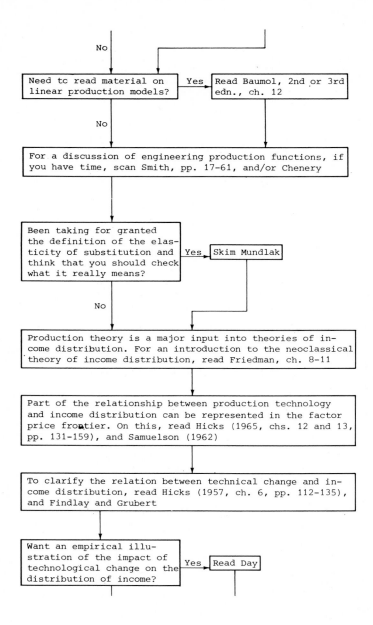

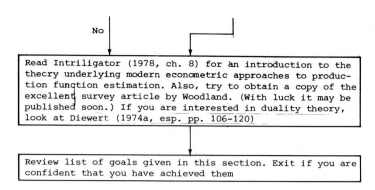

No

Read Intriligator (1978, ch. 8) for an introduction to the theory underlying modern econometric approaches to production function estimation. Also, try to obtain a copy of the excellent survey article by Woodland. (With luck it may be published soon.) If you are interested in duality theory, look at Diewert (1974a, esp. pp. 106-120)

Review list of goals given in this section. Exit if you are confident that you have achieved them

* Full titles are in the list of references below.

References for Chapter 4

Allen, R.G.D. (1967) *Macro-Economic Theory: A Mathematical Treatment*, St. Martin's.

Arrow, K.J., H.B. Chenery, B.S. Minhas and R.M. Solow (1961) 'Capital–Labor Substitution and Economic Efficiency', *Review of Economics and Statistics*, 45, August, 225–250.

Baumol, W.J. (1972) *Economic Theory and Operations Analysis*, 3rd edn., Prentice-Hall.

Berndt, E.R. and M.S. Khaled (1977) 'Energy Prices, Economies of Scale and Biased Productivity Gains in U.S. Manufacturing, 1947–1971', *Discussion Paper* no. 77–23, University of British Columbia, Department of Economics.

Brown, M. (1966) *On the Theory and Measurement of Technological Change*, Cambridge University Press.

Caves, R.E. (1963) *Trade and Economic Structure*, Harvard University Press, Cambridge, Mass.

Chenery, H.B. (1949) 'Engineering Production Functions', *Quarterly Journal of Economics*, 63, November, 507–531.

Christensen, L.R., D.W. Jorgenson and L.J. Lau (1971) 'Conjugate Duality and the Transcendental Logarithmic Production Function,' (abstract), *Econometrica*, 39, July, 255–256.

Christensen, L.R., D.W. Jorgenson and L.J. Lau (1973) 'Transcendental Logarithmic Production Frontiers', *Review of Economics and Statistics*, 55, February, 28–45.

Day, R.H. (1967) 'Technological Change and the Demise of the Sharecropper', *American Economic Review*, 57, June, 427–449.

Diewert, W.E. (1971) 'An Application of the Shepard Duality Theorem: A Generalized Leontief Cost Function', *Journal of Political Economy*, 79, May/June, 481–507.

Diewert, W.E. (1973) 'Separability and a Generalization of the Cobb–Douglas Cost, Production and Indirect Utility Functions', Research Branch, Department of Manpower and Immigration, Ottawa.

Diewert, W.E. (1974a) 'Applications of Duality Theory', in: M. D. Intriligator and D.A. Kendrick, eds., *Frontiers of Quantitative Economics*, vol. II, North-Holland Publishing Company.

Diewert, W.E. (1974b) 'Functional Forms for Revenue and Factor Requirements Functions', *International Economic Review*, 15, February, 119–130.

Dorfman, R., P. Samuelson and R. Solow (1958) *Linear Programming and Economic Analysis*, McGraw-Hill.
Douglas, P.H. (1948) 'Are there Laws of Production?', *American Economic Review*, 33, 1–49.
Findlay, R. and H. Grubert (1959) 'Factor Intensities, Technological Progress, and the Terms of Trade', *Oxford Economic Papers*, 11, 111–121.
Friedman, M. (1976) *Price Theory*, Aldine.
Frisch R. (1965) *Theory of Production*, D. Reidel and Rand McNally.
Haldi, J. and D. Whitcomb (1967) 'Economies of Scale in Industrial Plants', *Journal of Political Economy*, 75(4).
Hanoch, G. (1971) 'CRESH Production Functions', *Econometrica*, September, 695–712.
Hanoch, G. (1975) 'Production and Demand Models with Direct or Indirect Additivity', *Econometrica*, 43(3), 395–419.
Hasenkamp, G. (1976) 'A Study of Multiple-Output Production Functions: Klein's Railroad Study Revisited', *Journal of Econometrics*, 4(3), 253–262.
Henderson, J.M. and R.E. Quandt (1971) *Microeconomic Theory*, 2nd edn., McGraw-Hill.
Hicks, J.R. (1957) *The Theory of Wages*, Peter Smith.
Hicks, J.R. (1965) *Capital and Growth*, Oxford University Press.
Intriligator, M.D. (1971) *Mathematical Optimization and Economic Theory*, Prentice-Hall.
Intriligator, M.D. (1978) *Econometric Models, Techniques and Applications*, Prentice-Hall.
Krueger, A.O. (1974) 'The Political Economy of the Rent-Seeking Society', *American Economic Review*, 64(3), 291–303.
Lancaster, K. (1968) *Mathematical Economics*, Macmillan.
Leibenstein, H. (1966) 'Allocative Efficiency vs. X-Efficiency', *American Economic Review*, 61, June, 392–415.
Markowitz H. and A. Manne (1957) 'On the Solution of Discrete Programming Problems', *Econometrica*, 25, January, 84–87.
Mundlak, Y. (1968) 'Elasticities of Substitution and the Theory of Derived Demand', *Review of Economic Studies*, 35, 225–236.
Paul, R.S. and E.F. Haeussler (1973) *Introductory Mathematical Analysis for Students of Business and Economics*, Reston Publishing Co. Inc., Reston, Virginia.
Samuelson, P.A. (1949) 'International Factor Price Equalization Once Again', *Economic Journal*, 59, June.
Samuelson, P.A. (1962) Parable and Realism in Capital Theory: The Surrogate Production Function', *Review of Economic Studies*, 29(3), 193–206.
Smith, V.L. (1966) *Investment and Production*, Harvard University Press.
Takayama, A. (1972) *International Trade: An Approach to the Theory*, Holt, Rinehart and Winston.
Thirsk, W. (1974) 'Factor Substitution in Columbian Agriculture', *American Journal of Agricultural Economics*, 56, 73–84.
Vincent, D.P., P.B. Dixon and A.A. Powell (1979) 'The Estimation of Supply Response in Australian Agriculture: The CRESH/CRETH Production System', *International Economic Review*, forthcoming.
Woodland, A. (1976) 'Modelling the Production Sector of an Economy: A Selective Survey and Analysis', IMPACT Working Paper No. 0-04, Industries Assistance Commission, 608 St. Kilda Rd., Melbourne, mimeo, 90 pp.
Wymer, C.R. (1973) 'Computer Programs: Resimul Manual', London School of Economics, mimeo, 25 pp.

4.2. Background notes on some recent developments in production function theory

Because of your experience with consumer theory, our guess is that you can cope with production theory at a slightly higher level of mathematical sophistication than was required in Problem Sets 2 and 3. Consequently, some of the problems towards the end of this chapter (section D in Problem Set 4) involve rather long mathematical arguments. The economic theory, however, is quite straightforward and you should not lose sight of the main points while you grapple with the technicalities. Of course, grappling with the technicalities is essential if you are to make use of the theory in your own research or if you are to understand, with any confidence, the research results of others. While doing battle with the maths, it might be useful to have some rough historical perspective on how the theory has developed.

Modern production function theory started with the Cobb–Douglas[1] function,

$$Y = A \prod_{i=1}^{n} X_i^{\delta_i},$$

where Y and the X_i's are output and inputs and A and the δ_i's are parameters. Although the Cobb–Douglas function continues to play an important role in applied economics, it must be considered a very restrictive theoretical description of production technology. For example, in E4.3 you will discover that under the Cobb–Douglas specification, the elasticity of substitution between any pair of inputs is 1. Hence, if we adopt the Cobb–Douglas form as the underlying specification for an empirical study, we prevent the data from telling us that the elasticity of substitution differs from 1.

In 1961, Arrow et al. proposed a more general functional form, the CES. Under this specification, the elasticity of substitution between pairs of inputs is allowed to differ from 1. However, the elasticity of substitution between any pair of inputs is the same as that between any other pair. Hence, under the CES specification we prevent the data from telling us, for example, that farm machinery and labor are good substitutes whereas farm machinery and land are poor substitutes.

Since the CES function, there have been several generalizations.[2] The one that we focus on in Problem Set 4 is CRESH. The CRESH function, formulated by Hanoch (1971), allows elasticities of substitution to differ from 1 and from each other. In CRESH, however, if the elasticity of substitution between inputs i

---

[1] See Douglas (1948).
[2] See, for example, Hanoch (1975).

and j is twice (say) that between i and k, then the elasticity of substitution between any other input m and j is twice that between m and k.

The progression from Cobb–Douglas to CES to CRESH represents a steady relaxation of the prior restrictions on the elasticities of substitution. Thus, it places increasingly heavy burdens on the data. The estimation of the parameters of a CES production function requires more detailed data on inputs, outputs and prices than does the estimation of the parameters of a Cobb–Douglas function. Similarly, estimation of the parameters of CRESH is more ambitious than for CES. Theoretical generalizations of production functions have become of interest because of (a) improvements in data sets, e.g. the lengthening of consistent time series on input prices and quantities and output, and (b) the development of more powerful econometric theory and computing algorithms, especially the availability of packages capable of giving maximum likelihood parameter estimates in models involving many equations, parameters and theoretical restrictions on the parameter values.[3]

The most recent step in the generalization of the specification of production functions is the flexible functional form. With a flexible functional form we impose no prior restrictions on substitution elasticities beyond those which arise from their definition or from the assumptions of optimizing behavior. As well as improvements in data, and econometric theory and computing, the exploitation of flexible functional forms has awaited another development – duality theory.

The word 'duality' is used fairly loosely in economics. Usually it refers to the relationship between two theoretical constructions. They are said to be dual if all the important features of one are deducible from a knowledge of the other and vice versa. For example, those of you who are familiar with the theory of linear programming will know that the problems

$$\begin{pmatrix} \text{choose } x \geq 0 \\ \text{to maximize } c'x \\ \text{subject to } Ax \leq b \end{pmatrix} \quad \text{and} \quad \begin{pmatrix} \text{choose } y \geq 0 \\ \text{to minimize } y'b \\ \text{subject to } y'A \geq c' \end{pmatrix}$$

are said to be dual problems since we can deduce the solution of either one given the solution to the other. The particular duality proposition which is emphasized in recent production theory relates cost functions and production functions. You will find that under cost minimizing assumptions it is possible to deduce the production function given the cost function or to deduce the cost function given the production function.

Because of the duality between production functions and cost functions, it follows that if we can measure the parameters of the cost function then this is as

---

[3]   For example, see Wymer (1973).

good as measuring the parameters of the production function. Whatever is the purpose for investigating the production function, it can equally well be served by a knowledge of the cost function. Now what are the principal purposes for investigating production functions? Perhaps the most important is to allow us to derive the input demand equations. Given the production function (or cost function) we can derive equations showing how the demands for labor, capital, land and materials will vary in response to changes in output levels and factor prices. Such equations are a basic ingredient for applied general equilibrium models which are concerned with, among other things, the effects of changes in wages on the aggregate level and occupational composition of employment.

It turns out that from an algebraic point of view, the derivation of input demand functions from a given cost function is a comparatively easy task. You will discover *Shepard's lemma* which says that the demand function for input *i* can be derived by differentiating the cost function with respect to the price of input *i*. On the other hand, if we are given a production function, then to find the input demand functions we must solve a constrained minimization problem. Except where the production function has a very simple form (e.g. Cobb–Douglas or CES) the solution of the constrained minimization problem can be difficult and the input demand functions may have no convenient explicit representation. Therefore, if we propose to use a flexible production specification, i.e., one which imposes a minimum of prior restrictions on the elasticities of substitution, then it is better that we specify our explicit flexible functional form for the cost function rather than the production function. That way we avoid the tedious and perhaps unmanageable algebra which would be involved in moving from a necessarily complicated production function (simple functional forms will not have the required flexibility) to the input demand functions.

One final point before you start into the problems. Even where we are talking about flexible functional forms, we are often dealing with rather special cases. For example, in section D of the problem set we have, for simplicity, restricted attention to constant returns to scale production functions. We have also omitted technological change, and we have considered only production functions on the multiple-inputs–one-output type.[4]

---

[4] A detailed discussion of multi-input–multioutput production functions is in Frisch (1965, ch. 14). For an application of a multi-input–multioutput production function, see Hasenkamp (1976) or Vincent, Dixon and Powell (1979).

PROBLEM SET 4

A. Some Properties of Production Functions

Exercise 4.1. Properties of two-factor, linearly homogeneous[5] production functions

Consider a smooth (i.e. differentiable), concave production function $Y = F(K,L)$, where F is homogeneous of degree 1 in K and L (constant returns to scale).

Denote by y output per worker (L = number of workers), by k the capital–labor ratio, by η_{YL} and η_{YK} the partial elasticities of output (Y) with respect to labor (L) and capital (K), and by σ the elasticity of substitution between K and L.

(a) Show that y is a function (denote it by f) of k only; that is, output per worker can be explained in terms of capital per worker without reference to the level of output.

(b) Show that $F_K \equiv (\partial F/\partial K)$ and $F_L \equiv (\partial F/\partial L)$ (marginal productivities of capital and labor, respectively) also depend on k only.

(c) Show that $\eta_{YK} + \eta_{YL} = 1$. Under competitive equilibrium (i.e. marginal productivity pricing), what economic interpretation would you give to η_{YK} and to η_{YL}? Hence, what is the economic meaning of the equality $\eta_{YK} + \eta_{YL} = 1$?

(d) One measure of the ease with which factors may be substituted for each other in production is given by

$$\sigma = - \frac{d(K/L)}{K/L} \frac{F_K/F_L}{d(F_K/F_L)}, \tag{E4.1.1}$$

where it is understood that K/L is being varied while output is being held constant. σ is called the elasticity of substitution between capital and labor. You should check that it is a good indicator of 'ease of substitution'. Does it depend on the units in which K and L are measured? What sign does σ generally have?

---

[5] The expression 'linearly homogeneous' and 'homogeneous of degree 1' mean exactly the same thing.

Does σ increase or decrease as substitution between factors becomes easier? For the constant returns to scale case show that

$$\sigma = \frac{F_L F_K}{F F_{KL}} \, . \tag{E4.1.2}$$

With competitive pricing in a single-sector economy, show how the relative shares accruing to capital and labor will behave for small increases in K when $\sigma \gtrless 1$.

(e) Show for production functions which are homogeneous of degree 1 that any pattern of technical change can be written as a combination of Hicks neutral and Harrod neutral technical change.

Answer.   (a) $Y = F(K,L)$. By homogeneity of first degree,

$$Y = LF(K/L, 1). \tag{E4.1.3}$$

That is,

$$Y/L = F(K/L, 1)$$

or

$$\boxed{y = f(k)} \quad .$$

(b) To show that $\partial F/\partial K$ is a function of k only, we differentiate in (E4.1.3), obtaining

$$\frac{\partial F}{\partial K} = L \, \frac{\partial f(k)}{\partial K} = L f'(k) \, \frac{\partial k}{\partial K} = L f'(k) \, \frac{1}{L} = f'(k). \tag{E4.1.4}$$

To show that $\partial F/\partial L$ is a function of k only, we note that by Euler's theorem,

$$Y = \frac{\partial F}{\partial K} \, K + \frac{\partial F}{\partial L} \, L.$$

Hence

$$\frac{Y}{L} = \frac{\partial F}{\partial K} \, \frac{K}{L} + \frac{\partial F}{\partial L} \, ,$$

and thus

$$\frac{\partial F}{\partial L} = f(k) - kf'(k). \tag{E4.1.5}$$

(c)

$$\eta_{YK} = \frac{(\partial Y/\partial K)K}{Y} \quad \text{and} \quad \eta_{YL} = \frac{(\partial Y/\partial L)L}{Y}$$

by the usual definition of any elasticity as the ratio between marginal and average values. Therefore

$$\eta_{YK} + \eta_{YL} = \frac{(\partial Y/\partial K)K + (\partial Y/\partial L)L}{Y}$$

and since, by Euler's theorem,

$$(\partial Y/\partial K)K + (\partial Y/\partial L)L = Y,$$

we find that

$$\boxed{\eta_{YK} + \eta_{YL} = 1}$$

Denote the price of labor (wage) by w and that of capital (rental) by r. In competitive equilibrium, the price of any factor of production is equated to the value of its marginal product. Taking the price of Y as the numeraire (that is, setting $P_Y = 1$), we have

$$w = F_L, \quad r = F_K$$

so that

$$\eta_{YK} = \frac{rK}{Y} = S_K, \quad \eta_{YL} = \frac{wL}{Y} = S_L,$$

where S_K and S_L denote the shares of K and L, respectively, out of total output (or income). *Note*: in our case, $\eta_{YK} + \eta_{YL} = 1$. Hence, no 'adding-up' problem arises when factors are rewarded according to their marginal productivity. To what special characteristic of the production function may this be attributed?

(d) In fig. E4.1.1 we have sketched an isoquant $\alpha\beta\gamma\delta$. Imagine that we are at point γ with a labor–capital ratio of $(L/K)_0$ and a marginal rate of substitution of capital for labor (MRS_{KL}) given by $(F_K/F_L)_0$. Now we make a small increase in the labor–capital ratio; we move to a point such as β by increasing L and reducing K, but we keep output constant. We say that K and L are 'good' substitutes if a given percentage increase in L/K leads to only a small percentage increase in the MRS_{KL}, i.e. K and L are good substitutes in the region of γ if the slope of the isoquant does not change rapidly as we move from γ to β. Hence, L and K are good substitutes in the region of γ if

$$Z = \frac{[(F_K/F_L)_1 - (F_K/F_L)_0]/(F_K/F_L)_0}{[(L/K)_1 - (L/K)_0]/(L/K)_0}$$

is small.

Since it is convenient to define the elasticity of substitution so that it *in-*

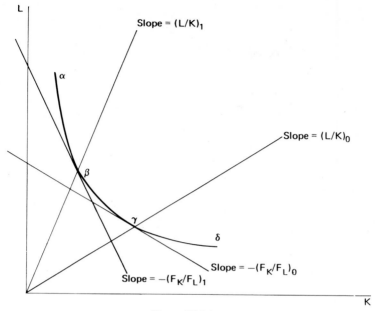

Figure E4.1.1

creases as ease of substitution increases, we use $1/Z$ rather than Z as our definition. That is, we define the elasticity of substitution by

$$\sigma = \frac{d(L/K)/(L/K)}{d(F_K/F_L)/(F_K/F_L)} .$$

(E4.1.6)

(E4.1.6) can also be written as

$$\sigma = -\frac{d(K/L)}{K/L} \frac{F_K/F_L}{d(F_K/F_L)} .$$

(E4.1.7)

In summary, σ is positive and higher values of σ indicate greater ease in substituting between capital and labor.

You are asked to show that under constant returns to scale, σ, as defined by (E4.1.7), is given by

$$\sigma = \frac{F_L F_K}{F F_{KL}} .$$

(E4.1.8)

We see from (E4.1.4) and (E4.1.5) that

$$F_K/F_L = f'(k)/(f(k) - kf'(k)).$$

Thus,

$$\frac{d(F_K/F_L)}{dk} = \frac{f''(k)}{f(k) - kf'(k)} + \frac{f'(k)f''(k)k}{(f(k) - kf'(k))^2} ,$$

i.e.

$$\frac{d(F_K/F_L)}{dk} = \frac{f''(k)f(k)}{(f(k) - kf'(k))^2} .$$

Now

$$\sigma = -\frac{F_K/F_L}{K/L} \; \frac{1}{(d(F_K/F_L)/dk)} , \quad \text{see (E4.1.7).}$$

Hence

$$\sigma = -\frac{f'(k)}{f(k) - kf'(k)} \; \frac{1}{k} \; \frac{(f(k) - kf'(k))^2}{f''(k)f(k)} ,$$

i.e.

$$\sigma = -\frac{f'(k)\,(f(k) - kf'(k))}{kf''(k)f(k)} . \tag{E4.1.9}$$

From (E4.1.4) and (E4.1.5) we see that the numerator of (E4.1.9) is $F_K F_L$. In simplifying the denominator, we use (E4.1.4) to obtain

$$F_{KL} = f''(k) \frac{\partial k}{\partial L} = -f''(k)k\frac{1}{L} . \tag{E4.1.10}$$

By substituting into (E4.1.9) we find that

$$\sigma = \frac{F_K F_L}{F_{KL} L f(k)} ,$$

i.e.

$$\sigma = \frac{F_K F_L}{F_{KL} F} .$$

With competitive pricing we have: capital share, $S_K = F_K K/F$. Hence

$$\frac{\partial S_K}{\partial K} = \frac{F_{KK}K + F_K}{F} - \frac{(F_K)^2 K}{F^2} . \tag{E4.1.11}$$

From Euler's theorem we know that

$$F_K K = F - F_L L$$

and also that[6] $F_{KK}K = -F_{KL}L$. On substituting these results into (E4.1.11), we see that

$$\frac{\partial S_K}{\partial K} = \frac{-F_{KL}LF + F_K F - F_K(F - F_L L)}{F^2},$$

i.e.

$$\frac{\partial S_K}{\partial K} = \frac{F_L F_K L}{F^2} \left(-\frac{F_{KL}F}{F_L F_K} + 1 \right),$$

i.e.

$$\frac{\partial S_K}{\partial K} = A \left(1 - \frac{1}{\sigma} \right),$$

where

$$A \equiv \frac{F_L F_K L}{F^2} > 0.$$

Therefore

$$\frac{\partial S_K}{\partial K} \gtrless 0, \quad \text{as } \sigma \gtrless 1.$$

We conclude that, depending on whether $\sigma \gtrless 1$, an increase in K will increase, leave unchanged, or decrease the relative share of K in output.

  (e) Any (factor-augmenting) technical change can be written in the general form

$$Y = F[a(t)K, b(t)L].$$

Because of homogeneity of first degree,

$$Y = a(t) F \left[K, \frac{b(t)}{a(t)} L \right]$$

so that $a(t)$ can be viewed as a (neutrally) shifting factor (Hicks neutrality), whereas $b(t)/a(t)$ can be viewed as a purely labor-augmenting factor (Harrod neutrality).

---

  [6] Remember that, since F is homogeneous of degree 1 in L and K, F_K is homogeneous of degree zero in L and K.

Exercise 4.2.   Factor price frontier

Answer the following questions assuming that the production function, $Y = F(K,L)$, is differentiable and homogeneous of degree 1.

(a) What is the definition of the factor price frontier (*FPF*)? (*Note*: all prices are defined in terms of the output Y, i.e. take $P_y = 1$.)

(b) If you draw its graph in the 'factor price' space, to what is the slope of the *FPF* curve equal at any point?

(c) What can you say about the general curvature of the *FPF* curve (e.g. strictly convex, concave, straight line, etc.)?

(d) What is the elasticity of the curve at any point?

(e) Suppose now that a technical change occurs. How will the *FPF* curve shift (if at all) if the technical change is Hicks-neutral? Harrod-neutral?

Answer.   (a) The *FPF* is the technological relationship between the marginal products (and, hence, under perfect competition, the prices) of the factors of production showing the maximal (or 'efficient') marginal product of one of the factors for any given (attainable) level of the other.

It can be expressed mathematically as

$$\frac{\partial Y}{\partial L} = G\left(\frac{\partial Y}{\partial K}\right) \quad \text{or} \quad \frac{\partial Y}{\partial K} = G^{-1}\left(\frac{\partial Y}{\partial L}\right). \tag{E4.2.1}$$

In examples where the particular form of F (and hence f) is given, we can eliminate k from (E4.1.4) and (E4.1.5) to obtain the particular form for G. Under competitive assumptions, we can substitute w (wage) $= \partial Y/\partial L$ and r (rental) $= \partial Y/\partial K$ (where the price of output serves as the numeraire). Then (E4.2.1) becomes a relationship between factor prices.

(b) By using (E4.1.4) and (E4.1.5), we see that the slope of the *FPF* is

$$\frac{dw}{dr} = \frac{d[f(k) - kf'(k)]}{d[f'(k)]} = \frac{f'(k)\,dk - f'(k)\,dk - kf''(k)\,dk}{f''(k)\,dk}$$

$$= -k < 0.$$

(c)

$$\frac{d(dw/dr)}{dr} = \frac{d(-k)}{d[f'(k)]} = \frac{-dk}{f''(k)\,dk} = \frac{-1}{f''(k)} > 0,$$

provided $f''(k) < 0$, a condition which will be satisfied if the production function exhibits diminishing marginal productivities for capital and labor. This means that the *FPF* (which is downward-sloping) is concave from above (under, we recall, constant returns to scale). It is of the general shape shown in fig. E4.2.1.

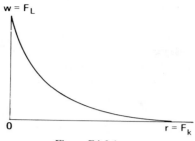

Figure E4.2.1

(d) Denote the elasticity by N_{wr}.

$$N_{wr} = \frac{dw}{dr}\frac{r}{w} = -k\frac{r}{w} = -\frac{Kr}{Lw} = \text{ratio of absolute factor shares.}$$

Hence, the elasticity of the *FPF* is an indicator of income distribution — under marginal productivity pricing — between the two factors of production.

(e) The basic property (or, definition) of Hicks-neutral technical change is that at any given capital–labor ratio (k), the ratio of factor marginal products remains unchanged, i.e. both increase by the same proportion. Thus, comparing the *FPF* before the technical change (FPF_0) to that after (FPF_1), the diagram will look like fig. E4.2.2, where FPF_1 is a radial expansion of FPF_0 (the slopes of the two *FPF*s along any ray through the origin are equal).

On the other hand, Harrod neutrality implies that at any given marginal productivity for capital the marginal productivity of labor increases at the (given) rate of technological change. For this case, the diagram is as in fig. E4.2.3 where the two curves divide any two vertical lines in the same proportion.

Exercise 4.3. Properties of the Cobb–Douglas production function

(a) Answer parts (a)–(c) of E4.1 for the case of the Cobb–Douglas production function:

$$Y = AK^{\alpha}L^{1-\alpha}, \quad 0 < \alpha < 1.$$

(b) What is the significance of the fact that η_{YK} and η_{YL} are constants for this production function?

(c) Calculate the elasticity of substitution for this production function using the expression for σ found in (E4.1.2).

(d) What is the relationship between the answers to parts (b) and (c) of this exercise? Relate your answer to part (d) of E4.1.

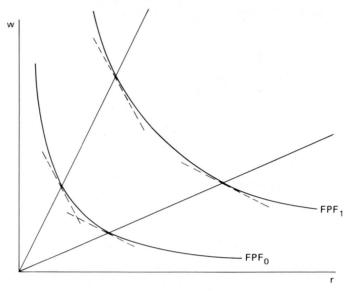

Figure E4.2.2

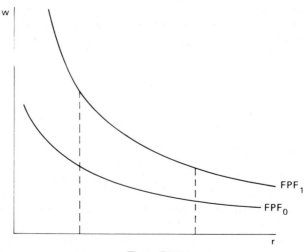

Figure E4.2.3

Answer.   (a) We are given

$$Y = AK^{\alpha}L^{1-\alpha}.$$

Hence

$$y = \frac{Y}{L} = \frac{AK^{\alpha}L^{1-\alpha}}{L} = AK^{\alpha}L^{-\alpha} = A\left(\frac{K}{L}\right)^{\alpha} = Ak^{\alpha},$$

$$\frac{\partial Y}{\partial K} = \alpha AK^{\alpha-1}L^{1-\alpha} = \alpha A \left(\frac{K}{L}\right)^{\alpha-1} = \alpha Ak^{\alpha-1},$$

$$\frac{\partial Y}{\partial L} = (1-\alpha)AK^{\alpha}L^{-\alpha} = (1-\alpha)A\left(\frac{K}{L}\right)^{\alpha} = (1-\alpha)Ak^{\alpha},$$

$$\eta_{YK} = \frac{(\partial Y/\partial K)K}{Y} = \frac{\alpha A(K/L)^{\alpha-1}K}{AK^{\alpha}L^{1-\alpha}} = \frac{\alpha AK^{\alpha}L^{1-\alpha}}{AK^{\alpha}L^{1-\alpha}} = \alpha,$$

$$\eta_{YL} = \frac{(\partial Y/\partial L)L}{Y} = \frac{(1-\alpha)A(K/L)^{\alpha}L}{AK^{\alpha}L^{1-\alpha}} = \frac{(1-\alpha)AK^{\alpha}L^{1-\alpha}}{AK^{\alpha}L^{1-\alpha}} = 1-\alpha.$$

Finally,

$$\eta_{YK} + \eta_{YL} = \alpha + (1-\alpha) = 1.$$

(b) We have seen that $\eta_{YK} = \alpha$ and $\eta_{YL} = 1-\alpha$, where α is a constant, $0 < \alpha < 1$. If we assume perfectly competitive factor and product markets, this means that the relative shares of factors (since $S_K = \eta_{YK}$ and $S_L = \eta_{YL}$) are totally independent of the relative (and, of course, absolute) amounts used of the factors K and L.

(c)

$$\sigma = \frac{F_K F_L}{FF_{KL}}.$$

Since

$$F_{KL} = \frac{\partial \alpha A(K/L)^{\alpha-1}}{\partial L} = \alpha AK^{\alpha-1}\frac{\partial(L^{1-\alpha})}{\partial L} = \alpha AK^{\alpha-1}(1-\alpha)L^{-\alpha},$$

$$\sigma = \frac{\alpha A(K/L)^{\alpha-1}(1-\alpha)A(K/L)^{\alpha}}{AK^{\alpha}L^{1-\alpha}\alpha AK^{\alpha-1}(1-\alpha)L^{-\alpha}} = \frac{\alpha AK^{\alpha-1}L^{1-\alpha}(1-\alpha)AK^{\alpha}L^{-\alpha}}{AK^{\alpha}L^{1-\alpha}\alpha AK^{\alpha-1}(1-\alpha)L^{-\alpha}}.$$

Therefore, $\boxed{\sigma = 1}$.

(d)   In view of part (d) of E4.1, we know that $\sigma = 1$ implies constant factor shares. And, in fact, in part (b) in E4.3 we have seen that these shares are constant.

Exercise 4.4.   A 'generalized' Cobb–Douglas production function

Consider now a 'generalized' Cobb–Douglas production function, $Y = AK^{\alpha}L^{\beta}$, where, generally, $\alpha + \beta \neq 1$ (but still, $0 < \alpha < 1$ and $0 < \beta < 1$), that is, homogeneity of degree other than 1. (Why homogeneity? Why different from 1?)

(a)   Assume that $\alpha + \beta > 1$. What does this imply for $\eta_{YK} + \eta_{YL}$? Why is it no longer possible to assume that all factors are paid according to their marginal products?

(b)   Answer part (a) for $\alpha + \beta < 1$.

Answer.

$$Y = AK^{\alpha}L^{\beta}.$$

Suppose now we multiply K and L by some $\lambda > 0$:

$$Y' = A(\lambda K)^{\alpha}(\lambda L)^{\beta} = \lambda^{\alpha}\lambda^{\beta} AK^{\alpha}L^{1-\alpha} = \lambda^{\alpha+\beta} Y.$$

This shows that Y is homogeneous of degree $\alpha + \beta$.

(a) $\alpha + \beta > 1$.

Using the method of E4.3, it is easy to see that

$$\alpha = \eta_{YK} \quad \text{and} \quad \beta = \eta_{YL}.$$

Hence

$$\eta_{YK} + \eta_{YL} > 1.$$

Therefore, under marginal productivity pricing, we would have

$$S_K + S_L > 1,$$

which would mean that the total factor payments were greater than production. This is an example of the adding-up problem referred to in E4.1.

(b)   If $\alpha + \beta < 1$, then

$$\eta_{YK} + \eta_{YL} < 1$$

(again, $\eta_{YK} = \alpha$ and $\eta_{YL} = \beta$). And again there is an adding-up problem, where now part of the product is not paid to the factors of production (when these are rewarded according to their marginal productivities).

B. Static optimization

Exercise 4.5. Optimization subject to neoclassical technology

The output of a farm is related to the inputs, labor and capital, by the function

$$Y = 100L^{1/2}K^{1/4}, \tag{E4.5.1}$$

where L and K are labor and capital. Find the following.

(a) The cost minimizing input levels for an output level Y if the rental on capital is r and the wage is w. How do you know your solution is a minimum?

(b) The long run cost function.

(c) The effect of an increase in Y on long run marginal cost.

(d) The demand for labor as a function of w, the level of capital inputs and the price of output, p (i.e. the short run demand curve for labor).

(e) The demands for labor and capital as functions of the factor prices, w and r, and the price of output, p (i.e. the long run factor demand equations).

(f) Imagine that the production function is $Y = 100L^{1/2}K^{1/2}$ rather than (E4.5.1). Can you still answer the question in (e)? What if $Y = 100L^{1/2}K^{3/4}$?

(g) Returning to (E4.5.1), do you find it reasonable that a farm production function where the arguments are capital and labor should exhibit decreasing returns to scale?

Answer.

$$Y = 100L^{1/2}K^{1/4},$$

$$\text{cost} = wL + rK.$$

(a) To find the cost minimum subject to producing a given output, Y, we form the Lagrangian

$$H = rK + wL + \lambda(Y - 100L^{1/2}K^{1/4}).$$

At the cost minimum we have

$$\frac{\partial H}{\partial K} = r - \frac{100}{4}\lambda L^{1/2}K^{-3/4} = 0 \tag{E4.5.2}$$

and

$$\frac{\partial H}{\partial L} = w - \frac{100}{2}\lambda L^{-1/2}K^{1/4} = 0. \tag{E4.5.3}$$

Hence,

$$\frac{w}{r} = \frac{2K}{L} \quad \text{or} \quad K = \frac{wL}{2r}.$$

Therefore

$$Y = 100 \left(\frac{wL}{2r}\right)^{1/4} L^{1/2} \tag{E4.5.4}$$

and so we obtain the optimal input levels as

$$L = \left(\frac{Y}{100}\right)^{4/3} \left(\frac{2r}{w}\right)^{1/3} \quad \text{and} \quad K = \left(\frac{Y}{100}\right)^{4/3} \left(\frac{2r}{w}\right)^{-2/3}. \tag{E4.5.5}$$

To see that we have found a minimum, we could check the second-order conditions. But in fact we can be sure that we have found a minimum simply because the production function is concave contoured (i.e. it has isoquants which are the conventional shape).

(b) The long run cost function is of the form

$$C = C(Y, w, r),$$

where $C(Y, w, r)$ is the minimum cost of producing the output level Y when the factor prices are w and r. Hence, from (a) we have

$$C = w \left(\frac{Y}{100}\right)^{4/3} \left(\frac{2r}{w}\right)^{1/3} + r \left(\frac{Y}{100}\right)^{4/3} \left(\frac{2r}{w}\right)^{-2/3},$$

i.e.

$$C = \tfrac{3}{2} w \left(\frac{1}{100}\right)^{4/3} \left(\frac{2r}{w}\right)^{1/3} Y^{4/3}. \tag{E4.5.6}$$

(c) Long run marginal cost (MC) is

$$MC = \frac{\partial C}{\partial Y} = 2w \left(\frac{1}{100}\right)^{4/3} \left(\frac{2r}{w}\right)^{1/3} Y^{1/3}. \tag{E4.5.7}$$

Hence MC increases with Y. (Alternatively, we could have derived (E4.5.7) by recognizing that MC equals λ in (E4.5.2)–(E4.5.4).)

(d) Assume a profit maximizing farm. Then in the short run the farm puts

$$\frac{\partial \text{profit}}{\partial L} = 0,$$

where

$$\text{profit} = \pi = pY - wL - rK$$

$$= 100 \, pL^{1/2} K^{1/4} - wL - rK,$$

and K, p, w and r are exogenously given. Hence

$$\frac{\partial \pi}{\partial L} = -w + 50pL^{-1/2} K^{1/4} = 0.$$

Therefore

$$L = \left(\frac{50p}{w}\right)^2 K^{1/2} \tag{E4.5.8}$$

is the short run demand curve for labor.

(e) In the long run, the farm will choose K, L and Y to maximize

$$\pi = pY - wL - rK$$

subject to

$$Y = 100L^{1/2}K^{1/4}. \tag{E4.5.9}$$

We can solve the problem in two steps. First, whatever level Y is chosen for output, we know that the factor inputs must minimize the costs of producing Y. Hence from (a) we have

$$L = \left(\frac{Y}{100}\right)^{4/3} \left(\frac{2r}{w}\right)^{1/3}$$

and

$$K = \left(\frac{Y}{100}\right)^{4/3} \left(\frac{2r}{w}\right)^{-2/3}. \tag{E4.5.10}$$

The second stage of our problem is to choose Y to maximize

$$\pi = pY - C(Y, r, w),$$

where C was found in part (b), i.e. C is the minimum cost of producing Y, given w and r.

We choose Y so that

$$\frac{\partial \pi}{\partial Y} = p - \frac{\partial C}{\partial Y} = 0, \quad \text{i.e } p = MC. \tag{E4.5.11}$$

We also require that

$$\frac{\partial^2 \pi}{\partial Y^2} < 0. \tag{E4.5.12}$$

Expression (E4.5.12) is included to ensure that we choose a *maximizing* value for Y. However, since we have already found that MC increases with output, (E4.5.12) will be satisfied at all levels of Y.

By substituting from (E4.5.7) into (E4.5.11) we obtain

$$Y = (50)^4 p^3 w^{-2} r^{-1}. \tag{E4.5.13}$$

Finally, we substitute into (E4.5.10), generating the long run demand functions as

$$L = \frac{50^4}{2} p^4 w^{-3} r^{-1} \tag{E4.5.14}$$

and

$$K = \frac{50^4}{4} p^4 w^{-2} r^{-2}. \tag{E4.5.15}$$

(f) With the production function given by

$$Y = 100 L^{1/2} K^{1/2},$$

we can follow the methods of parts (a) and (b) to find that the cost minimizing input levels and the cost function are

$$L = \frac{1}{100} \left(\frac{r}{w} \right)^{1/2} Y,$$

$$K = \frac{1}{100} \left(\frac{w}{r} \right)^{1/2} Y$$

and

$$C = \frac{1}{50} r^{1/2} w^{1/2} Y.$$

Hence

$$MC = \frac{1}{50} r^{1/2} w^{1/2}.$$

This is also the average cost, i.e. marginal cost equals average cost and is independent of the output level. When we turn to the second part of the profit maximizing problem of part (e), i.e. the selection of the optimum level for output, we find three possibilities.

(i) If $p < \frac{1}{50} r^{1/2} w^{1/2}$, then the optimal level for output is zero, i.e. $Y = 0$.

(ii) If $p = \frac{1}{50} r^{1/2} w^{1/2}$, then the level of output is indeterminate. The farm can make zero profit (but no more than zero) at any level of output.

(iii) If $p > \frac{1}{50} r^{1/2} w^{1/2}$, then there is no finite profit maximizing output level. Profit can always be increased by producing more.

When $Y = 100 L^{1/2} K^{3/4}$, it is again possible to derive input demand functions showing the cost minimizing input levels required to produce given output levels at given factor prices. However, on attempting the second stage of the profit maximizing problem, we find that MC (and average cost) declines with increases in Y. With a fixed product price p — p does not decline with increases in Y — there is no finite solution for the optimum value of Y.[7]

To sum up, we have found in part (e) that the profit maximizing model with given prices has a 'sensible' solution if the production function exhibits decreasing returns to scale. But once we postulate constant or increasing returns to scale, we run into difficulties. When marginal cost curves are either flat or declining, the 'exogenously-given-prices' model has nothing with which to explain limitations on output. Consequently, in models where there are constant or increasing returns to scale, you usually will find that outputs are limited by considerations of market sizes. For example, such models may allow for increases in outputs to reduce product prices and/or increase factor prices.

(g) One possible explanation is that there is a left-out factor, e.g. land. The production function might exhibit constant returns to scale if written with land, capital and labor as arguments. By using the form (E4.5.1), there is an implicit assumption that land is a fixed factor.

Exercise 4.6. *Optimization in a two-sector model*

A country can produce food (F) with land and labor according to the following production function:

$$F = 3L_F^{1/3} T_F^{2/3},$$

where L_F and T_F are, respectively, the numbers of man-hours of labor and acres of land devoted to food production. The country can produce cloth at a rate of four units per man-hour of labor devoted to cloth production. No land is required for cloth production.

(a) The country faces constant world market prices for both goods. If food prices are \$ 4.00 per unit and cloth prices are \$ 1.00 per unit, and the country has a labor force of 108 million man-hours per year and a cultivable land area of 64 million acres, how should it distribute its resources so as to maximize the value of production?

(b) How is the labor input to the two sectors affected by an increase in the labor force? By an increase in the amount of cultivable land? What assumptions in the model cause these results to hold?

---

[7] You may be able to find Y such that $p = MC$. But remember the second-order condition (E4.5.12)! It may also be worth pointing out that a continuously declining MC curve does not always mean an 'infinite solution' for the profit maximizing problem. If average cost never falls below p, then the optimum value for Y will be zero.

Answer. (a) The problem for the country is to choose food production and cloth production to maximize the value of production. It is clear that all land and labor will be used and that at the optimal allocation of labor, the value of the marginal product of labor in both uses will be the same. Hence

$$4 \ \frac{\partial F}{\partial L_F} = \frac{\partial C}{\partial L_C},$$

where F and C are food and cloth production. Therefore

$$4 L_F^{-2/3} T_F^{2/3} = 4.$$

Hence

$$L_F = T_F$$

and

$$L_F = 64 \times 10^6$$

$$L_C = 44 \times 10^6.$$

(b) Any increase in the labor force will be entirely devoted to cloth production. This is because the value of the marginal product of labor is constant in cloth production but declining in food production. On the other hand, an increase in land will raise the value of the marginal product of labor in food production. Hence labor will be shifted from cloth to food until the value of the marginal product in food is driven down to 4.

Exercise 4.7. A planning problem

(a) The manufacturing sector of Douglasia is endowed with 100 units of capital and operates under the production function

$$Q = AL^{1/2} K^{1/2},$$

where Q is the quantity of output, L and K are the inputs of labor and capital, respectively, and A is a constant equal to 100.

The planning board of Douglasia seeks to maximize Q by transferring labor (assumed to be unlimited in supply) from the agricultural sector. Assume that it must pay a wage which is equal to the marginal productivity of labor and which must not fall below the subsistence wage w_s, which is equivalent to five units of the output Q. What will be the output of the manufacturing sector?

(b) If the planners' preference (or objective) function W — expressed in monetary terms — includes both Q and the amount of employment in the manufacturing sector (L) explicitly and is defined over the relevant range as

$$W = V_1 Q + V_2 L, \quad V_1 = 2 \quad \text{and} \quad V_2 = 4,$$

where V_1 and V_2 are the relative weights of Q and L in the objective function W, what is the most which the planners would be willing to pay for an additional unit of K?

Answer. (a) $A = 100, K = 100, Q = 1000 L^{1/2}$. Since $\partial Q / \partial L = 500 L^{-1/2} > 0$, the more L the better, under the objective of maximizing Q. However, we have the additional constraint $\partial Q / \partial L \geq 5$ (= subsistence wage), and since $\partial^2 Q / \partial L^2 = -250 L^{-3/2} < 0$, our constrained maximum implies $\partial Q / \partial L = 5$. That is, $500 L^{-1/2} = 5$, i.e. $L^{1/2} = 100$. That is, $Q^* = 100\,000$, where the asterisk superscript to Q indicates that this is the (constrained) maximizing level of manufacturing output.

(b) We assume that the most the planners would be willing to pay for an additional unit of capital is the value of the resulting increase in W.

In part (a) we have seen that for $K = 100$, and for the constraint $\partial Q / \partial L \geq 5$ (which, effectively, reduces to $\partial Q / \partial L = 5$, as shown above), we had $Q_1 = 100\,000$ and $L_1 = (L^{1/2})^2 = 10\,000$, giving $W_1 = 2(100\,000) + 4(10\,000) = 240\,000$, where the one subscripts refer to the first situation (i.e. where $K = 100$).

If now K is increased to $K_2 = 101$, the new optimum for L will satisfy

$$\frac{\partial Q}{\partial L} = 50\sqrt{(101)}L_2^{-1/2} = 5.$$

That is,

$$L_2^{1/2} = 10\sqrt{(101)} \quad \text{and} \quad L_2 = 100 \times 101 = 10\,100.$$

Therefore,

$$Q_2 = 100\sqrt{(101)}\ 10\sqrt{(101)} = 1000 \times 101 = 101\,000$$

and so

$$W_2 = 2(101\,000) + 4(10\,100) = 242\,400.$$

And, finally,

$$dW = W_2 - W_1 = 242\,400 - 240\,000 = 2400.$$

Therefore, 2400 is the most which the planners would be willing to pay for an additional unit of K.[8] *Note*: an alternative, and very neat, approach to the

---

[8] This answer is in terms of welfare units. It translates to $dW/V_1 = 1200$ in terms of output units.

solution of part (b) would be to start directly from dW/dK and to calculate its values for our data (remember that both Q and L depend on K):

$$\frac{dW}{dK} = 2 \frac{\partial Q}{\partial K} + 2 \frac{\partial Q}{\partial L} \frac{\partial L}{\partial K} + 4 \frac{\partial L}{\partial K}.$$

$\partial Q/\partial K = 500$ as is easily evaluated for the data from part (a). $\partial Q/\partial L = w_s$, and since the marginal product of labor is fixed, L/K is fixed. Hence, $\partial L/\partial K$ is obtained by noting that $L/K = 10\,000/100 = 100$, so that $\partial L/\partial K = 100$. We see again that

$$dW/dK = 2 \times 500 + 2 \times 5 \times 100 + 4 \times 100 = 2400.$$

Exercise 4.8. The construction of the production possibilities frontier from a set of production functions and resource endowments

Most firms and virtually all other relevant decision units (societies as a whole, for example) produce more than one product and face the choices that are implicit in a production possibilities frontier. Consider a firm producing two goods, the quantities of output of which are Y_1 and Y_2. The total supplies of the only two inputs are in the short run fixed at $\bar{X}_1$ and $\bar{X}_2$ and the production functions for the two products are

$$Y_1 = f_1(X_{11}, X_{21}) \tag{E4.8.1}$$

and

$$Y_2 = f_2(X_{12}, X_{22}), \tag{E4.8.2}$$

where X_{ij} is the amount of input i devoted to the production of good j.

Since the inputs are limited by the total amounts available, we write the constraints

$$X_{11} + X_{12} \le \bar{X}_1 \tag{E4.8.3}$$

and

$$X_{21} + X_{22} \le \bar{X}_2. \tag{E4.8.4}$$

The relationships (E4.8.1)–(E4.8.4) together with the non-negativity constraints

$$X_{ij} \ge 0, \quad \text{for all } i,j, \tag{E4.8.5}$$

define the production possibilities *set* for the firm in the short run.

(a) The production possibilities *frontier* for this firm is a particular boundary of the production possibilities set and is the locus of points in output space

(Y_1, Y_2) which are Pareto optimal. Thus, a point on the production possibilities frontier can be located by fixing the output of one good and maximizing the output of the other subject to constraints (E4.8.1)–(E4.8.5).

Assume that the achievement of any output combination on the production possibilities frontier requires the full employment of both factors of production. Also assume that the non-negativity constraints, (E4.8.5), are never binding. (Can you justify these assumptions?) Under these assumptions, carry out the optimization mentioned above and show that it leads to the requirement that all points on the production possibilities frontier must satisfy the relationship

$$\frac{\partial Y_1/\partial X_{11}}{\partial Y_1/\partial X_{21}} = \frac{\partial Y_2/\partial X_{12}}{\partial Y_2/\partial X_{22}}. \tag{E4.8.6}$$

(b) When we treat (E4.8.3) and (E4.8.4) as equalities, the resulting equations (E4.8.3') and (E4.8.4'), together with (E4.8.1), (E4.8.2) and (E4.8.6), define the production possibilities *frontier*. Explain why and explain the relationship between these equations and the Edgeworth–Bowley box diagram.

(c) The shape of the production possibilities frontier (or, alternatively, the convexity properties of the production possibilities set described by the frontier and the non-negativity constraints on output levels) is of particular importance in the computation of efficient patterns of resource allocation. For example, you may recall the difficulties encountered in E3.10 on account of the irregular shape of the production possibilities frontier. (If you decided to skip E3.10, you should be ready to tackle it when you have completed this exercise.)

For the present, we ask you to consider the shape of the production possibilities frontier in a society in which two goods are produced: coal and corn. In the production of each good there is a specific factor (mines and agricultural land, respectively) assumed to be nontransferable and in given supply. The only other factor is labor, which can be allocated between the two activities in any way which is compatible with the total supply of labor available (assumed to be 100 man-days).

Assume that the two production functions have the following forms:

$$x_1 = 2L_1^{1/2}; \quad x_2 = L_2^{1/2},$$

where x_1 is the output of corn, x_2 the output of coal, L_1 the amount of labor devoted to the production of corn, and L_2 the amount of labor devoted to the production of coal.

Derive an equation representing the production possibilities frontier for this economy. Graph a few points. Does it describe a convex production possibilities set? Why or why not? Now assume that the production function for coal is as follows:

$$x_2 = L_2^2.$$

Derive the new production possibilities frontier for the economy. Explain the difference in curvatures of the production possibilities frontiers in the two cases.

(d) Now consider the original case (part (a)) with two production functions and two factors of production, neither of which are specific to any production process. If both production functions are characterized by constant returns to scale, will the production possibilities frontier be linear?

What do you conclude determines the curvature of the production possibility frontier? If you have difficulty with the question, read Caves (1963, pp. 31–35) and Samuelson (1949, pp. 183–186).

Answer.   (a)   Let (Y_1^*, Y_2^*) be a point on the production possibilities frontier. Let (X_{11}^*, X_{21}^*), (X_{12}^*, X_{22}^*) be the input vectors used to produce Y_1^* and Y_2^*. Then it must be true that $X^* = (X_{11}^*, X_{21}^*, X_{12}^*, X_{22}^*)$ maximizes

$$Y_1 = f_1(X_{11}, X_{21})$$

subject to

$$f_2(X_{12}, X_{22}) = Y_2^*,$$
$$X_{11} + X_{12} = \overline{X}_1$$

and

$$X_{21} + X_{22} = \overline{X}_2.$$

(Since we are assuming that points on the production possibilities frontier involve full employment of both factors, we write the resource constraints as equalities.)

Using the Lagrangian function

$$L = f_1(X_{11}, X_{21}) + \lambda [f_2(X_{12}, X_{22}) - Y_2^*]$$
$$+ \mu_1(X_{11} + X_{12} - \overline{X}_1) + \mu_2(X_{21} + X_{22} - \overline{X}_2),$$

we derive the necessary conditions for X^* to maximize Y_1 subject to the constraints. It is necessary that there exists $(\lambda^*, \mu_1^*, \mu_2^*)$ such that $(X^*, \lambda^*, \mu_1^*, \mu_2^*)$ solves the following set of equations: the constraint equations plus

$$\frac{\partial f_1}{\partial X_{11}} + \mu_1 = 0; \qquad \frac{\partial f_1}{\partial X_{21}} + \mu_2 = 0, \qquad\qquad \text{(E4.8.7a)}$$

$$\frac{\lambda \partial f_2}{\partial X_{12}} + \mu_1 = 0; \qquad \frac{\lambda \partial f_2}{\partial X_{22}} + \mu_2 = 0. \qquad\qquad \text{(E4.8.7b)}$$

(We are assuming that the sign constraints on the X_{ij}'s are not binding. This allows the various conditions in (E4.8.7) to be written as equalities.)

Eliminating λ, μ_1, and μ_2, we obtain

$$\frac{\partial f_1/\partial X_{11}}{\partial f_1/\partial X_{21}} = \frac{\partial f_2/\partial X_{12}}{\partial f_2/\partial X_{22}} ,$$

demonstrating (E4.8.6).

We can conclude that the following set of equations will be satisfied by any output vector (Y_1, Y_2) and the corresponding input vectors where (Y_1, Y_2) is on the production possibilities frontier:

$$Y_1 = f_1(X_{11}, X_{21}), \tag{E4.8.1}$$

$$Y_2 = f_2(X_{12}, X_{22}), \tag{E4.8.2}$$

$$X_{11} + X_{12} = \overline{X}_1, \tag{E4.8.3'}$$

$$X_{21} + X_{22} = \overline{X}_2, \tag{E4.8.4'}$$

$$\frac{\partial Y_1/\partial X_{11}}{\partial Y_1/\partial X_{21}} = \frac{\partial Y_2/\partial X_{12}}{\partial Y_2/\partial X_{22}} . \tag{E4.8.6}$$

$\left. \vphantom{\begin{matrix}1\\2\\3\\4\\5\end{matrix}} \right\} A$

These equations were generated under the assumptions of (i) full employment of factors and (ii) no binding non-negativity constraints. A sufficient condition for assumption (i) to be valid is that all the first derivatives of f_1 and f_2 are positive for any input vectors, i.e. extra inputs of either factor can always contribute to increasing the output of either good. A sufficient condition for assumption (ii) to be valid is that the marginal product of each factor, i, in the production of each good, k, becomes very large as the ratio $X_{ik}/X_{jk}, i \neq j$, becomes very small. Under this condition, it will always be optimal to use a nonzero input of both factors to produce any nonzero output of either commodity.

(b) List A gives five equations in six variables $(Y_1, Y_2, X_{11}, X_{21}, X_{12}, X_{22})$. In principle, we can generally eliminate four of these, leaving us with a relation between Y_1 and Y_2: $Y_1 = \varphi(Y_2)$.
This will be the production possibilities frontier. The relationship between the equations in list A and the Edgeworth–Bowley box can be explained as follows: (E4.8.3') and (E4.8.4') determine the size of the box, (E4.8.1) and (E4.8.2) give the isoquants inside the box; and when (E4.8.6) is satisfied, we are on the contract curve, i.e. the locus of tangent points between the isoquants.

(c) Write $L_1 = 100 - L_2$. Then

$$x_1 = 2L_1^{1/2} = 2(100 - L_2)^{1/2}$$

so that

$$x_1^2 = 4(100 - L_2)$$

or

$$L_2 = 100 - x_1^2/4$$

and by substitution we find that the equation for the production possibilities frontier is

$$x_2 = (100 - x_1^2/4)^{1/2}.$$

The slope of the frontier is

$$\frac{dx_2}{dx_1} = \frac{-[100 - (x_1^2/4)]^{-1/2}}{2} \frac{x_1}{2}$$

$$= -\frac{x_1}{4x_2},$$

which is less than zero in the relevant range.

$$\frac{d^2x_2}{dx_1^2} = \frac{d}{dx_1} \left(-\frac{1}{4} \frac{x_1}{x_2} \right) = -\frac{1}{4} \left[\frac{x_2 - x_1(dx_2/dx_1)}{x_2^2} \right],$$

and since

$$\frac{dx_2}{dx_1} < 0,$$

we have shown that

$$\frac{d^2x_2}{dx_1^2} < 0.$$

Thus, the transformation curve has a negative slope and is concave (i.e. it lies above its chord). With the axes considered as lower boundaries, the production set is convex.

Now, change the x_2 production function and substitute to obtain the equation for the new production possibilities frontier

$$x_2 = \left(100 - \frac{x_1^2}{4} \right)^2.$$

Then

$$\frac{dx_2}{dx_1} = -2 \left(100 - \frac{x_1^2}{4} \right) \frac{2x_1}{4} = -\left(100 - \frac{x_1^2}{4} \right) x_1 = -x_2^{1/2} x_1,$$

which is less than zero in the relevant range. But

$$\frac{d^2x_2}{dx_1^2} = -\left(100 - \frac{3x_1^2}{4} \right).$$

x_1 can take any value from 0 to 20. ($x_1 = 20$ when $L_1 = 100$.) Hence $(d^2x_2)/(dx_1^2)$ changes sign in the relevant range. In fact,

$$\frac{d^2x_2}{dx_1^2} \gtrless 0, \quad \text{for } x_1 \gtrless \frac{20\sqrt{3}}{3}.$$

Thus, the transformation curve has a negative slope but is not concave. We can explain the difference in curvature in the two cases as follows. At small values of x_1 the marginal product of a unit of labor in the production of x_1 is high (check this). As more labor is transferred to x_1 production, diminishing returns to scale reduce the marginal product of labor in x_1. Hence, more and more labor must be transferred from x_2 in order to increase x_1 by one unit. If x_2 is subject to diminishing returns, the transfer of labor from x_2 will raise the marginal product of labor in x_2. Therefore, the transfer of a given amount of labor from x_2 reduces x_2 production by more and more. So with diminishing returns to scale in both industries we have two reasons why more and more x_2 must be given up to get one more unit of x_1 as x_1 increases (which is why $(d^2x_2)/(dx_1^2) < 0$). First, it becomes harder to produce x_1 and, secondly, the sacrifice in production of x_2 increases. But when there are increasing returns to scale in x_2, the second reason no longer holds. Now as resources are transferred from x_2 the marginal product of labor in x_2 falls. In the example given in this problem, the marginal product of labor in x_2 falls sufficiently fast that eventually less x_2 must be given up to get one more unit of x_1 as x_1 increases (that is, $(d^2x_2)/(dx_1^2)$ becomes positive).

(d) No. A linear production possibilities frontier implies that an increase of, say, k units of x_2 can always be achieved by the sacrifice of one unit of x_1. But this is a very special case. More generally we would expect that if x_2 were large, we would be forced by the scarcity of factors to use an 'unsuitable factor mix' in its production. The initial reductions in x_2 can be made by sacrificing combinations of inputs from x_2's production, which are more suitable for production of x_1. This type of argument leads us to expect a concave production possibilities frontier.

Exercise 4.9. The construction of a production function

Economists often treat the firm's production function as data and implicitly assume that the decision-making required to 'reach' the production function is carried out efficiently.[9] They confine themselves to questions such as how the

---

[9] The literature on X-efficiency is an exception, see for example, Leibenstein (1966) and Krueger (1974). These authors argue that efficiency in the use of given sets of inputs varies with the economic environment — the competitiveness of markets, the levels of tariffs, etc.

input levels are chosen under the assumption that any given set of inputs will be used so as to maximize the size of the output. The current exercise and E4.12–E4.14 give explicit attention to preproduction-function questions, i.e. questions of the form: how will the firm use a given set of inputs so as to maximize its output? In this exercise we ask you to derive

(a) the production function,

(b) the input demand functions (inputs as functions of output level and factor prices), and

(c) the cost function for a trucking firm whose output is measured by the number, m, of truck-miles moved per day and whose daily inputs are the number, G, of gallons of gasoline and the number, H, of hours of truck-driver labor. The operating conditions are assumed to be as follows.

(1) The total outlays comprise: (i) wages of the drivers amounting to $\$ w$ per hour, and (ii) costs of gasoline, which is bought at $\$ p$ per gallon.

(2) Gasoline usage per truck-mile increases with driving speed so that

$$G \geq Am + Bsm,$$

where s is driving speed measured in miles per hour, and A and B are positive parameters

(3) The trucking firm owns and keeps in operating shape many trucks and thus can use one, two, or more of them depending on its needs.

Hint: (i) The preproduction-function decision variable is s. In deriving the production function you will eliminate s by expressing it in terms of H and G under the assumption that s is always chosen to maximize m. (ii) Do not worry if you are unable to express the production function in explicit form. An implicit form

$$\psi(m,H,G) = 0$$

is quite acceptable and turns out to be easy to work with in part (b). However, it is possible to obtain the explicit form

$$m = f(H,G).$$

Answer. (a) The production function. For given input levels G and H, the firm will choose s to maximize

$$m$$

subject to

$$G \geq Am + Bsm$$

and

$$H \geq m/s.$$

The first of these constraints relates gasoline consumption to miles and speed while the second says that hours employed must be at least as great as miles divided by speed. Thus, for given values of the inputs G and H, we see that output, m, is limited according to

$$m \le \frac{G}{A + Bs} \tag{E4.9.1}$$

and

$$m \le sH. \tag{E4.9.2}$$

Since the right-hand side of (E4.9.1) is a decreasing function of s and the right-hand side of (E4.9.2) is an increasing function of s, it follows that the maximum value for m can occur only when s is chosen so that

$$\frac{G}{A + Bs} = sH.$$

Hence, the optimal speed, $s^* = s^*(G, H)$, will satisfy

$$G = s^* H(A + Bs^*) \tag{E4.9.3}$$

and both constraints (E4.9.1) and (E4.9.2) will be satisfied as equalities. In particular,

$$s^* = m/H. \tag{E4.9.4}$$

On combining (E4.9.3) and (E4.9.4) we obtain the production function

$$Bm^2 + AHm - GH = 0. \tag{E4.9.5}$$

Eq. (E4.9.5) is in an implicit form. We generate an explicit form by applying the quadratic formula, giving

$$m = -\frac{AH}{2B} + \frac{\sqrt{[(AH)^2 + 4BGH]}}{2B}. \tag{E4.9.6}$$

(The other root of (E4.9.5) can be ignored since it gives a negative value for m.) Check that the production function (E4.9.6) exhibits constant returns to scale. Can you show that the marginal products, $\partial m/\partial H$ and $\partial m/\partial G$, are both positive?

(b)   The input demand functions. We choose G and H to minimize

$$pG + wH$$

subject to (E4.9.5) where we regard m as exogenously given. (It is only for algebraic convenience that we work with (E4.9.5) rather than (E4.9.6).)

The first-order conditions are

$$p - \lambda H = 0. \tag{E4.9.7}$$

$$w + \lambda Am - \lambda G = 0 \tag{E4.9.8}$$

and

$$Bm^2 + AHm - GH = 0. \tag{E4.9.9}$$

We substitute from (E4.9.7) into (E4.9.8) and find that

$$G = \frac{Hw}{p} + Am.$$

Now we substitute for G into (E4.9.9):

$$Bm^2 + AHm - \frac{H^2 w}{p} - AHm = 0.$$

From here we quickly find that the input demand equations are

$$H = m\, B^{1/2} \sqrt{(p/w)} \tag{E4.9.10}$$

and

$$G = m\, (A + B^{1/2} \sqrt{(w/p)}). \tag{E4.9.11}$$

(c) The cost function. The minimum cost of producing m when the factor prices are w and p is given by

$$C(m, w, p) = wH + pG,$$

where H and G are defined by (E4.9.10) and (E4.9.11). Hence,

$$C(m, w, p) = 2\, m\, B^{1/2} (wp)^{1/2} + mAp. \tag{E4.9.12}$$

Exercise 4.10.   Class interests and induced technical change

Consider an economy whose capital stock K and number of laborers L are given. The aggregate production function is

$$Y = f(AK, BL),$$

where for a given set of parameters (A, B) the production function describes a set of isoquants which are convex to the origin.

The research and development facilities of the society may expand the production possibilities by altering A or B or both. They are assigned a fixed budget

to carry out their investigations, and given this they face an innovation possibilities function,

$$g(A,B) = 0,$$

as illustrated in fig. E4.10.1. The problem is to determine the optimal pattern of
technological change. (You may consider the introduction of new techniques as
instantaneous and ignore dynamic considerations.)

(a) Explain what you understand by the innovation possibilities function.
Classify the types of technical progress associated with increases in A and B.

(b) What decision rules would you prescribe for the research and development section if the social goal is to maximize income?

(c) Assume now that although labor markets are competitive, and that, for
this reason, labor must be paid its marginal product, the owners of capital
collude in the determination of research and development priorities. What decision rules should they follow in order to maximize their collective income? (In
parts (b) and (c) give your decisions rules an economic interpretation.)

(d) Compare the pattern of technological progress and income distribution
which results from the institutional assumptions in parts (b) and (c). Is it possible to say whether the capitalists will increase or decrease A/B compared with
the income maximizers?

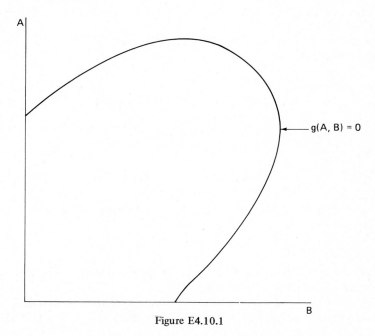

Figure E4.10.1

Answer.   (a)   By concentrating research effort in various directions, society may change the production function in different ways. Two types of technical progress are available in the given model: labor-augmenting or Harrod-neutral technical progress, and capital-augmenting or Solow-neutral technical progress (review Allen (1967, pp. 236–258) if these terms are unfamiliar). If a large proportion of the resources available for research is devoted to labor-augmenting technical progress (i.e. increasing B), then the increase in A will be small and vice versa. Hence, the innovation possibilities function gives the various combinations of capital- and labor-augmenting technical progress available to society from the fixed research budget.

(b)   The income maximizing problem is to choose A and B to maximize

$$f(AK, BL) \tag{E4.10.1}$$

subject to

$$g(A, B) = 0.$$

In fig. E4.10.2, we have drawn isoquants of the form

$$F(A, B) \equiv f(AK, BL) = w_i, \quad i = 1, 2, 3,$$

i.e. we have sketched combinations of A and B, which together with society's given factor endowments K and L, allow output levels of w_1, w_2 and w_3.

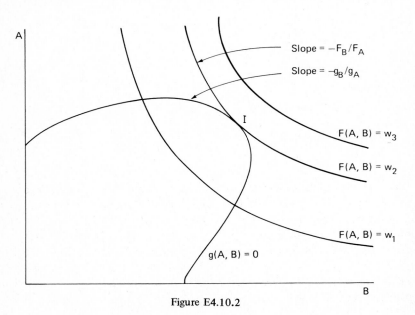

Figure E4.10.2

(Assuming that the $K-L$ isoquants — for given A and B — are convex to the origin, it is clear that the $A-B$ isoquants are also convex to the origin.) Fig. E4.10.2 places the income maximizing combination of A and B at the point I and shows that the income maximizing decision rules are that A and B should be chosen to satisfy

$$g_B/g_A = F_B/F_A \quad \text{and} \quad g(A,B) = 0, \tag{E4.10.2}$$

where g_A, g_B, F_A and F_B are partial derivatives of g and F. It follows from the definition of F that $F_A = Kf_K/A$ and $F_B = Lf_L/B$, where f_L and f_K are the marginal products of labor and capital. Thus (E4.10.2) may be re-expressed as

$$g_B/g_A = \frac{ALf_L}{BKf_K} \quad \text{and} \quad g(A,B) = 0. \tag{E4.10.3}$$

(c) The capitalists' problem is to choose A and B to maximize

$$f(AK, BL) - f_L L$$

subject to

$$g(A,B) = 0.$$

That is, they choose A and B to maximize $F(A,B) - BF_B$ subject to $g(A,B) = 0$. This implies that they should choose A and B so that

$$\frac{-BF_{BB}}{F_A - BF_{BA}} = \frac{g_B}{g_A} \tag{E4.10.4}$$

and

$$g(A,B) = 0. \tag{E4.10.5}$$

Alternatively, we may express rule (E4.10.4) as

$$\frac{AL}{BK} \left(\frac{f_L - f_{LL}L}{f_K - f_{LK}L} \right) = \frac{g_B}{g_A}.$$

The two sets of decision rules can now be interpreted. (E4.10.2) shows that if society wishes to maximize output, then it should equate the marginal rate of transformation between A and B (i.e. g_B/g_A) with the marginal rate of substitution between A and B in *production* (i.e. F_B/F_A). On the other hand, if the objective is profit maximization, then the marginal rate of substitution between A and B in *generating profits* should be equal to the marginal rate of transformation between A and B. The marginal rate of substitution between A and B in profit generating equals

$$\frac{\text{marginal profit from an increase in } B}{\text{marginal profit from an increase in } A} = \frac{\partial(f - Lf_L)/\partial B}{\partial(f - Lf_L)/\partial A},$$

giving the left-hand side of (E4.10.4).

(d) The colluding capitalists will lower total income (since in general they move away from I in fig. E4.10.2) but increase the absolute income of capitalists (since the capitalists' income must be at least as great as in the initial situation). Hence, the income of labor and the labor share of income will fall. For deciding the direction in which the capitalists will move A/B from the income maximizing solution, the critical question is whether capital and labor are easily substitutable. For example, if capital and labor are very poor substitutes, then labor augmenting technical progress may in fact lower the marginal product of labor (and wages) sufficiently to induce the capitalists to choose a higher value for B/A than would be chosen by the income maximizers. On the other hand, if capital and labor substitute easily, then labor augmenting technical progress will raise the marginal product of labor and it may be in the capitalists' best interest to lower B/A relative to the income maximizing value. Without further information no firmer conclusions are possible.

Exercise 4.11. Technological change, factor supplies and income distribution

Using a two-factor, two-commodity, perfectly competitive model with constant product prices, discuss the following.

(a) The effect of Hicks-neutral technological change in the capital intensive sector on the distribution of income between capital and labor.

(b) The effect of an increase in the supplies of labor on the absolute and relative amounts of income going to capital and labor. What is the effect on the wage?

(c) Would you get analogous results if you used a one-sector model? Be sure that you understand the difference.

Note: in both parts (a) and (b) assume that the two production functions are homogeneous of degree 1. You may also want to assume that the relative factor intensities of the two technologies are unambiguous, i.e. the same one of the two technologies is the more capital intensive at every set of factor prices. This requirement of no 'factor intensity reversal' will be met as long as any two isoquants representing the two technologies do not intersect more than once. (Why is this sufficient?)

Answer.   (a) Consider the two goods shown in fig. E4.11.1, where A is capital intensive relative to B. (Why is it permissible to represent each technology by a

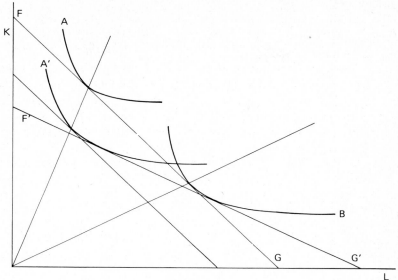

Figure E4.11.1

single isoquant?) The isoquants *A* and *B* represent outputs which (at the given goods prices) exchange for equal value in the market.

The line *FG*, which may be considered an isocost function, gives the (unique) equilibrium factor-price ratio in the economy. Any other factor-price ratio would yield differences in profitability between the two sectors. If you do not understand why, reread Findlay and Grubert (1959). Would a unique equilibrium factor-price ratio exist in the presence of factor intensity reversal? Explain why or why not.

Isoquant *A'*, representing an output equal to that represented by *A*, shows Hicks-neutral technical progress in the capital intensive sector, leaving the cost minimizing capital–labor ratio unchanged at the original equilibrium factor prices. If the factor prices did not change, which sector would become more profitable? The new equilibrium factor price line is *F'G'*, showing a shift in prices (and therefore in factor shares) to capital. Notice that although no change in factor supply has been specified, the capital–labor ratio in both sectors has fallen, increasing the marginal product of capital relative to the marginal product of labor in both sectors.

Given the higher profitability in the production of *A* following the introduction of the new technique, but prior to the change in factor prices, we may suspect that the factor-price adjustment was brought about by changes in the

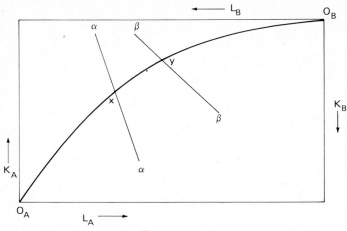

Figure E4.11.2

distribution of resources and output between the two sectors, namely in the expansion of sector A relative to sector B. To see this process more clearly, we can examine the effects of Hicks-neutral technical change by looking at an Edgeworth–Bowley box (fig. E4.11.2). The contract curve $O_A O_B$ shows A to be the more capital intensive good. Hicks-neutral technical progress in industry A can be represented merely by reassigning output levels to the A isoquants, e.g. increasing all the outputs by α percent. The position of the contract curve is unaltered. Next, we translate the effects of Hicks-neutral technical change from the box diagram to the transformation curve.

For any output of B shown on the contract curve, the corresponding output of A has increased α percent, and hence the shift in the transformation curve is of the form shown in fig. E4.11.3. Since the product prices are unchanged, the output of B falls while that of A rises. This can be seen by noting the shift in production from I to II.

Now return to fig. E4.11.2. The reduction in the production of B must move us back along the contract curve toward O_B, e.g. from point x to y. But as we move toward O_B, the factor-price lines (i.e. $\alpha\alpha$ and $\beta\beta$ in the diagram) become flatter,[10] indicating an increase in the rental–wage ratio. Also, since the factor quantities are constant, there is an increase in the capital share. The fall in the capital–labor ratio in both sectors can be seen in fig. E4.11.2 by constructing

[10]   Sketch in some isoquants to convince yourself. Remember that we are assuming linearly homogeneous production functions.

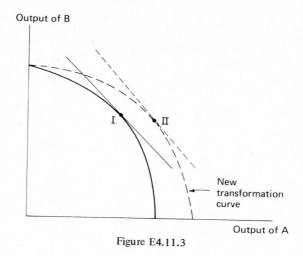

Figure E4.11.3

rays from each origin (O_A and O_B) to points x and y. The slopes of these rays indicate the factor intensity of each sector before and after the change in technology.

(b) Given the constancy of the relative prices of the two commodities, one can show (as was suggested above) that in the case where the isoquants intersect only once (as in fig. E4.11.1), factor proportions and the factor-price ratio are uniquely determined. It should be clear from the above discussion that the equilibrating mechanism in this case is the alteration of the distribution of output between sectors. Given this result, we observe that the wage—rental ratio will remain unchanged after the increase in labor supply, while labor's absolute and relative income will increase. How will the distribution of output between the two sectors change?

(c) The results in the one-sector case are as follows: (1) Hicks-neutral technological change has no effect on distribution, and (2) the relative share of labor will increase (decrease) if the elasticity of substitution between capital and labor is greater than (less than) 1.

Why was the elasticity of substitution not relevant to the problem for the two-sector model? Remember that in a single-sector model all factor substitution must take place directly, in production. In a multisector model, factor substitution takes place both directly in production and indirectly through shifts in the composition of output among sectors of differing factor intensities.

C. An introduction to linear models

Exercise 4.12.   Optimization with linear technologies

Three methods of producing Z are known: to produce 100 units of output,
   (1)   process A requires 20 man-days of labor and 10 days of machine time;
   (2)   process B requires 10 man-days of labor and 20 days of machine time;
and
   (3)   process C requires 17.5 man-days of labor and 16 days of machine time.
   Each process is divisible and operates under constant returns to scale independent of the other processes.
   (a)   Assume 20 man-days and 20 machine-days are available. Set up and solve the output maximization 'primal' linear programming problem and do the same for its dual. Interpret the dual variables. Find the marginal rate of substitution between machine-days and labor-days at the output maximizing point.
   (b)   Construct the marginal productivity of labor curve given that machine time is fixed at 20 days.
   (c)   Using your results from parts (a) and (b), find the *MP* of machine days when the factor input levels are 20 man-days and 20 machine-days. If machines are rented by the day, and if both factors are paid their marginal product in kind, how much of the product will be left for management? Why?

Answer.   (a)   *Primal.* Maximize

$$100(x_1 + x_2 + x_3)$$

(E4.12.1)

subject to

$$\begin{bmatrix} 20 & 10 & 17.5 \\ 10 & 20 & 16 \end{bmatrix} \begin{bmatrix} x_1 \\ x_2 \\ x_3 \end{bmatrix} \leq \begin{bmatrix} 20 \\ 20 \end{bmatrix}$$

$$x_1, x_2, x_3 \geq 0.$$

To solve the problem, set up a graph and observe that process C is dominated by the others (see fig. E4.12.1). The point *III* showing the factor inputs necessary to produce 100 units of output with process C alone lies above the 100 isoquant, illustrating that process C will never be used. Hence, we know that $x_3 = 0$. It is also clear from the diagram that within the feasible set, z is the point on the highest isoquant. Hence both factors are fully used. We could complete the

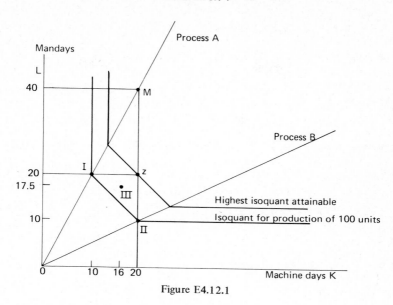

Figure E4.12.1

solution geometrically, but it is more convenient to solve for x_1 and x_2 algebraically. We have

$$20x_1 + 10x_2 = 20$$

and

$$10x_1 + 20x_2 = 20.$$

Therefore $x_1 = x_2 = \frac{2}{3}$, $x_3 = 0$.
Dual. Minimize

$$20p_1 + 20p_2 \qquad\qquad\qquad\text{(E4.12.2)}$$

subject to

$$[p_1, p_2] \begin{bmatrix} 20 & 10 & 17.5 \\ 10 & 20 & 16 \end{bmatrix} \geq 100\,[1, 1, 1]$$

and $p_1, p_2 \geq 0$.

Since the first two activities are nonzero in the primal, from the 'equilibrium theorem' of linear programming we know that the first two constraints are binding in the dual. Hence

$$20p_1 + 10p_2 = 100$$

and

$$10p_1 + 20p_2 = 100,$$

giving the dual solution

$$p_1 = p_2 = 3\tfrac{1}{3}.$$

You should check to see that the third dual constraint is satisfied and that the values of the primal and dual problems are the same.

Interpretations of the dual variables. One possible interpretation of the dual variables can be obtained by asking the following question: what is the lowest value that the firm should put on its productive resources in terms of output? That is to say, what is the lowest number of units of output that the firm should accept in exchange for its machine and labor endowments? Let p_1 and p_2 be the appropriate values per man-day and machine-day, respectively. Then certainly p_1 and p_2 should be such that

$$20p_1 + 10p_2 \geq 100.$$

This is because process A can be operated to give 100 units of output if we retain 20 man-days and 10 machine-days. Similarly, consideration of processes B and C shows that p_1 and p_2 should satisfy

$$10p_1 + 20p_2 \geq 100$$

and

$$17.5p_1 + 16p_2 \geq 100.$$

Finally, p_1 and p_2 should be non-negative. Hence, the problem of finding the minimum appropriate value for the firm's resources becomes that of minimizing $20p_1 + 20p_2$ subject to the constraints mentioned above. But this is precisely the dual problem. So a reasonable interpretation of the dual variables is that they give the appropriate values for the firm's resources when it is considering disposal of these resources.

Another interpretation of the dual variables can be seen from the duality theorem. This important theorem of linear programming says that the optimal values for the objective functions of the primal and dual problems (for problems which have feasible and bounded solutions) will be equal. The first interpretation of the dual variables given above should help to convince you that this theorem is true.

Applying the duality theorem in our problem gives

optimal value of primal = output

$$= 100(x_1^* + x_2^*)$$

$$= Lp_1^* + Kp_2^*$$

= optimal value of dual,

where the asterisks denote the optimal levels of variables and L and K are availabilities of man-days and machine-days, respectively.

Consider a small increase, dL, in the availability of man-days. K is held constant. Then

$$dx = (dL)p_1^* + (dp_1^*)L + (dp_2^*)K,$$

where x denotes output. Normally a small change in the weights in the objective function of a linear program will not affect the optimum values for the variables. The geometrical picture to keep in mind is given in fig. E4.12.2. Hence in the usual case

$$dp_1^* = dp_2^* = 0 \quad \text{and} \quad dx = (dL)p_1^*.$$

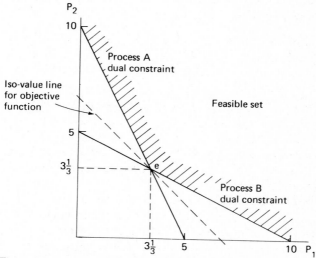

Figure E4.12.2. This figure illustrates the dual problem (E4.12.2). It is not necessary to show the third dual constraint because it does not reduce the feasible region and can play no role in the solution. Also notice that a small change in L will rotate the dotted objective line slightly, but it will not change the solution away from point e.

That is

$$dx/dL = p_1^*.$$

Similarly

$$dx/dK = p_2^*.$$

Therefore p_1^* and p_2^* can be interpreted as the marginal productivities of man-days and machine-days. With this interpretation, the dual variables are often called 'shadow prices'. They give the prices which the firm should be willing to pay for extra units of the various resources. We also note that the marginal rate of substitution between machine- and man-days is given by

$$MRS_{KL} = - \left(\frac{dL}{dK} \right)_{dx=0}.$$

Then assuming that $dp_1^* = dp_2^* = 0$, we find that

$$- \left(\frac{dL}{dK} \right)_{dx=0} = \frac{dx/dK}{dx/dL} = \frac{p_2^*}{p_1^*}$$

Hence

$$MRS_{KL} = \frac{3\frac{1}{3}}{3\frac{1}{3}} = 1.$$

(b) We use fig. E4.12.1 to help answer this question. With $K = 20$ and L between zero and 10, labor is the only scarce factor. We use process B alone, and the appropriate production function is

$$x = 100x_2 = 100 \frac{L}{10} ,$$

giving

$$MP_L = 10.$$

With L greater than 10 but less than 40, both processes will be used and both resources will be scarce. In this second stage we have

$$20x_1 + 10x_2 = L$$

and

$$10x_1 + 20x_2 = 20.$$

Hence

$$x = 100(x_1 + x_2) = 3\frac{1}{3} (L + 20),$$

giving

$$MP_L = 3\tfrac{1}{3}.$$

Finally for $L > 40$, capital is the only scarce resource and MP_L falls to zero. The marginal product of labor function is shown in fig. E4.12.3.

Summarizing, we have

$$MP_L = 10, \quad \text{for } 0 \le L < 10,$$
$$= 3\tfrac{1}{3}, \quad \text{for } 10 < L < 40,$$
$$= 0, \quad \text{for } L > 40.$$

We still have not determined the MP_L at $L = 10$ and $L = 40$, i.e. at the break points between the stages. The reason is that $\partial x/\partial L$ does not exist for these values of L, i.e. the total product curve is not smooth at these points (see fig. E4.12.4). It is interesting to return to fig. E4.12.2 and to notice that for $L = 10$, $K = 20$, the dotted objective function will lie coincident with the constraint boundary B. With $L = 40$, $K = 20$, the objective function is coincident with boundary A. In these two cases the dual solution is not unique. Hence there is no well-defined MP_L (or MP_K). Also, in terms of our second interpretation of the dual variables we note that for small changes in the primal resource availabilities (which are the dual objective weights) we can no longer treat the dual solution as unchanged, i.e. we do not have $dp_1^* = dp_2^* = 0$. In this case our second interpretation of the dual variables (i.e. as shadow prices) breaks down.

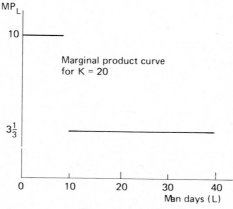

Figure E4.12.3

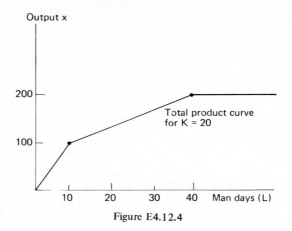

Figure E4.12.4

(c) From the dual solution and the interpretation of the dual variables, we know that with resource endowments of $K = 20$, $L = 20$,

$$MP_L = 3\tfrac{1}{3}; \quad MP_K = 3\tfrac{1}{3}.$$

Hence total factor payments $= 3\tfrac{1}{3} \times 20 + 3\tfrac{1}{3} \times 20 = 133\tfrac{1}{3}$. From the primal solution

$$x = 100(x_1 + x_2)$$
$$= 100(\tfrac{2}{3} + \tfrac{2}{3})$$
$$= 133\tfrac{1}{3}.$$

Total factor payments exhaust the total product, leaving nothing for management. This result was certainly to be expected in view of the duality theorem of linear programming – see the solution to (a). Alternatively, given that the production function used here is homogeneous of degree 1, we should not be surprised that there is no 'adding-up' problem (see E4.1 (c) and E4.4).

Exercise 4.13. An illustration of Samuelson's (non)substitution theorem [11]

Consider the input–output type of technologies shown in table E4.13.1 for a 100-worker economy producing 'primary' and 'secondary' goods.

---

[11]   For a short clear statement of Samuelson's proposition and its significance, read Baumol (1972, ch. 20, section 4.1).

Table E4.13.1

Inputs	Primary good		Secondary good	
	A	B	1	2
P goods	0	0	7	3
S goods	2	3	0	0
Labor	40	25	50	60
Production	10	10	10	10

(a) Show graphically that technology B alone will be used to produce primary goods and that technology 2 alone will be used to produce secondary goods. Show that shifts in society's demands for the two goods will not affect the choice of production technologies. *Hint*: treat the commodity inputs as negative outputs. Then for each technology, plot the 'output' combination of the two goods which would be generated if the entire labor endowment were devoted to using the technology. Draw the obvious lines. If you have trouble, see Dorfman, Samuelson and Solow (1958, pp. 219–227).

(b) Suppose there were two primary factors in the economy. Would the choice of technology in general be independent of the pattern of society's commodity demands?

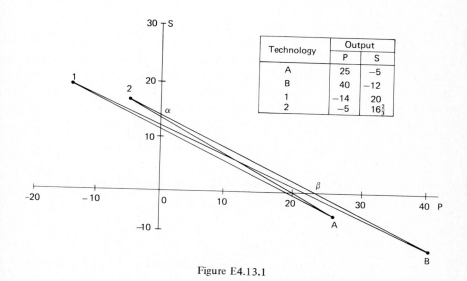

Figure E4.13.1

Answer.   (a) The results of applying all 100 labor units to the various technologies are indicated in fig. E4.13.1.

By inspecting the figure, we see that the economy's production possibilities (in the absence of external trade which would allow negative 'outputs' to be made up by imports) are defined by the triangle $\alpha\beta0$. Assuming that society is not satiated, the optimal output combination of goods S and P will occur on the production possibilities frontier $\alpha\beta$. Achievement of any point on this frontier requires the operation of technologies B and 2. Hence, irrespective of the pattern of society's commodity demands, only technologies B and 2 will be required.

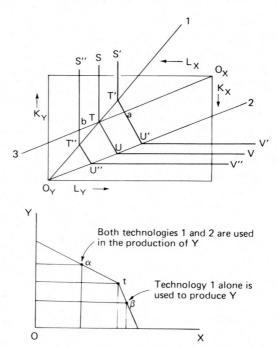

Figure E4.13.2. For simplicity we have illustrated a case in which there are no intermediate inputs. Each technology requires only capital and labor. The $K-L$ ratios for the two Y-producing technologies are shown by the rays O_y1 and O_y2. $STUV$, $S'T'U'V'$ and $S''T''U''V''$ are typical isoquants for the production of Y (see fig. E4.12.1). The ray O_X3 shows the only $K-L$ ratio available for the production of good X. Notice that after production of X is expanded past that available at point T, there will be unemployment of capital. Points α, t and β on the transformation frontier correspond to points a, T and b in the box diagram.

(b) Fig. E4.13.2 is the Edgeworth—Bowley box and the production possibilities frontier for an economy in which there are two factors of production, two commodities, *one* technology for producing good X and *two* technologies for producing good Y. In the particular case illustrated, increases in the demand (from zero) for good X lead to a transfer from technology 2 towards technology 1 in the production of good Y. Thus, we can conclude that in the two-factor model, the choice of technology is not, in general, independent of the composition of society's product demands.

Exercise 4.14. Income distribution in Ricardia

Ricardia is a country producing only wheat and is endowed with two types of agricultural land: 60 acres of good land and 40 acres of not-so-good land. On an acre of good land, 2 man-years are required to produce a gross output of 50 bushels of wheat, while on one-half acre of not-so-good land 2 man-years are required to produce 30 bushels. (It is assumed that the indicated input proportions for each type of land are fixed.) There are a very large number of laborers available to Ricardia. However, to employ a laborer for one year, capitalists must pay a wage of 10 bushels in advance. Assume that capitalists have a wage fund of 2000 bushels, i.e. sufficient to employ 200 laborers. Use a linear programming approach to answer the following.

How many bushels of wheat will be produced?

What will be the marginal social product of a unit of employed labor, i.e. what is the additional output allowed by a 10 bushel increase in the wage fund?

Indicate the rent (in bushels per year) imputed to the two types of land; the functional distribution of income between rent, profit and wages, and the capitalists' rate of return.

Answer. The linear programming maximization problem facing Ricardia is: maximize

$$z = 50X_1 + 60X_2$$

subject to

$$2X_1 + 4X_2 \leq 200,$$

$$X_1 \leq 60,$$

$$X_2 \leq 40,$$

$$X_1 \geq 0$$

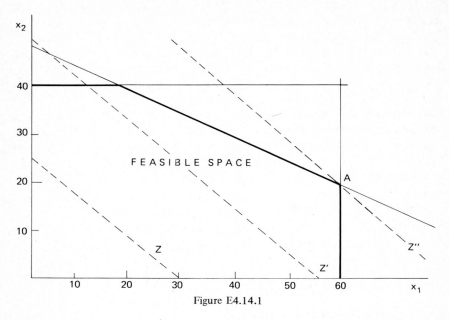

Figure E4.14.1

and

$$X_2 \geq 0,$$

where X_1 is the acres of good land used and X_2 the acres of not-so-good land used.

Fig. E4.14.1 shows the feasible space and different levels of the objective function on contours, Z, Z', and Z''. The optimum is at point A, where the constraint on poor land is not binding. Solving the two equations,

$$2X_1 + 4X_2 = 200,$$

$$X_1 = 60,$$

we obtain

$$X_1 = 60,$$

$$X_2 = 20,$$

total output = 4200.

The dual problem is to choose non-negative values for u_1, u_2, and u_3 to minimize

$$z^* = 200u_1 + 60u_2 + 40u_3$$

subject to

$$2u_1 + u_2 \geq 50$$

and

$$4u_1 + u_3 \geq 60.$$

From the quantity solution ($X_1 = 60$, $X_2 = 20$) we know that u_3, the rent on poor land, is zero. Why? We may use the knowledge that both types of land are used in the optimal solution to convert the dual constraint inequalities to strict equalities. Why? Thus, we arrive at the solution of the dual: u_1, the marginal product of employed labor is 15 bushels, and u_2, the rent on good land, is 20 bushels.

Assuming that the capitalists rent the land from land-owners, the capitalists' annual return is

$$\pi = \text{output} - \text{rents} - \text{wages},$$

which is

$$\pi = 4200 - 20(60) - 0(40) - 10(200) = 1000,$$

and the functional income distribution is

$$
\begin{aligned}
\text{rent} &= 1200 \text{ bushels} \\
\text{profits} &= 1000 \text{ bushels} \\
\text{wages} &= 2000 \text{ bushels} \\
\hline
\text{Total product} &= 4200 \text{ bushels}
\end{aligned}
$$

The capitalists realize a net return of 1000 bushels on a 'wage fund' of 2000 bushels. Hence their rate of return is 50 percent.

Exercise 4.15. A factor-price frontier for an economy with linear technologies

Consider the following simple economy. The only output is corn. There are two known ways of producing corn. The first requires 200 man-days and 500 units of capital to produce 1000 bushels. The second technology requires 100 man-days and 800 units of capital to produce 1000 bushels. Within the confines of each technology, there are no possibilities of substitution.

(a) Draw two of the family of isoquants for corn production. If there are exactly 500 units of capital and 100 man-days available for production, what is the maximum which can be produced? At this maximum production point what is the marginal rate of substitution of capital for labor?

(b) Draw the factor-price frontier for this simple economy. What is the relationship of this factor-price frontier to the dual of the linear-programming problem implicit in part (a)?

Assuming the same economy-wide input availabilities as above, what is the ratio of the return per unit of capital to the wage of labor?

Now, assume alternatively that unlimited supplies of labor can be made available to the economy (perhaps from immigration or from that old standby, the reserve army of the unemployed) at the rate of one-half bushel of corn per man-day. What is the maximum return per unit of capital that can be paid? What would be the factor input proportions? Does your answer depend on the quantity produced or the amount of capital available?

(c) Now assume that a new farming technology is invented which requires 700 units of capital and 150 man-days of labor to produce 1000 bushels of corn. Draw two of the new family of isoquants and the factor-price frontier.

(d) Assume that a technological change has occurred such that, using the first technology, only 400 units of capital and 200 man-days of labor are required to produce 1000 bushels of corn. Draw a new factor-price frontier and one of the new isoquants. Using the Hicks definition of the factor intensity of a

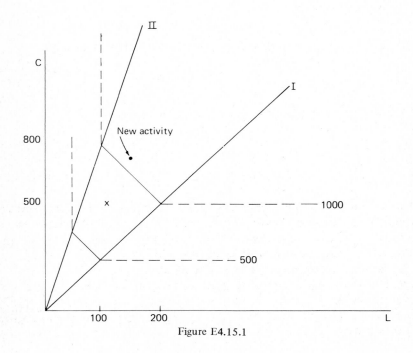

Figure E4.15.1

technological change, would you say that the overall technology of the society has undergone a labor-saving, capital-saving, or a neutral technological change? Would your answer to this question be different if the change in technology had been a proportional reduction in both inputs rather than merely a reduction in the capital input?

Answer. (a) From fig. E4.15.1 it is clear that a combination of the two activities will be used in production at the endowment point (x). To find the production levels, solve

$$200x_1 + 100x_2 = 100$$

and

$$500x_1 + 800x_2 = 500$$

to obtain $x_1 = \frac{3}{11}$ and $x_2 = \frac{5}{11}$, which give a corn output level of $1000(\frac{3}{11}) + 1000(\frac{5}{11}) = 727.3$.

The marginal rate of substitution is given by the negative of the slope of the isoquant, i.e.

$$-\frac{800 - 500}{100 - 200} = 3.$$

(b) Let r be the return per unit of capital and w be the wage rate. The input coefficients for the two processes are

$$a_L^1 = \frac{200}{1000} = 0.2; \quad a_C^1 = \frac{500}{1000} = 0.5,$$
$$a_L^2 = \frac{100}{1000} = 0.1; \quad a_C^2 = \frac{800}{1000} = 0.8.$$

Define the price of corn as 1. Then the factor-price frontier (FPF) for each technology is defined by

$$wa_L^i + ra_C^i = 1, \quad i = 1, 2.$$

The economy-wide FPF is shown in fig. E4.15.2 as the outer sections of the two individual technology FPF's. The factor-price frontier is simply a boundary of the set of feasible solutions to the dual of the linear-programming problem in part (a). At point A in fig. E4.15.2 both technologies are being used. This solution was found in part (a) to be optimal. Therefore, the equilibrium values of w and r are determined by solving the two FPFs simultaneously:

$$0.2w + 0.5r = 1,$$

$$0.1w + 0.8r = 1.$$

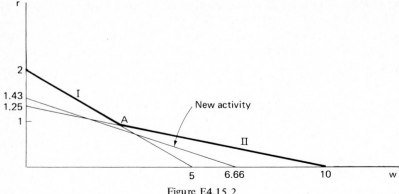

Figure E4.15.2

or $r = \frac{10}{11}$, $w = \frac{30}{11}$, so that $r/w = \frac{1}{3}$. Note that w/r is equal to 3, the value found previously for the marginal rate of substitution between capital and labor. Do you understand why the ratio of factor prices is equal to the marginal rate of substitution in production? For $w = \frac{1}{2}$, the maximal r is found to be 1.8. At this configuration of factor prices, only activity I is used, independently of the level of capital and (hence) output.

(c) The new activity is dominated by the others in that it requires more input per unit of output than a combination of I and II (see fig. E4.15.1). Similarly, its FPF lies inside the joint FPF of I and II (see fig. E4.15.2).

(d) The technical change is Hicks-capital-saving (labor-using) since for a

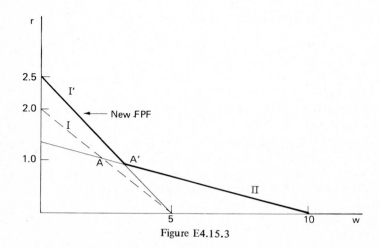

Figure E4.15.3

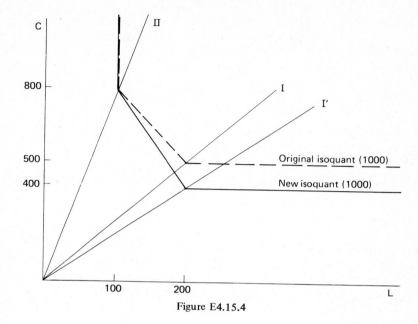

Figure E4.15.4

given C/L ratio the marginal product of labor increases relatively more than the marginal product of capital. Along ray I a proportionate reduction in capital and labor input would be Hicks-neutral for that particular process, but Hicks-capital-saving for the technology of the economy as a whole, as represented by any mixture of the I and II activities. (See figs. E4.15.3 and E4.15.4.)

D. Theoretical developments underlying modern production function econometrics

Exercise 4.16. *Some formal analysis of the standard cost minimizing model*

Assume that the firm chooses the levels X_1, X_2 ...,X_n, of its n inputs so that they minimize the cost, $\Sigma_i p_i X_i$, of producing a given output, Y, subject to the constraint $Y = f(X_1,...,X_n)$, where $p_1,...,p_n$ are input prices and f is a differentiable strictly quasiconcave production function.

(a) Show that the input demand functions,

$$X_i = g_i(Y, p_1,...,p_n), \quad i = 1,...,n,$$

are homogeneous of degree zero in prices, i.e. for any $\alpha > 0$, we have

$$g_i(Y, \alpha p_1, ..., \alpha p_n) = g_i(Y, p_1, ..., p_n).$$

Hence, establish the *homogeneity restriction*,

$$\sum_{j=1}^{n} \frac{\partial g_i}{\partial p_j} p_j = 0, \quad i = 1, ..., n. \qquad (E4.16.1)$$

(b) Show that if f is homogeneous of degree 1 (constant returns to scale) then g_i is homogeneous of degree 1 in Y. In fact, the input demand functions can be written as

$$X_i = Y h_i(p_1, ..., p_n), \quad i = 1, ..., n. \qquad (E4.16.2)$$

(c) Establish the *symmetry restriction*, i.e.

$$\frac{\partial g_i}{\partial p_j} = \frac{\partial g_j}{\partial p_i}, \quad \text{for all } i \neq j. \qquad (E4.16.3)$$

Hint: if you are uncertain about how to proceed with this problem, you could get some ideas by reviewing E2.6.

(d) Establish the nonpositiveness of the own-price substitution effect, i.e.

$$\frac{\partial g_i}{\partial p_i} \leq 0, \quad \text{for all } i. \qquad (E4.16.4)$$

Also show that the matrix of own and cross price derivatives $[\partial g_i / \partial p_j]_{n \times n}$ is negative semidefinite.

Hint: if you have difficulty with this problem, you should review E2.10.

(e) Discuss the similarities and differences between the analysis of this exercise and the analysis which led to the 'triad' (see E2.1–E2.7).

Answer.   (a) The cost minimizing problem is to choose $X_1, ..., X_n$ to minimize

$$\sum_{i=1}^{n} p_i X_i \qquad (E4.16.5)$$

subject to

$$Y = f(X_1, ..., X_n).$$

Let $\bar{X}_1, ..., \bar{X}_n$ be the problem solution for the output level, $\bar{Y}$, and the list of input prices $\bar{p}_1, ..., \bar{p}_n$. Let $\bar{\bar{X}}_1, ..., \bar{\bar{X}}_n$ be the problem solution when output is maintained at $\bar{Y}$, but the input prices are changed to $\alpha \bar{p}_1, ..., \alpha \bar{p}_n$ where $\alpha > 0$, $\alpha \neq 1$. Assume that

$$\sum \bar{p}_i \bar{\bar{X}}_i \neq \sum \bar{p}_i \bar{X}_i. \qquad (E4.16.6)$$

If $\Sigma \bar{p}_i \bar{X}_i > \Sigma \bar{p}_i \bar{\bar{X}}_i$, this would contradict the fact that $\bar{X}_1,...,\bar{X}_n$ is the problem solution when the prices are $\bar{p}_1,..,\bar{p}_n$. On the other hand, if $\Sigma \bar{p}_i \bar{X}_i < \Sigma \bar{p}_i \bar{\bar{X}}_i$, we would have

$$\sum_i \alpha \bar{p}_i \bar{X}_i < \sum_i \alpha \bar{p}_i \bar{\bar{X}}_i,$$

and this would contradict the fact that $\bar{\bar{X}}_1,...,\bar{\bar{X}}_n$ is the problem solution when the prices are $\alpha \bar{p}_1,...,\alpha \bar{p}_n$. We may conclude that

$$\sum_i \bar{p}_i \bar{X}_i = \sum_i \bar{p}_i \bar{\bar{X}}_i.$$

This also allows us to conclude that

$$\bar{X}_i = \bar{\bar{X}}_i, \quad \text{for all } i. \tag{E4.16.7}$$

If (E4.16.7) were not valid, (E4.16.5) would have alternative solutions, a possibility which is ruled out by the *strict* quasiconcavity of the production function.

By establishing (E4.16.7), we have proved, for all i, that

$$g_i(Y,p_1,...,p_n) = g_i(Y,\alpha p_1,...,\alpha p_n)$$

when $\alpha > 0$. On applying Euler's theorem, we obtain, (E4.16.1),

$$\sum_{j=1}^{n} \frac{\partial g_i}{\partial p_j} \, p_j = 0, \quad i = 1,...,n.$$

(b) Let $\bar{X}_1,...,\bar{X}_n$ and $\bar{\bar{X}}_1,...,\bar{\bar{X}}_n$ be problem solutions for the output levels $\bar{Y}$ and $\bar{\bar{Y}}$ with the price list being maintained at $p_1^*,...,p_n^*$ in both situations. Assume that

$$\frac{\Sigma p_i^* \bar{X}_i}{\bar{Y}} \neq \frac{\Sigma p_i^* \bar{\bar{X}}_i}{\bar{\bar{Y}}}.$$

For example, assume that

$$\frac{\Sigma p_i^* \bar{X}_i}{\bar{Y}} < \frac{\Sigma p_i^* \bar{\bar{X}}_i}{\bar{\bar{Y}}}, \tag{E4.16.8a}$$

i.e.

$$\Sigma p_i^* \left(\frac{\bar{X}_i \, \bar{\bar{Y}}}{\bar{Y}} \right) < \Sigma p_i^* \bar{\bar{X}}_i. \tag{E4.16.8b}$$

We notice that

$$f\left(\frac{\bar{X}_1 \, \bar{\bar{Y}}}{\bar{Y}},...,\frac{\bar{X}_n \, \bar{\bar{Y}}}{\bar{Y}} \right) = \frac{\bar{\bar{Y}}}{\bar{Y}} f(\bar{X}_1,...,\bar{X}_n) = \frac{\bar{\bar{Y}}}{\bar{Y}} \bar{Y} = \bar{\bar{Y}}.$$

(This follows from the linear homogeneity of f.)

Hence, the input list $\overline{X}_1 \overline{\overline{Y}}/\overline{Y},...,\overline{X}_n \overline{\overline{Y}}/\overline{Y}$ is compatible with the output level $\overline{\overline{Y}}$. Thus (E4.16.8) contradicts the fact that $\overline{\overline{X}}_1,...,\overline{\overline{X}}_n$ is the cost minimizing solution for the output level $\overline{\overline{Y}}$ and the price list $p_1^* ...,p_n^*$. Similarly, we could obtain a contradiction from the assumption that

$$\frac{\Sigma p_i^* \overline{X}_i}{\overline{Y}} > \frac{\Sigma p_i^* \overline{\overline{X}}_i}{\overline{\overline{Y}}} .$$

We conclude, therefore, that

$$\frac{\Sigma p_i^* \overline{X}_i}{\overline{Y}} = \frac{\Sigma p_i^* \overline{\overline{X}}_i}{\overline{\overline{Y}}} . \tag{E4.16.9}$$

Then by the strict concavity of f (which rules out alternative optima) we have

$$\frac{\overline{X}_i}{\overline{Y}} = \frac{\overline{\overline{X}}_i}{\overline{\overline{Y}}} , \quad i = 1,...,n.$$

Hence,

$$\frac{g_i(\overline{Y},p_1^*,...,p_n^*)}{\overline{Y}} = \frac{g_i(\overline{\overline{Y}},p_1^*,...,p_n^*)}{\overline{\overline{Y}}} , \quad i = 1,...,n.$$

If we choose $\overline{\overline{Y}} = \alpha \overline{Y}, \alpha > 0$, we obtain

$$g_i(\alpha \overline{Y},p_1^*,...,p_n^*) = \alpha g_i(\overline{Y},p_1^*,...,p_n^*). \tag{E4.16.10}$$

Since the choices of $p_1^*, p_2^*,...,p_n^*, \overline{Y}$ and α are arbitrary, (E4.16.10) is sufficient to demonstrate that g_i is homogeneous of degree 1 in Y. It may be written in the form

$$g_i(Y,p_1,...,p_n) = Y g_i(1,p_1,...,p_n) = Y h_i(p_1,...,p_n),$$

where

$$h_i(p_1,...,p_n) \equiv g_i(1,p_1,...,p_n).$$

(c) We return to the problem (E4.16.5). The first-order conditions for an optimum are

$$p_i = \lambda f_i, \quad i = 1,...,n \tag{E4.16.11}$$

and

$$Y = f(X_1,...,X_n), \tag{E4.16.12}$$

where we use the notation $f_i = \partial f/\partial X_i$. By totally differentiating (E4.16.11) and (E4.16.12) we find that

$$dp_i = (d\lambda)f_i + \lambda \sum_{j=1}^{n} f_{ij} \, dX_j$$

and

$$dY = \Sigma f_i \, dX_i,$$

where

$$f_{ij} = \partial^2 f/(\partial X_i)(\partial X_j).$$

In matrix notation, these equations may be presented as

$$\begin{bmatrix} f_{11}, \ldots f_{1n} & p_1 \\ \vdots & \vdots & \vdots \\ f_{n1}, \ldots f_{nn} & p_n \\ p_1, \ldots p_n & 0 \end{bmatrix} \begin{bmatrix} dX_1 \\ \vdots \\ dX_n \\ d\lambda/\lambda^2 \end{bmatrix} = \begin{bmatrix} dp_1/\lambda \\ \vdots \\ dp_n/\lambda \\ \lambda \, dY \end{bmatrix},$$

i.e.

$$\begin{bmatrix} F & P \\ p' & 0 \end{bmatrix} \begin{bmatrix} dX \\ d\lambda/\lambda^2 \end{bmatrix} = \frac{1}{\lambda} \begin{bmatrix} dp \\ \lambda^2 \, dY \end{bmatrix}.$$

Hence,

$$\begin{bmatrix} dX \\ d\lambda/\lambda^2 \end{bmatrix} = \frac{1}{\lambda} Q \begin{bmatrix} dp \\ \lambda^2 \, dY \end{bmatrix},$$

where Q is the inverse[12] of the bordered Hessian. Because the bordered Hessian is symmetric, Q is symmetric. Thus,

$$\frac{\partial X_i}{\partial p_j} = \frac{1}{\lambda} Q_{ij} = \frac{1}{\lambda} Q_{ji} = \frac{\partial X_j}{\partial p_i},$$

i.e.

$$\frac{\partial g_i}{\partial p_j} = \frac{\partial g_j}{\partial p_i}, \quad \text{for all } i \neq j. \tag{E4.16.13}$$

---

[12] Are you worried about the existence of the inverse? If so, refer to footnote 14 in Chapter 2.

(d) We consider two situations. In the first the input price vector is $\bar{p}$. In the second it is $\bar{\bar{p}}$ with $\bar{p} \neq \bar{\bar{p}}$.[13] In both situations the output level is the same, say Y^*. Where $\bar{X}$ and $\bar{\bar{X}}$ are the optimal input vectors for the two situations [14] we note that

$$\bar{p}'\bar{\bar{X}} > \bar{p}'\bar{X} \qquad\qquad\qquad\qquad\qquad (E4.16.14)$$

and

$$\bar{\bar{p}}'\bar{X} > \bar{\bar{p}}'\bar{\bar{X}}. \qquad\qquad\qquad\qquad\qquad (E4.16.15)$$

The first of these inequalities means that when the producer is faced with the initial prices, $\bar{p}$, the input bundle $\bar{\bar{X}}$ is more expensive than the bundle $\bar{X}$. If $\bar{p}'\bar{\bar{X}}$ were less than $\bar{p}'\bar{X}$, then the vector $\bar{X}$ could not be the cost minimizing input vector for the production of Y^* in the initial situation. If $\bar{p}'\bar{\bar{X}}$ were equal to $\bar{p}'\bar{X}$, then $\bar{\bar{X}}$ and $\bar{X}$ would be alternative optima, a possibility which is ruled out by the strict quasiconcavity of the production function. The justification for inequality (E4.16.15) is similar to that for (E4.16.14).

From here, we follow the form of the argument given in E2.10 to obtain (E4.16.4) and to show that $[\partial g_i/\partial p_j]$ is negative semidefinite.

(e) In this exercise we have analysed the cost minimizing model (E4.16.5). Our objective has been similar to that in E2.1–E2.7. In these earlier exercises we used the utility-maximizing model to establish econometrically useful restrictions on the form of household commodity demand functions. Here we have used the cost minimizing model to establish restrictions on the form of producer input demand functions.

In mathematical terms, our utility-maximizing model consisted of maximizing a strictly quasiconcave objective function subject to a linear constraint, whereas our cost minimizing model involved minimizing a linear objective function subject to meeting a strictly quasiconcave constraint. However, the similarity between the formal structure of the two models can be emphasized if we note that the optimal consumption bundle, $X_1,...,X_n$, for a utility-maximizing household will minimize

$$\sum_i p_i X_i \qquad\qquad\qquad\qquad\qquad (E4.16.16)$$

subject to

$$\bar{U} = U(X_1,...,X_n),$$

---

[13] We assume that relative prices have changed, i.e. $\bar{p} \neq \beta\bar{\bar{p}}$ where β is a scalar.
[14] We may assume that $\bar{X} \neq \bar{\bar{X}}$. With a differentiable, strictly quasiconcave production function, a change in relative input prices will produce a change in the cost minimizing input vector. (Examine figs. E2.10.1 and E2.10.2, interpreting the curves as isoquants.)

i.e. the optimal bundle will be the least costly vector of commodities with which the household can reach its utility-maximizing level $\overline{U}$. [15]

On the basis of (E4.16.16), we could derive the *compensated* demand functions, i.e.

$$X_i = r_i(\overline{U}, p_1,...,p_n), \quad i = 1,...,n. \tag{E4.16.17}$$

These functions give the household demands as we vary prices and the utility level (rather than the expenditure level). Because (E4.16.16) is strictly analogous to (E4.16.5), we can apply (E4.16.3) and (E4.16.1) to (E4.16.17). Hence

$$\frac{\partial r_i}{\partial p_j} = \frac{\partial r_j}{\partial p_i}, \quad i \neq j,$$

i.e.

$$\left(\frac{\partial X_i}{\partial p_j}\right)_{\mathrm{d}U=0} = \left(\frac{\partial X_j}{\partial p_i}\right)_{\mathrm{d}U=0} \tag{E4.16.18}$$

and

$$\sum_{j=1}^{n} \frac{\partial r_i}{\partial p_j} p_j = 0, \quad i = 1,...,n,$$

i.e.

$$\sum_{j=1}^{n} \left(\frac{\partial X_i}{\partial p_j}\right)_{\mathrm{d}U=0} p_j = 0. \tag{E4.16.19}$$

When we use (E2.9.1), we see that (E4.16.18) and (E4.16.19) quickly lead to the symmetry and homogeneity restrictions (E2.6.2) and (E2.2.1).

Exercise 4.17. *Some properties of cost functions*

Adopt the standard cost minimizing model. Then let

$$C = C(Y, P_1,...,P_n)$$

be the minimum cost of producing output Y, when prices are $P_1, P_2,...,P_n$.

(a) Certainly C is a nondecreasing function of Y and the P_i's. Show that it is homogeneous of degree 1 in prices.

(b) If the production function is homogeneous of degree 1, show that C is homogeneous of degree 1 with respect to Y, i.e. show that C can be written as

$$C = Y\chi(P_1,...,P_n).$$

[15] $\overline{U}$ is the value of the objective function in the problem of choosing $X_1,...,X_n$ to maximize $U(X_1,...,X_n)$ subject to $p'X = Y$, where Y is the household's budget.

(c) Establish *Shepard's lemma* by showing that

$$\frac{\partial C(Y, P_1,...,P_n)}{\partial P_i} = X_i, \quad \text{for all } i,$$

where X_i is the cost minimizing level for input i, i.e. in the notation of E4.16,

$$\frac{\partial C(Y, P_1,...,P_n)}{\partial P_i} = g_i(Y, P_1,...,P_n), \quad \text{for all } i.$$

(d) Show that C is concave in prices, i.e.

$$C(Y, \alpha\bar{P}_1 + (1-\alpha)\bar{\bar{P}}_1,..., \alpha\bar{P}_n + (1-\alpha)\bar{\bar{P}}_n)$$

$$\geq \alpha C(Y, \bar{P}_1,...,\bar{P}_n) + (1-\alpha)C(Y, \bar{\bar{P}}_1,...,\bar{\bar{P}}_n),$$

where $(\bar{P}_1,...,\bar{P}_n)$ and $(\bar{\bar{P}}_1,...,\bar{\bar{P}}_n)$ are any two-price vectors and α is any number between 0 and 1.

(e) Given a legitimate [16] cost function of the form

$$C = C(Y, P_1,...,P_n),$$

suggest a general method for deducing the underlying production function. If the cost function has the form

$$C = Y P_1^{1/2} P_2^{1/2}, \tag{E4:17.1}$$

what is $f(1, 4)$, where f is the production function?

More generally, if

$$C = A \, Y P_1^{\delta_1} P_2^{\delta_2},...,P_n^{\delta_n}, \tag{E4.17.2}$$

where A, $\delta_1,...,\delta_n$ are positive parameters with $\Sigma_i \delta_i = 1$, what is the form of the production function, $f(X_1,...,X_n)$? What are the input demand functions? What is the equation to the factor-price frontier?

Answer.   (a) Usually it is assumed that C is an increasing function of Y and the P_i's. However, if a particular input is not used, then increases in its price will not affect C. Also, if there is a 'lumpy' input, it is possible that expansions in Y could be achieved without additional cost.

To show that C is homogeneous of degree 1 in prices, we note that

$$C(Y, P_1,...,P_n) = \sum_i P_i g_i(Y, P_1,...,P_n),$$

where the g_i are the cost minimizing input demand functions studied in E4.16. Since the g_i are homogeneous of degree zero in prices, we have

---

[16]   That is, the cost function is a nondecreasing function of the P_i's and Y, it is homogeneous of degree 1 in the P_i's, and it is concave in the P_i's.

$$C(Y, \alpha P_1, ..., \alpha P_n) = \sum_i \alpha P_i g_i(Y, \alpha P_1, ..., \alpha P_n)$$

$$= \alpha \sum_i P_i g_i(Y, P_1, ..., P_n)$$

$$= \alpha C(Y, P_1, ..., P_n),$$

for any $\alpha > 0$. Hence C is homogeneous of degree 1 in prices.

(b) If the production function, f, is homogeneous of degree 1, then the input demand functions, g_i, are homogeneous of degree 1 in Y (see E4.16, part (b)). Hence

$$C(\alpha Y, P) = \sum_i P_i g_i(\alpha Y, P)$$

$$= \sum_i P_i \alpha g_i(Y, P)$$

$$= \alpha C(Y, P), \tag{E4.17.3}$$

where α is any positive number and we use the notation $P = (P_1, ..., P_n)$. (E4.17.3) shows that C is homogeneous of degree 1 in output. Consequently, we can write

$$C(Y, P) = YC(1, P),$$

i.e.

$$C(Y, P) = Y\chi(P),$$

where

$$\chi(P) \equiv C(1, P).$$

(c) We know that

$$C(Y, P) = \sum_j P_j g_j(Y, P).$$

Hence

$$\frac{\partial C(Y, P)}{\partial P_i} = g_i(Y, P) + \sum_j P_j \frac{\partial g_j}{\partial P_i}. \tag{E4.17.4}$$

Applying the symmetry restriction, (E4.16.3), we can rewrite (E4.17.4) as

$$\frac{\partial C(Y, P)}{\partial P_i} = g_i(Y, P) + \sum_j P_j \frac{\partial g_i}{\partial P_j}. \tag{E4.17.5}$$

Now we apply the homogeneity restriction, (E4.16.1), to obtain

$$\frac{\partial C(Y, P)}{\partial P_i} = g_i(Y, P). \tag{E4.17.6}$$

(E4.17.6) implies that, given the cost function, we can find the input demand functions simply by differentiation.

(d) We adopt a shorter notation and restate our problem as follows: show that

$$C(Y, \alpha\bar{P} + (1-\alpha)\bar{\bar{P}}) \geq \alpha C(Y, \bar{P}) + (1-\alpha)C(Y, \bar{\bar{P}}).$$ (E4.17.7)

The left-hand side of (E4.17.7) is given by

$$
\begin{aligned}
\text{LHS (E4.17.7)} &= \sum_i (\alpha\bar{P}_i + (1-\alpha)\bar{\bar{P}}_i)g_i(Y, \alpha\bar{P} + (1-\alpha)\bar{\bar{P}}) \\
&= \alpha \sum_i \bar{P}_i g_i(Y, \alpha\bar{P} + (1-\alpha)\bar{\bar{P}}) \\
&\quad + (1-\alpha) \sum_i \bar{\bar{P}}_i g_i(Y, \alpha\bar{P} + (1-\alpha)\bar{\bar{P}}).
\end{aligned}
$$

Certainly

$$\sum_i \bar{P}_i g_i(Y, \bar{P}) \leq \sum_i \bar{P}_i g_i(Y, \alpha\bar{P} + (1-\alpha)\bar{\bar{P}})$$ (i)

and

$$\sum_i \bar{\bar{P}}_i g_i(Y, \bar{\bar{P}}) \leq \sum_i \bar{\bar{P}}_i g_i(Y, \alpha\bar{P} + (1-\alpha)\bar{\bar{P}}).$$ (ii)

(These two inequalities reflect the fact that $g_i(Y,\bar{P})$, $i = 1,...,n$ and $g_i(Y,\bar{\bar{P}})$, $i = 1,...,n$, are the cost minimizing input vectors for producing Y when the prices are $\bar{P}$ and $\bar{\bar{P}}$, respectively.) By substituting from (i) and (ii), we see that

$$\text{LHS (E4.17.7)} \geq \alpha \sum_i \bar{P}_i g_i(Y, \bar{P}) + (1-\alpha) \sum_i \bar{\bar{P}}_i g_i(Y, \bar{\bar{P}}),$$

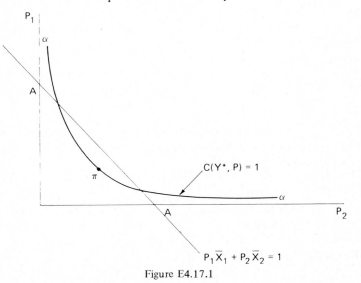

Figure E4.17.1

i.e.

$$\text{LHS (E4.17.7)} \geq \alpha C(Y, \bar{P}) + (1-\alpha)C(Y, \bar{\bar{P}})$$

$$= \text{RHS (E4.17.7)}.$$

(e) Our problem is as follows. Given the cost function $C = C(Y,P)$, how can we determine what production level is possible with the input vector $\bar{X}$, say. That is, can we find $f(\bar{X})$? We consider a two input case.

In fig. E4.17.1 we have sketched two curves. The first, AA, is a straight line showing the various *price combinations*, (P_1, P_2), at which our input vector $\bar{X}$ costs $ 1. (Take note, the figure has prices on the axes – the $\bar{X}_i$'s are constants.) The second curve, $\alpha\alpha$, shows the various price combinations, (P_1, P_2), at which the minimum cost of producing the output Y^* is $ 1. The shape of $\alpha\alpha$ reflects the fact that C is concave in prices.

We can see from the diagram that

$$f(\bar{X}) < Y^*. \tag{E4.17.8}$$

Notice that the cost of the input vector $\bar{X}$ at the price vector π is less than $ 1. Therefore if $\bar{X}$ were capable of generating Y^* we would have

$$C(Y^*, \pi) < 1.$$

However, $C(Y^*, \pi) = 1$ and therefore we must accept (E4.17.8). Thus, it appears that

$$f(\bar{X}) < Y^*$$

if there exists

$$\pi \geq 0 \tag{E4.17.9}$$

such that

$$C(Y^*, \pi) > \pi_1 \bar{X}_1 + \pi_2 \bar{X}_2.$$

(E4.17.9) says that the vector $\bar{X}$ is incapable of producing Y^* if we can find a price vector π such that the minimum cost of producing Y^* at π is greater than the cost of the input vector $\bar{X}$ at π.

Now consider fig. E4.17.2. The straight line AA again shows the price combinations at which our input vector, $\bar{X}$, costs $ 1. On the other hand, the curve $\gamma\gamma$ is sketched further from the origin than $\alpha\alpha$. $\gamma\gamma$ shows the price combinations for which the minimum cost of producing Y^{**} is $ 1. (Notice that since $\gamma\gamma$ lies outside $\alpha\alpha$, Y^{**} is less than Y^*.) The question to be considered is whether or not $\bar{X}$ is capable of producing this smaller output level Y^{**}.

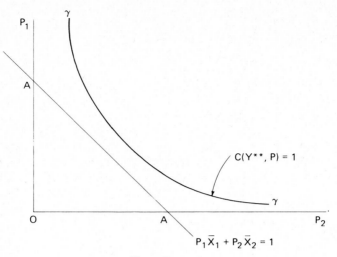

Figure E4.17.2

Intuitively, it would seem that

$$f(\bar{X}) > Y^{**}. \tag{E4.17.10}$$

Notice that at every price combination shown along AA, the cost of producing Y^{**}, is less than \$ 1 whereas the cost of buying $\bar{X}$ is equal to \$ 1. Then because of the homogeneity of C with respect to prices, we know that

$$C(Y^{**}, P) < P'\bar{X}, \quad \text{for all } P \geq 0. \tag{E4.17.11}$$

Thus, if the input vector $\bar{X}$ were capable of producing no more than Y^{**}, then $\bar{X}$ would be *economically irrelevant*, i.e. $\bar{X}$ would never be a chosen input vector. If $f(\bar{X}) \leq Y^{**}$, then (E4.17.11) says that there is no price vector which makes $\bar{X}$ a cost minimizing input vector for any production level. At every price vector we can produce at least as much as $f(\bar{X})$ for less than it would cost to buy $\bar{X}$. Hence we can accept (E4.17.10) subject to a proviso: provided that $\bar{X}$ is an economically relevant input vector, then

$$\left. \begin{array}{l} C(Y^{**}, P) < P'\bar{X}, \quad \text{for all } P \geq 0 \\[6pt] \text{implies that } f(\bar{X}) > Y^{**}. \end{array} \right\} \tag{E4.17.12}$$

In fig. E4.17.3 we have brought the previous two figures together. Our argument so far shows that if $\bar{X}$ is an economically relevant input vector, then

$$f(\bar{X}) = \bar{Y}.$$

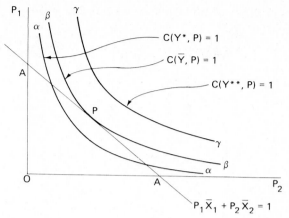

Figure E4.17.3

This suggests that for a given $\overline{X}$, provided that it is economically relevant, the output level can be determined by solving the programming problem: choose P_1, P_2, $Y \geq 0$ to minimize [17]

$$Y \qquad \text{(i)}$$

subject to

$$P'\overline{X} = 1 \qquad \text{(ii) (E4.17.13)}$$

and

$$C(Y, P) = 1. \qquad \text{(iii)}$$

Before we move to some specific examples in which we use (E4.17.13), it might be useful to make two comments about economically irrelevant input bundles. First, if $\overline{X}$ is economically irrelevant (as is shown in fig. E4.17.4), we should not expect to be able to deduce $f(\overline{X})$ from the cost function. Since $\overline{X}$ is never a cost minimizing input, a small change in $f(\overline{X})$ will not affect the cost function, i.e. the cost function is independent of $f(\overline{X})$. Secondly, if $\overline{X}$ is economically irrelevant, problem (E4.17.13) will not yield a misleading solution. In fact, the problem will have no solution in which all the P_i's are positive (see fig. E4.17.4). This allows us to conclude that if $\overline{X}$ is economically relevant, then $f(\overline{X})$ is the solution to (E4.17.13). If $\overline{X}$ is not economically relevant, then we will be

---

[17] In terms of fig. E4.17.3, output is falling as we move out from the origin across the curves $\alpha\alpha$, $\beta\beta$, and $\gamma\gamma$.

alerted by finding that at least one of the sign constraints on the P_i's in (E4.17.13) will be binding.

At this stage we are ready to consider the specific example in which $C(Y,P)$ is given by (E4.17.1) and $\bar{X} = (1,4)$. Provided that $\bar{X}$ is economically relevant, we

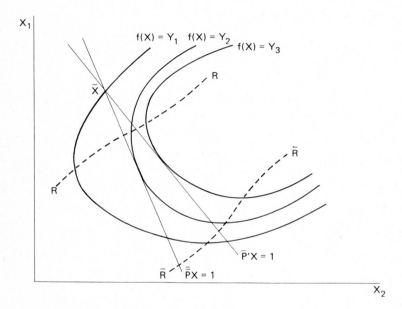

Figure E4.17.4. This figure shows an isoquant map in which the economically relevant inputs are between the 'ridge' lines RR and $\bar{R}\bar{R}$. (If the ridge lines are the axes – marginal products are never negative – then the problem of irrelevant input vectors does not arise.) Our aim is to illustrate the proposition that if $\bar{X}$ is economically irrelevant, then (E4.17.13) has no solution in which all the P_i's are positive. We consider the irrelevant input vector $\bar{X}$ and sketch a line through it of the form $\bar{P}_1 X_1 + \bar{P}_2 X_2 = 1$, noting that the line is tangent to the Y_3-isoquant. We emphasize that $\bar{P}_1$ and $\bar{P}_2$ are strictly positive and that whatever values they have, it is always possible to sketch a steeper line such as $\bar{\bar{P}}_1 X_1 + \bar{\bar{P}}_2 X_2 = 1$, where $\bar{\bar{P}}_1$ and $\bar{\bar{P}}_2$ are also positive but such that the new line is tangent to a lower isoquant. The critical question is whether $\bar{P}_1, \bar{P}_2$ can be part of a solution for problem (E4.17.13). If we find that the answer is no, then (since $\bar{P}_1$ and $\bar{P}_2$ were chosen quite arbitrarily, apart from being positive), we will have found that (E4.17.13) has no solution in which P_1 and P_2 are both positive. To see that $\bar{P}_1$ and $\bar{P}_2$ cannot be part of a solution for (E4.17.13) we note that if $P = \bar{P}$, then (iii) in (E4.17.13) would require that the problem solution be Y_3. But Y_3 cannot be a problem solution because $Y = Y_2, P = \bar{\bar{P}}$ is consistent with the constraints, but has $Y_2 < Y_3$.

can find $f(X)$ by choosing Y, P_1 and P_2 to minimize Y subject to

$$P'\bar{X} = 1,$$
$$YP_1^{1/2}P_2^{1/2} = 1$$

and

$$P \geq 0.$$

Hence, we can find Y by choosing $P \geq 0$ to minimize

$$Y = \frac{P_1\bar{X}_1 + P_2\bar{X}_2}{P_1^{1/2}P_2^{1/2}},$$

i.e.

$$f(\bar{X}) = \min_{P \geq 0} \left\{ \frac{P_1\bar{X}_1 + P_2\bar{X}_2}{P_1^{1/2}P_2^{1/2}} \right\}.$$

Alternatively,

$$1/f(\bar{X}) = \max_{P \geq 0} \{P_1^{1/2}P_2^{1/2} \mid P_1\bar{X}_1 + P_2\bar{X}_2 = 1\}. \tag{E4.17.14}$$

The first-order conditions for the problem on the right-hand side of (E4.17.14) are

$$\tfrac{1}{2}P_1^{-1/2}P_2^{1/2} = \lambda\bar{X}_1,$$
$$\tfrac{1}{2}P_1^{1/2}P_2^{-1/2} = \lambda\bar{X}_2$$

and

$$P_1\bar{X}_1 + P_2\bar{X}_2 = 1.$$

From here we find that $P_i = 1/(2\bar{X}_i), i = 1,2$. Thus,

$$1/f(\bar{X}) = (2\bar{X}_1)^{-1/2}(2\bar{X}_2)^{-1/2},$$

i.e.

$$f(\bar{X}) = 2\bar{X}_1^{1/2}\bar{X}_2^{1/2}.$$

In particular, $f(1,4) = 4$.

In the more general problem where $C(Y,P)$ is given by (E4.17.2),

$$1/f(X) = \max_{P \geq 0} \left\{ AP_1^{\delta_1}P_2^{\delta_2}...P_n^{\delta_n} \mid \sum_i P_iX_i = 1 \right\}. \tag{E4.17.15}$$

The first-order conditions are

$$\delta_i(AP_1^{\delta_1}...P_n^{\delta_n}) = \lambda P_iX_i, \quad i = 1,...,n$$

and

$$\sum_i P_i X_i = 1.$$

Hence,

$$\lambda = A P_1^{\delta_1} \dots P_n^{\delta_n},$$

and we find that

$$P_i = \delta_i / X_i, \quad i = 1,\dots,n.$$

Now we substitute back into (E4.17.15) to obtain the production function

$$f(X) = B X_1^{\delta_1} X_2^{\delta_2} \dots X_n^{\delta_n}, \tag{E4.17.16}$$

where B is the constant $1/A\, \delta_1^{\delta_1}\, \delta_2^{\delta_2} \dots \delta_n^{\delta_n}$. (You could check (E4.17.16) by deriving the implied cost function. Make sure you get back to (E4.17.2).)

The input demand functions may be derived by differentiating the cost function (E4.17.2) with respect to the P_i's (see part (c)). Hence, the input demand functions are

$$X_i = \frac{\delta_i A \, Y P_1^{\delta_1} \dots P_n^{\delta_n}}{P_i}, \quad i = 1,\dots,n. \tag{E4.17.17}$$

Alternatively you could derive (E4.17.17) by using (E4.17.16) in the standard cost minimizing problem.

In deriving the factor-price frontier we take the price of output as the numeraire, i.e. the price of output is 1. Then since the factor-price frontier is formed by the combinations of factor prices, $P_1,\dots,P_n$, which are compatible with the equation:

cost of 1 unit of output = value of 1 unit of output,

we have $C(1,P) = 1$, i.e. the factor-price frontier is defined by

$$A P_1^{\delta_1} P_2^{\delta_2} \dots P_n^{\delta_n} = 1.$$

Exercise 4.18. The Allen definition of the elasticity of substitution

Consider the two-factor cost minimizing model: choose X_1, X_2 to minimize

$$P_1 X_1 + P_2 X_2 \tag{E4.18.1}$$

subject to

$$Y = F(X_1, X_2).$$

Show that

$$-\left\{ \frac{d(X_1/X_2)}{X_1/X_2} \frac{F_1/F_2}{d(F_1/F_2)} \right\}_{dY=0} = \frac{\eta_{12}}{S_2}, \tag{E4.18.2}$$

where η_{12} is the cross-elasticity of demand for input 1 with respect to changes in P_2. (In terms of the notation of E4.16, $\eta_{12} = (\partial g_1/\partial P_2)(P_2/g_1)$.) S_2 is the share of input 2 in total costs, i.e.

$$S_2 = P_2 X_2/(P_1 X_1 + P_2 X_2).$$

F_1 and F_2 are the marginal products of inputs 1 and 2. We have added the subscript $dY = 0$ to the left-hand side of (E4.18.2) to emphasize that we are concerned with the effect on the marginal rate of substitution between inputs 1 and 2, F_1/F_2, as we move around an isoquant (see fig. E4.1.1).

On comparing (E4.18.2) with (E4.1.1) you will see that (E4.18.2) implies that the elasticity of substitution between factors 1 and 2, σ_{12}, is given by

$$\sigma_{12} = \eta_{12}/S_2.$$

This suggests one possibility for generalizing the definition (E4.1.1) for applications in which there are many factors of production. We can adopt the Allen definition that the elasticity of substitution between inputs i and j is

$$\sigma_{ij} = \eta_{ij}/S_j, \quad i \neq j, \quad i,j = 1,...,n. \tag{E4.18.3}$$

This, however, is not the only plausible generalization. See E4.19.

Show that if σ_{ij} is defined by (E4.18.3), then

$$\sigma_{ij} = \sigma_{ji}, \quad \text{for all } i \neq j. \tag{E4.18.4}$$

Answer. The first-order conditions for a solution of (E4.18.1) are

$$\left. \begin{aligned} \lambda F_1 &= P_1, \\ \lambda F_2 &= P_2 \\ Y &= F(X_1, X_2). \end{aligned} \right\} \tag{E4.18.5}$$

If we eliminate λ, we obtain the demand system

$$X_i = g_i(Y, P_1, P_2), \quad i = 1, 2. \tag{E4.18.6}$$

In elasticities form, we have

$$x_1 = \eta_{11} p_1 + \eta_{12} p_2 + \epsilon_1 y$$

and

$$x_2 = \eta_{21} p_1 + \eta_{22} p_2 + \epsilon_2 y, \tag{E4.18.7}$$

where

$$\eta_{ij} = \frac{\partial g_i}{\partial P_j} \frac{P_j}{g_i}, \quad \text{for } i,j = 1,2,$$

$$\epsilon_i = \frac{\partial g_i}{\partial Y} \frac{Y}{g_i}, \quad \text{for } i = 1,2$$

and the lower-case symbols denote percentage changes in the variables defined by the corresponding upper-case symbols. For example

$$y = 100 \frac{dY}{Y}.$$

Next we note that (E4.18.5) implies that

$$F_1/F_2 = P_1/P_2.$$

Hence[18]

$$\frac{d(F_1/F_2)}{F_1/F_2} = p_1 - p_2. \qquad (E4.18.8)$$

Also,

$$\frac{d(X_1/X_2)}{X_1/X_2} = x_1 - x_2. \qquad (E4.18.9)$$

Now we see that the left-hand side of (E4.18.2) can be obtained by substituting

$$p_1 - p_2 = 1 \qquad (E4.18.10)$$

and

$$y = 0 \qquad (E4.18.11)$$

into (E4.18.7) and computing $-(x_1 - x_2)$. That is, we impose a 1 percent increase in P_1/P_2 (or F_1/F_2), we fix Y, and we compute the resulting percentage change in X_2/X_1. On using (E4.18.10) and (E4.18.11) in (E4.18.7) we have

$$-(x_1 - x_2) = (\eta_{21} - \eta_{11})(1 + p_2) + (\eta_{22} - \eta_{12})p_2,$$

i.e.

$$\text{LHS}(E4.18.2) = (\eta_{21} - \eta_{11} + \eta_{22} - \eta_{12})p_2 + (\eta_{21} - \eta_{11}). \qquad (E4.18.12)$$

---

[18]   Recall that if U and V are any two variables, then

$$\frac{d(U/V)}{U/V} = u - v,$$

where $u = dU/U$ and $v = dV/V$. See, for example, Takayama (1972, pp. 35–38).

Via the homogeneity restriction (E4.16.1), we know that

$$\eta_{21} + \eta_{22} = \eta_{11} + \eta_{12} = 0.$$

Hence, (E4.18.12) reduces to

$$\text{LHS}(E4.18.2) = \eta_{21} - \eta_{11}.$$

Next, we apply the symmetry restriction, (E4.16.3), and find that

$$\text{LHS}(E4.18.2) = \eta_{12} \frac{S_1}{S_2} - \eta_{11},$$

i.e.

$$\text{LHS}(E4.18.2) = \eta_{12} \frac{S_1}{S_2} + \eta_{12}$$

$$= \frac{\eta_{12}}{S_2}.$$

Eq. (E4.18.4) follows from the symmetry restriction, (E4.16.3), as follows:

$$\frac{\partial g_i}{\partial P_j} = \frac{\partial g_j}{\partial P_i}.$$

Hence,

$$\frac{\partial g_i}{\partial P_j} \frac{P_j}{g_i} \frac{C}{P_j g_j} = \frac{\partial g_j}{\partial P_i} \frac{P_i}{g_j} \frac{C}{P_i g_i},$$

where

$$C = \sum_k P_k X_k,$$

i.e.

$$\eta_{ij}/S_j = \eta_{ji}/S_i.$$

Exercise 4.19. Alternative definitions of the elasticity of substitution

Adopt the production function

$$Y = 2X_1^{1/2} (X_2^{1/2} + X_3^{1/2}). \tag{E4.19.1}$$

Assume that input prices, P_1, P_2 and P_3 are each 1.
 (a) Compute the matrix of Allen elasticities of substitution (AES).
 (b) Compute the matrix of direct elasticities of substitution (DES).

(c) In making the computations for parts (a) and (b), did you need to know the value of Y? Why not?

(d) Explain why differences between the AESs and the DESs arise only when we have more than two factors of production.

Answer.   We start by deriving the cost minimizing input demand functions. Assume that X_1, X_2 and X_3 are chosen to minimize

$$\sum_i P_i X_i$$

subject to

$$Y = 2 X_1^{1/2} (X_2^{1/2} + X_3^{1/2}).$$

Then the first order-conditions are

$$\Lambda X_1^{-1/2} (X_2^{1/2} + X_3^{1/2}) = P_1, \tag{i}$$

$$\Lambda X_1^{1/2} X_2^{-1/2} = P_2, \tag{ii}$$

$$\Lambda X_1^{1/2} X_3^{-1/2} = P_3 \tag{iii}$$

and

$$2 X_1^{1/2} (X_2^{1/2} + X_3^{1/2}) = Y, \tag{iv}$$

where Λ is the Lagrangian multiplier.

From (i) and (ii) we obtain

$$\frac{X_2 + X_2^{1/2} X_3^{1/2}}{X_1} = \frac{P_1}{P_2}, \tag{v}$$

and from (ii) and (iii) it follows that

$$\left(\frac{X_2}{X_3}\right)^{-1/2} = \frac{P_2}{P_3},$$

i.e.

$$X_3 = X_2 \left(\frac{P_2}{P_3}\right)^2. \tag{vi}$$

Now we use (vi) to eliminate X_3 from (v):

$$X_1 = \frac{P_2 X_2}{P_1} \left(1 + \frac{P_2}{P_3}\right). \tag{vii}$$

Next we use (vi) and (vii) to eliminate X_1 and X_3 from (iv). This gives

$$Y = 2 X_2 \left(\frac{P_2}{P_1}\right)^{1/2} \left(1 + \frac{P_2}{P_3}\right)^{3/2}.$$

Hence, the input demand functions are

$$X_2 = \tfrac{1}{2} Y \left(\frac{P_1}{P_2}\right)^{1/2} \left(\frac{P_3}{P_2 + P_3}\right)^{3/2}$$

$$X_3 = \tfrac{1}{2} Y \left(\frac{P_1}{P_3}\right)^{1/2} \left(\frac{P_2}{P_2 + P_3}\right)^{3/2}$$

$$\left.\right\} \quad \text{(E4.19.2)}$$

and

$$X_1 = \tfrac{1}{2} Y \frac{P_2^{1/2} P_3^{1/2}}{P_1^{1/2} (P_2 + P_3)^{1/2}} .$$

The demand system, (E4.19.2), can be rewritten in d ln or percentage change form as [19]

$$x_1 = y + \tfrac{1}{2}p_2 + \tfrac{1}{2}p_3 - \tfrac{1}{2}p_1 - \tfrac{1}{2}\left(\left(\frac{P_2}{P_2 + P_3}\right)p_2 + \left(\frac{P_3}{P_2 + P_3}\right)p_3\right),$$

$$x_2 = y + \tfrac{1}{2}p_1 - \tfrac{1}{2}p_2 + \tfrac{3}{2}p_3 - \tfrac{3}{2}\left(\left(\frac{P_2}{P_2 + P_3}\right)p_2 + \left(\frac{P_3}{P_2 + P_3}\right)p_3\right),$$

$$x_3 = y + \tfrac{1}{2}p_1 - \tfrac{1}{2}p_3 + \tfrac{3}{2}p_2 - \tfrac{3}{2}\left(\left(\frac{P_2}{P_2 + P_3}\right)p_2 + \left(\frac{P_3}{P_2 + P_3}\right)p_3\right),$$

$$\left.\right\} \quad \text{(E4.19.3)}$$

where the lower-case symbols denote percentage changes in the variables defined by the upper-case symbols. For example,

$$x_i = 100 \frac{dX_i}{X_i} .$$

Next we use the information that $P_2 = P_3 = 1$ and rewrite (E4.19.3) as

$$x_1 = y - \tfrac{1}{2}p_1 + \tfrac{1}{4}p_2 + \tfrac{1}{4}p_3,$$

$$x_2 = y + \tfrac{1}{2}p_1 - \tfrac{5}{4}p_2 + \tfrac{3}{4}p_3,$$

$$x_3 = y + \tfrac{1}{2}p_1 + \tfrac{3}{4}p_2 - \tfrac{5}{4}p_3.$$

$$\left.\right\} \quad \text{(E4.19.4)}$$

We are now ready to compute the matrices of substitution elasticities.

(a) Under the Allen definition, the elasticity of substitution between factors i and j is measured by

$$\sigma_{ij}^A = \eta_{ij}/S_j, \quad i \neq j. \qquad \text{(E4.19.5)}$$

[19] For a discussion of logarithmic differentiation, see Takayama (1972, pp. 35–38).

With $P_1 = P_2 = P_3 = 1$, it quickly follows from (E4.19.2) that the cost shares, S_j, $j = 1, 2, 3$, are

$$S_1 = \tfrac{1}{2}, \quad S_2 = \tfrac{1}{4} \quad \text{and} \quad S_3 = \tfrac{1}{4}. \tag{E4.19.6}$$

We can read the elasticities, η_{ij}, from (E4.19.4). Then on applying (E4.19.5) and (E4.19.6) we obtain the matrix of Allen elasticities of substitution at $P_1 = P_2 = P_3 = 1$:

$$\sigma^{A}(P_1 = P_2 = P_3 = 1) = \begin{bmatrix} * & 1 & 1 \\ 1 & * & 3 \\ 1 & 3 & * \end{bmatrix}.$$

(b)   Under the 'direct' definition, the elasticity of substitution between factors i and j is measured by

$$\sigma_{ij}^{D} = - \left\{ \frac{\mathrm{d}(X_i/X_j)}{X_i/X_j} \frac{F_i/F_j}{\mathrm{d}(F_i/F_j)} \right\}_{\mathrm{d}Y=0,\,\mathrm{d}X_k=0,\,\forall k \neq i,j}$$

Hence, the direct elasticity of substitution between i and j is computed by allowing a 1 percent increase in F_i/F_j (i.e. P_i/P_j) and recording the associated percentage change in the ratio X_j/X_i, *holding Y and all other factor inputs constant.* For example, to compute σ_{12}^{D}, we set [20]

$$\begin{aligned} y &= 0; \quad x_3 = 0, \\ p_1 &= 1; \quad p_2 = 0, \end{aligned} \tag{E4.19.7}$$

and compute $-(x_1 - x_2)$ from (E4.19.4). That is, to compute σ_{12}^{D} we solve for $-(x_1 - x_2)$ from the equations

$$\left. \begin{aligned} x_1 &= -\tfrac{1}{2} + \tfrac{1}{4} p_3, \\ x_2 &= \tfrac{1}{2} + \tfrac{3}{4} p_3, \\ 0 &= \tfrac{1}{2} - \tfrac{5}{4} p_3. \end{aligned} \right\} \tag{E4.19.8}$$

(E4.19.8) implies $p_3 = 0.4, x_1 = -0.4, x_2 = 0.8$ and thus $\sigma_{12}^{D} = 1.2$.

----

[20]   Notice that our answer for $-(x_1 - x_2)$ would be the same if $p_1 = 6$ and $p_2 = 5$. All that is important is that $p_1 - p_2 = 1$. You might like to check this assertion in your calculations. Intuitively, we are examining a movement around an '$X_1 X_2$ isoquant' defined by $\overline{Y} = F(X_1, X_2, \overline{X}_3)$. We get the same movement as long as we fix the percentage change in F_1/F_2 (or P_1/P_2), i.e. as long as we fix $p_1 - p_2$.

By similar calculations we can find σ_{13}^D and σ_{23}^D. Our solution is

$$\sigma^D (P_1 = P_2 = P_3 = 1) = \begin{bmatrix} * & 1.2 & 1.2 \\ 1.2 & * & 2 \\ 1.2 & 2 & * \end{bmatrix}.$$

(c) Measures of the elasticity of substitution are concerned with the 'shape',[21] of n-dimensional isoquants

$$\bar{Y} = F(X_1,...,X_n).$$

Under constant returns to scale (notice that (E4.19.1) exhibits constant returns to scale), the shape of an isoquant at any point depends on the relative factor inputs, e.g. the ratios X_2/X_1, $X_3/X_1,...,X_n/X_1$. Hence, if we know the relative factor prices, which (with a homothetic production function) is enough to determine the relative factor inputs, we can know the elasticities of substitution. We do not need to know the absolute value of Y.

(d) In a two-factor model, the DES between factors 1 and 2 is

$$\sigma_{12}^D = -\left\{ \frac{d(X_1/X_2)}{X_1/X_2} \frac{F_1/F_2}{d(F_1/F_2)} \right\}_{d\,Y=0}. \tag{E4.19.9}$$

In E4.18 we found that the right-hand side of (E4.19.9) is equal to η_{12}/S_2, i.e. the right-hand side of (E4.19.9) equals σ_{12}^A. Thus, in a two-factor model,

$$\sigma_{12}^D = \sigma_{12}^A.$$

The difficulty when we define an elasticity of substitution between factors 1 and 2 in a three or more factor model is to decide what to hold constant as we vary P_1/P_2. Under the direct definition we fix the levels of other factor inputs, but we allow other prices to vary. By contrast, the Allen definition involves a change in P_1/P_2 with other prices held constant, but with other input quantities varying.

Exercise 4.20. The CES production function

The constant returns to scale version of the CES (constant elasticity of substitution) production function is

---

[21] That is, elasticities of substitution are defined in terms of ratios of marginal products (the slopes of isoquants) and the rates at which the ratios of marginal products change as we change relative factor inputs.

$$Y = A \left[\sum_{i=1}^{n} \delta_i X_i^{-\rho} \right]^{-1/\rho}, \qquad\qquad (E4.20.1)$$

where Y is output, the X_i's are inputs and A and the δ_i's are positive parameters. ρ is a parameter whose value is greater than -1, but not equal to zero. It is also convenient to assume that the value of A is defined so that

$$\sum_i \delta_i = 1.$$

(a) Check that (E4.20.1) implies constant returns to scale.

(b) Derive the input demand functions (cost minimizing inputs as functions of prices and the output level).

(c) 'Linearize' the input demand functions by expressing percentage changes in demands as linear functions of percentage changes in prices and the output level.

(d) Show that both the Allen and direct elasticities of substitution between any pair of inputs, k and j, are given by

$$\sigma_{kj} = \frac{1}{1+\rho},$$

irrespective of the output level and input prices.

(e) Show that as $\rho \to 0$, (E4.20.1) reduces to a Cobb–Douglas form. In particular, show that

$$\lim_{\rho \to 0} Y = A \prod_{i=1}^{n} X_i^{\delta_i}.$$

(f) Show that as $\rho \to \infty$, (E4.20.1) reduces to a Leontief form. In particular,

$$\lim_{\rho \to \infty} Y = \min \{AX_1, AX_2,..., AX_n\}.$$

(g) Discuss possible methods for estimating the elasticity of substitution, σ, for a two-input, one-output, production process where the production function is assumed to be CES and data exists on output levels, input levels and input prices.

Answer.   (a) Where α is any positive number, we have

$$A \left[\sum_i \delta_i (\alpha X_i)^{-\rho} \right]^{-1/\rho} = \alpha A \left[\sum_i \delta_i X_i^{-\rho} \right]^{-1/\rho}.$$

Hence (E4.20.1) implies constant returns to scale.

(b) The cost minimizing problem is to choose $X_i, i = 1,...,n$, to minimize

$$\sum_i P_i X_i$$

subject to

$$Y = A \left[\sum_i \delta_i X_i^{-\rho} \right]^{-1/\rho}.$$

The first-order conditions are

$$P_k = \Lambda A \left[\sum_i \delta_i X_i^{-\rho} \right]^{-((1+\rho)/\rho)} \delta_k X_k^{-(1+\rho)}, \quad k = 1,...,n$$

and

$$Y = A \left[\sum_i \delta_i X_i^{-\rho} \right]^{-1/\rho}.$$

Hence

$$\frac{P_k}{P_i} = \frac{\delta_k X_k^{-(1+\rho)}}{\delta_i X_i^{-(1+\rho)}}, \quad \text{for all } i,$$

i.e.

$$X_i = \left(\frac{P_i \delta_k}{P_k \delta_i} \right)^{-(1/(1+\rho))} X_k, \quad \text{for all } i.$$

We substitute this last expression into the production function to obtain

$$Y = A \left[\sum_i \delta_i \left(\frac{P_i \delta_k}{P_k \delta_i} \right)^{(\rho/(1+\rho))} \right]^{-1/\rho} X_k.$$

From here we find that the input demand functions have the form

$$X_k = Y \frac{1}{A} \left[\sum_i \delta_i \left(\frac{P_i \delta_k}{P_k \delta_i} \right)^{(\rho/(1+\rho))} \right]^{1/\rho}, \quad k = 1,...,n,$$

i.e.

$$X_k = Y \left(\frac{1}{A} \right) \delta_k^{(1/(1+\rho))} P_k^{-(1/(1+\rho))} \left[\sum_i \delta_i^{(1/(1+\rho))} P_i^{(\rho/(1+\rho))} \right]^{1/\rho},$$

$$k = 1,...,n. \tag{E4.20.2}$$

(c) Logarithmic differentiation of (E4.20.2) yields

$$x_k = y - \left(\frac{1}{1+\rho} \right) p_k + \frac{1}{\rho} \sum_i S_i \left(\frac{\rho}{1+\rho} \right) p_i, \tag{E4.20.3}$$

where

$$S_i = (\delta_i^{(1/(1+\rho))} \, P_i^{(\rho/(1+\rho))}) / [\sum_i \delta_i^{(1/(1+\rho))} \, P_i^{(\rho/(1+\rho))}]$$

and the lower-case x's, p's and y are percentage changes in the variables denoted by the corresponding upper-case symbols. If we multiply both sides of (E4.20.2) by P_k we find that

$$S_k = P_k X_k / \sum_k P_k X_k,$$

i.e. the S_k's are cost shares.

Finally, we rewrite (E4.20.3) as

$$x_k = y - \sigma(p_k - \sum_i S_i p_i), \quad k = 1,...,n, \tag{E4.20.4}$$

where σ is the positive parameter defined by $\sigma = 1/(1+\rho)$.

Eq. (E4.20.4) has a straightforward interpretation. It says that in the absence of changes in relative input prices, the percentage change in the use of input k will equal the percentage change in output — a 10 percent increase in output requires a 10 percent increase in the use of all inputs. (This result follows from the linear homogeneity of (E4.20.1).) Next, we see that if P_k increases relative to a weighted average of the percentage increases in all input prices, then X_k will increase more slowly than Y. The weights used in calculating the average of all input prices are the cost shares.

(d)   From (E4.20.4) we have

$$\eta_{kj} = \sigma S_j, \quad \text{for all } j \neq k, \tag{E4.20.5}$$

where η_{kj} is the cross-elasticity of demand for input k with respect to changes in the price of input j. (To obtain (E4.20.5), we put $p_j = 1$ in (E4.20.4) and all other price changes and the output change to zero.)

The Allen elasticity of substitution between inputs k and j is

$$\sigma_{kj}^A = \eta_{kj}/S_j = \sigma.$$

For computing the direct elasticity of substitution between inputs k and j, we put

$$y = 0,$$

$$x_i = 0, \quad \text{for all } i \neq k, j,$$

and

$$p_k - p_j = 1.$$

Then we compute $-(x_k - x_j)$. Under (E4.20.4), we find that

$$-(x_k - x_j) = \sigma(p_k - p_j).$$

Hence

$$\sigma_{kj}^{\Delta} = \sigma.$$

(e) Eq. (E4.20.1) implies that

$$\ln\left(\frac{Y}{A}\right) = \frac{\ln\left[\sum_{i=1}^{n} \delta_i X_i^{-\rho}\right]}{-\rho}. \tag{E4.20.6}$$

As $\rho \to 0$, both the numerator and denominator of the right-hand side of (E4.20.6) approach zero. (Remember that $\sum_i \delta_i = 1$). Therefore, we apply L'Hospital's rule: [22]

$$\lim_{\rho \to 0}\left(\ln\left(\frac{Y}{A}\right)\right) = \lim_{\rho \to 0}\left\{\frac{\dfrac{d}{d\rho}\left(\ln\left(\sum_{i=1}^{n} \delta_i X_i^{-\rho}\right)\right)}{\dfrac{d}{d\rho}(-\rho)}\right\}.$$

Hence,

$$\lim_{\rho \to 0}\left(\ln\left(\frac{Y}{A}\right)\right) = \lim_{\rho \to 0}\left\{\frac{\sum_i (\ln X_i) X_i^{-\rho}\delta_i}{\sum_i \delta_i X_i^{-\rho}}\right\},$$

i.e.

$$\lim_{\rho \to 0}\left(\ln\left(\frac{Y}{A}\right)\right) = \sum_i \delta_i \ln X_i = \ln\left(\prod_{i=1}^{n} X_i^{\delta i}\right)$$

and

$$\lim_{\rho \to 0} Y = A \sum_{i=1}^{n} X_i^{\delta i}. \tag{E4.20.7}$$

(f) Again we write

$$\ln\left(\frac{Y}{A}\right) = -\frac{1}{\rho}\ln\left[\sum_i \delta_i X_i^{-\rho}\right]. \tag{E4.20.8}$$

---

[22] According to L'Hospital's Rule, if $\lim_{x \to a} f(x) = 0$ and $\lim_{x \to a} g(x) = 0$ and both $f'(x)$ and $g'(x)$ exist, then

$$\lim_{x \to a} \frac{f(x)}{g(x)} = \lim_{x \to a} \frac{f'(x)}{g'(x)}$$

provided that the limit on the right exists or is ∞ or $-\infty$. An excellent elementary discussion of L'Hospital's Rule is in Paul and Haeussler (1973, ch. 9).

Let

$$X_M = \min_i \{X_i\},$$

i.e. X_M is the smallest of the X_i's. Now rewrite (E4.20.8) as

$$\ln \left(\frac{Y}{A} \right) = -\frac{1}{\rho} \ln \left[\sum_i \delta_i \left(\frac{X_M}{X_i} \right)^\rho \right] + \ln X_M. \qquad (E4.20.9)$$

Since each of the X_M/X_i is between 0 an 1, and at least one of them is equal to 1,

$$\lim_{\rho \to \infty} \ln \left[\sum_i \left(\frac{X_M}{X_i} \right)^\rho \delta_i \right] = k, \qquad (E4.20.10)$$

where

$$k = \ln \left(\sum_{i \in R} \delta_i \right)$$

and R is the set of inputs such that $X_i = X_M$ for $i \in R$.
On applying (E4.20.9) and (E4.20.10) we see that

$$\lim_{\rho \to \infty} \ln \left(\frac{Y}{A} \right) = \ln X_M.$$

Thus,

$$\lim_{\rho \to \infty} Y = A X_M = A \min_i \{X_i\}. \qquad (E4.20.11)$$

A confusing aspect of the last two results, (E4.20.7) and (E4.20.11), concerns units. For example, it appears that as $\rho \to \infty$, the CES production function approaches the particular Leontief production function in which *one* unit of each input is required to produce A units of output. If, however, we had written the production function (E4.20.1) as

$$Y = A^* \left[\sum_{i=1}^n \delta_i^* \left(\frac{X_i}{T_i} \right)^{-\rho} \right]^{-1/\rho}$$

where the T_i's are a positive parameters, then we would have found that

$$\lim_{\rho \to \infty} Y = A^* \min_i \left\{ \frac{X_i}{T_i} \right\}.$$

(g) No answer is provided. We suggest that you read Intriligator (1978, ch. 8, esp. sec. 8.3).

Exercise 4.21. *The CRESH production function*

The constant returns to scale version of the CRESH (constant ratios of elasticities of substitution, homothetic) production function can be written in the
implicit form as

$$\sum_{i=1}^{n} \left(\frac{X_i}{Y}\right)^{h_i} \frac{Q_i}{h_i} = \kappa, \tag{E4.21.1}$$

where Y is output, the X_i's are inputs and the Q_i's, h_i's and κ are parameters.
Each h_i is less than 1, but not equal to zero. Each Q_i is positive and the Q_i's and
κ are normalized so that $\Sigma_i\, Q_i = 1$. In general, κ can have either sign, but clearly
if each of the Q_i/h_i has the same sign, then κ must have their common sign.

(a) Check that (E4.21.1) implies constant returns to scale.

(b) Assume that $X_1, X_2,...,X_n$ are positive. Check that the marginal product
of each input is positive.

(c) Check that the marginal rate of substitution of input j for input i (i.e.
the number of units of j required to replace 1 unit of i at a given level of output)
decreases as we increase X_i/X_j.

(d) Assume that $X_1,...,X_n$ are positive. Check that there is a unique positive
value of Y which satisfies (E4.21.1).

(e) Check that (E4.21.1) reduces to a CES form when $h_i = h$ for all i.

(f) Show that for a cost minimizing firm,

$$x_i = y - \frac{1}{1 - h_i} \left(p_i - \sum_{j=1}^{n} S_j^* p_j\right),$$

where x_i, y and p_i denote percentage changes in X_i, Y and P_i, and S_j^* is a
'modified' cost share for the jth input defined by

$$S_j^* = \frac{S_j/(1 - h_j)}{\sum_k S_k/(1 - h_k)}. \tag{E4.21.2}$$

S_j is the unmodified cost share, i.e.

$$S_j = P_j X_j / \sum_{j=1}^{n} P_j X_j.$$

(g) What is the AES between inputs i and j? What is the DES between inputs
i and j? Can you explain how CRESH got its name? *Hint*: for parts (f) and (g),
do not try to obtain explicit forms for the input-demand functions. (You
can't!) Express the first-order conditions in percentage change form and eliminate the percentage change in the Lagrangian multiplier.

Answer.   (a) Consider any vector of inputs $(\bar{X}_1,...,\bar{X}_n)$. The output producible from this input vector is $\bar{Y}$, where $Y = \bar{Y}$ satisfies the equation

$$\sum_{i=1}^{n} \left(\frac{\bar{X}_i}{Y}\right)^{h_i} \frac{Q_i}{h_i} = \kappa. \tag{E4.21.3}$$

If $Y = \bar{Y}$ satisfies (E4.21.3) then $Y = \alpha \bar{Y}$ satisfies

$$\sum_{i} \left(\frac{\alpha \bar{X}_i}{Y}\right)^{h_i} \frac{Q_i}{h_i} = \kappa,$$

where α is any positive number. Thus (E4.21.1) exhibits constant returns to scale.

(b) To find the marginal product of input k, we allow X_k to change, but hold all the other input levels constant. Then the change in the left-hand side of (E4.21.1) will be given by

$$\frac{Q_k X_k^{h_k-1}}{Y^{h_k}} \, dX_k - \sum_{i=1}^{n} \frac{X_i^{h_i} Q_i}{Y^{h_i+1}} \, dY = 0.$$

Hence

$$\frac{dY}{dX_k} = Q_k \left(\frac{X_k}{Y}\right)^{h_k-1} \Bigg/ \sum_{i=1}^{n} Q_i \left(\frac{X_i}{Y}\right)^{h_i}. \tag{E4.21.4}$$

The expression on the right-hand side of (E4.21.4) is the marginal product of input k. It is positive because the Q_i's are positive.

(c)

$$MRS_{ij} = \frac{\partial Y/\partial X_i}{\partial Y/\partial X_j}$$

$$= \frac{Q_i(X_i/Y)^{h_i-1}}{Q_j(X_j/Y)^{h_j-1}}.$$

With (h_i-1) and (h_j-1) both negative, MRS_{ij} will decrease as we increase X_i and decrease as we reduce X_j.

Hence, MRS_{ij} will decrease as we increase X_i/X_j at a given level of output, holding all other inputs constant.

(d) First we notice that

$$\frac{\partial \text{ LHS (E4.21.1)}}{\partial Y} = - \sum_{i=1}^{n} Q_i X_i^{h_i} Y^{-h_i-1} < 0,$$

i.e. for any given positive vector $(X_1,...,X_n)$, the left-hand side of (E4.21.1) is a monotonically decreasing function of Y over positive values of Y. Next, we see that

$$h_i > 0 \quad \text{implies} \quad \lim_{Y \to 0} \left\{ \left(\frac{X_i}{Y} \right)^{h_i} \frac{Q_i}{h_i} \right\} = \infty,$$

$$h_i > 0 \quad \text{implies} \quad \lim_{Y \to \infty} \left\{ \left(\frac{X_i}{Y} \right)^{h_i} \frac{Q_i}{h_i} \right\} = 0,$$

$$h_i < 0 \quad \text{implies} \quad \lim_{Y \to 0} \left\{ \left(\frac{X_i}{Y} \right)^{h_i} \frac{Q_i}{h_i} \right\} = 0,$$

$$h_i < 0 \quad \text{implies} \quad \lim_{Y \to \infty} \left\{ \left(\frac{X_i}{Y} \right)^{h_i} \frac{Q_i}{h_i} \right\} = -\infty.$$

Hence,

$$\lim_{Y \to 0} \quad \text{LHS(E4.21.1)} \quad = \quad \infty, \quad \text{if } h_i > 0 \text{ for } any \ i$$

$$= \quad 0, \quad \text{if } h_i < 0 \text{ for } all \ i.$$

$$\lim_{Y \to \infty} \quad \text{LHS(E4.21.1)} \quad = \quad -\infty, \quad \text{if } h_i < 0 \text{ for } any \ i$$

$$= \quad 0, \quad \text{if } h_i > 0 \text{ for } all \ i.$$

We now have three cases.

Case 1: $h_i > 0$ for all i. $\kappa > 0$. In this case, LHS(E4.21.1) falls monotonically from ∞ to 0 as we increase Y from 0 to ∞. Hence at a unique positive value for Y,

$$\text{LHS(E4.21.1)} = \kappa.$$

Case 2: $h_i < 0$ for all i. $\kappa < 0$. In this case, LHS(E4.21.1) falls monotonically from 0 to $-\infty$ as we increase Y from 0 to ∞. Hence, at a unique positive value for Y,

$$\text{LHS(E4.21.1)} = \kappa.$$

Case 3: $h_i < 0$ for some i, $h_i > 0$ for some i. In this case, LHS(E4.21.1) falls monotonically from $+\infty$ to $-\infty$ as we increase Y from 0 to ∞. Hence, irrespective of the sign of κ, it will be true that at a unique positive value for Y,

$$\text{LHS(E4.21.1)} = \kappa.$$

(e) If $h_i = h$ for all i, then (E4.21.1) becomes

$$\sum_{i=1}^{n} \left(\frac{X_i}{Y}\right)^h Q_i = \kappa h.$$

(*Note*: the restriction on κ implies that $\kappa h > 0$.) Hence,

$$A \left(\sum_{i=1}^{n} \delta_i X_i^{-\rho}\right)^{-1/\rho} = Y, \tag{E4.21.5}$$

where

$$\rho = -h, \tag{i}$$

$$\delta_i = Q_i \tag{ii}$$

and

$$A = (\kappa h)^{-1/h}. \tag{iii}$$

(E4.21.5) is the CES form (E4.20.1). Notice that ρ, as defined in (i), satisfies $\rho > -1$; the δ_i's, as defined in (ii) satisfy $\Sigma_i \delta_i = 1$ and $\delta_i > 0$ for all i; the A as defined in (iii) satisfies $A > 0$.

(f) The cost minimizing problem for the firm is to choose $X_1,...,X_n$, to minimize

$$\sum_i P_i X_i$$

subject to

$$\sum_{i=1}^{n} \left(\frac{X_i}{Y}\right)^{h_i} \frac{Q_i}{h_i} = \kappa.$$

The first-order conditions are

$$P_k = \Lambda \frac{X_k^{h_k - 1}}{Y^{h_k}} Q_k, \quad k = 1,...,n \tag{E4.21.6}$$

and

$$\sum_{i=1}^{n} \left(\frac{X_i}{Y}\right)^{h_i} \frac{Q_i}{h_i} = \kappa. \tag{E4.21.7}$$

We follow the hint and express (E4.21.6) and (E4.21.7) in percentage change form:

$$p_k = \lambda + (h_k - 1)x_k - h_k y, \quad k = 1,...,n \tag{E4.21.8}$$

and

$$\sum_{i=1}^{n} h_i(x_i - y) W_i = 0,$$ (E4.21.9)

where

$$W_i = \left(\frac{X_i}{Y}\right)^{h_i} \frac{Q_i}{h_i}, \quad i = 1,...,n.$$

Notice that by multiplying (E4.21.6) through by X_k, we can show that

$$h_k W_k / \sum_i h_i W_i = S_k, \quad \text{for all } k,$$

i.e. the $h_k W_k$ are proportional to the cost shares. Hence (E4.21.9) may be re-written as [23]

$$\sum_{i=1}^{n} S_i x_i = y.$$ (E4.21.10)

Now we return to (E4.21.8) and rearrange it as

$$x_k = \left(\frac{1}{h_k - 1}\right)(p_k - \lambda + h_k y), \quad \text{for all } k.$$ (E4.21.11)

By multiplying both sides by S_k, aggregating and using (E4.21.10), we find that

$$y = \sum_k \left(\frac{S_k}{h_k - 1}\right)(p_k - \lambda + h_k y).$$

Hence

$$\lambda = -y \frac{\left(1 - \sum_k \frac{h_k S_k}{h_k - 1}\right)}{\sum_k \left(\frac{S_k}{h_k - 1}\right)} + \sum_k S_k^* p_k.$$

That is,

$$\lambda = y + \sum_k S_k^* p_k,$$ (E4.21.12)

where S_k^* is the modified cost share defined in (E4.21.2). Finally we substitute from (E4.21.12) into (E4.21.11), obtaining

$$x_i = y - \left(\frac{1}{1 - h_i}\right)(p_i - \sum_j S_j^* p_j), \quad \text{for all } i.$$ (E4.21.13)

---

[23] Can you show that (E4.21.10) is valid in any cost minimization problem where the production function is homogeneous of degree 1?

The interpretation of (E4.21.13) is similar to that of (E4.20.4). In the absence of changes in relative input prices, the use of all inputs change in the same proportion as output. However, if P_i increases relative to a weighted average of all input prices, X_i will increase more slowly than Y. The weights used in computing the average of the input prices are 'modified' cost shares rather than cost shares as in the CES case. More importantly, (E4.21.13) generalizes (E4.20.4) by allowing the responsiveness of X_i, to changes in P_i relative to other input prices, to depend on i. That is, the coefficient $1/(1 - h_i)$, on the relative price term in (E4.21.13) has an i subscript.

(g) From (E4.21.13) we see that

$$\eta_{ij} = S_j^*/(1 - h_i), \quad \text{for all } i \neq j.$$

The Allen elasticity of substitution between inputs i and j is

$$\sigma_{ij}^A = \eta_{ij}/S_j = \frac{S_j^*/(1 - h_i)}{S_j}, \quad \text{for all } i \neq j.$$

Hence,

$$\sigma_{ij}^A = \left(\frac{1}{1 - h_i}\right)\left(\frac{1}{1 - h_j}\right)\left(\frac{1}{\sum_k S_k/(1 - h_k)}\right), \quad \text{for all } i \neq j. \quad \text{(E4.21.14)}$$

To compute the DES between inputs 1 and 2, say, we set

$$\left. \begin{aligned} y &= 0; \quad x_k = 0, \quad \text{for } k > 2, \\ p_1 &= 1; \quad p_2 = 0, \end{aligned} \right\} \quad \text{(E4.21.15)}$$

and compute $(x_2 - x_1)$ from (E4.21.13). On substituting from (E4.21.15) into (E4.21.13), we find that

$$p_k = S_1^* + \sum_{j>2} S_j^* p_j, \quad \text{for all } k > 2, \quad \text{(E4.21.16)}$$

i.e. all the p_k, for $k > 2$, have the same value and we can conclude from (E4.21.16) that

$$p_k = \frac{S_1^*}{1 - \sum_{j>2} S_j^*} = \frac{S_1^*}{S_1^* + S_2^*}, \quad \text{for all } k > 2.$$

Next, we note that

$$x_1 = -\frac{1}{1 - h_1}\left(1 - S_1^* - \frac{\sum_{j>2} S_j^* S_1^*}{S_1^* + S_2^*}\right).$$

This expression simplifies to

$$x_1 = -\frac{1}{1 - h_1}\frac{S_2^*}{S_1^* + S_2^*}.$$

For x_2 we have

$$x_2 = -\frac{1}{1-h_2}\left(-S_1^* - \frac{\sum\limits_{j>2} S_j^* S_1^*}{S_1^* + S_2^*}\right).$$

This expression simplifies to

$$x_2 = \frac{1}{1-h_2}\frac{S_1^*}{S_1^* + S_2^*}.$$

From here we find that

$$\sigma_{12}^D = (x_2 - x_1) = \frac{\left(\dfrac{1}{1-h_1}\right)S_2^* + \left(\dfrac{1}{1-h_2}\right)S_1^*}{S_1^* + S_2^*}.$$

In general

$$\sigma_{ij}^D = \frac{\left(\dfrac{1}{1-h_i}\right)S_j^* + \left(\dfrac{1}{1-h_j}\right)S_i^*}{S_i^* + S_j^*}, \qquad \text{for all } i \neq j. \qquad (E4.21.17)$$

If $h_i = h$ for all i (the CES case), both (E4.21.14) and (E4.21.17) simplify to

$$\sigma_{ij}^A = \sigma_{ij}^D = \frac{1}{1-h}$$

Also, it is clear that CRESH is named from (E4.21.14):

$$\frac{\sigma_{ij}^A}{\sigma_{rt}^A} = \frac{\left(\dfrac{1}{1-h_i}\right)\left(\dfrac{1}{1-h_j}\right)}{\left(\dfrac{1}{1-h_r}\right)\left(\dfrac{1}{1-h_t}\right)}, \qquad \text{for all } i,j,r,t, \ i \neq j, \ r \neq t.$$

The ratios of the Allen elasticities of substitution are constant.

Exercise 4.22.   An example of a flexible functional form: the generalized Leontief function

Consider the per unit cost function [24]

$$\frac{C}{Y} = \sum_{i=1}^{n}\sum_{j=1}^{n} b_{ij} P_i^{1/2} P_j^{1/2} \qquad (E4.22.1)$$

---

[24]   In this exercise we assume that the underlying production function exhibits constant returns to scale. More generally, we could write

$$C = k(Y)\sum_{i}^{n}\sum_{j}^{n} b_{ij} P_i^{1/2} P_j^{1/2},$$

where k is a monotonically increasing function of Y.

where $b_{ij} > 0$ for all i and j, and $b_{ij} = b_{ji}$ for all $i \neq j$.

(a) Is (E4.22.1) a legitimate (see E4.17) unit cost function; is it homogeneous of degree 1 in prices, an increasing function of prices and concave in prices?

(b) Derive the input demand functions implied by (E4.22.1).

(c) Consider an arbitrary unit cost function

$$\frac{C}{Y} = \Gamma(P_1,...,P_n).$$ (E4.22.2)

Use the notation

$$\Gamma(P) \equiv \Gamma(P_1,...,P_n),$$

$$\Gamma_i(P) \equiv \frac{\partial \Gamma(P)}{\partial P_i}$$

and

$$\Gamma_{ij}(P) \equiv \frac{\partial^2 \Gamma(P)}{\partial P_i \partial P_j} ,$$

i.e. $\Gamma(P)$ is the cost per unit of production when the input price vector is P. Γ_i is the demand for input i per unit of output when the price vector is P, and Γ_{ij} is the derivative with respect to P_j of the demand per unit of output for input i.

How should the b_{ij} be set if we wish to use the functional form (E4.22.1) as a second-order approximation to (E4.22.2) in the region of the point $P = \overline{P}$? Can you explain why (E4.22.1) is classified as a 'flexible functional' form? Why is it called a *generalized Leontief* function?

Answer.   (a)   Where α is any positive number, we see that (E4.22.1) implies that

$$\alpha \frac{C}{Y} = \sum_{i=1}^{n} \sum_{j=1}^{n} b_{ij}(\alpha P_i)^{1/2}(\alpha P_j)^{1/2}.$$

Hence C/Y is homogeneous of degree 1 in prices.

Since all the b_{ij} are positive, it is clear that C/Y, as defined in (E4.22.1), is an increasing function of each of the P_j's.

To establish concavity, we must prove that

$$\sum_i \sum_j b_{ij}(\alpha \overline{P}_i + (1-\alpha)\overline{\overline{P}}_i)^{1/2}(\alpha \overline{P}_j + (1-\alpha)\overline{\overline{P}}_j)^{1/2}$$
$$\geq \alpha \sum_i \sum_j b_{ij}\overline{P}_i^{1/2}\overline{P}_j^{1/2} + (1-\alpha)\sum_i \sum_j b_{ij}\overline{\overline{P}}_i^{1/2}\overline{\overline{P}}_j^{1/2}$$ (E4.22.3)

for any pair of price vectors, $\overline{P} = (\overline{P}_1,...,\overline{P}_n)$ and $\overline{\overline{P}} = (\overline{\overline{P}}_1 ...,\overline{\overline{P}}_n)$, and any number α between 0 and 1.

Since all the b_{ij} are positive, (E4.22.3) certainly will be valid if

$$(\alpha \bar{P}_i + (1-\alpha)\bar{\bar{P}}_i)^{1/2} (\alpha \bar{P}_j + (1-\alpha)\bar{\bar{P}}_j)^{1/2} \geq \alpha \bar{P}_i^{1/2} \bar{P}_j^{1/2} + (1-\alpha)\bar{\bar{P}}_i^{1/2} \bar{\bar{P}}_j^{1/2},$$

for all i and j,

i.e. if

$$(\alpha \bar{P}_i + (1-\alpha)\bar{\bar{P}}_i)(\alpha \bar{P}_j + (1-\alpha)\bar{\bar{P}}_j)$$
$$\geq \alpha^2 \bar{P}_i \bar{P}_j + (1-\alpha)^2 \bar{\bar{P}}_i \bar{\bar{P}}_j + 2\alpha(1-\alpha)(\bar{P}_i \bar{P}_j \bar{\bar{P}}_i \bar{\bar{P}}_j)^{1/2},$$

i.e. if

$$(\bar{P}_i \bar{\bar{P}}_j + \bar{\bar{P}}_i \bar{P}_j) \geq 2(\bar{P}_i \bar{P}_j \bar{\bar{P}}_i \bar{\bar{P}}_j)^{1/2},$$

i.e. if

$$(\bar{P}_i \bar{\bar{P}}_j)^2 + (\bar{\bar{P}}_i \bar{P}_j)^2 - 2\bar{P}_i \bar{P}_j \bar{\bar{P}}_i \bar{\bar{P}}_j \geq 0,$$

i.e if

$$(\bar{P}_i \bar{\bar{P}}_j - \bar{\bar{P}}_i \bar{P}_j)^2 \geq 0.$$

This last expression is valid and therefore we may conclude that (E4.22.3) is valid. Hence, C/Y, as defined by (E4.22.1), is concave in prices.

(b) We apply Shepard's lemma and obtain

$$X_i = \frac{\partial C}{\partial P_i} = Y \sum_j b_{ij}(P_j/P_i)^{1/2}, \quad \text{for } i = 1,...,n. \tag{E4.22.4}$$

(c) We must, *if possible*, set the b_{ij}'s so that

$$\sum_i \sum_j b_{ij} \bar{P}_i^{1/2} \bar{P}_j^{1/2} \quad = \Gamma(\bar{P}), \tag{i}$$
$$\sum_j b_{ij}(\bar{P}_j/\bar{P}_i)^{1/2} \quad = \Gamma_i(\bar{P}), \quad i = 1,...,n, \tag{ii}$$
$$\tfrac{1}{2} b_{ij}(\bar{P}_i \bar{P}_j)^{-1/2} \quad = \Gamma_{ij}(\bar{P}), \quad i \neq j \tag{iiia}$$

and

$$-\tfrac{1}{2} \sum_{j \neq i} b_{ij} \bar{P}_j^{1/2} \bar{P}_i^{-3/2} \quad = \Gamma_{ii}(\bar{P}), \quad i = 1,...,n. \tag{iiib}$$

By insisting on (i)–(iii), we are requiring the approximate function to give in the region of $P = \bar{P}$, the true values for unit cost and for the first and second derivatives of unit cost with respect to prices. The question to be answered is whether we can, in fact, choose values for the b_{ij}'s to satisfy (i)–(iii).

According to (iiia) we must set

$$b_{ij} = 2 \Gamma_{ij}(\bar{P})(\bar{P}_i \bar{P}_j)^{1/2}, \quad \text{for all } i \neq j. \tag{E4.22.5}$$

Then by substituting (E4.22.5) into (ii) we find that the b_{ii} must be set according to

$$b_{ii} = \Gamma_i(\bar{P}) - 2 \sum_{j \neq i} \Gamma_{ij}(\bar{P}) \bar{P}_j, \quad i = 1,...,n. \tag{E4.22.6}$$

Since Γ is a per unit cost function, it is homogeneous of degree 1 in prices. Therefore Γ_i is homogenous of degree zero in prices [25] and

$$\sum_{j \neq i} \Gamma_{ij}(\bar{P}) \bar{P}_j = - \Gamma_{ii}(\bar{P}) \bar{P}_i.$$

We rewrite (E4.22.6) as

$$b_{ii} = \Gamma_i(\bar{P}) + 2 \Gamma_{ii}(\bar{P}) (\bar{P}_i\bar{P}_i)^{1/2}, \quad i = 1,...,n. \tag{E4.22.7}$$

Now we check that (E4.22.5) and (E4.22.7) are consistent with (i) and (iiib). When we substitute (E4.22.5) and (E4.22.7) into the left-hand side of (i), we obtain

$$\text{LHS(i)} = \sum_i \Gamma_i(\bar{P}) \bar{P}_i + 2 \sum_i \sum_j \Gamma_{ij}(\bar{P}) \bar{P}_j\bar{P}_i.$$

The second term is zero since $\sum_j \Gamma_{ij}(\bar{P}) \bar{P}_j$ is zero for all i. The first term is $\Gamma(\bar{P})$ since Γ is homogeneous of degree 1 in prices. Hence

$$\text{LHS(i)} = \Gamma(\bar{P}) = \text{RHS(i)}.$$

Finally, we substitute (E4.22.5) into (iiib).

$$\text{LHS(iiib)} = - \sum_{j \neq i} \Gamma_{ij}(\bar{P}) \bar{P}_j/\bar{P}_i.$$

Hence,

$$\text{LHS(iiib)} = \frac{\Gamma_{ii}(\bar{P}) \bar{P}_i}{\bar{P}_i} = \Gamma_{ii}(\bar{P}) = \text{RHS(iiib)}.$$

Eq. (E4.22.1) is classified as a *flexible* functional form because it is rich enough in paramters to approximate any legitimate unit cost function. In this exercise we have found that with a suitable choice of values for the b_{ij}'s (i.e. if the b_{ij} are set according to (E4.22.5) and (E4.22.7)), (E4.22.1) can give a local second-order (i.e. correct up to the second-order derivatives in the region of a particular price vector) approximation to any legitimate cost function.

Eq. (E4.22.1) is only one member of a growing family of flexible functional forms. [26] To see why it is called the generalized Leontief form, consider the special case in which $b_{ij} = 0$ for all $i \neq j$. Then (E4.22.1) reduces to

[25]   Remember that Γ_i is the demand for input i per unit of output. If we double all prices, then the input of i per unit of output will be unchanged.

[26]   Other flexible functional forms include the generalized Cobb–Douglas, the translog, and the generalized square root quadratic. See Diewert (1971, 1973, 1974b); Christensen, Jorgenson and Lau (1971, 1973) and Berndt and Khaled (1977).

$$\frac{C}{Y} = \sum_i b_{ii} P_i. \tag{E4.22.8}$$

For this unit cost function the underlying production function has the Leontief form

$$Y = \min_i \left\{ \frac{X_i}{b_{ii}} \right\}.$$

Exercise 4.23. *Direct specification of the input demand functions*

An econometrician [27] recently used the theoretical specification [28]

$$X_i(t) = K_i \, Y(t) \left(\prod_{j=1}^{n} P_j(t)^{\eta_{ij}} \right) \epsilon_i(t), \quad i = 1, \ldots, n, \tag{E4.23.1}$$

where K_i and η_{ij} are parameters to be estimated,[29] and $X_i(t)$, $Y(t)$ and $P_j(t)$ are the tth observations of the level of farm use of input i, the level of farm output and the price of input j. $\epsilon_i(t)$ is a disturbance term with an expected value of 1. To increase the precision of the parameter estimates, the econometrician imposed the prior restrictions

$$\sum_{j=1}^{n} \eta_{ij} = 0, \quad \text{for all } i, \tag{E4.23.2}$$

and

$$\frac{\eta_{ij}}{\bar{S}_j} = \frac{\eta_{ji}}{\bar{S}_i}, \quad \text{for all } i \neq j, \tag{E4.23.3}$$

where $\bar{S}_j$ is the average over all observations of the cost share for input j.

One student criticized the specification claiming that it was ad hoc, and that it was not derived from an underlying model in which inputs are chosen to minimize costs subject to a production function constraint. Do you find the criticism persuasive?

Answer. In his defence, the econometrician can argue that he has used what the theory of cost minimization has to offer, the homogeneity and the sym-

---

[27] Thirsk (1974).
[28] This specification is particularly attractive from an econometric point of view — it is linear in logs.
[29] Notice that η_{ij} is the elasticity of demand for input i with respect to changes in price j.

metry restrictions (see (E4.16.1) and (E4.16.3) [30]).[31] We assume that his principal concern is not with estimating the coefficients of the underlying production function, but rather with estimating the own- and cross-price elasticities of the input demand functions. If, in fact, the student wished to know the production function, a local[32] approximation in the region of the sample means for the X_i's could be derived by generating the cost function from (E4.23.1) and working back to the production function by the method of E4.17. Alternatively, an approximate production function could be deduced by a method similar to the one used in E3.14 where we worked back to the utility function from a system of commodity demand functions.

The approach in (E4.23.1) is rather similar to that of econometricians who specify explicit forms for cost functions rather than production functions. In both cases, theoretical results from the cost minimization model are applied, but the algebra involved in solving a constrained minimization problem is avoided.

---

[30]   (E4.16.3) may be written as

$$\frac{\partial g_i}{\partial P_j} \frac{P_j}{g_i} \frac{C}{P_j g_j} = \frac{\partial g_j}{\partial P_i} \frac{P_i}{g_j} \frac{C}{P_i g_i} , \quad \text{for all } i \neq j,$$

i.e.

$$\eta_{ij}/S_j = \eta_{ji}/S_i, \quad \text{for all } i \neq j.$$

[31]   He has not imposed the sign restrictions studied in E4.16 part (d). However, it is usual to check the consistency of parameter estimates with sign restrictions after estimation, rather than impose the sign restrictions prior to estimation.

[32]   (E4.23.1) is not globally consistent with the cost minimizing model. For example, as we move away from average cost shares, (E4.23.1) will violate the symmetry restriction.

INDEX